Back Channel Negotiation

Syracuse Studies on Peace and Conflict Resolution
Louis Kriesberg, *Series Editor*

Back Channel Negotiation

Secrecy in the Middle East Peace Process

Anthony Wanis-St. John

SYRACUSE UNIVERSITY PRESS

For a listing of books published and distributed by Syracuse University Press,
visit our Web site at SyracuseUniversityPress.syr.edu.

ISBN: 978-0-8156-3275-7

Library of Congress Cataloging-in-Publication Data

Wanis-St. John, Anthony

Back channel negotiation : secrecy in the Middle East peace process / Anthony Wanis-St. John. — 1st ed.

p. cm. — (Syracuse studies on peace and conflict resolution)

Includes bibliographical references and index.

ISBN 978-0-8156-3275-7 (cloth : alk. paper)

1. Arab-Israeli conflict—Peace. 2. Diplomatic negotiations in international disputes—Case studies. I. Title.

DS119.7.W339 2010

956.05—dc22

2010042957

Manufactured in the United States of America

Dedicated to Claudia,
Isabela, Christopher, and Emilio,
my family "back channel"

Contents

Tables and Figure

Tables

Figure

Preface

Over the years, I have benefitted from support around the globe in my pursuit of knowledge of the Middle East peace process. Initial research support came from the Program on Negotiation at Harvard Law School. Years later, a postdoctoral fellowship was granted by the Palestinian-American Research Council. The Middle East peace process has passed through more than a decade and half of turbulence, and in that time I have progressively presented the cases and ideas found in this book and gained insight from the feedback of colleagues at venues such as the United States Institute of Peace, the International Studies Association, and the International Association for Conflict Management. The scholars who meet as the Washington Interest in Negotiation (WIN) group at the Nitze School of Advanced International Studies, Johns Hopkins University, founded by Bill Zartman, provided intellectual support and led me to look at the "other side of the coin": if secrecy and exclusion characterize back channel negotiations, then inclusion and civil society roles in peace negotiations could characterize another facet of negotiation.

Bert Spector, managing editor of *International Negotiation,* invited me to further explore the tension between secrecy and inclusion as guest editor of an issue of the journal titled *Peace Processes, Secret Negotiations and Civil Society,* which was published as volume 13, number 1 in 2008. I would also like to thank several colleagues and mentors for their insights, feedback, and intellectual engagement over the years, including Pamela Aall, Ron Fisher, Abdul Aziz Said, Lou Kriesberg, Darren Kew, Omar Dajani, Jeff Helsing, Dean Pruitt, David Matz, Neil Caplan, Bill Zartman, Aharon Klieman, Saadia Touval, Moty Cristal, Roger Fisher, Howard Raiffa, David Metcalfe, Keith Fitzgerald, Mike Wheeler, Mahdi Abdel Hadi, and many others. Saadia, my friend and mentor, passed on to better life as this book was completed. Jeff Rubin, who inspired it all, passed away when

I was just beginning my research. He was intrigued by the back channel topic. Thanks also to those who agreed to be interviewed over the years and to those who helped me locate information and people, including Mahmoud al-Neirab, Salah Elayan, Firaz Yaghi, Nadia Sartawi, Dr. Mahdi Abdel Hadi, Arie Nadler, and so many others. For their diligence as my research assistants I wish to thank Christoff Luehrs, Sara Cady, and Reva Hoosier-Thomas of American University's School of International Service.

At Syracuse University Press, I am grateful to Lou Kriesberg, who always believed in this book, as well as to Mary Selden Evans, Annelise Finegan, Marcia Hough, Lisa Renee Kuerbis, Kay Steinmetz, Fred Wellner, and D. J. Whyte.

Abbreviations

BCN   back channel negotiation

CAPS   Comprehensive Agreement on the Permanent Status

CIA   Central Intelligence Agency

DCI   Director of Central Intelligence

DFLP   Democratic Front for the Liberation of Palestine

DoP   Declaration of Principles

ECF   Economic Cooperation Foundation

FAFO   Institute of Applied Social Science in Oslo

FAPS   Framework Agreement on the Permanent Status

FATAH   The PLO's main centrist political party. Reverse acronym of Arabic *H*arakat al-*T*ahrir al-Watani al-*F*ilastini. English: Palestinian Movement for National Liberation

FCN   front channel negotiation

FMLN   Farabundo Martí de Liberación Nacional

FRD   Further redeployment (of Israeli troops out of Palestinian territory)

HAMAS   Palestinian religious nationalist organization with both social welfare and military wings. Arabic: Harakat al-Muqawama al-Islamiya. English: Islamic Resistance Movement

IAEA   International Atomic Energy Agency

IDF   Israel Defense Forces

JLC	Joint Liaison Committee (Palestinian Israeli body set up by Article X of the DoP)
MIJ	Movement for Islamic Jihad
OSCE	Organization for Security and Cooperation in Europe
PFLP	Popular Front for the Liberation of Palestine
PISGA	Palestinian Interim Self Governing Authority
PLC	Palestinian Legislative Council
PLO	Palestine Liberation Organization
PNA/PA	Palestinian National Authority
PNC	Palestine National Council
PSF	Palestinian Preventive Security Force
SALT	Strategic Arms Limitation Talks
SHAS	Israeli religious political party representing the Sephardic Jews. Hebrew: Shomrei Torah Sephardim. English: Sephardi Torah Guardians
UNSC	United Nations Security Council
YESHA	Organization representing Israeli settlers. Hebrew: Yehuda, Shomron, 'Azza. English: Judea, Samaria, Gaza-Israeli Settlers Organization

Back Channel Negotiation

1

Analyzing the Palestinian-Israeli Peace Process

A nation that cannot be trusted to maintain the confidentiality of sensitive exchanges . . . will be crippled in negotiations.
—HENRY KISSINGER[1]

Secrecy has long been a tool used by diplomats and politicians in their negotiations with adversaries. Perplexingly, secret negotiations can and often do take place in parallel with open and acknowledged "front channel" negotiations. Front channel negotiators meet with their counterparts and are often subject to intense scrutiny by the public, political parties, and media. However, different negotiators are sometimes sent to negotiate with their counterparts, but their encounters are kept secret from the front channel negotiators, the media, political and other actors, as well as the public. I term these secret encounters "back channel negotiation" (BCN). In this book, I explore the back channel negotiations of the Palestinian-Israeli peace process.

The Palestinian-Israeli conflict is not really a very old conflict, dating back only to the early 1900s, when the British Army wrested Palestine from the crumbling Ottoman Empire and committed itself to prepare Palestine for Arab self-rule under a "mandate" from the League of Nations, while also promising to create a Jewish national home in the same country. The solutions to this conflict are not particularly elusive or mysterious. On the contrary, various facets of a solution have been well known and debated among the interested parties at least since 1967 when Israel took over the remaining Palestinian territories that were then under Jordanian and Egyptian control (the West Bank and the Gaza Strip, respectively). And yet it is a conflict that has proven highly resistant to all attempts to resolve it; diplomats and scholars term this *intractability*.[2] In

1

this book, we confront the painful irony that some methods for peacemaking have had the unintended consequence of inflaming the conflict and sustaining its intractability.

High-profile mediators from the United Nations to the United States have tried and failed to resolve it for the past five and one-half decades. For the Palestinians, the open wound of this conflict has meant displacement and dispossession of what today has grown to approximately 4 million refugees, loss of land and property, and generations prevented from having normal lives in the land of their origins. In the West Bank and Gaza, people have endured a violent military occupation. For the Israelis, the conflict has meant a constant, nagging insecurity about attacks on civilians and the fear that conflict will reignite beyond its borders to wider wars with neighboring countries such as Iran, Syria, and Iraq, or even into a "civilizational" war pitting Islam against Judaism. The Palestinian-Israeli conflict, despite its relative scale, has become the paradigm of conflicts considered to be intractable.

For the United States and others, the continuation of this conflict has meant tense relations with Arab countries and, worse still, with populations who identify with Islam and have begun to see the conflict through a religious prism. For Arab states, the conflict has been used to justify undemocratic rule at home and a foreign policy hostile to Israel (and by extension, to the United States). To date, only two states—Egypt and Jordan—have a formal peace with Israel, and both concluded that peace at least partly on the misplaced hope that a resolution of the Palestinian question would follow. The definitive resolution of this conflict would bring numerous benefits on global as well as regional levels, not to mention the direct benefits of peace so long sought by Palestinians and Israelis.

The contemporary Palestinian-Israeli peace process is part of broader effort to bring about Arab-Israeli peace. The Palestinian-Israeli dimension of this concerns the political status of the territory and Palestinian inhabitants of the West Bank (an area lying to the west of the Jordan River) and the Gaza Strip (a Palestinian enclave on the Mediterranean coastal plain), and the conditions under which Israel will accept any change in their political status. Historical narratives of the conflict are far more common than analyses of the negotiations, and such narratives are beyond the scope of this book.[3]

My intention with this book is to thoughtfully strengthen efforts to make a just peace rather than simply to criticize the efforts of peacemakers. The study of peacemaking is far less developed than the study of war, and there is still much to learn about how to resolve the world's existing conflicts while preventing future ones. It is my hope that this book will contribute to that effort, first of all by telling the story of the most significant Palestinian-Israeli attempts to make peace. These are worth applauding—whatever their defects. It is also my purpose to honor those efforts by turning an analytical eye to them. This book is not about taking sides or casting blame either for the conflict's origins or for the current state of affairs. It is about frankly discussing the art and science of the peacemakers.

The Decision to Negotiate with the Enemy: Using Secret Channels

One of the most difficult decisions that leaders face is the decision to negotiate with their enemies in an effort to put an end to conflict and initiate cooperative, peaceful relations. Much is at stake: the physical survival of the country or national group may well depend on this decision. For the leader making this decision, political and even physical survival may be put at risk.

If we try to put ourselves in the place of such a leader, we can imagine the painful dilemmas involved. How does such a leader explain to the people that they must now make peace with those against whom they were fighting and dying? And what shall the leader do about members of his or her own society who are opposed to making peace with the enemy? Will the enemy negotiate in good faith? Will the leader be more successful in peacemaking than in making war? The decision to enter negotiations is by no means an easy one. Leaders of groups and countries at war must confront this choice, despite the risks and dilemmas involved.

Once a decision is made to negotiate, solemn delegations of men and women are then dispatched on missions to seek the best terms for ending hostilities. It is a strange fact of international affairs (and of domestic dispute resolution as well) that, more frequently than may be supposed, by mutual accord, leaders will quietly and simultaneously send a second delegation to negotiate with the other party. The first delegation will most likely face press conferences before, during, and after their negotiations with their counterparts. Every word they say (and any words they don't say) will be scrutinized. The second delegation, on the other hand, will conduct its work in the utmost secrecy. The press, the public, political factions, and even ministers within the government will not know about this second delegation.

Even the first delegation may not know that its work is being duplicated. Only the leader and a close circle of advisers will know about both efforts.

The negotiations that everyone knows about may proceed as planned, but to the surprise of all, the breakthrough agreements are often reached and drafted in the secret talks. I call these secret negotiations "back channels," borrowing a term popularized by former U.S. secretary of state Henry Kissinger in his memoirs, as he wrote about the need to isolate policy making from widespread leaks among discontented officials and to more tightly control negotiation strategies from the White House, rather than through the U.S. State Department's channels.[4]

I formally define back channel negotiation as *secret, official negotiations among the parties to a dispute that supplement or replace open, existing front channel negotiations*. For negotiations to conform to this definition, the negotiators are not typically "freelancers"; that is, they must have some accountability to and official empowerment from their respective leadership. Otherwise, the exercise is not truly negotiation but rather "people-to-people" diplomacy, Track II diplomacy, or another variant of an unofficial, problem-solving approach that, although important in the construction of peaceful relations, is removed from official decisions and commitments about war and peace. Track II and back channel negotiation, however, can be combined in a hybrid form of diplomatic engagement. Back channels are in a sense a gray or even black market for official negotiations: they are transactional spaces and relationships in which the parties seek alternative arrangements while deliberately excluding others, often sidelining negotiators of lower rank who are conducting negotiations in parallel and who don't know about the secret negotiations. Early negotiation research sought and found explanations for secrecy in negotiations by examining the effect of publicity on negotiators. Negotiators occasionally use publicity and make public commitments to help them avoid making concessions. But once inflamed, the pressures of constituents and principals—audiences—become severe constraints that can leave the parties worse off. And so negotiators seek the cloak of secrecy for signaling and eventually for full negotiations with a delegate from the other side. They cast off the secrecy only once agreements are reached and can be publicized for all parties.[5] This dilemma of publicity is part of the cause for the back channels examined in this book. In addition to secrecy, the Palestinian-Israeli back channels became a fully parallel system of negotiation, often operating in simultaneity with open, acknowledged channels.

The Diplomatic "Black Market"

During the past eight years, there has been a return to armed conflict between Israeli governments that openly disavow the peace process and irregular Palestinian forces that were never part of it in the first place. The Palestinian National Authority struggled to coax its internal opposition to a ceasefire while persuading the Israeli government that a negotiated, comprehensive peace would be better for all than unilateral solutions.

The Palestinian-Israeli peace process, as of late 2010, has stagnated. There have been relatively few significant open negotiations since 2001. Negotiations from 2001 onward have been mostly limited to attempts to deescalate the violence that erupted in late 2000, or to implement previously negotiated commitments, negotiations about restarting negotiations, and pragmatic discussions of issues such as the handover of a checkpoint from the Israeli military to Palestinian security forces or the softening of an economic closure of Palestinian territory and access to Palestine for humanitarian agencies. Ceasefire arrangements have been mediated between Israel and Palestinian militant groups and among the various Palestinian political factions.

Instead of negotiating on the basis of "land for peace" the Israeli government has implemented a unilateral "disengagement" plan that removed its soldiers and settlers from one small part of the Palestinian territories occupied by Israel, the Gaza Strip, even as Israel constructs a barrier around the remaining Palestinian territory, the West Bank, carving out large parts of it for Israeli settlements.

If there is ever to be a permanent agreement between the Israelis and Palestinians, it seems highly likely that it will be negotiated in a back channel. All of the major signed agreements between Israel and the PLO so far have been attained using BCN—alone or in combination with front channels.

Some Characteristics of Back Channel Negotiations

Who are back channel negotiators? In international negotiations, especially those involving questions of war and peace, back channel negotiators tend to be individuals who are closer hierarchically to the top decision makers than are front channel negotiators, which helps explain why they are able to more authoritatively explore a wider range of options and to commit to tentative agreements more readily than are front channel negotiators. A back channel negotiator might be a private individual who has special access to a president or prime minister, or he or she could be a specially empowered national security advisor or other high-ranking foreign affairs officer. In some cases, both the front and back channel negotiations are handled by the same chief negotiator. When back channel negotiators succeed in reaching agreement while their front channel counterparts fail, negotiation theorists and practitioners need to look harder at the differences between front and back channels, since many of the classic variables often examined for correlation to success or failure remain constant: the conflict history and dynamics, the international and regional structure, domestic political factors, the parties' cultural context, and power asymmetries.

BCN negotiators sometimes have their origin in freelance operations without official status or the knowledge of the head of government, but they always leverage strong links to official decision makers to gain official status when they show promise of reaching agreement. BCN overlaps with—but is also different from—Track II diplomacy, which is a deliberate strategy of engaging either officials or "near influentials" from opposing groups for the purpose of dismantling the psychological barriers that prevent the parties from imagining and exploring solutions to their conflict and taking steps toward resolving it.[6] Track II work is typically not considered official negotiation, nor is it designed to result in an officially endorsed agreement, even though officials and former officials are sometimes key participants in Track II efforts. Secret Track II efforts can, however, become BCN if the Track II participants either acquire an official mandate (and are thus empowered to make commitments on behalf of the party they represent) or if a draft agreement emerges from the Track II work that is then endorsed by the official decision makers.

Although back channel negotiations take place in secret, practitioners are not shy about admitting their back channels ex post facto. Henry Kissinger, for example, has described how, as national security advisor in the Nixon and Ford administrations, he kept the U.S. secretary of state in the dark about his diplomatic initiatives in the Middle East, China, and Russia.[7] Kissinger also secretly negotiated with the North Vietnamese in Paris while sidelining both the U.S. ambassador in France and the rest of the U.S. State Department.[8] As secretary of state, he conducted numerous secret negotiations with the Soviets.[9]

Sometimes the back channel is a third party, someone "unofficial" who goes between the parties as a messenger engaging in officially sanctioned, but secret and thus disavowable, diplomacy. Journalists were used as secret negotiators in the Cuban Missile Crisis and the efforts to free the U.S. hostages held in Iran from 1979 to 1980.[10] At other times, BCN is specifically used to *avoid the interference of third parties.* While Russia and the United States led a mediation initiative known as the Minsk Group, which was sponsored by the Organization for Security and Co-operation in Europe (OSCE), to deescalate the conflict between Armenia and Azerbaijan, the Armenian government's top national security official made a direct trip to the Azeri capital to negotiate terms himself, cutting out OSCE and the superpowers and reaching a ceasefire arrangement directly with the Azeris.[11] Former Israeli back channel negotiator Uri Savir considered U.S. mediation during the period 1996 to 2000 to be a "critical mistake" that prevented "creativity, trust and mutual understanding of interests" to emerge.[12] Abu Alaa, who often led Palestinian back channel delegations, also felt that one of the advantages of using back channels was that it prevented the United States from playing a mediation role and to encourage direct understandings among the parties: "the most important thing in the secret negotiations is to educate, to teach the other side about your real concern. And to listen from him about his real concern. [The] third parties' . . . concern is to conclude something, to sign and to finish."[13]

In another notable case of BCN, Jacobus Coetsee, South Africa's minister of justice, police, and prisons, opened a back channel in 1985 to prisoner number 466/64, Nelson Mandela, in order to make "discreet contact" with the leaders of the African National Congress. Over the next few years, Minister Coetsee met with Mandela in prisons, hospitals, and private homes. He subsequently informed South African president PW Botha about the talks, who then gave them his authorization, thus upgrading them to official secret talks. Botha demanded that other cabinet members initially be kept in the dark.[14]

A Typology of Back Channel Negotiation

BCN is a variant of bargaining models that have been subject to analysis for the past several decades, and the differences would appear to impact both the process and outcomes. For this reason, I believe BCN merits consideration as a special "type" of negotiation worthy of separate analysis. A typology of BCN in which several characteristics vary while maintaining an overall conformity with the image of BCN as secret negotiation is presented here. In offering a typology of BCN it is therefore idealized, although in reality there may be greater fluidity and overlap among the categories offered here. Additionally, some of these instances of BCN may involve the use of a third party who acts as the secret conduit in place of direct, secret contacts.

- Secret *prenegotiations* (for exploring the possibility of negotiations, direct or third party)
- *Direct secret* negotiations (with no parallel open activities)
- *Mediated secret* negotiations (with no parallel open activities)
- *Intermittent, sequential* use of open and secret channels of negotiation (direct or third party)
- Secret negotiations conducted in *parallel* with open negotiations (direct or third party or both)

These variants of BCN all share the sine qua non characteristic of secrecy. They are assumed to be neither inherently sinister nor benevolent in intent. Intentionality regarding good faith participation in negotiation is likely to be independent from the type of BCN used. The various forms of BCN result from their placement along a continuum of simultaneity and multiplicity of channels.

On one end of the continuum, in the first variant, back channel negotiation efforts are the only discussions taking place between the parties and may be of such a preliminary nature that their chief purpose is to explore the feasibility of further diplomatic contact or conflict deescalation. In this instance, the parties most likely do not have communication channels, or perhaps do not have diplomatic relations, and are possibly in a state of war or other form of violent conflict. Due to the uncertainties regarding cost of entry and outcome, they may simply need to ascertain whether or not further negotiations should be conducted. If further negotiations are contemplated, the type of negotiation used and the level of party involvement need to be determined. In this prenegotiation use of BCN, unofficial parties and former officials may be present.

In the second variant, BCN appears as a single, secret channel in which the parties are officially represented and are actually negotiating to reach an agreement. Once again, normal negotiation and communication channels are not present or are dysfunctional: there is no front channel. The features that most distinguish this variant from the first are the representation and intention of the parties. The representation is official and deliberate. These typically are not lower-ranking agents removed from the inner circle of the decision makers, but trusted envoys. Their intent is to reach some kind of agreement, not simply to explore the feasibility of substantive negotiation.

Alternately, this variant can be structured by a third-party mediator who acts as the secret conduit between noncommunicative or confrontational parties. The third party, as well as the principal parties, are officially represented. However, here, too, one or more of the parties may use unofficial agents in order to create additional deniability and distance from the mediated effort.

The fourth variant is characterized by intermittent and sequential use of back and front channels. In this instance, one might inquire as to the timing of the sequencing. The secret channels might be used only while political risks of negotiation are high. They can be followed by open sessions or conferences designed to legitimate concessions and celebrate agreements. The front channels may simply be used for the purpose of representation or posturing. The parties are officially represented and move between front and back channels according to need or preference. In this variant, the parties may be most concerned about uncertainties regarding cost of entry and emergence of spoilers. If an agreement in principle is reached in a back channel, it may, for example, lead to front channel negotiations. If spoilers emerge or threaten the stability of a negotiation process, back channels may alternate with front channels.

Finally, the fifth and most complex variant is where back channel negotiations take on an almost entirely separate existence, occurring in parallel with existing front channel negotiations. At this end of the continuum of multiplicity and simultaneity of channels, BCN realizes its full capacity as an alternative negotiation channel. The rich possibilities for negotiating at two separate tables are fully realizable here: the projection of a public negotiating posture while retaining a closely held channel where decision makers contemplate deviations from policy and costly concessions. The full ability to use the channels in strategic ways, to use them to subtly signal preferences and areas of flexibility, is best realized when there are parallel channels. Uncertainties that impact negotiators using this method are likely to concern information about the other party's

Table 1. Variants of Back Channel Negotiation

	Variant	Uses
1	Secret prenegotiations	Determine the feasibility of further negotiations in a front channel. May be conducted by unofficial agents and be a quasi–Track II initiative.
2	Direct, secret negotiations	Classic secret negotiation or secret diplomacy: official representation in a secret channel, which is the only venue of negotiation.
3	Mediated, secret negotiations	Classic secret mediation: official third parties go between official parties who will not or cannot communicate.
4	Intermittent, sequential use of open and secret channels	Preparation and negotiation for the attainment of a final agreement that will eventually be revealed to the public and constituents. Front or back channels are chosen intermittently and according to the kind of uncertainty experienced (cost of entry and spoilers).
5	Secret channels in parallel with open negotiations	Strategic shifts in policy, manipulation of subparties and internal spoilers, protection of the back channel for use in the early phases of a staged peace process. Corresponds most closely with uncertainties about information and outcome.

preferences or uncertainties about the outcome of the negotiation and any consequent impact on the top-level decision makers.

In each of the prior two variants, the configuration may also include a third party. Some cases, however, show evidence of conflict parties who opt for back channels in order to escape the heavy hand of a third-party front channel effort.

Other configurations and variations may exist, and these five may not be so neatly separable in practice, so this typology is offered tentatively. Table 1 summarizes this typology.

Back Channels in the Palestinian-Israeli Conflict

Back channels have been extensively used throughout the years of the Palestinian-Israeli peace process. Yasir Arafat, as chairman of the Palestine Liberation Organization, announced the PLO's recognition of Israel in December 1988 in

Geneva before the UN General Assembly meeting, and his announcement set in motion direct talks between officials of the U.S. government and the PLO, as a prelude to direct peace talks between the PLO and Israel. However, the officials of the PLO and Israel had already been meeting quietly for at least three years before that. They continued to do so even after the United States-PLO dialogue faltered.

At that time, the PLO and Israel did not formally conclude any peace accords. The Israelis were still attached to the century-old fantasy that the final path to resolve the Palestinian question ran through Jordan. The leaders of Israel's major political parties were in a difficult position that required them to share power. In attempting to find the most expedient route to power they could either block each other or build a temporary alliance of convenience. Then, as now, Israeli governments tended to be weak because of this dynamic; they often owe allegiance to divergent and opposing political tendencies. The PLO's leadership was then in exile in Tunisia and the Palestinians of the West Bank and Gaza were engaged in an unarmed uprising against the Israeli military occupation; the first intifada.

In January 1991, the United States organized a multinational coalition to reverse the August 1990 Iraqi invasion of Kuwait. Once the Iraqi surrender was signed, the United States decided to leverage its new diplomatic standing and honor its commitment to pursue Arab-Israeli peace by organizing a comprehensive peace conference.[15] The conference took place in Madrid, Spain, in October 1990. The PLO was officially excluded from that conference, so non-PLO figures had to negotiate with the Israeli government delegates. As those talks ground on without any progress, a secret initiative was launched in Norway in 1993 that brought together high-level PLO officials and Israeli academics connected to their government. When these talks began to show promise, the Israeli academics were joined by high-level Israeli officials. All this took place while the talks sponsored by the United States that had begun in Madrid sputtered on in Washington, D.C.

It was during the secret talks held near Oslo, Norway, that the first agreement between the PLO and Israel was drafted and initialed in late 1993. When knowledge of the breakthrough came out, both outside observers and insiders were amazed at the progress of the back channel negotiators, and some were resentful because they had not been invited to the secret table. Others—both Israelis and Palestinians—complained that "too much was given away" at the secret table from which they had been excluded. Content with their work, leadership on both sides made affirmative decisions to continue and deepen the pattern of conducting secret negotiations in parallel with open ones. Many observers concluded—with unmeasured exuberance—that the back channel approach had been instrumental in the successful breakthrough at Oslo.

Palestinians, Israelis, and people all over the world harbored the hope in 1993 that this first breakthrough, whatever its flaws, would eventually lead to a full and comprehensive peace between Palestinians and Israelis and to a reversal of the Israeli military occupation of the two remaining "pieces" of British Mandate Palestine: the West Bank and the Gaza Strip. Palestinians hoped that the peace process would lead to full international recognition of their state and claims to land and compensation, while Israelis hoped to live without the anxiety and uncertainty of constant conflict locally and internationally.

I shared all of these hopes, but I also had strong concerns about the peace process and its many flaws. I began to systematically study this and other peace processes, hoping to understand the factors involved in their success and failure. By September 1994, within one year of the signing of the Oslo peace accord (known as the Declaration of Principles), I began to suspect that the peace process itself could contain the seeds of its own destruction. After taking a closer look, I found it hard to sustain my initial elation and optimism and published my concerns in a monograph at Harvard's Program on Negotiation.[16] My concerns arose from a desire to *see the peace process succeed*.

After Oslo, both the PLO and Israel continued to set up both open and secret channels, in parallel with each other. This continued throughout the life of the peace process and up to its death throes.

The use of secrecy in diplomacy was a well-known issue and had been a topic of some controversy among policy makers prior to the end of World War I. Debate among scholars of diplomacy followed as newer types of diplomacy began to take hold in a world in which new countries and former colonies demanded a place at the tables of global decisionmaking. "Conference diplomacy," supposedly more consistent with the ideals of democratic decision making and open societies for which the World Wars were fought, became a global standard. But then as now, real decisions of global importance continued to be made behind closed doors.

Back channels, a special use of secret diplomacy, almost never came under any scrutiny at all in either academic or policy-making circles, even as studies of negotiation emerged as a scientific endeavor in their own right in political science and social psychology. Certainly, Kissinger's memoirs and other works provided ample historical evidence that international negotiations are often characterized by back channels operating in parallel with front channels. Only one scholar, Aharon Klieman, paid serious analytical attention to this phenomenon, exploring several instances of Israel's reliance on this kind of diplomacy in his 1988 monograph.[17]

Confusion of Causes and Effects Regarding Peace Processes

Although much descriptive writing on the Palestinian-Israeli conflict concerns itself with polemics and blame, academia spends time testing existing theories on this high-profile international conflict. In undertaking this project, I felt that more fundamental research needed to be done. Polemics and theory testing seemed tired, sterile, and futile if the goal is ultimately to make a difference. There was much that remained to be discovered and understood about Palestinian-Israeli negotiations, and official archives would not become available for decades (and only to the extent that they existed in the first place). There also was and is much to learn about back channel negotiation in general, such as why leaders resort to it in the first place and, perhaps more critically, what happens when you rely on it for several years throughout a peace process. No one had posed such questions before, and I thought then, as I do now, that it was more important to create knowledge about this phenomenon of negotiating in two channels at once while also seeking to understand how the initially promising Palestinian-Israeli peace process had been abandoned in favor of military confrontation. Back channel negotiation is one of the key defining characteristics of the peace process. The failure of policy makers, negotiators, and academics to properly understand it represents a serious gap in our knowledge of peacemaking.

From my own experience mediating conflicts within corporations and between unions and management of public institutions, I could see very clearly some of the basic drivers of the executive use of secrecy because I had personally experienced them; the boisterous rights-based demands of a fractious constituency on the union side and the preoccupation with image, resources, and reappointments that concern management and board members on the negotiation team often contributed to fiery clashes in which even the mediator's blood was on the floor. Quiet dinners, coffee breaks, and clandestine meetings between delegation heads were often more effective than days of expert facilitation. But in the backs of their minds, secret negotiators could anticipate being accused of "being in bed with the enemy." This phenomenon was clearly not limited to the international political sphere.

By the year 2001, opponents of the peace process had succeeded in derailing it completely. Breakaway factions on the Palestinian side were resorting to suicide bombings and guerrilla attacks against Israelis. The Israeli armed forces resorted to a military reoccupation of the West Bank and Gaza, assassinations of militant leaders, and the demolition of Palestinian neighborhoods. Thousands of civilian Palestinians and Israelis have lost their lives. Israel systematically destroyed the Palestinian National Authority's civil structures, including police and security, further weakening the moderates under Yasir Arafat and thereby strengthening militancy. Israelis elected as prime minister a former general, Ariel Sharon, one of the most vehement opponents of the peace process and long-time proponent of the annexation of Palestinian territory and expulsion of Palestinians. Pundits and academics alike seemed to confuse these symptoms of the failure of the peace process with its causes.

I was not satisfied with "explanations" that blamed the international or domestic context for the continuation of the conflict. Contextual factors, including the political mood among Palestinians and Israelis or the domestic pressures and foreign policies of the United States, were themselves things that varied and could be influenced. Certainly the Bush administration's lukewarm commitment to the peace process and rejection of Arafat did not help, but neither could the United States shoulder all the blame. After all, the parties had been negotiating the terms of peace directly (openly and secretly) from 1993 to 2001 under extremely trying circumstances and against a long historical record of failure. The European Union, the United Nations, and Russia had all attempted to support the peace process, but it was beyond the power of any of these actors to jump-start something that already lay dying in early 2001.

Context, then, was clearly not the only place to look for explanations. It would be critical to look at the *process* and *substance* of the negotiations carried out in these years. That is exactly what I set out to do with this book, to take a deeper look at the process and substance of the secret and open Palestinian-Israeli negotiations in order to get answers to what I considered the two most critical questions: how does back channel negotiation work, and what impact does it have on the overall negotiations. The working image of back channels I had in mind emerged around the practice of setting up two negotiation tables sometimes operating simultaneously, one openly and one secretly. In detail, this book sets out to answer the following two questions:

1. *Function.* How does back channel negotiation work? What motivates Palestinian and Israeli leaders to choose back channels over other modes of negotiation and communication? How do they put it into action? What are the operational details of such negotiations? Are issues dealt with differently in back channels than in "front" channels? What role, if any, do third parties such as the United States, Egypt, or Norway play in back channels?

2. *Impact.* What effect does back channel negotiation have on the Palestinian-Israeli peace process specifically and on peace processes in general? What are the intended consequences of using back channels? How do they compare with actual results? What, if any, are the *unintended* consequences of using back channels? This latter question, it seems to me, is particularly important. By seeking answers to that, we may be in a better position to provide advice and guidance to leaders confronting the dilemmas of peacemaking in violent conflicts.

Negotiation practitioners have long understood that attaining agreement is not a sufficient criterion of success. It is the implementation and duration of an agreement that proves its worth. Because implementation of peace process agreements is so fragile, I pay attention to the question of secret negotiation's impact on implementation. If, for example, secret negotiations are used to avoid arousing bureaucratic or popular opposition to a new policy, swift and complete implementation would be desirable. If implementation is only partial or if it is delayed or if it fails altogether, it is appropriate to ask about the negative consequences of the secrecy. In any case, negotiated agreements of importance—whether conducted secretly or openly—often must be "shopped around": stakeholders will need to be persuaded that the new policy is worth supporting. If this task is neglected due to a strategic or tactical need for secrecy, not only can implementation suffer, the sustainability of the negotiation process itself may be put at risk.

For readers interested in the state of our knowledge on international negotiations and the theories concerning them, the final chapter of the book proposes hypotheses derived from the Palestinian-Israeli cases of back channel negotiation, as compared to their front channel negotiations. In this real-world laboratory of critical negotiations, the leaders, the conflict, and the domestic and international context were all "controlled" for; that is, they did not vary across back or front channels. And yet the results obtained in the channels were very different. Thus, a detailed, structured comparison of what the negotiators were doing differently in the different channels yielded findings relevant to those who actually conduct such negotiations and those who study them.

Readers who would prefer to focus on the story of the Palestinian-Israeli negotiation episodes will find the historical-analytical chapters more tempting than the policy and theory implications of the final chapter. In either case, both the structure of this book and the concepts relevant to back channel negotiation remain to be explained here.

How the Historical Negotiations Are Examined

The central chapters of the book tell the story of the negotiations in a structured way, as I systematically take a look at how certain aspects of the negotiations differed across time and across channels. In particular, I look at seven aspects of the negotiations and how they differed.

1. *Issues negotiated.* What are the negotiators trying to deal with? Is there a shared agenda? Do they have differing or competing agendas? What is discussable? Is anything "undiscussable" in a particular channel? If the issues are the same, are they dealt with differently across channels?

2. *Extent of secrecy and publicity.* Because publicity and secrecy are mirror images, it's important to know how much of one versus the other the negotiators were exposed to and what effect it had on them. In Palestinian-Israeli negotiations, publicity and secrecy were used simultaneously. Secret channels were sometimes protected but then "leaked"; front channels were subject to scrutiny but sometimes protected.

3. *People and groups included or excluded.* We know that constituencies, audiences, political allies, and the different parts of government bureaucracies can all exercise pressure and influence on leaders and negotiators. So it is important to identify who is invited to which negotiation table and why. What are the reactions of the parties excluded from back channels? Do they protest quietly? Do they mobilize for political action? Do they take actions to support or block the peace process?

4. *Proximity of the negotiator to the leaders.* How much access does the negotiator have to his or her leader? Is there a difference between front and back channel negotiators in this regard? One working assumption in the course of this research

was that back channel negotiators tend to be "closer" to top decision makers, whereas front channel negotiators are more distant and have less access to the top.

5. *Autonomy of the negotiators.* We know from decades of negotiation research that optimal solutions to complex, shared problems are often not found when parties simply stake out severe positions. Creative, "out-of-the-box" thinking is often associated with agreements that provide the most value to the most parties. To have this creativity, delegates need a certain degree of flexibility in their negotiation instructions. Do negotiators in one channel have more freedom to make demands and concessions, think creatively, and make commitments than negotiators in the other channel? Is this autonomy affected by the proximity of the negotiator to the leader?

6. *Role of third parties.* In international conflicts, third parties often try to (or are invited to) intervene diplomatically by brokering deals, carrying messages, and acting as guarantors of the process and outcome. But they are almost never disinterested or entirely neutral. Are third parties excluded from back channel negotiations? If not, do they mediate differently?

7. *Strategic use of multiple channels.* What motivates leaders to use both back and front channels simultaneously? Do they have different purposes or hopes for each channel? Do the channels affect each other? Are the channels used completely in parallel to each other, or do they follow each other sequentially in time? Are accords from one channel filtered into another channel?

These seven sets of questions offer insights into several analytical aspects of international negotiations and permit us to structure the findings of this research coherently. Chapters 3, 4, and 5 contain the bulk of the narrative of Palestinian-Israeli negotiations and stay close to this structure. Chapters 2 and 6 serve as bookends to the main case chapters and tell the story of the genesis and demise of the peace process. As such they are written in a more straightforward narrative, although the analytical elements are highlighted. Chapter 7 concludes the synthesis of the case findings and the analysis of BCN.

Separation of Interim and Permanent Status Issues

Palestinian-Israeli negotiations have followed a pattern known as "incrementalism" that was embedded in the Camp David Accords of September 17, 1978:

the separation of the negotiation agenda into two interdependent parts, *interim* issues and *permanent status* issues.[18] The interim issues were to be negotiated and implemented during a *transitional* period of five years in which the Israeli military government and armed forces were withdrawn from West Bank and Gaza territory while an elected Palestinian National Authority was to progressively assume governmental functions. In contrast, permanent status talks are to lead to a permanent settlement of the Palestinian-Israeli conflict based on UN Security Council Resolutions 242 (1967) and 338 (1973) and were to commence "not later than the beginning of the third year of the interim period."[19]

Front channels and secret channels have been used for both the interim and permanent status negotiations. The interim issues have concerned the arrangements for Israeli withdrawal of its military from selected Palestinian territories and the assumption of civil and security powers by Palestinian institutions. The systematic exclusion of certain Palestinian militant and political groups from the peace process meant that the interim period negotiations have been strongly characterized by negotiations over security cooperation between the PLO and Israel against such militant groups. Indeed, the interim period negotiations were all predicated on an overarching bargain of security cooperation in exchange for limited autonomy for the Palestinians and limited withdrawals by the Israelis, and no discussion of the permanent status issues. Table 2 presents the agreements reached by Israel and the PLO.

Looming very large in the background, the permanent status issues were not so easily separated from the interim arrangements. Five final status issues remain:

- Status of Arab East Jerusalem (currently occupied by Israel)
- The future of Israeli settlements in the occupied territories
- The future of Palestinian refugees and the exercise of their right of return to property in Israel, Jerusalem, the West Bank, and Gaza
- Final borders and political status of Palestine
- Israel's security concerns

Declared positions of the parties are presented in table 3 and described in simplified language that does not account for the wide breadth of debate within each side on these volatile and contentious issues.

Table 2. Chronology of Agreements, 1993 to 2003

Agreements	Dates of negotiation	Scope	BCN/FCN
1 Declaration of Principles on Interim Self-Government Arrangements, Sept. 13, 1993 [and four side letters]	Jan. 1993 to Sept. 1993	Mutual recognition, framework for conducting the rest of the peace process.	BCN/FCN
2 Cairo Agreement, Feb. 9, 1994	Oct. 13, 1993 to Jan. 9, 1994	Security aspects of initial IDF withdrawal.	BCN/FCN
3 Israeli-Palestinian Security Agreement, Mar. 31, 1994	Mar. 6 to 31, 1994	Interim; limited to Hebron in aftermath of massacre at Ibrahimi Mosque.	BCN/FCN
4 Economic Agreement (Paris Protocol), Apr. 29, 1994	Nov. 1993 to Apr. 29, 1994	Interim; limited to economic issues.	FCN
5 Agreement on the Gaza Strip and Jericho Area, May 4, 1994 (incorporating both the Cairo Agreement and Paris Protocol)	Sept. 13, 1993 to May 4, 1994	Interim; initial Israeli withdrawal.	BCN/FCN
6 Agreement on the Preparatory Transfer of Powers and Responsibilities, Aug. 29, 1994	July 5, 1994 to Aug. 29, 1994	Interim; spheres of authority.	BCN/FCN
7 Interim Agreement on the West Bank and Gaza Strip ("Oslo II"), Sept. 28, 1995	Dec. 6, 1994 to Sept. 24, 1995	Interim; comprehensive. Palestinian political and security authority, Israeli withdrawal timetable and scope.	BCN/FCN
8 Framework for the Conclusion of a Final Status Agreement (Stockholm or Beilin-Abu Mazen Agreement), Oct. 31, 1995	Sept. 1, 1994 to Oct. 31, 1995	Permanent; framework agreement.	BCN
9 Israel-PLO Permanent Status Negotiations [joint communiqué]	May 5-6, 1996	Permanent.	FCN
10 Hebron Protocol, Note for the Record, and Agreed Minute, Jan. 15, 1997	Aug. 1996 to Jan. 15, 1997	Interim; implementation of Interim Agreement.	BCN/FCN

(continued)

20   Back Channel Negotiation

Table 2. Chronology of Agreements, 1993 to 2003 *(continued)*

Agreements	Dates of negotiation	Scope	BCN/FCN
11 Wye River Memorandum, Oct. 23, 1998	Back channels from May to Oct. 1998; Summit Oct. 15 to 23, 1998	Interim; implementation of Interim Agreement.	BCN/FCN
12 The Sharm el-Sheikh Memorandum on Implementation Timeline of Outstanding Commitments of Agreements Signed and the Resumption of Permanent Status Negotiations, September 4, 1999	1999	Renegotiation of renegotiated agreement, resumption of permanent status.	BCN/FCN
13 Protocol Concerning Safe Passage Between the West Bank and the Gaza Strip, Oct. 5, 1999	1999	Interim.	FCN
14 Israeli-Palestinian Joint Statement, Jan. 27, 2001	Jan. 21 to 27, 2001	Permanent, following failure of Clinton summit, Taba, and back channels.	FCN/BCN
15 Geneva Accords (the "Virtual Agreement"), Dec. 2003	2001 to 2003	Permanent, comprehensive.	BCN

Table 3. Final Status Issues, with Some Traditional Israeli and Palestinian Policies

Final status issue	Israel	Palestine
1 Jerusalem	Unified halves (East and West) of Jerusalem comprise the eternal capital of Israel, including the Old City and its holy sites. The city is to be expanded and joined to settlements in East Jerusalem.	Arab East Jerusalem is occupied territory since the June 1967 war. East Jerusalem (including the Old City) is "al-Quds" the capital of Palestine. The city should not be divided; both states to have their capital within a shared municipality. Compensation is due to the Palestinians evicted from West Jerusalem.
2 Refugees	Israel has no moral or legal responsibility for the refugees. They cannot return to Israel, except in very small numbers for family reunification. Their return is a demographic bomb that implies the destruction of Israel. Arab states should accept them as citizens.	The refugee problem was caused by Israel; they were mostly expelled from their homes by force. Refugees have a right of return to their lands and properties in Israel under international law. They are also entitled to compensation for homes, businesses, and property lost when they were made refugees.
3 Borders	The borders of the West Bank and Gaza prior to June 1967 are not relevant. Negotiate with the Palestinians over what parts of the West Bank they will give up and what parts they retain. The territory will not become a sovereign state. Palestinian territories need not be connected to each other.	All of the Gaza Strip and the West Bank, including East Jerusalem, are occupied territory and are the territorial basis for the state of Palestine and must be evacuated by the Israeli armed forces and settlers. Together they amount to approximately 27 percent of Mandate Palestine. Any territorial exchanges should be made on the basis of equal value and area.
4 Settlements	The vast bulk of the settlements, especially those constructed in and around East Jerusalem and along the Green Line (pre-June 1967 border between Israel and the West Bank) and the settlements in the Jordan Valley and elsewhere, to be incorporated into Israel.	All settlements to be evacuated and the territory returned to the Palestinian owners and communities for private or public use. In some cases, settlers who wish to become Palestinian citizens may stay.

(continued)

Table 3. Final Status Issues, with Some Traditional Israeli and Palestinian Policies *(continued)*

	Final status issue	*Israel*	*Palestine*
5	Security	Jordan Valley is the Israeli "security border." There can be no Palestinian army and no presence of any international peacekeeping troops in Israel or the territories west of the Jordan River. All border crossings, ports, and airspace must be controlled by Israel.	Crossings between the West Bank and Jordan, and between Gaza and Egypt, must be controlled by the Palestinian state. Israeli troops must be withdrawn from all the occupied territories. Palestinians to maintain their own internal security forces. United Nations or other international peacekeeping troops needed to protect Palestinians and reassure Israelis.

2

The Search for Peace in the Palestinian-Israeli Conflict, 1973 to 1991

I have come to you so that together we should build a durable peace based on justice to avoid the shedding of one single drop of blood.
—ANWAR EL-SADAT[1]

The search for peace in the Palestinian-Israeli conflict did not originate in Washington, Stockholm, or Geneva. Nor did it commence in the 1990s. It dates all the way to the conflict's origins when Palestinian notables, officials of the Hashemite royal family (that was later to rule Jordan), and Zionist leaders attempted to find elusive common ground in the early years of the British Mandate in Palestine. All their attempts failed. Major diplomatic efforts undertaken by the United States, the United Nations, and others followed each of the five major Arab-Israeli wars of 1948, 1956, 1967, 1973, and 1982. These too utterly failed to resolve any aspect of the Palestinian-Israeli conflict. In each of those efforts, the Palestinians and their leadership were consistently excluded from the discussions on their own fate.[2]

Getting to the negotiation table would, for the Palestinians, be an intrinsic major diplomatic goal and consume vast political resources. The United States and Israel ended up negotiating with the PLO, directly but secretly, precisely because they came to realize that the PLO was indispensable to a peace settlement. Their self-imposed limitation of refusing the PLO official diplomatic recognition was one of the original drivers of the secrecy that enshrouded their early contacts even after the PLO abandoned its rejection of Israel and recognized its right to exist.

Rather than recount nearly a century of what Professor Neil Caplan has so aptly termed "futile diplomacy," this chapter sets out the major attempts to

23

resolve the Palestinian self-determination question of the past three decades.[3] The narratives described here are organically linked. Taken together, they show that the systematic attempts to exclude Palestinian leaders from political discussions and the failure of Israel and the PLO's military approaches paved the way for direct and secret talks between them. The origins of the major patterns of later PLO-Israel peacemaking are found in this period, including the reliance on a step-by-step incrementalist approach and Israel's preference for ceding some degree of civil authority (but not real sovereignty) to the Palestinians.

Negotiating Palestine, Avoiding the Palestinians

At a summit of the Arab League in Rabat, Morocco, on October 28, 1974, the PLO was recognized by the Arab states as the "sole, legitimate representative of the Palestine people."[4] With this move the PLO moved closer to becoming the indispensable party in any diplomatic efforts regarding the West Bank and Gaza. It signaled that the Arab states viewed the PLO as an independent actor and that the future peace of the region would depend on the emergence of an independent Palestine not controlled by any of them. The PLO was transformed from an instrument of proxy war used by the Arab states against Israel into a more independent actor. Nevertheless, the PLO was not offered a seat at any diplomatic table.

In the wake of the October 1973 War that pitted Israel against Egypt and Syria, Henry Kissinger's vigorous shuttle diplomacy resulted in separate disengagement agreements between Israel and Egypt (January 18, 1974) and between Israel and Syria (May 31, 1974).[5] By September 4, 1975, the second Israeli-Egyptian disengagement agreement known as "Sinai II" was signed in Geneva, further separating the forces in the Sinai and more deeply involving UN troops as peacekeepers.[6] As one of the concessions made by the United States in exchange for Israel's compliance with Sinai II, Kissinger made a commitment that the United States would not deal with the PLO until it had accepted UN Security Council Resolutions 242 (1967) and 338 (1973)[7] and as long as the PLO refused to recognize Israel's right to exist.[8]

While he was busy obtaining Israeli commitment to the Sinai II disengagement agreement, Kissinger sent his own high-level envoy to meet with the PLO, deputy director of Central Intelligence, lieutenant general Vernon Walters (he would later become ambassador to the UN, among other high-level diplomatic posts). At the PLO's invitation, General Walters met with Hani al-Hasan, executive member of the PLO Central Committee, in Morocco in November 1973 and again in March 1974. Despite the possibilities their meeting held, Kissinger gave Walters remarkably little room to negotiate and limited him to warning the PLO against attacks on Jordan, Israel, and also against U.S. targets. (The PLO had assassinated two U.S. officials in Sudan in March 1973 and had been expelled from Jordan in September 1970 after attempting to overthrow the monarchy.) When Kissinger gave Walters his orders to go, Walters responded, "but I'm the Deputy Director of the CIA, I'm probably number five on their hit list." Kissinger responded, "I'm the Secretary of State. I'm probably number one on their list. Go!" Of the three PLO officials with whom Walters met, two would be killed in Palestinian infighting.[9]

The assumption of the U.S. presidency by Jimmy Carter in January 1977 provided an opportunity for reenergized outside leadership to intervene in the peace process.[10] The Carter presidency signaled Henry Kissinger's exit from public life and left Carter with the difficult challenge of converting the disengagement agreements Kissinger had brokered into true peace settlements. On June 21, 1977, Menachem Begin became prime minister of Israel after his secular right-wing Likud Party prevailed in the Knesset elections. He publicly committed the Israeli government to expanding settlements in the occupied West Bank and Gaza. Carter's secretary of state, Cyrus Vance, was then sending out feelers through the Egyptians to see if the PLO would accept UN Security Council Resolution 242 in order to become a potential negotiating partner in the Arab-Israeli peace process.[11] Ultimately, the United States continued its policy of excluding the PLO, following the maxim that politics is the art of the possible. The diplomatic separation of Egypt from the Palestinians, Jordan, and Syria had already been encompassed during Sadat's overtures for U.S. mediation, and Sadat was firmly tracking a path toward peace with Israel that neither the United States nor the Israelis could quite comprehend. Sadat's frustration with the United States' incrementalism and Israel's lack of initiative on a more comprehensive peace led him to his dramatic trip to Jerusalem on November 19, 1977. The trip and further Egyptian concessions elicited no reciprocal movement from Israel toward a more comprehensive peace and resulted in Egypt's isolation within the Arab world.

Almost two years into his presidency, Jimmy Carter invited the leaders of Israel and Egypt to a peacemaking summit. From September 5 to September 17,

1978, President Carter, Prime Minister Begin, and President Sadat met at Camp David and hammered out two framework agreements. The first agreement set out the basis for future negotiations on a full Israeli-Egyptian peace treaty, and the second set out interim Palestinian autonomy arrangements for the West Bank and Gaza Strip.[12] The first agreement ultimately culminated in a full-fledged Egypt-Israel peace treaty that was signed on March 26, 1979, after more vigorous personal diplomacy by Carter. The second agreement was reneged upon by Israel's secular right-wing Likud government, despite sustained mediation by Carter, Secretary of State Cyrus Vance, and special U.S. negotiator Sol Linowitz.[13]

The Camp David Accords served as the model and benchmark for future patterns of Arab-Israeli diplomacy concerning the Palestinians' political status. It envisioned three separate negotiation processes: Egypt, Israel, and Jordan along with representatives of the population of the West Bank and Gaza would negotiate an agreement creating an "elected self-governing authority in the West Bank and Gaza" and providing for a limited withdrawal of Israeli troops. This was to lead to a "transitional period" of three to five years in duration. The transitional period was the hallmark of the incrementalist strategy of negotiation. It seemed necessary because of the gap between el-Sadat's demand for Palestinian independence in all of the West Bank and Gaza prior to June 1967, including East Jerusalem, and the Israeli offer to concede only "administrative" autonomy to the Arab residents of some parts of the occupied territories. This strategy reflected an American bridging proposal to defer negotiation on the core issues that generated the most positional demands and the least mutual concessions.[14]

The final status negotiations were to start before the third year of the transitional period. These talks would be held by and among Egypt, Israel, Jordan, and West Bank and Gaza Palestinian leaders elected during the transitional period.

A "separate but related committee" would negotiate the terms of the Jordanian-Israel peace treaty, "taking into account the agreement reached on the final status of the West Bank and Gaza."[15]

Palestinians, whether West Bank or Gaza civic leaders or PLO political officials, were all excluded from the post–Camp David Egyptian-Israeli negotiations dealing with the creation of a Palestinian Self-Government Authority and its powers. Foreign minister Moshe Dayan informally consulted with West Bank and Gaza notables regarding Palestinian preferences on their political status and was confounded by the plethora of political perspectives he encountered. While

Dayan was under the impression that the Israeli occupation was beneficial and enlightened toward the Palestinians, he disagreed with Prime Minister Begin on the degree and scope of Jewish settlements to be built in the occupied territories.[16]

Prime Minister Begin and his minister of agriculture, a former general named Ariel Sharon, began implementing aggressive plans to build Israeli settlements in the West Bank despite Begin's pledge to freeze all settlements during negotiations and publicly commit Israel to this in a side letter to the Camp David Framework for Peace.[17] Although Egyptian-Israeli talks on the Palestinian autonomy issue continued under the watch of special negotiator Sol Linowitz for a short time after Carter left office, the Israeli invasion of Lebanon in 1982 led Egypt to recall its ambassador from Israel and finally withdraw from all negotiations over Palestinian autonomy. Linowitz asserts that considerable progress was made on his negotiations with the Israelis over the powers to be assumed by the eventual Palestinian National Authority. He confesses that he could not resolve the issues of territorial sovereignty, water rights, internal/external security responsibilities, or the fate of East Jerusalem, all critical to the viability of a peace process.[18] The agreement remained a dead letter.

Strangely enough, a single U.S. diplomat, the U.S. ambassador to Lebanon, Robert Dillon, was at the same time having direct dealings with PLO leaders operating in Beirut. The relationship is said to have yielded political benefits to both sides but was never fully developed or widely acknowledged.[19] Most critical, this channel seems never to have been utilized for the purpose of engaging directly on the efforts to resolve the Palestinian-Israeli conflict. In August 1979, President Carter's ambassador to the United Nations, Andrew Young, in his term as president of the UN Security Council, was forced to resign because of the political fallout from having met informally with the PLO's representative at the United Nations.[20] On October 21, 1979, Moshe Dayan, the Israeli foreign minister (he had been defense minister during the 1967 War), resigned his cabinet post due to his disagreements with Begin over the scope and purpose of Israeli settlement of the West Bank. He had previously been sidelined from the autonomy negotiations.[21]

The failure to implement the provisions on Palestinian autonomy in the Camp David framework agreement undoubtedly helped foster among Palestinian political leaders a renewed sense that no Arab state or other third party—including Egypt, the United States, and the Soviet Union—could be counted on to negotiate the terms of their self-determination or to otherwise represent their interests with Israel.

In 1981, the year before the Israeli invasion of Lebanon began, President Sadat met with a group of prominent British and French Jews in Paris. The meeting had been arranged by Austrian chancellor Bruno Kreisky, who had been quietly busy trying to arrange contacts between the PLO and Israeli opposition leaders under the organizational pretext of meetings of Socialist International. Just prior to his trip, Sadat summoned the PLO ambassador in Cairo, Said Kemal, to advise him on the inevitability of peacemaking with Israel and how to sequence diplomatic moves. He recommended approaching prominent Jewish individuals and organizations abroad first, who would in turn work with the Israeli government. Washington should be approached last. He strongly recommended that Kemal meet with professor Stephen Cohen, a Canadian academic who had worked with Harvard University social psychologist Herbert Kelman on Israeli-Palestinian problem-solving workshops in the 1970s.[22] Cohen and Kemal met with Arafat's consent and knowledge, but when news of his meetings with Cohen leaked out, Kemal had to step down from his PLO post. Nevertheless, they continued to meet with the knowledge of Yasir Arafat.[23]

The peace treaty between Egypt and Israel therefore did not in itself facilitate the attainment of a comprehensive regional peace because it resulted in what Begin had most desired: a separate peace between Egypt and Israel not conditional upon or linked to any agreements related to Palestine or any other Arab country. On the contrary, the possibility of open, meaningful negotiations with Jordan, Lebanon, Syria, and—most critical—the Palestinians, became more remote. Several further political developments helped to tarnish the image among Egyptians of this landmark peace agreement and compromised Egypt's position as a leader of pan-Arab nationalism.[24]

When negotiations over Palestinian autonomy finally broke down, Israel attempted to unilaterally impose its own vision of regional order and Palestinian autonomy. Israel's military government in the West Bank began trying to create a non-PLO leadership in Palestinian villages. "Pro-PLO mayors in the larger cities were dismissed, and the number of deportations, curfews, house demolitions, property seizures and imprisonment without trial increased."[25] Israel declared that it had annexed East Jerusalem in 1980 and extended Israeli law into the Syrian Golan Heights in 1981. Israel launched an airstrike on Iraq that destroyed that country's Osirak nuclear reactor in June 1981. In October 1981, on the eighth anniversary of the commencement of the October 1973 War, Egyptian president Anwar el-Sadat was assassinated by Islamic militants in the Egyptian Army. Armed confrontation between the PLO and Israel continued on the Israeli-Lebanese border and ultimately led to the invasions of Lebanon in 1978 and 1982. The future of regional peace seemed ever more remote. During the final phases of the Israeli withdrawal from Egypt in April 1982, Israel failed to return to Egypt the Red Sea area of Taba in the Sinai Desert (although this issue was later settled by arbitration). Egypt had played a central role in the creation of the PLO and was one of its remaining allies in the Arab world after the PLO's problems with Syria, Lebanon, and Jordan. In this context, Egypt's political isolation after making its "separate peace" contributed to the PLO's search for other allies among the Persian Gulf states, such as Iraq and Kuwait.

One consequence of the PLO's continued exclusion from the negotiation table and the failure of the talks sponsored by the United States to make any progress on Palestinian autonomy was an escalation of direct military confrontation between Israel and the PLO. The PLO had by then set up a virtual "state-within-a-state" within Lebanon, taking advantage of and exacerbating the civil war that had left a political vacuum in Lebanon. Israel and the PLO continued their confrontation on the Israeli-Lebanese border. President Carter had personally exchanged "harsh" messages with Prime Minister Begin on Israeli incursions into Lebanon, and the United States continued to be concerned about the fighting during the Reagan administration.[26]

In May 1981, the United States sent a special presidential envoy, Philip Habib, to forestall an outright Israeli invasion of Lebanon. He negotiated a fragile PLO-Israeli ceasefire by July 24, 1981. Secretary of State Alexander Haig had been briefed in May on the Israeli invasion plans by Defense Minister Sharon and is reported to have expressed only mild concern, which Sharon allegedly interpreted as a "green light." Despite Habib's ceasefire, Israel launched a massive invasion on June 6, 1982, and set out to trap the PLO combatants in Beirut so that Israel's Lebanese militia ally, the right-wing Christian Phalange movement, could eliminate the Palestinians living in Beirut.[27] The destruction of Beirut and the toll of the invasion on Palestinian and Lebanese civilians quickly turned President Reagan and his administration against it. Habib found himself again pressed into service from retirement.[28]

Hampered by heavy Israeli shelling of Beirut and direct harassment by Israeli forces, prevented from negotiating directly with the PLO and Arafat by Kissinger's prior commitment to Israel, Habib negotiated the August 1982 evacuation of the PLO troops from Lebanon into exile in Tunis and elsewhere. He hoped that the evacuation would stop the killing, deprive Sharon of his primary casus belli and buy time for deeper regional peacemaking.[29] Unfortunately, it accomplished only the first goal, and only temporarily at that. Habib conducted his negotiations with the PLO through the Lebanese foreign minister, Shafik al-Wazzan. Other U.S.-PLO intermediaries were at work in parallel with Habib's efforts, including a serious French effort to mediate the PLO's evacuation[30] and some direct contacts between U.S. officials and PLO/Fatah leader Hani al-Hasan.[31]

Building on Habib's momentary triumph, President Reagan presented a major policy speech on September 1, 1982, signifying that American diplomacy would embark on a "fresh start" in the Middle East. Reagan specifically mentioned the Palestinian people's "legitimate rights" and "just requirements" to self-government in association with Jordan, while also affirming steadfast support for Israeli security.[32] The new initiative had been developed by Haig's replacement, the incoming secretary of state, George Shultz, who viewed the resolution of the Palestinian question as central to any overall resolution of the Arab-Israeli conflict.[33] The Palestinian issue was on the agenda, but the PLO was still being avoided.

Reagan's speech infuriated the Israeli prime minister, provoking his "shock and outrage,"[34] and Defense Minister Sharon responded to the United States' "fresh start" by renewing the Israeli assault on Beirut.[35] While that city agonized and burned throughout September, a massacre of Palestinian refugees in West Beirut was committed by the Lebanese Phalange forces who were then under the operational command of the IDF.[36] The news of the massacre provoked international revulsion and began turning Israeli public opinion against the war.[37]

Habib's continuing efforts to deescalate the conflict foundered against numerous obstacles. Habib was replaced by National Security Council official Robert "Bud" McFarlane, whose policy recommendations led the United States to become a direct combatant in the Lebanese civil war, rather than a broker of international peace. The "fresh start" that was supposed to crown Philip Habib's efforts became a victim of the catastrophic suicide bombings of the U.S. embassy (April 18, 1983) and U.S. Marine compound (October 23, 1983) in Beirut.[38]

Direct negotiations between officials of the PLO and the Israeli government did not start until 1984 and took place entirely in secret. Their existence continues to be denied by some of the officials involved. It was not until a Palestinian popular uprising started in December 1987 that Israeli governments started pondering the possibility of a PLO role in the administration of the occupied territories, which they could no longer dominate with impunity. The next two sections consider those first direct, secret contacts that would set the foundation for the following two decades of Palestinian-Israeli negotiations.

The Earliest Official Secret Contacts Between Israel and the PLO

Due to the failure of any political party to achieve an outright electoral majority in Israel's 1984 elections, a "national unity" government was forged from an alliance of convenience between the two principal parties, Labor and Likud. The coalition took power in September 1984. Yitzhak Rabin (of the Labor Party) became defense minister while Shimon Peres (also Labor) shared a rotating prime ministry with Yitzhak Shamir of (the Likud Party). Peres served as prime minister for the first two years of the coalition government, and Shamir served as prime minister for the last two years. The Likud-Labor "cohabitation" (as some called it) at the highest levels of government provided new opportunities for departures from traditional diplomacy because the government itself manifested divergent views on peacemaking and the Palestinians.

Reuven Hazak, second in command at Israel's domestic counterintelligence agency Shin Bet, was assigned in July 1984 to keep a watch on Stephen Cohen, the Canadian academic who had recently informed Yitzhak Shamir of his interactions with Egyptian officials and the PLO. Cohen persuaded Hazak that he intended no harm to the state of Israel and that to the contrary, they could work together. They jointly came up with a strategy to goad Shamir toward negotiating directly with his archenemy, the PLO. According to one diplomatic history, Cohen obtained official authorization to establish secret contacts with the PLO on behalf of the Shin Bet, under the pretext of obtaining information on the fate of Israeli MIAs (soldiers missing in action) in Lebanon; Shamir is said to have approved of this venture, although he denies it.[39] Cohen separately met with Arafat in Tunis and succeeded in persuading him that secret talks between the PLO and the Israelis could prepare the way for an official peace process.[40] At that time,

Arafat coined the phrase "secret kitchen" for such talks, referring to secret negotiations for preparing both the "ingredients" and the "courses" to be "served" in front channel negotiations.

Peres describes the secret channel opened to the PLO during his term as prime minister, and he does not deny authorizing those missions. Shamir, Rabin, and Peres discussed them at their ministerial meetings during the years of the national unity government.[41] Peres, however, does not claim that this channel was opened to explore a political settlement with the Palestinians, but only to discuss the MIA issue.

On February 11, 1985, Jordan and the PLO announced their intention to form a joint negotiating team. After a future Israeli withdrawal from the occupied territories, they would create a confederation of the Arab states of Jordan and Palestine that would span both banks of the Jordan River.[42] Although this outcome was exactly what Reagan and Shultz had called for in their September 1982 policy announcement, no U.S. engagement followed this announcement.[43] By healing their rift with and linking themselves to the Jordanians, whom the Israelis and the United States preferred as a negotiation partner, the PLO was reversing its long exclusion from negotiations and making itself an indispensable part of a future peace process.[44]

Israel sent one of its high Shin Bet officials, Yossi Genosar, to New York in June 1985 to meet with Said Kemal, the restored PLO representative in Egypt, in order to conduct a kind of prenegotiation session that was being supervised by an interesting list of Israeli leaders, all of whom would play key roles in the peace process over the following two decades: Ehud Barak, then chief of military intelligence; Shimon Peres, prime minister; Yossi Beilin, the then cabinet secretary; Yitzhak Rabin, minister of defense; and Avraham Shalom, head of Shin Bet.[45]

Genosar and Kemal met again in London during August 1985, where the PLO made proposals that can only be considered remarkable in light of the early stage of high-level Palestinian-Israeli contact and compared to what they eventually agreed upon nearly a decade later—a decade during which much blood was spilled during the first intifada and the Gulf War and further violence by Israeli soldiers, settlers, and Palestinians. In the course of these secret contacts, the PLO in 1985 proposed to its Israeli counterparts a peace process beginning with Palestinian self-rule in Gaza and leading to a Palestinian confederation with Israel.[46] The "Gaza-first" proposal had been first discussed by Egyptian president Anwar el-Sadat, U.S. secretary of state Cyrus Vance, and Shimon Peres in the context of the Camp David Accords on Palestinian autonomy.[47] However, the idea that the PLO itself would propose a Palestinian confederation with Israel seems nothing less than stunning in its boldness.

In late 1985, Peres recruited Shlomo Gazit, a retired general who was the first military governor of the West Bank and a former head of military intelligence, to carry out a secret mission to the PLO in Geneva. His nonofficial status gave him "deniability" and therefore distanced him somewhat from the shaky Israeli coalition government. A Palestinian assassination attempt in Cyprus claimed three Israeli lives in September and led to a reprisal Israeli airstrike on October 1, 1985, against the PLO headquarters-in-exile in Tunis, killing seventy-five Palestinians and Tunisians and nearly killing Arafat and other top leaders. On October 7, 1985, an extremist but marginal Palestinian faction hijacked the Italian cruise ship *Achille Lauro* on its passage between Egypt and Israel. In light of those events, Prime Minister Peres and Defense Minister Rabin cancelled the Gazit mission to Geneva.[48]

The early attempts by the PLO and Israel to settle their dispute resulted only in the exchange of ideas without any commitment. The content of those ideas eventually found their way into the formal agreements made between the PLO and Israel ten years later.

The Fading Jordanian Role

Shimon Peres called for an international peace conference on the Middle East in his speech before the UN General Assembly in October 1985. King Hussein and Shimon Peres had already met secretly in London on July 19 order to develop a plan for joint rule of the West Bank (their so-called condominium plan) that was supposed to emerge from the envisioned international conference and met again there on October 5, 1985. Nevertheless, U.S. officials such as George Shultz concluded that "neither Hussein nor Peres was politically strong enough to deliver the concessions needed to make the peace process work, even though their own thinking was not far apart."[49]

Arafat was attacked militarily but also was courted secretly by Israel, challenged by extremist terrorist factions within the Palestinian movement, and in early 1986, found himself and the PLO openly abandoned by Hussein who had opted for healing the political rift that had developed between Syria (also hostile to the PLO) and Jordan. The rift between the PLO and Jordan developed over the questions of American engagement with the PLO. The PLO insisted on direct channels, while the United States insisted on detailed PLO commitments to UN Security Council Resolutions 242 and 338. Jordan was the intermediary in these exchanges, which ended up straining and breaking Jordanian-PLO relations.[50] A summit meeting between Arafat and Hussein took place on January 25, 1986, but resulted in a complete rupture. No joint PLO-Jordanian cooperation in international diplomacy could be envisaged. Hussein, as noted above, appeared to already have shifted from the PLO to Israel as a potential partner in the joint rule of the West Bank.

This reliance by the United States and Israel on first Egypt and later Jordan to "deliver" the PLO, or to assume political representation of West Bank and Gazan Palestinians and thus bypass the PLO, was to have significant implications for the broader regional peace process because it relied on sustained and solid Jordanian-PLO cooperation with the PLO as a submissive junior partner at best. This approach also depended on the political will of Jordan's Hashemite Kingdom to assert its claim to represent the Palestinians, which itself implied further armed confrontation with the PLO—an unlikely scenario—which the Jordanians had already given up. By September 1970, Jordan had already endured a year of escalating confrontations with various infighting Palestinian factions who were all opposed to any Jordanian peacemaking with Israel. Some of these factions were determined to overthrow the monarchy. In response, Jordan, with Israeli backing, attacked PLO military and refugee camps and expelled the PLO from Jordan in a military operation that cost thousands of Palestinian civilians and fighters their lives. The episode is known as "Black September."[51]

These diplomatic events foreshadowed the eventual necessity for both Israel and the United States to deal directly with the PLO in a sustained manner and laid the political groundwork for the intensified and ongoing use of multiple channels of diplomacy.

Secret Prenegotiations Between Israel and the PLO

The continued difficulties of using the Jordanians as proxies for negotiations with the Palestinians possibly prompted Peres to send Shlomo Gazit and Yossi

Genosar to Paris to meet with Hani al-Hasan, executive member of the PLO Central Committee and PLO ambassador to Egypt Said Kemal on February 21, 1986. Professor Stephen Cohen joined the group as well. Fourteen years later, at the start of the second intifada, Gazit would recall: "I was the first one to negotiate with the PLO in secret."[52] The pretext for these negotiations continued to be the possibility of obtaining PLO intelligence on the fate of Israeli MIAs in Lebanon, in exchange for ongoing dialogue on the terms of Israeli-Palestinian coexistence and political matters.[53] A second meeting took place in Brussels on March 12, 1986, in which, significantly, it appears that both the Israeli and Palestinian delegations proposed the simultaneous use of an international conference leading to bilateral open negotiations and secret parallel negotiations. The difference between their proposals seemed to be how much importance to assign to the official negotiations; the Israelis proposed that the front channels be a facade, while the Palestinians responded that the front channels had an intrinsic importance that should not be dismissed.

A third meeting took place in Paris on April 3, 1986. The Israelis declined an invitation from Yasir Arafat to meet with him in Tunis. The delegations further developed the idea that an international conference would be attended by prominent West Bank and Gaza Palestinians, but not by PLO officials from the Palestinian Diaspora, who would work only in the secret channel. Agreements would be drafted in the secret channel and finalized in the open one,[54] a proposal that is nearly an exact prototype of the parallel Madrid/Oslo negotiations that took place from 1991 to 1993. Shimon Peres readily acknowledges that he initiated these negotiations, although he claims they were limited in scope to the MIA issue alone. He also argues that "Shamir knew of these missions: they were discussed in our discreet 'prime ministers' troika,' which was made up of Shamir, Rabin and myself."[55] Shamir, however, denies knowledge of those talks.[56]

The third member of the troika, defense minister Yitzhak Rabin, also explored some secret channels of negotiation with Palestinians. A member of his staff, Eitan Haber (who became Rabin's chief of staff when Rabin became prime minister in 1994) initiated a series of approximately twelve secret negotiation sessions for Rabin with Palestinian mayors from the West Bank and Gaza in 1987. There were two purposes for these meetings. Rabin hoped to forestall social unrest that some Israeli observers anticipated in the days before the intifada while also checking to see if any Palestinian leaders would make concessions to Israel rather than rely on the PLO as the representative of Palestinian national-ism and leadership.

Haber claims that the secrecy of these meetings was to protect the Pales-tinian mayors from being assassinated by hard-line elements of the PLO due to their meetings with Israeli officials, although Rabin too could take advantage of the secrecy for his own political protection. After the meetings with Rabin, arrangements were made for follow-up meetings between the mayors and two Israeli envoys, Yossi Genosar of the Shin Bet and Shlomo Gazit, the retired head of Israeli military intelligence. Haber and Rabin concluded that the Palestinian mayors could not substitute for the PLO itself and that some feared reprisals from the PLO were they to be accused of talking with the Israelis. Only among the Tunis-based PLO would the Israelis be able to find Palestinian leaders willing to take responsibility for peacemaking with Israel.[57]

The Israeli Ban on Contact with the PLO

As the frequency of meetings between Israelis and Palestinians (including PLO officials) increased, a small but growing sector of the Israeli electorate began supporting the idea of direct negotiations with the PLO. The Likud members of the national unity coalition government in Israel began seeking ways to pro-hibit such meetings by legislation. Their efforts dovetailed with the Labor Party's desire to outlaw Kach, the racist political party of Brooklyn-born rabbi Meir Kahane, which openly advocates the wholesale expulsion of all Palestinian Arabs from Israel, the West Bank, and Gaza Strip. A Labor-Likud deal resulted in twin laws passed on August 5, 1986, one excluding Kach from participation in govern-ment and the other criminalizing Israeli contacts with the PLO. Only journalists and academics attending conferences were exempted from the anti-PLO legisla-tion and the three-year prison sentence it prescribed.[58] A new barrier had been erected to "dialogue with the enemy."

Besides the obvious benefit of not having to disavow their publicly declared antinegotiation postures, there was at least one reason PLO and Israeli officials found the "secret kitchen" idea appealing: external parties with an interest in the conflict—whether interested superpowers such as the United States and, at that time, the Soviet Union, or regional players such as Syria—could be excluded from negotiations processes as they tended to use the parties and any negotiations for their own strategic benefit, in addition to or in substitution for the interests of the parties themselves.[59]

During the period that contact with the PLO was forbidden to Israeli citizens, the communications between the PLO and Israel then actually increased. The PLO set out to meet with the different political parties and coalitions in Israeli politics in order to build "a bridge between Arabs and Israelis," according to senior PLO official (and later, prime minister) Mahmoud Abbas.[60] Three major encounters took place between PLO officials, groups of Oriental Jews, and representatives of the Israeli Peace Now movement. These were held in Romania (1986); Hungary (1987); and Toledo, Spain (1989). Palestinian leader Hanan Ashrawi called them "a series of exploratory rehearsal dialogues . . . hosted by a variety of third parties, to 'normalize' the negotiations option and to set its terms of reference." At the very least, these talks "contributed incrementally to identifying the basic issues and creating a pool of possible approaches and agendas."[61]

The Peres-Hussein Channel and the Unwilling Americans

On April 11, 1987, in the midst of the Israeli national unity government, Foreign Minister Peres donned a wig and traveled to London to meet secretly with King Hussein.[62] There, Peres and Hussein agreed on the modalities of setting up an international peace conference under UN auspices. The conference would deal with the most difficult issues, especially the issue of Palestinian self-determination, in separate bilateral committees. Jordan was to be Israel's counterpart by representing the Palestinians, who would not be permitted to participate independently. The conference would confer legitimacy on the ongoing quiet diplomacy between Jordan and Israel while resulting in the permanent marginalization of the PLO and the establishment of a joint Israeli-Jordanian arrangement for the West Bank.[63] Peres hoped to have U.S. secretary of state George Shultz adopt the London Agreement as a U.S. initiative and propose it openly to Jordan and Israel, so that Likud prime minister Yitzhak Shamir would accept the "American plan."[64] Peres sent Yossi Beilin secretly to brief Shultz's aide Charlie Hill on the agreement, which accorded well with Shultz's plan to propose "shared, overlapping or interwoven sovereignties across Israel, the West Bank and Jordan" as his preferred basis for peace in the region. Beilin urged Shultz to take on the initiative and claimed to speak for both Jordan and Israel. By April 20, Peres had informed Shamir himself about what had transpired in London. Peres states that he had fully briefed Shamir both before and after the London trip and that Shamir had consented to the initiative.[65]

In any case, Shamir had his aide Eliyakim Rubinstein (who would later head the Israeli delegation to the Israeli-Palestinian talks that emerged from Madrid in 1991) call Shultz and explain that Shamir was opposed to any UN conference that Shamir feared would give a regional role to the PLO and to the Soviet Union. On April 24, Shamir sent minister without portfolio Moshe Arens as his personal envoy to ask Shultz to distance himself from the Peres-Hussein London Agreement, thus bypassing Foreign Minister Peres and keeping him in the dark about the Arens trip.[66] Shultz explained that Hussein needed the conference as cover to provide him legitimacy for negotiating on behalf of the Palestinians. The Soviets had already agreed to play only a symbolic role. Shultz left Hussein the task of persuading Shamir, which ultimately led to the collapse of the London Agreement.[67]

Hussein then secretly hosted Shamir at his London residence on July 18, 1987. After their meeting, Shamir sent envoy Dan Meridor to Shultz to brief him, without the knowledge of the Israeli embassy in Washington. Hussein also conveyed his impressions of the meeting to Shultz. Their respective versions of the meeting seemed contradictory to the Americans, with Hussein portraying Shamir as "hopeless" while Meridor painted a rosy picture of their secret encounter.[68]

In September, Shultz renewed his efforts to cajole the parties to attend an internationally sponsored peace conference and hoped to take advantage of an impending Reagan-Gorbachev summit to invite Shamir and Hussein to Washington. This time Shultz succeeded in persuading Shamir that a United States-Soviet Union "summit" at which the Soviets were present but not influential would not damage Israel while still providing Hussein with the cover he required. But at Shultz's October 20, 1987, meeting with King Hussein, the tables had turned. The Shamir-Hussein channels of direct, secret communication had convinced King Hussein that Shamir was an unsuitable partner for constructive peace talks. Now it was Hussein's turn to decline Shultz's efforts.[69]

Peres laments that, had this effort succeeded, the next chapter in Palestinian-Israeli affairs might have been averted or, at least, might have been less costly to the two sides.[70]

Back Channel with Likud

Once started on the road of dialogue, the PLO sought to cast its net as wide as possible. The PLO would no longer limit its official exploratory negotiations to only anti-Zionist Jews, left-wing secular Israelis, or Oriental Jews disaffected with the ruling political elite. Since Shamir and the secular right dominated government policy making regarding peace with the Palestinians, the PLO decided to open direct channels to the Likud leadership. Shamir had been constantly briefed by his intelligence chiefs on their contacts with the PLO in any case.[71] In the West Bank, Sari Nusseibeh, a Fatah member (Arafat's party within the PLO) and at that time a professor at Birzeit University; and Faisal al-Husseini, Fatah leader and head of New Orient House, the Palestinian quasi-governmental institution in East Jerusalem, met with Likud Central Committee member Moshe Amirav, an associate of then prime minister Yitzhak Shamir, throughout July and August 1987.[72] Together they produced a Document of Principles that contained the contours of a relatively far-reaching peace agreement between Israel and the PLO. These efforts collapsed when Shamir ordered Amirav to refrain from making contact with the Palestinians. Faisal al-Husseini was arrested by the Israeli military (then controlled by Shamir's Labor Party rival, defense minister Yitzhak Rabin). According to al-Husseini, news of the channel was leaked to an Israeli newspaper sympathetic to the Labor Party.[73] Shamir had evidently been kept informed of Amirav's negotiations with the Fatah leaders by Amirav and other Likud members who were marginally involved in the effort. Unhappy with the far-reaching mutual concessions foreshadowed in the draft, Shamir dismissed Amirav from the internal committees of the Likud Party and disowned Amirav's work. Shamir now has little to say about that remarkable early draft agreement, other than to claim that "he [Amirav] was not a serious man." Significantly, he does not directly disavow his knowledge and oversight of the Amirav initiatives,[74] he only disdains the man and his efforts. Arafat and his colleagues apparently saw the Likud back channel as Shamir's attempt to steal Shimon Peres's thunder and torpedo the Peres-Hussein talks.[75]

The Palestine National Council (PLO's parliament-in-exile) as a whole progressively moved to legitimize such contacts, even though some Palestinian militant factions continued to oppose them and went as far as to kill PLO officials who participated in talks with Israelis.[76] These conferences and contacts encouraged the growth of a new network of Palestinians and Israelis interested in moving beyond the enemy images they had of each other and holding dialogues on issues of mutual concern. They were not negotiations between the state of Israel and the PLO, and the participants were not empowered to enter into binding agreements with each other. Nonetheless, real negotiations between authorized Israeli and Palestinian negotiators were taking place in secret at that time.

The New Arab Rebellion: The First Intifada

In the years between 1936 and 1939, an uprising known as the Arab Rebellion took place in Palestine. It was mostly directed against the British Mandate authorities in control of Palestine because of their admission of ever larger numbers of Jewish refugees from Europe into Palestine and the economic effects of land and job losses incurred by the Palestinian Arabs. The Arab Rebellion became the backdrop for a series of secret negotiations among prominent Arab nationalists and Zionist leaders under the auspices of the Palestine Mandate authorities, even as Jewish extremists carried out revenge attacks against Arab civilians and British officials. As a result of a series of diplomatic encounters between the Arabs and British, the "London Conferences" at St. James Palace, there was renewed Arab cooperation with the British government, but also a new campaign of violence by Jews against the Arabs and British.[77]

In an historical parallel, a massive civil uprising (intifada in Arabic) erupted on December 7, 1987, in the Gaza Strip and quickly spread to the West Bank. It constituted an expression of Palestinian rage against the continuing Israeli occupation and its effects. The intifada was waged by diverse methods: Palestinian noncooperation with the military government, massive demonstrations, stone-throwing against troops, and nonviolent protest.

In early 1988, two new Palestinian organizations emerged from the shadow of the secular nationalist movements operating under the PLO umbrella, Harakat al-Muqawama al-Islamiya (HAMAS, the Islamic Resistance Movement) and the Movement for Islamic Jihad. Early in its existence, HAMAS appears to have been encouraged by Israel, in keeping with the policy of looking for ways to weaken the PLO. At first HAMAS filled in the enormous gap in social services neglected by the Israeli occupation authorities, especially in overcrowded Gaza. During the intifada, they created a paramilitary wing that espoused violent methods of resistance, including attacks on Israeli soldiers and civilians. The main Israeli response was use of repressive force against Palestinians in the West Bank and Gaza: closing of universities and other social institutions, mass arrests without trial, house demolitions, suppression of protests, deportation, beatings, imprisonment, and extrajudicial assassinations.[78]

The intifada, like the Arab Rebellion fifty years before it, was a major political uprising that provoked a repressive military response. The intifada and the Arab Rebellion both provided the catalyst for exploratory negotiations between Palestinians and Israelis in an effort to move away from an ongoing violent confrontation. It served as the catalyst for much new diplomatic activity, which is analyzed in the following text, and ultimately led to the first open Palestinian-Israeli negotiations that would be held under the sponsorship of the superpowers at Madrid in 1991 as well as to the Oslo back channel that resulted in a the historic Declaration of Principles in 1993.

Reentry of the United States in Middle East Peacemaking

The intifada succeeded in arousing a surprising amount of concern among leaders and ordinary citizens in Israel and the United States, as well as in Europe and the rest of the world. At the urging of American Jewish leaders, Israeli politicians, and even President Mubarak of Egypt, Secretary of State Shultz decided to travel to the region in early 1988 to assess the possibility of relaunching the peace initiative he had first proposed in September 1982. Shultz's new initiative proposed to accelerate the program of negotiation envisioned in the Camp David Accords and explicitly endorsed rapid onset of permanent status negotiations (to commence after one year, instead of the five envisioned in the Camp David Accords) without regard to the success or failure of the negotiations on the transitional stage. It incorporated the Peres-Hussein understandings by calling for a joint Jordanian-Palestinian delegation.[79] Also integral to the new Shultz Initiative was a suspension of Israeli settlements and a Palestinian suspension of the intifada.[80]

The negotiations were to be initiated at an international conference and followed up by active U.S. mediation in all phases. Like Menachem Begin before him, Likud prime minister Shamir opposed key aspects of the plan, and the PLO resented being excluded. The Soviets and Syria were cool to the plan. Only

Egypt openly endorsed it. As at Camp David, front channel negotiations on the Israeli-Palestinian conflict demonstrated the strengths and limitations of this method and some of the inherent limitations of third-party interveners such as the United States.

Challenged by the spontaneous onset of the intifada and the local leadership that emerged from it, the PLO expended efforts building grassroots support in the occupied territories, providing financial assistance to families whose homes were demolished or whose salary earners were imprisoned. As the intifada and the Israel's iron-fisted response to it raged on, the Tunis-based PLO struggled to coordinate civil disobedience activities directly with the "Unified National Leadership of the Uprising," as the internal leadership of the intifada called itself.[81]

Shultz had already received some pragmatic proposals from Palestinian leaders in the West Bank and Gaza concerning Palestinian self-rule. At the same time, Shamir launched his own concept for Palestinian administrative autonomy. Seizing the moment, Shultz introduced his ambitious diplomatic timetable to Shamir's and Peres's aides (separately), as well as to local Palestinian leaders and Jordanian officials. His plan was to visit the region in February 1988. He proposed that autonomy talks begin and that Israeli and Palestinian elections be held with the new Palestinian self-governing authority being inaugurated within one year, by February 1989.[82]

Shultz earlier recognized that Palestinians were at the heart of the conflict and therefore at the heart of the solution. This observation led him to predict that Palestinians would not participate in his newest peace plan unless they felt that transitional autonomy arrangements would lead to a satisfactory final status. Shultz's plan therefore included an important additional element that he termed the "interlock." By December 1988, negotiations should begin on final status of the Palestinian territories, regardless of the status of the autonomy talks.[83] Thus Shultz wisely recognized the parties' need to minimize political uncertainties regarding negotiation outcomes prior to engaging in them.

During Shultz's February 1988 shuttle diplomacy trip to Israel and the Palestinian territories, Shultz and his Middle East team had further separate meetings with aides to Peres and Shamir. The Likud-led faction within the cabinet and the Knesset mounted an effort to discourage Shultz from continuing, but Shamir himself encouraged Shultz, going so far as to ask Shultz to convey to King Hussein that he was "ready to negotiate final status . . . sovereignty." The local

Palestinian leadership had been contacted by Shultz's team and were willing to meet with him but at the last moment were prevented from doing so, according to Shultz, by PLO directives. King Hussein too gave Shultz only mixed support. On this basis, Shultz issued letters of invitation from the United States government for the international conference to all the parties in March 1988, complete with his "interlock" concept.[84] No invitation was sent to the PLO, to no one's surprise.

Without prior warning, King Hussein announced Jordan's explicit renunciation of administrative responsibilities and claims to the West Bank on July 31, 1988.[85] King Hussein also declined to represent the Palestinians in any further regional diplomatic efforts. The Jordanian "partner" identified and assiduously courted by Israel and the United States had washed his hands of the Palestinian dilemma beyond his borders, leaving Israel and the United States little choice but to engage the Palestinians themselves. Although Israel's options for a negotiating partner continued to narrow, the Israeli coalition government continued a policy of openly rejecting the PLO. Israel instead continued to follow a policy of deporting local leaders associated with the intifada while simultaneously echoing the longstanding Israeli complaint about the lack of strong local leaders who could represent Palestinian interests[86]—a complaint that had carried over from the Arab-Zionist conflict of early 1900s.

The United States seemed to be approaching the realization that if it wanted to continue to promote a regional peace process and play a role in the same, it had no other option than to initiate direct, high-level contact with the PLO. News and images of the intifada, as well as the failure of the IDF to control it by repressive force, continued to make constant headlines and put pressure on the U.S. administration to address the situation.

At a speech given at the Wye Plantation in September 1988, Shultz bequeathed his initiative to the next American administration, affirming "the right of Palestinians to participate actively in every stage of negotiations," a dramatic but long overdue shift in U.S. policy.[87]

Palestinian Recognition of Israel: New Back Channels

Prior to the Palestinian declaration of statehood and the implicit recognition of Israel in November 1988, a delegation of Israelis led by Dr. Ephraim Sneh (a reserve IDF general who had once headed the military government in the West

Bank) and a delegation of PLO officials led by Hani al-Hasan met in Paris for three meetings during August and September 1988. Professor Stephen Cohen and PLO ambassador Said Kemal were also present. The first two dramatic encounters were characterized by "an atmosphere of elation and mutual trust." The Israeli agenda was to see if the PLO could control the intifada and reduce the level of violence, in exchange for a reduction in Israeli repressive measures, prior to the general elections in Israel, scheduled for the end of the year.[88]

A fourth meeting, to be held after the election on November 3, 1988, never took place due to Peres's electoral defeat to Shamir. The failure of these talks convinced the Palestinians that Israel could neither make bold political decisions in favor of peace nor set aside the use of force. Israelis concluded that the PLO could not control the intifada by itself. The secrecy in which these talks were held was a product not only of their illegality under Israeli law but may also have stemmed from the need to exclude Shamir and the Likud Party because Shamir would have tried to end the talks had he known about them, or at least would have tried to turn them into an election issue, painting Labor as lawbreakers and traitors. All attempts from 1978 to 1988 to address the Palestinian-Israeli conflict while excluding the Palestinian leadership had failed.

The PLO–United States dialogue: Front and Back Channels

Between July and December 1988, the United States and the PLO attempted to move beyond their tactical clandestine contacts and come to agreement on the terms of a higher-level diplomatic "dialogue" to be held between them, predicated on the PLO's acceptance of UN Security Council Resolutions 242 (1967) and 338 (1973), explicit recognition of Israel, and the PLO's renunciation of violence. Several channels of communication operated simultaneously: the Swedish government acting as mediator-facilitator, the CIA, the good offices of a U.S. citizen of Palestinian origin, and others all pushed the U.S. administration and the PLO toward a dialogue.[89]

At that time, the U.S. government began to communicate with PLO officials in Ankara, Algiers, and Tunis through U.S. diplomats in those capitals.[90] Additionally, prominent American Jewish figures met with Yasir Arafat in the hopes of laying the groundwork for open, official contacts among Israel, the PLO, and the United States.[91] Some negotiations over the terms of the PLO's acceptance of the United States' conditions for a dialogue between Tunis and Washington were also handled by the CIA, but the Swedish back channel produced direct exchanges of correspondence between the high-level decision makers: Secretary of State Shultz and Arafat.[92]

Mohamed Rabie, an American citizen of Palestinian origin who had links to the PLO leadership, approached William Quandt, senior Brookings Fellow and former NSC official in charge of Middle East affairs in the Nixon and Carter administrations. King Hussein's surprise renunciation of claims and responsibilities for the West Bank had definitively created a political vacuum for the United States regarding the Palestinian-Israeli conflict. Quandt therefore arranged meetings between high-level State Department officials and Rabie in order to explore the possibility of a United States-PLO dialogue[93] that could legitimate the PLO as the elusive negotiating partner for Israel that some U.S. policy makers believed was missing from the Middle East peace efforts.[94]

The Palestine National Council (PNC), the Palestinian parliament-in-exile, held its historic nineteenth meeting in Algiers and on November 15, 1988, issued a declaration of Palestine's statehood that implicitly recognized Israel in the context of the "two-state solution" originally proposed by the UN forty years before.[95] The declaration was embraced not only by PLO supporters in the West Bank and Gaza but also by the Israeli peace movement and center left parties, which mobilized public opinion in order to articulate a clear demand that the government commence negotiations with the PLO over the status of the West Bank and Gaza.[96] The PNC envisioned that the way to the two-state solution was by creating an international conference sponsored by the United Nations.

The U.S. government was also moving toward open diplomatic engagement with the PLO, despite expressing serious reservations about the independent Palestinian state called for at the Algiers PNC meeting. In November 1988, Shultz declined to recommend to the attorney general that Yasir Arafat be granted a U.S. visa to attend a UN General Assembly session, hoping to exercise further leverage over the PLO and thus force the PLO to make an explicit recognition of Israel.

The secret Swedish back channel was precisely the forum for assuring both Shultz and Arafat in advance that their respective interests would be met by the terms and procedure of the dialogue. At that moment, Shultz's dilemma was not due to a lack of information but rather a lack of certainty regarding outcome.

Information was in overabundance. His recollection provides some insight into the problems of the statesman involved in complex negotiations: "Everyone knew that something was brewing. Rumors abounded. People tried either to take credit for or to kill the prospective development. Messages—usually false messages— flew back and forth. I shut my ears to all the noise except for what the Swedes and I communicated to one another."[97]

Ultimately, Arafat delayed in making public the text that the Swedes had shown Shultz and that all had approved. Instead, Arafat decided to go back to the PLO Executive Council about the policy shift before making the declaration public. The Executive Council approved Arafat's declaration recognizing Israel's right to exist and to live in peace and informed the Swedes that Arafat would in fact make the policy public in his address to the UN General Assembly, whose venue had been changed to Geneva in light of Shultz's denial of the Arafat visa request.[98]

Arafat made his explicit declarations to the UN General Assembly in Geneva, in which he accepted United States' conditions for dialogue on December 13, 1988 (with even more explicit clarifications to the press on December 14, 1988),[99] and President Reagan ordered the United States-PLO dialogue to start.[100] Rabie proposed to Arafat that the official dialogue with the United States be supplemented by "a private channel" that would be composed of former officials, academics, and Middle East experts who could impact public opinion—the very essence of a Track II effort. Arafat approved.

The official United States-PLO dialogues consisted of four rounds of meetings between U.S. ambassador to Tunisia Robert Pelletreau and a high-level PLO delegation, although many other working-level meetings were held. Little progress was made, possibly because the U.S. side spent much of the time asking the Palestinians about their reactions to Israeli prime minister Yitzhak Shamir's proposals for local elections in the West Bank and Gaza as the path to limited autonomy—a plan designed to displace the PLO and block the emergence of a sovereign Palestinian state (discussed in the following). Two other obstacles were the vociferous Israeli opposition to the dialogue (led by then deputy foreign minister Binyamin Netanyahu) and communication failures within the United States-PLO dialogue.[101]

Furthermore, the use of several other simultaneous channels of diplomatic contact served to undermine both the United States' and the PLO's investment in their dialogue. These channels were the third-party efforts of Egypt and the Soviet Union.[102] The Soviets, interested in bolstering their fading status as a regional and global actor, continued to seek a role in Middle East politics and not simply a part assigned by the United States. Egypt maintained its direct communication with Yasir Arafat himself, who was excluded from the United States-PLO dialogue.

A new president, George H. W. Bush, was elected in the United States and inherited Shultz's diplomatic achievements in the Middle East. President Bush's secretary of state, James Baker, began using Egyptian good offices to obtain Arafat's acceptance of his conditions for a new regional peace effort, bypassing the United States' own fading dialogue with the PLO. Unfortunately, Baker's early efforts were in support of Yitzhak Shamir's watered-down plan for Palestinian administrative autonomy through elections.

The Israeli Autonomy Plan of 1989

In May 1989 Shamir, at the helm of the newly solidified Likud-led government, proposed a plan for local elections in the West Bank and Gaza, hoping to forestall any withdrawal of the Israel Defense Force and Israeli settlers from Palestinian territory while also dampening the intifada. The local elections plan did not have even the modest reach of the autonomy arrangements sketched out in the Camp David Accords. The elections plan was first drafted in early 1989 by Joel Singer, who would later play a key role in the 1993 Oslo back channel as well as each and every episode of Israeli-Palestinian negotiations that followed until 1996. Singer was a lawyer in private practice who had served for several years in the Israel Defense Force's international law department and had participated in the Camp David summit, as well as Israel-Lebanon and Taba dispute negotiations. He wrote the elections plan at the request of Yitzhak Rabin, then defense minister in the national unity government. Rabin submitted it to Shamir, who adopted it as his own.[103] Shamir's plan excluded negotiations on territorial status and self-determination issues. Not surprisingly, West Bank and Gaza Palestinians declined to participate in implementing the Shamir plan.[104] The PLO was not entirely out of the picture, however.

U.S. secretary of state James Baker inherited the United States-PLO dialogue from his predecessor, George Shultz, and used it to pressure the PLO to accept being formally excluded from negotiations that were to lead to local elections and autonomy. The PLO showed some willingness to accede to Baker's demands. Shamir, however, disavowed his own elections/negotiation plan on June 28, 1989.[105]

Further Israel-PLO Back Channels

Even while these early United States-PLO contacts were proceeding, Yitzhak Rabin, then defense minister in the coalition government, had opened his own back channel to Tunis through Arab members of the Israeli Knesset.[106]

Apparently, at Rabin's initiative as defense minister, Israel opened up exploratory discussions with imprisoned intifada leaders whom Rabin considered to be a front for the PLO. The purpose of these talks, in some respects reminiscent of South Africa's negotiations with Nelson Mandela while he was imprisoned,[107] was to see whether or not this newly emerging, non-Tunis Palestinian leadership would participate in an elections plan designed to exclude the PLO while ending Israel's problems in the occupied territories. According to one Palestinian informed about these discussions, the Israelis unilaterally broke them off.[108] However, Rabin was not the only government official looking to the PLO as a potential negotiation partner.

During the second half of the national unity government, when Yitzhak Shamir became prime minister, Ezer Weizman, nephew of Chaim Weizman, one of Israel's founding statesman, became science minister. The younger Weizman had been commander of the Israel Air Force at the pinnacle of his military career and defense minister under Menachem Begin, but he resigned from Likud to protest Begin's delays in the negotiation of the Palestinian autonomy arrangements embodied in the Camp David Accords.[109] As science minister from the Labor opposition, he violated the ban on contact with the PLO by secretly meeting with the PLO representative in Switzerland, Nabil Rimlawi, and also addressed a letter to Yasir Arafat. When the contacts were revealed, Shamir attempted to fire Weizman during a cabinet meeting. Rabin suggested the compromise of keeping Weizman as minister, but without portfolio. Rabin's suggestion was implemented.[110]

During that time, Yitzhak Shamir's own party as well as right-wing parties allied with him demanded that Shamir not participate in any Baker peace initiatives. After Shamir succeeded in consolidating his government and excluding the Labor Party from his new government in March 1990, Shamir's noncooperation with the United States worked against the modest achievements of the

United States-PLO dialogue and further derailed Baker's initial peace plans. In any case, the United States-PLO dialogue was officially suspended by President Bush in June 1990 after a Palestinian splinter faction aligned with Iraq attempted an armed incursion into Israel.[111]

U.S. officials were to some extent reacting to the strong Israeli opposition to the dialogue, but they were also confounded by the PLO's inability to reign in dissidents opposed to recognition of and negotiations with Israel in the absence of any corresponding Israeli recognition of the Palestinian right to a state. The other factor in the suspension of the dialogue was the ongoing confrontation between the Bush administration and Shamir over the issue of ongoing construction of Israeli settlements on Palestinian property in East Jerusalem, the West Bank, and Gaza. This confrontation ironically brought the United States into closer alignment with Israel because of the widespread condemnation Israeli policies aroused. Baker, and even President Bush himself, publicly and privately opposed the settlements. Several prominent land seizures, funded in part by the Likud Party, led to intense outbreaks of killings of Palestinians, both protesters and bystanders. In response to pressures from the United States, Shamir and Likud defiantly declared their intentions to resettle newly arrived Soviet émigrés in East Jerusalem. Negotiations at the United Nations at the end of May over how to address the new settlements and the Israeli killings of Palestinians led only to a U.S. veto of a proposed Security Council resolution that would have authorized a Security Council investigation.[112]

The suspension of the official United States-PLO dialogue and the deterioration of this fragile bilateral relationship once again politically isolated the PLO. This in turn helped persuade Yasir Arafat that the United States was simply an unreliable partner in peacemaking. Iraq was the remaining regional power and appeared to be a strong diplomatic, political, and military counterweight to Egypt, Syria, Iran, and Israel. It had been supported militarily and politically by the United States as a bulwark against Iran's Islamic revolution and its leader, Saddam Hussein, was increasingly vocal in speaking out on behalf of Palestinian rights. At an Arab League summit, Hussein called attention to the massive Soviet immigration to Israel and the United States' inability to moderate Israeli policies when the PLO had accepted both negotiation and exclusion from them. Iraq would nonetheless prove to be an embarrassing ally for both the United States and the PLO.

After the Persian Gulf War: The International Peace Conference

As the cold war approached its final throes, a new geopolitical event shook the Middle East. Iraq invaded its small, oil-rich neighbor Kuwait on August 2, 1990. In response, the Bush administration began organizing a broad multilateral coalition to reverse Iraq's annexation of Kuwait. Five months later, on January 16, 1991, the Persian Gulf War erupted and altered the political balance in the region. Israel had been attacked with Iraqi missiles, but U.S. management of the crisis effectively prevented Israel from participation in the fighting because Israeli participation had the potential to split the military coalition, in which Arab armies participated on the allied front.

The PLO was ostracized for Yasir Arafat's support for a diplomatic solution to the Iraqi invasion, even though numerous Palestinians spoke out against the Iraqi annexation of Kuwait, drawing parallels to their own occupation by Israel.[113] The PLO leadership paid undue attention to president of Iraq Saddam Hussein's pretense of linkage; Iraq would withdraw from Kuwait if Syria withdrew from Lebanon, and Israel withdrew from both Lebanon and the Palestinian territories. It would take Yasir Arafat's death in 2004 for the PLO leadership to rebuild a bridge to the Kuwaiti government, culminating in a public Palestinian apology and Kuwait's public statements of forgiveness during an official visit by the prime minister of Palestine Ahmed Qurei and the new PLO chairman Mahmoud Abbas in December 2004.

In the aftermath of both the cold war and the Persian Gulf War, a new regional political backdrop for Palestinian-Israeli peace was being created in which positive coordination between the United States Soviet Union was possible.

On March 9, 1991, less than one month after Iraq's surrender, U.S. secretary of state James Baker embarked on a vigorous mission of shuttle diplomacy to take advantage of the newly changed context of Palestinian-Israeli relations and to promote an open Arab-Israeli peace process. His nearly eight months of unrelenting efforts culminated in the Madrid Peace Conference of October 1990, at which national delegations from Israel, Lebanon, Syria, and a joint Jordan-Palestine delegation convened, with official observers from the Gulf Cooperation Council and the United Nations.[114]

The conference provided the international legitimacy needed for each party to engage in direct bilateral talks (between Israel and each of the Arab delegations) with the expectation that this might eventually result in full peace accords and diplomatic relations between Israel and each of the Arab states with which it was still in a state of war. In the case of the Palestinians, still without a state of their own, Baker hoped to at least get them to the table together to negotiate the terms of interim self-government as a first step toward dealing with the big issues such as the political status of the Palestinians.

In any case, the Madrid Peace Conference was structured so that the opening plenaries were followed up by two independent but linked "tracks" of negotiations. The principal track consisted of bilateral talks between Israel and each of the Arab delegations, and all delegations to Madrid were persuaded to begin their bilateral discussions in the immediate aftermath of the Madrid Peace Conference. The bilaterals formally commenced on November 3, 1991, and then were moved to Rome and Washington, D.C., in early 1992. Supplementing the bilaterals was a set of multilateral negotiations that were structured around five negotiating committees that focused on issues that concerned everyone in the region and beyond: regional economic development, water, refugees, environment, and arms control/security. The multilateral track was inaugurated in Moscow on January 28, 1992, and (it was hoped) would explore and develop substantive solutions that could be plugged back into the bilaterals.[115]

3

The Madrid Peace Conference and the Washington Track, 1991 to 1993

Traditionally, only collaborators or people with questionable national credentials had conducted talks with Israeli officials . . . popular perceptions presented such meetings as "normalization" under occupation or suspicious secret deals/sell-outs.

—HANAN ASHRAWI, spokeswoman for
Palestinian delegation in Washington[1]

It took nearly forty-three years after the establishment of the state of Israel for Palestinian and Israeli negotiators to openly sit down to peace talks. The world watched as the Madrid Peace Conference was followed by a bilateral track of Palestinian-Israeli negotiations held mostly in Washington, D.C. Paradoxically, their efforts were soon eclipsed by PLO-Israel negotiations being conducted in parallel, but also in complete secrecy. To analyze and understand the secret negotiations, it is necessary to understand the content and conduct of the open negotiations.

The Context of the Madrid Peace Conference

On October 30, 1991, delegations from Israel, Lebanon, Syria, and a joint Jordanian-Palestinian delegation convened in Madrid, Spain, to inaugurate the open peace process. The United States and Soviet Union were the conveners of the conference, but it was really Secretary of State James Baker who had manipulated the parties into attending. At the insistence of Israel's government, the Palestinian delegates could neither be members of the Palestine Liberation Organization

52

(PLO) nor Arab residents of East Jerusalem. Nor could they attend the conference under their own auspices. Jordan was once again required to provide the fig leaf of diplomatic representation for the Palestinians: Jordan's diplomatic delegation incorporated notable Palestinians from the West Bank (excluding Jerusalem) and Gaza. Even though several of the Palestinian delegates were openly affiliated with the PLO, they were not the core, top-level leadership. A separate Palestinian-Israeli bilateral "track" followed up the Madrid conference in Washington, D.C., and met for ten rounds of intense but ultimately fruitless negotiations between 1991 and 1993 (the "Washington track"). With the PLO's exclusion from the Madrid Peace Conference and the ensuing Washington track and the relative distance of the Israeli negotiators from top Israeli decision makers, the wrong parties again seemed to be trying to negotiate an end to the core issue of Arab-Israeli political hostility.

Israeli and Palestinian front channel negotiations demonstrated their limitations, given the difficulty of the issues being negotiated and the political constraints of the negotiators. Proposals advanced by the Israeli side demonstrated a retreat from Israeli commitments under the Camp David Accords (discussed in chapter 2) and were predicated on the concept of personal but not territorial autonomy for Palestinians, under continued Israeli sovereignty. The Palestinian side wanted to negotiate the formation of the "Palestinian Interim Self-Governing Authority" with a view toward independent Palestinian statehood.[2]

The Madrid Peace Conference seemed to exemplify the classic, large multilateral sessions that had so often proven ineffective in prior Middle East peacemaking. Despite their shortcomings, large conferences were long seen as desirable, essential elements of peacemaking by would-be third-party interveners in Middle East conflicts because they brought all the relevant parties together, permitted the third party great leverage, and conferred legitimacy on the process of negotiation with one's enemy. In other words, despite their proven track record of ineffectiveness, they provided some protection to each party to the peacemaking process.

Under the auspices of the United States and the Soviet Union, Israel and the surrounding Arab states Syria, Lebanon, and Jordan attended as parties. The Jordanian delegation provided diplomatic cover for a delegation of Palestinians who would succeed in attaining direct negotiations with their Israeli counterparts. This marked the first time that Palestinians had official representation at an international peace conference on the conflict that so intimately involves them.[3]

James Baker III: Resurrecting the Peace Conference

Secretary of State James Baker took advantage of the United States' regional political leverage in the Middle East following the liberation of Kuwait and surrender of Iraq. The postwar military balance and diplomatic conditions were propitious for a U.S. effort to relaunch peace initiatives in the Middle East just as Henry Kissinger had done in an analogous historical moment following the 1973 Middle East war. The futility of Iraqi attempts to militarize the Arab-Israeli conflict, the political weakness of the PLO and Jordan's King Hussein, as well as Israel's demonstrated dependence on U.S. military technology and power projection all combined with a popular, energized U.S. presidency willing to take domestic political risks for a foreign policy victory. The conditions had seldom been better for Secretary Baker to undertake a new round of regional shuttle diplomacy throughout 1991 in order to persuade the regional players to attend the peace conference he was planning.[4]

What was unique about his shuttle diplomacy was the fact that he met repeatedly with the Palestinian "notables"—the local leadership—from Jerusalem, the rest of the West Bank, and Gaza to negotiate the terms of their inclusion at the peace conference.[5] Although it is true that Baker worked within the constraints of Shamir's demand that Israel be permitted to control which Palestinians could be participants in their own delegation, Baker must be credited for being among the first U.S. statesmen to seek out the Palestinians as partners in the peace process.

Analysis

The long-awaited opening plenary session of the Madrid Peace Conference proved that at least some delegates had come ready for confrontation rather than diplomacy. Prime Minister Shamir lost no time labeling the Syrians as terrorists, and the Syrian foreign minister Farouk al-Sharaa set aside his prepared speech to accuse Shamir of complicity in the September 17, 1948, assassination of Counte Folke Bernadotte, the first UN-appointed mediator who tried to arrange a ceasefire in the fighting that followed the declaration of the state of Israel. A Palestinian delegate at Madrid, Dr. Saeb Eraqat, riled Shamir by putting on the traditional Palestinian kaffiyeh headdress to assert the long-suppressed Palestinian identity and to hint at the PLO's support for the non-PLO delegation.[6] It was hardly an auspicious start for a peace conference of such historic importance.

Yet the delegations in attendance at the Madrid Peace Conference somehow sustained the fragile momentum beyond the opening plenary sessions. Israel and each of the attending Arab delegations held bilateral negotiation sessions before they even left Madrid, thus initiating the bilateral "tracks" whose existence was the only real criterion of a successful outcome of the Madrid Peace Conference.

The Madrid Peace Conference and the front channel bilateral negotiations are analyzed in this chapter according to a structured framework of seven critical international negotiation factors chosen to help isolate the differences, similarities, strengths, weaknesses, and interactions between front and back channel negotiations. The following seven factors are explained in the introductory chapter in detail:

- Issues negotiated
- Secrecy and publicity
- Exclusion and inclusion of subparties
- Proximity of negotiators to decision makers
- Autonomy of the negotiators
- Third parties: presence and role
- Strategic use of front and back channels

Issues Negotiated in the Washington Track

At the beginning of the Palestinian-Israeli bilaterals, the delegations could not agree on how to talk to each other; the process of negotiation was itself in dispute. The Palestinians quickly insisted on meeting directly with the Israelis (and thus without Jordanian tutelage). At first the Israelis refused to compromise on this.

After they resolved this issue, they failed to overcome their differences over what to talk about, the substance of the negotiation agenda. Their procedural and substantive differences arose because their end goals and assumptions were in conflict. The Israeli delegation worked on the assumption that Palestinian autonomy would be built on a functional, administrative structure with no territorial base or sovereign powers—essentially the concepts Menachem Begin proposed to the United States and Egypt in the Camp David process.

The Palestinian delegation worked on the assumption that autonomy could be limited but that the limitations would only be temporary. The goal was always clear to anyone who was paying attention: local autonomy was only seen as a bridge to independent statehood, with the minimum requisite territorial base on the entire West Bank and Gaza and with a national capital in East Jerusalem. These were fundamental differences that could not be ignored or finessed. In terms of process differences, the Palestinians preferred to represent themselves while the Israelis worked hard to deny them the legitimacy that would come from self-representation. They pushed hard for a joint Palestinian-Jordanian delegation.

The Palestinian-Israeli track moved very slowly toward a common agenda for negotiation. The first two rounds of Palestinian-Israeli talks, and part of the third, were dedicated solely to the *procedural* dispute over Palestinian participation.[7] The question was whether or not the Palestinian delegation could meet alone with the Israelis and if its status was equal to that of the other Arab states negotiating with Israel (Syria, Lebanon, and Jordan). Israel's delegation, to its credit, conceded that the Palestinian delegation could speak for itself. The procedural question had been addressed; however, there remained the far more difficult substantive differences to negotiate over.

With the procedural issue behind them, from the third round onward, the delegations began exchanging incompatible drafts of documents outlining general concepts and details of interim arrangements. The Palestinian documents did not meet the minimum requirements of the Israeli delegation. The Israeli proposals also fell far short of what the Palestinian delegation was instructed to seek. Thus there was always a large gap between the proposals submitted by each side. An examination of the key documents exchanged demonstrates the incompatibility of their perspectives.[8] Simply put, the two delegations were working on the basis of vastly different assumptions. With time, the Israeli drafts became more detailed and provided initial responses to some Palestinian concerns while still retaining Israeli control over territory, lawmaking, settlers, natural resources, security, and other sets of issues.

Nevertheless, one Palestinian advisor to the delegation wrote that "a small exhausting step had been made toward Israeli acceptance of Palestinian central authority during the interim period . . . there is yet another progress, but only insofar as unraveling the incoherence of the Israeli model can be considered progress. Still it is not without utility for the battle for public opinion and third-party intervention to oppose the force of logic to the logic of force."[9]

Embedded in this Palestinian analysis are elements important for the present analysis; the "battle for public opinion" that Mansour mentions refers to the Palestinians' use of the newfound publicity to convey the legitimacy of the Palestinian desire for self-determination to non-Palestinian audiences who were watching the unfolding of the peace process. Audiences were critical in the unfolding of the Washington bilateral talks. The "third-party intervention" Mansour mentions refers to the Palestinians' need for superpower patronage—a strong advocate to bolster the argument for legitimacy and back up the Palestinian claim with diplomatic, political, and economic leverage.

The Israeli delegation focused on the enumeration of civil powers that a Palestinian governing "council" could exercise in the lives of Palestinian people in the West Bank and Gaza. The Palestinian delegation had a more classic approach to the peace negotiations; the Palestinians sought an interim, provisional government with a defined territorial base and broad powers of governance. The Palestinian goal was to have a state on all the territory of the West Bank and Gaza by the conclusion of the interim period.

This disagreement on the substance of the negotiations was directly related to the competing frameworks under which their track could operate. The Palestinian delegation, for their part, pursued a "two-pronged approach." While they were offering proposals on the composition of the Palestinian Interim Self-Governing Authority (PISGA), they felt that a number of other serious concerns had to be brought up with the Israelis because they directly affected the personal safety of the Palestinian delegation, the status of Palestinian territory, and the protection of Palestinian civilians. In this regard, they articulated their view that East Jerusalem was occupied Palestinian territory, that settlements had to be halted immediately, and that the Geneva Convention Relative to the Protection of Civilian Persons in Time of War was applicable to the Palestinian people and territory under occupation, among other concerns.[10] Other Palestinian constituencies and political groups opposed to the peace process felt that these demands were not even legitimate subjects of negotiation, but rather should have been *preconditions* to negotiation. The Palestinian delegation was in a sense burdened by this dual role, and the Israeli delegation did not "engage" on the overarching issues that concerned their counterparts.[11] This only exacerbated the problematic role of publicity because issues that could not be addressed at the negotiation table inevitably ended up in press releases and media statements.

The question of the overarching framework for the negotiations was problematic from the beginning. There was no lack of political and legal frameworks to guide the negotiations, only a lack of political will to choose among them and find an agreed basis for negotiations over substance. For example, the Camp David Accords set forth Prime Minister Begin's autonomy plan for the Palestinians and were more detailed than UN Security Council Resolution 242 (1967) and Resolution 338 (1973).[12] However, the UN resolutions incorporated the "land for peace" principle as the basis of peace in the region, calling for Israeli withdrawal from territories occupied in the 1967 and 1973 wars. Israel argued that Resolution 242, if it applied to the Palestinians at all, applied only to the final status negotiations, not interim autonomy talks or the far more limited Israeli goals for the Washington talks. In short, the Israeli argument rested on the contention that the resolutions applied only to existing states. Jordan and Egypt, after all, had been running the West Bank and Gaza, respectively, from 1948 until the 1967 War, not the PLO.

The Palestinian delegation argued that their terms of reference and letter of invitation to the Madrid conference explicitly invoked UN Resolutions 242 and 338, which embodied the legal principles that supported their aspirations to establish a Palestinian state in the West Bank and Gaza Strip. Additionally, a Letter of Assurances from the United States to the Palestinian delegation explicitly invoked the relevant UN Security Resolutions as the framework for negotiation, without limiting their application to only the issues related to the permanent status phase of negotiations.[13]

Over time, the two delegations' work seemed to converge slightly, but the fact remains that they did not establish a common working agenda and instead argued first over legal and diplomatic status of the Palestinian delegation, then over the terms of reference, and only later began offering each other their ideas on the substance of how Palestinians would live during the interim period.

In essence, the Washington talks demonstrated two incompatible visions of the peace process. On the Palestinian side, the requirement of certainty regarding the final status (a Palestinian state on all of the West Bank and Gaza, dismantlement of Jewish settlements, repatriation of the refugees, etc.) was a precondition to negotiating on interim issues.

The Israeli delegation, at first reflecting the ideological intransigence of Yitzhak Shamir, was not offering anything the Palestinians felt they could work with. The motivation for Shamir was the need for certainty regarding the prevention of the emergence of a Palestinian state while possibly conceding only administrative responsibilities to the Palestinian people while preventing them from achieving territorial sovereignty. This motivation did not completely carry over into the Rabin government, but the Israeli delegation in Washington received no new negotiation guidance, despite having requested it when the Israeli government changed.[14] However, the working assumption on the Israeli side continued to be that interim negotiations should not predetermine the outcome of the permanent status negotiations, which prevented any discussion of the endgame of the Palestinian state.

The positional distance between the two official delegations therefore remained significant and was one of the factors that impeded real progress: negotiations are difficult if parties cannot agree on what they are negotiating over. This was not the case in the Oslo channel, which is the subject of the following chapter.

The Role of Secrecy and Publicity

There was little or no secrecy in the Palestinian-Israeli negotiations that emerged from the Madrid Peace Conference. On the contrary, both parties saw the utility of the public relations opportunity provided by the Washington talks. The few quiet diplomatic episodes that occurred in this case are discussed in the following but appear to have had no impact on the conduct or outcome of the negotiations.

The Madrid Peace Conference provided the Palestinians and Israelis a prime opportunity to change global opinion about their conflict. For the Palestinians, it was a chance to make their case in the arena of the news media. For the Israelis, it was an opportunity to shift public opinion in their favor after acquiring a negative public image during the years of the intifada when cameras transmitted the images of the fighting to anyone with a television set around the world. From the perspective of the third party—such as the United States—interested in getting both the Israelis and Palestinians committed and "locked in" to a new course of diplomatic engagement, the preference would be for more rather than less publicity focused on the conference.

Previous conferences on Middle East peace, when measured against their goals, had uniformly yielded poor results, if any at all, except for the Rhodes conference, at which UN envoy Ralph Bunche skillfully obtained ceasefire and disengagement agreements from all the belligerents. In both substantive goals and procedural dynamics, Middle East conferences had been either of a minimalist or comprehensive model. Baker followed and modified Kissinger's 1973 "minimalist" conference example.[15] The high-profile conference would not have to result in an agreement to succeed but simply commit the parties to proceed quietly in bilateral or trilateral subsets on their own or under the auspices of the United States.[16]

The three-day-long Madrid Peace Conference was itself a veritable media show,[17] which facilitated two contradictory behaviors. In the spotlight of the international media, the Israeli and Arab delegations traded acerbic accusations calculated to lay blame for the conflict at each others' doorsteps. At the same time, simply by being there, they demonstrated a degree of engagement in a process that conferred recognition of each parties' legitimacy. This was, after all, the first time that Palestinians and Israelis were negotiating together in public view. Their public appearance together communicated some measure of mutual acceptance, even if this acceptance was conditional, instrumental, and opportunistic rather than truly conciliatory.

The Madrid Peace Conference was structured so as to provide maximum media coverage to the opening plenaries. The ensuing bilateral talks were eagerly anticipated by large groups of media correspondents. Eliyakim Rubinstein points to the interplay between the negotiators and the media that helped constrain the atmosphere of the negotiations: "with open negotiations you have the media and you have to give the media its work."[18]

The Palestinian-Israeli track continued in Rome and in Washington D.C., where according to the minimalist model, the talks should have proceeded quietly. Nevertheless, the intense asymmetries of power between the two parties[19] can help explain the consistent use the Palestinian delegation made of media exposure and public relations. Hanan Ashrawi, a Palestinian academic with a Ph.D. in English literature from the University of Virginia became the delegation's spokesperson and acted as a conceptual "translator," making the Palestinian goals and the obscure details of negotiations salient to the global public. She had also been a central figure in the preliminary negotiations with U.S. secretary of state James Baker over the terms of reference and the substance of the negotiations. Technically, Ashrawi and others were only advisors to the Palestinian delegation. Because of their residency in Jerusalem, Israel did not accept them as part of the negotiation team. Ashrawi recalls that upon arrival in Madrid, "the press, I decided, would be a partner in my battle for legitimacy and the truth."[20]

One of the principal tasks of the Palestinian delegates and their advisors at Madrid was to establish themselves as the legitimate diplomatic representative of the Palestinian people. For decades, Palestinians in the West Bank and Gaza had been declaring their inability and unwillingness to negotiate with Israel in place of the PLO. The members of the Washington delegation explicitly associated themselves with the banned PLO and pressured the United States and Israel to concede that the Palestinians needed to negotiate separately from the Jordanians. At Madrid, a first bilateral meeting of the joint Palestinian-Jordanian and Israeli delegations concluded with a televised handshake among the three delegation heads and a joint press statement.[21]

The second round of bilateral talks between Israelis and Palestinians was to begin on December 4, 1991, in Washington, D.C. Instead of appearing for the negotiation at the appointed time, the Israeli delegation's spokesman, Binyamin Netanyahu, held a preliminary press conference. Ashrawi retaliated in kind.[22] Ashrawi writes that when the negotiation session was finally scheduled, the State Department refused the Palestinian delegation entry to a conference room separate from the Jordanian delegation. The delegation heads conducted what became known as "couch diplomacy" or "corridor diplomacy," sitting on couches in the corridors of the State Department without the delegations ever meeting.[23] Active public relations efforts only served to highlight the procedural issues that were in dispute. "Our press briefings became debates by proxy, and the substance of our talks the public property of all interested parties and individuals."[24]

Hassan Asfour, a PLO official who oversaw the Washington track while also participating in the Oslo talks downplays differences between issues negotiated in the front versus the back channel, but emphasizes the difficulty posed to the negotiators by publicity. "When the negotiation is focused on by the media, it's difficult. [Our] taboos [could not be broken]. If you ask the parties for compromise, you will be focused on by the media; and also you know the Israelis, they had many taboos at the time, one of them about the PLO itself."[25]

The delegations regularly held press conferences before, during, and after negotiation rounds and also provided media commentary on the unfolding events in Israel and Palestine. There can be no question that, for both procedural and strategic reasons, the Palestinian-Israeli track was virtually conducted in front of television cameras and flash bulbs, except for several informal sessions the parties conducted in parallel with formal sixth and seventh rounds (these are the so-called side channels, which are discussed in the following section on strategic use of multiple channels). Even in the informal talks the parties could not establish a common negotiation agenda. These only served to underscore the disparity between the delegations' respective goals and assumptions about the outcome of the negotiation process.

Exclusion and Inclusion of Subparties

The Madrid Peace Conference and the Palestinian-Israeli bilateral track that was conducted in Washington present a mixed panorama regarding the question of whether or not important parties were excluded from the negotiations. At first, from October 1991 to June 1992, the Likud-led government was negotiating with non-PLO Palestinians. Labor and all Center and Left Israeli political parties were excluded from the government and therefore from negotiations. The PLO and several Islamic opposition groups were excluded on the Palestinian side. But a more complex picture comes into focus as I look in detail at the emerging dynamics of the Washington track.

Over time, the PLO exercised control over the Washington delegation with an ever firmer hand. On the Israeli side, Labor and a left-wing coalition party, Meretz, displaced Likud as the governing factions from July 1992 onward. The public nature of the talks and the delegations' extensive use of press conferences assured that all interested parties were aware of the Washington talks. In this sense, Likud excluded Labor operationally from the negotiation process but could not deny Labor any critical knowledge of those negotiations. The open secret that the PLO was controlling the Palestinian delegation guaranteed that Likud could only have the illusion (or delusion) of excluding the PLO.[26]

An aspect of exclusion that is related to the discussion in the previous section on issues concerns what Zartman called the problem of acceptable spokespersons in the resolution of international and internal conflicts: "the issue of valid spokespersons, usually a precondition for negotiations, becomes the major issue in the conflict."[27] Both Palestinians and Israelis have had historical difficulty moving beyond denial of legitimacy to their counterpart leaders and spokespersons, which obviously creates a major impediment to peace negotiations. The Israeli government's attempt to exclude the PLO, and its exclusion of the Labor Party by virtue of being a Likud-dominated government, constitute the main exclusionary aspects of the Madrid Peace Conference and the bilateral tracks. Both of these conditions changed over the course of the negotiations as the Labor Party replaced the Likud Party, and the PLO continually emerged as the executive conferring a mandate on the Palestinian delegation. Nevertheless, the gradual inclusion of the PLO and Labor did not change the tenor of the Washington talks. To understand why nothing changed, it is necessary to understand that the Israeli front channel negotiators remained the same over time. Despite the electoral triumph of a more pronegotiation government, the negotiators' distance from the Israeli decision makers continued to grow. Their negotiation flexibility did not increase. On the contrary, it became more constrained.[28] These two factors warrant further discussion.

Shamir continued to be opposed to the conduct of peace talks with the PLO.[29] One of his expressed regrets at not winning the last election in which he ran, which took place during the first year of the Washington track, is that he could not continue to take advantage of a weak PLO in order to ultimately destroy it.[30] At the time of the Madrid Peace Conference, when he was prime minister, he was intensely opposed to dealing with the PLO. Both major parties, Labor and Likud, hoped to make some arrangements about the Palestinians without dealing with the PLO. Likud and parties to its right looked to Jordan as the future Palestinian state, and some extreme Right parties went so far as advocating the "transfer" or expulsion of the Palestinians out of the West Bank and Gaza. Labor put some effort into having King Hussein take responsibility for the West Bank. During the post–Camp David I and II years, Israel attempted to cultivate an alternative leadership among the non-Diaspora Palestinians.

During the intifada, an alternative Palestinian leadership appeared to have emerged without the initial assistance or coordination of the PLO but was not seen as a negotiation partner. Despite all of this effort to avoid the PLO, secret Israeli overtures to the PLO were made during those years, partially because Israel thought the PLO to be responsible for the intifada.

In this context, Shamir conditioned his government's attendance at Madrid on the exclusion of certain Palestinians. PLO officials were of course excluded.

Residents of East Jerusalem were also deemed persona non grata due to the implication that could be drawn about his government's willingness to negotiate the status of East Jerusalem still considered by nearly every country in the world to be occupied territory. This left the prominent civic leaders in the West Bank and Gaza, all of whom refused to disavow the PLO, despite their differing political affiliations within it.

But was the PLO really excluded? PLO officials were prevented from attending the Madrid Peace Conference and were not physically present at the meetings of the Palestinian-Israeli track. The Palestinian delegation made occasional public declarations of affiliation with or support of the PLO and had constant consultations with PLO officials. Of course, none of this could persuade the Shamir government to acknowledge that it was, in fact, negotiating with the PLO by proxy.[31] After surviving a plane crash in the Libyan desert, Yasir Arafat met with the Palestinian delegation openly in April in Cairo. He met with them again in Amman in June 1992 to tacitly signal Shamir that the delegation was "a team receiving its instructions from its leadership [the PLO] while participating in the decision-making process."[32]

Although the PLO acquiesced in being overtly excluded from the Madrid Peace Conference and the Washington track, it remained very much involved in monitoring the work of the Palestinian delegation. One of the leaders of the Palestinian delegation termed the dialectic between the PLO and the "insider" delegation "*fax politica*—politics via the fax machine."[33] The PLO accomplished two apparently contradictory tasks: it assented to being excluded from Madrid even while it exerted great efforts to control the Palestinian delegation from the PLO's Tunis headquarters by drafting negotiation directives and background studies for the Palestinian delegation.[34] Hassan Asfour, a Tunis-based PLO official who negotiated at Oslo, was the secretary of the PLO's follow-up committee that monitored all the developments in the Washington track. According to Asfour, no piece of paper went from the Palestinian delegation to the Israeli delegation without being vetted by Yasir Arafat and his principal deputy, Mahmoud Abbas (known by the patronymic Abu Mazen).[35]

The extent of PLO involvement in guiding the Palestinian delegation was so well understood that U.S. secretary of state Warren Christopher made explicit reference to it at his meeting with the Palestinians on August 3, 1993. In that meeting he was perplexed that the Palestinian delegation refused to provide him with the official PLO response to a second U.S. "bridging" proposal. The Palestinians were refusing to hand it over despite Arafat's explicit instructions to do so because of their own assessments regarding its inadequacy. Christopher had been assured that he would receive it by the Egyptian government. His admonishment to the delegation served as an opportunity for them to urge direct American engagement with the PLO. The direct Israel-PLO back channel in any case was well underway by that time, and the back channel negotiators were only five weeks away from finalizing and initialing their breakthrough.

The PLO moves in the front channel were part of a PLO strategy to minimize the potential for progress in the Washington track and therefore to demonstrate to Rabin that the PLO was in control of the Palestinian delegation in Washington as well as the Palestinian delegation at Oslo.[36] To the Palestinians working in Washington, such as legal advisor Camille Mansour, it seemed in retrospect that their negotiation instructions were meant to steer the Israelis closer to Oslo.[37] Attempts to exclude parties from negotiation only succeed in getting those parties to redouble their efforts to make their presence felt, as will be discussed in the final section on back-front channel interactions.

While it is true that the PLO was working with the Palestinian delegation behind the scenes, there were PLO officials who did not want the organization to be denied legitimacy by being excluded from the frontline negotiations. Some also did not relish the thought that the delegation might actually become an alternative leadership, replacing the weakened PLO. Political survival and gaining Israeli recognition for the PLO were certainly motivating factors on the PLO side. Both Abu Alaa and Hassan Asfour affirmed the PLO's desire to be "the" negotiation partner for the Israelis, and although accepting of their nominal exclusion from the front channels, they both exercised official oversight of it. Both welcomed the preeminence eventually accorded to the back channel more for its conferral of legitimacy on the PLO than for any substantive breakthrough it achieved.[38]

Although the PLO could not be prevented from exercising oversight of the Washington track, these negotiations finally came to a dead halt in December 1992. At that time, the Palestinian delegation in Washington refused to attend sessions with its Israeli counterparts in response to the Israeli deportation of some four hundred Palestinians accused of belonging to HAMAS. This left Yasir Arafat and the PLO leadership in Tunis without any links to the Israelis, even while HAMAS continued to gain ground in Gaza and the West Bank. It was at that point, during the lull in the Washington negotiations, that Arafat invited Norwegian academic Terje Rød Larsen to Tunis to ask his assistance in setting up a formal back channel with the Israeli government.[39]

The religious nationalist groups such as HAMAS and Islamic Jihad that had arisen in Gaza and the West Bank were also excluded from participation in the Washington track and had never been part of the PLO, which after all is an umbrella group of diverse political parties, factions, and militias. Although they may not have participated in the peace process even if invited, their exclusion was to have grave consequences later when their renewed attacks on Israeli soldiers and civilians helped to galvanize the religious and secular right in Israel, which led to the 1995 assassination of Rabin, the defeat of the Labor government in 1996, and the political return of Likud from 1996 to 1999 and again in 2001. The exclusion of the militant Islamist parties and militias from the political process at the very least contributed to their further political militancy and militarization and contributed to extremism within Israeli politics.

On the Israeli side, there was no great impediment to political participation. The open, acknowledged nature of the negotiations implied that the Israeli government's cabinet ministers all knew about and approved the involvement of the Shamir government in the negotiation process. At the time of Madrid, all cabinet ministers were united behind Shamir, who had by then succeeded in forming a government without an alliance-based national unity structure. The solidity of the Shamir government did however imply that the other major party—Labor— was excluded from policy making and decision making. During the 1992 Israeli elections, while the track was in its first full year of meetings, the peace plank of the Labor Party platform called for more effective peacemaking with the Palestinians and Syrians. In effect, Labor had been excluded and wanted to get in on the game by getting back into the government.

In the 1992 prime ministerial elections in Israel, Shamir's former defense minister Yitzhak Rabin handily defeated Shamir, ushering in a Labor government that had formed a coalition with another Center-Left coalition, Meretz. Thus in the midst of the Washington track, Israel's top governmental policy making and decision making changed hands completely from the hard-line Right to the center and left of the Israeli political spectrum. The electoral outcome was influenced by the Bush administration's withholding of $10 billion that Israel had requested under a U.S. loan guarantee program. Ostensibly to be used to resettle Jewish immigrants from the Soviet Union, Israel was found to be using a previous $400 million loan guarantee to expand settlements in Palestinian territory. The Bush administration's refusal led to a highly acrimonious confrontation between the two governments, and the new loan guarantees were granted to Israel only after Shamir's defeat.

There was broad Israeli political participation in the highest levels of decision making on the negotiations that prepared for and conducted the Madrid Peace Conference and the subsequent negotiations. Neither the Shamir government nor the Rabin government that followed it sought the permission or agreement of the opposing party while it conducted the negotiations. Both parties had a turn at managing the peace process according to their preferences. While in power, each party excluded the other from decision making regarding the peace process. Under both governments, however, the same individual (the chef de cabinet of the prime minister, Eliyakim Rubinstein, a long-standing civil servant) led the Israeli delegation in Washington without any shift in his negotiation mandate. Rabin's failure to change the delegation or at least its instructions was a disappointment to domestic constituencies that were propeace. It was also difficult for the Palestinian delegation to understand because they were avid followers of Israeli politics and hoped and believed that the Labor platform would ultimately lead to direct contacts with the PLO or at least some moderation in the Washington track.

When parties are excluded from a negotiation process, they will pursue their interests in one of two ways: either they seek political power or access to it; or, if this is not permitted to them, they become rejectionists and spoilers. Rabin's foreign minister and longtime rival Shimon Peres was instructed to focus on the multilateral talks with their regional working groups because Rabin wanted to keep control of the Washington track himself. It is not surprising in this regard to note that Peres, long proactive in the pursuit of different peace initiatives and finding himself sidelined from the front channel peace process, adopted the nascent secret channel that vied with the Washington track for progress. "Rabin hated Peres," said Yoel Singer, a legal advisor to the Israeli foreign ministry and one of the two Israeli officials sent to the competing back channel in Oslo.[40]

On the Israeli side, the major parties excluded each other; but each got their turn managing the Washington negotiations and had the consent of their respective political allies, which, to be sure, are not always to be counted on. Cabinet ministers and military officers were aware of and participated in policy making on the Washington track. On the Palestinian side, the PLO, though nominally excluded, became increasingly assertive, acting like any government sitting in a faraway capital while its negotiators do their work and report in.

The level of exclusion of subparties was not high with regard to the Washington talks. And yet there were some dimensions of exclusion. These only reinforced the creation of alternate channels. A far more intense kind of exclusion was operative in the secret Oslo channel, and is the subject of the next chapter.

Proximity of Decision Makers

The Palestinian delegation coordinated closely with the Tunis leadership, although their contact was sometimes subject to the intercession of lower-level PLO officials. Nevertheless, the Palestinian civil society leaders were not in PLO or Fatah inner circles, and none were in daily contact with Yasir Arafat and his top aides. Several layers within the PLO organizational structure separated the top leadership from the Palestinian negotiators, none of whom had gone into exile with the PLO leaders and fighters after their evacuation from Beirut.

On the Israeli side, the Shamir government deliberately undermined its own negotiators in order to actually derail the Washington track because Shamir felt that Israel would benefit from appearing to negotiate in good faith while simultaneously consolidating Israeli settlements in the West Bank and Gaza. Shamir retrospectively admitted this when he confirmed to the Israeli newspaper *Maariv*, "I would have carried on autonomy talks for ten years . . . and meanwhile we would have reached half a million people in Judea and Samaria (West Bank)."[41] The change to the Rabin government begs the question of why the delegation in Washington was not changed. Certainly the head of the delegation had been a loyal civil servant who worked under governments run by both of the major parties. But neither he nor anyone else on the Israeli delegation was in Rabin's or Peres's respective inner circles. Decision making was retained by Rabin, whose "distance" from the Israeli delegation in Washington increased.

The locus of decision making on both sides seemed to stay with top-level decision makers who failed to provide the flexibility their respective delegations desired and requested, thus depriving their delegations of the negotiation autonomy needed to consider creative solutions that lay outside the bounds of the maximal aspirations expressed in negotiating instructions. Decision makers on both sides jealously guarded flexibility and negotiation mandates, manipulating and perhaps even undermining the work of their respective front channel delegations. This issue of distance from the top decision makers is linked to the next factor, the relative autonomy of negotiators.

Autonomy of Negotiators

The relative autonomy of negotiators really refers to their ability to transcend narrow negotiation instructions; move beyond tightly held positions; and reach optimal, creative solutions that provide mutual benefit to as many parties and subparties as possible. In particular, I want to discover whether and to what degree negotiator autonomy differs in front and back channels.

The Palestinian delegation saw what little autonomy it had progressively erode over time as Arafat exerted more and more control over the mandate given to the delegation. Ashrawi recalls that "at first, Abu Mazen wanted the Washington talks to succeed and adopted flexible policy positions and negotiations guidelines since he had no 'alternative leadership' preoccupation. Later on, as the back channel negotiations took a serious turn and showed signs of genuine progress, Abu Mazen began to issue more hard-line instructions in a deliberate attempt to block the Washington talks and to clear the way for the Oslo backstage negotiations."[42] At later stages of negotiation, "PLO instructions were becoming more rigid and demanding. While I held on to our basic negotiating strategy, the leadership was averse even to creating an impression of progress on technical issues. I began to wonder then whether a back channel was already in operation and asked Abu Ammar (Arafat) and Abu Mazen. Both denied it."[43]

Dr. Sari Nusseibeh, the president of al-Quds University in Jerusalem and a prominent Jerusalemite, was a member of the PLO Steering Committee that supervised both the bilateral and multilateral talks that emerged from the Madrid and Moscow conferences. His recollection of the Washington talks is that negotiators sought above all to "hold on to their positions and to announce this as soon as they stepped out of the negotiating room. It was just as important in the minds of those people in the room to address the world at large as it was for them to address their counterparts. It was very constrained."[44]

Israel's change of government in the midst of the Washington track provided an obvious opportunity for the Israeli negotiation strategy to shift toward the political platform of the victorious Labor Party. Eliyakim Rubinstein, the delegation head, recalls no difference in negotiation instructions when the Israeli government changed over from Likud to Labor. Uri Savir, the director general of the Israeli foreign ministry and one of the two Israeli officials to go to Oslo for the back channel believes that the two governments' *intentions* were different. Unlike Shamir, Rabin wanted the Washington channel to succeed, at least at first. The difference, according to Savir, is that Rabin wanted a "low-cost" arrangement to come out of the Washington talks and so, kept the hard-line delegates there with their instructions intact. When the secret Oslo channel was functioning in parallel with the Washington talks, Rabin changed nothing because he wanted to "test" the PLO and see where they would be more flexible.[45] This preference prevented him from changing the negotiation mandate of Rubinstein, and this in turn was the Israeli contribution to the failure of the front channel talks. "The fact is we had a limited mandate . . . a bigger role was given to the people who went to Oslo."[46]

Although Rubinstein was expecting a shift in his negotiating brief, there seemed to be an ongoing reluctance to empower him with any new negotiating authority or flexibility. Rubinstein recalls that Rabin had made the decision "at the political level to talk to Arafat and his people and go beyond the real negotiations [in Washington] . . . much beyond what the late Prime Minister Rabin was ready to O.K. to us [in] the Washington group even when we asked for [more] 'rope,' that is, 'negotiating room.'"[47] Both Israeli and Palestinian delegations at the Washington talks grew increasingly frustrated with each other, as well as with the constraints under which they conducted their historic front channel negotiations.

Presence and Role of Third Party

The United States was the intermediary that convened the Madrid Peace Conference and built the consensus for it among the parties that attended, capitalizing on the changed regional balance after the Persian Gulf War. The Washington track spanned two U.S. administrations and a change of party control. During the Republican Bush administration, the third-party role with the regard to the Palestinian-Israeli negotiations was characterized by a cautious stance and included little or no direct mediation. The United States applied pressure on the Shamir government and the Palestinian delegates to attend the conference but then withdrew from any active intermediary role. The Clinton administration tried new techniques as it became active in the negotiations, but these did not have the intended impact. The United States' role served its purpose in convening the conference but was not useful for either delivering Israeli concessions to the Palestinians or for reducing the expectations of the Palestinians. Once the United States had served its purpose, both sides' decision makers moved away from the U.S. presence in the negotiations and sought each other directly in the Oslo channel.

William Quandt observed that, at the Madrid conference, the U.S. government "seemed determined to play the part of convener, but not yet that of mediator."[48] While both Palestinians and Israelis were apt to accuse the Bush administration of partiality to "the other side," Baker and the U.S. Middle East team refrained from direct mediation at the Madrid Peace Conference and the Palestinian-Israeli track.

Nevertheless, the U.S. government described its role as that of the "honest broker," a label that obscures the close strategic United States-Israel relationship. Typically, U.S. candidates for national public office vie with each other in expressing pro-Israel sentiments. The historically close relationship did not prevent the Palestinian delegation from actually counting on the intervention of the United States, precisely because of this close relationship in the hope that only an Israeli ally as reliable as the United States could exercise leverage over the Israeli government in the peace process. This dynamic is well understood in international mediation theory; third-party states intervene in conflicts to protect and satisfy their core interests rather than for humanitarian purposes. Weak parties not allied with the intervening state accept intervention in the expectation that the intervener will "deliver" the ally.[49] The interest-driven intervention of third-party mediators is not without its problems, however, and the intervener's interests may be held more important than those of the principal parties, eventually leading the parties to reject such intervention.

As noted earlier, the United States did in fact exercise a surprising amount of leverage over the $10 billion loan guarantee that President Bush successfully held up in order to pressure Prime Minister Shamir into freezing settlements in

Palestinian territory while also encouraging the Arab states to attend the Madrid Peace Conference. This earned Bush (and Baker) the enmity of the Israeli Right and the acceleration of the settlement project, while the United States helped Rabin to win against Shamir in the 1992 Israeli elections.

On the other hand, for the Palestinians, even this gesture of conditionality was insufficient. The Palestinians hoped for active mediation. Ashrawi claimed that "the Palestinian call for a more active and effective American involvement . . . continued unheeded . . . this ineffectuality undermined the official negotiations and was a contributing factor leading to the alternative back channel negotiations in Oslo between the PLO and representatives of the Israeli government."[50] At one point, the Palestinian delegation sent an official memorandum to James Baker reminding him of the commitments implied in the Letter of Assurances, detailing Israel's human rights violations alleged to be taking place during the negotiations process, and finally, calling for a renewal of the United States-PLO dialogue.[51]

For their part, the Israeli government wished to avoid having to make substantive concessions, even to the United States, and has consistently expressed a preference for minimal U.S. involvement, except for situations in which (like their Palestinian counterparts) they feel the United States could and should "deliver the other side."

The Palestinian dissatisfaction with the quality of the United States' third-party intervention carried over into the new Clinton administration. After the Clinton inauguration, a crisis developed over the issue of killings of Palestinians by Israelis and of Israelis by Palestinians. In December 1992, Rabin had ordered the deportation of more than four hundred Palestinians accused of belonging to HAMAS. They were dropped off in a no-man's-land zone within Lebanon. Despite UN Security Council Resolution 799 that obliged Israel to return the deportees, no progress was made, and the Washington track was essentially frozen by the nonparticipation of the Palestinian delegation. U.S. secretary of state Warren Christopher visited the region to support a return to the negotiation table. The Palestinian delegation asked for American policy clarifications and diplomatic support on key issues in exchange for a resumption of talks, but according to the participants, the promised support fell far short.[52]

With the new American administration and foreign policy team led by Warren Christopher, the Palestinian delegation returned to the negotiation table while the deportation crisis was still unfolding. They had been obliged to return by Arafat himself, who was complying with Rabin's demand that the Washington channel must operate as a condition for continued Israeli participation in Oslo.[53]

When talks finally resumed (ninth round, April 27, 1993), they assumed a new format in keeping with Clinton's pledge of "full partnership." The United States decided to hold separate negotiations with the Israeli and Palestinian delegations in Washington and become a more active intermediary. A trilateral meeting was called in order to present an American document constructed from its separate consultations. The PLO issued instructions through the follow-up committee to the delegation to the effect that they should refuse to attend such a meeting without a preparatory meeting with the Americans and equal opportunity of prior review, on a par with the Israeli delegation. The Americans declined to provide prior review of the document and Tunis ordered the delegation to not even discuss the American document, which the Palestinians thought backtracked on issues that the Israelis had conceded earlier.[54] Ashrawi observed that "the language of Tunis [PLO headquarters] was becoming more strident in direct proportion to the quiet progress made in the secret talks under way in Oslo."[55]

The tenth round of talks in Washington took place between June 15 and July 1, 1993. The American team continued with its attempt to draft a bridging proposal and focused exclusively on direct American-Palestinian negotiations. The delegation insisted on the inclusion of East Jerusalem under eventual Palestinian territorial jurisdiction and the removal of the settlements.[56]

Hanan Ashrawi told the United States-Middle East team that "if American positions [concerning the nature of the Palestinian interim government] continue to be so rigid and you insist in being an obstacle to the peace, the natural conclusion will be to address the Israelis directly without you," which the PLO was already doing at the time in Norway, unbeknownst to Ashrawi and her colleagues on the Palestinian or Israeli delegations.[57]

U.S. intervention was at first insufficiently assertive for the Palestinians and potentially too coercive for the Israelis. Later the quality of U.S. intermediation (separate, direct negotiations with the delegations) was perceived by the Palestinians as being too manipulative and insufficiently neutral. The quality of the United States' presence, or lack of presence (depending on one's preference and perspective), may indeed have been a reason for the Israelis and the PLO to turn to back channels where that presence would not be a factor at all, a motivation that has been suggested by back channel negotiators in other international conflicts.[58]

Strategic Use of Multiple Negotiation Channels

The Washington track was the first acknowledged negotiation process between official Israeli and Palestinian delegations. In a sense, it was the pattern from which the parties would deviate later by deliberately establishing a separate back channel whenever they set up a front channel. There were two brief experiments with quasi back channels within the framework of the Washington track. In an effort to transform the lack of progress, the PLO leadership proposed that the Washington track adopt an unofficial and informal negotiation process to supplement (not replace) the formal talks. Abu Mazen conceived of them as a "side channel" in which the parties could set aside formalities and protocol and "probe matters without inhibition." The two delegations divided into three bilateral committees addressing Palestinian concerns on land, economic issues, and human rights.[59]

According to the legal advisor to the Palestinian delegation, the informal channel began operating in round six (Washington D.C., August 24 to September 24, 1992) and round seven (Washington, D.C., October 21 to November 20, 1992) in order to "get clarification" on these issues and probed "whether there was any reasonable expectation [that the Israeli delegation] might acquiesce in practice in what they refused to acknowledge in principle." Mansour believed that the informal efforts only served to confirm "many of the Palestinian fears."[60] The fact that they were utilized, albeit briefly (they continued into round eight), calls attention to the structural difficulties of the formal negotiations. The informal talks should have operated as a kind of noncommittal brainstorming session that could contribute any "product" to the formal channel. However, the delegation members were the same in the formal and informal talks, and the desired informality eluded the parties. Abu Mazen complains that the informal sessions amounted to a "rigid framework of meetings whose duration, venue, and composition were set in advance" and which failed "largely because neither party understood the main purpose behind them."[61]

A second quasi back channel within the Washington track opened up when Ashrawi and Faisal al-Husseini met secretly with foreign minister Shimon Peres and Rabin's envoy (a former military governor of the West Bank) Ephraim Sneh for the purpose of seeing if there were a way for Israel to avoid any compliance with the Security Council resolution on the Palestinian deportees. Arafat refused Ashrawi's request for explicit approval of these meetings and recommended that they be handled at lower levels first, in order to hammer out agreement on details before high-level leaders got involved. The initiative went no further.[62] According to Abu Mazen, at this time, the PLO itself quietly sent word through Russian and Egyptian intermediaries to the Israeli leaders requesting the opening of direct secret talks. According to Abu Mazen, Rabin declined the offer.[63] According to one of his closest advisors, Rabin "didn't believe—even for a moment—that something would emerge from such meetings."[64] Nearly simultaneously, the Oslo process had its humble beginnings, although Rabin was at first excluded from the small circle of Israelis who knew about it at that moment.

There was a five-month lull between the eighth and ninth rounds of the Washington track, in part because of the Palestinian delegation's decision to protest the expulsion to Lebanon of four hundred Palestinians. In January 1993, one month after the ninth round concluded in Washington, the secret talks in Oslo began. The Palestinian and Israeli delegations in the Washington rounds were excluded from the circle of those who knew about the existence of the secret channel.

The origins of the Oslo channel have been attributed to Hanan Ashrawi, who inadvertently contributed to their activation when she invited Israeli professor Yair Hirschfeld and Dr. Ron Pundik to a meeting at her house in Ramallah. Professor Hirschfeld was involved with the multilateral negotiation working groups on economic development issues. The PLO-appointed head of the Palestinian multilateral delegation, Ahmed Qurei (known by his patronymic, Abu Alaa) was scheduled to be in London at the same time Hirschfeld would be there attending a multilateral meeting. Ashrawi suggested that Hirschfeld make contact with Qurei there to work directly on economic issues of interest to the Israeli and Palestinian delegations to the multilaterals. Their meeting is what laid the foundation of the Oslo channel.[65]

Hassan Asfour, the PLO official who was overseeing the Washington track while also participating at Oslo, as well as Israeli delegation head Eliyakim Rubinstein and Palestinian spokesperson Hanan Ashrawi (both of whom participated and knew only of the Washington process at the time) concur that draft proposals, preparatory materials, briefing documents, and substantive concepts migrated from the Washington process to Oslo, which further establishes a substantive link between the two.[66] Rubinstein goes further than establishing a simple link and argues that "a lot of the material that people had in Oslo was based on most of the material that we [in the front channel] had at the time. . . . In retrospect, I think, one can say that without the infrastructure of Madrid and Washington, the Oslo Agreement wouldn't have been possible."[67]

When the Washington track began, it operated as the sole venue for negotiation. Eventually the delegations developed their own informal lateral "channel" in a failed experiment to inject creativity and clarity in the negotiations. It continued concurrently with the Oslo channel, and the actual members of the Washington track on both sides knew nothing about the existence of the Oslo channel until it was publicly revealed.

The multiplicity of channels provided the parties with strategic opportunities. At the point when the PLO was seeking increased Israeli commitment to the direct talks in Oslo, the Israeli government wanted to test the seriousness of PLO leadership. Among Rabin's conditions for continuing the Oslo channel at an upgraded level included the exclusion of East Jerusalem from Palestinian interim self-rule. In Oslo, the PLO officials conceded this.[68] Yet the PLO gave contradictory instructions to the Palestinian delegation in Washington, once it resumed participation in talks following the deportation crisis. They were to continue to insist on interim Palestinian self-rule in East Jerusalem. The adoption of contradictory negotiations stances in back and front channels, the first relatively flexible and the second relatively firm, appears to have been a tactic designed to induce the Israeli government to take the back channel negotiations more seriously. In a sense, the leader is setting up competing negotiation teams and giving advantages to one that are denied to the other.

On August 30, 1993, the existence of the Oslo channel was officially acknowledged by Norwegian foreign minister Johan Jørgen Holst, who played an increasingly active intermediary back channel role between the PLO and the Israeli government during July and August of 1993. The day after this announcement, the eleventh round of the Washington track was scheduled to begin. Its work was overshadowed by the revelation of the Oslo Declaration of Principles and the details that were leaked about it, especially the "Gaza-Jericho first" concept that had been opposed by the Palestinian delegation to the Washington talks.

The drafts negotiated in Norway by the back channel negotiators could have, and theoretically should have, been finalized and signed in the Washington track. Joel Singer, one of the Oslo negotiators, noted that "if life were simple, content being negotiated in secret could be finished in the front channel. But life is not simple."[69] It is difficult to imagine how the Washington delegations could have been persuaded to finalize an agreement on the basis of one of the Oslo drafts because it was so different from the work they were doing. Nevertheless, negotiators in the front channel such as Faisal al-Husseini regretted their exclusion on the grounds that their work was unjustifiably cut short. If they had input into the Oslo documents or had been permitted to finish negotiating them, "further Israeli concessions were possible. It was worth a try."[70]

The revelation of the secret channel in Oslo and the agreement reached there definitively put an end to the Israeli-Palestinian open negotiations in Washington and caused great consternation among the participants of those talks on both sides. In this regard, the overlap of multiple channels had reached the limit of its strategic and tactical utility. Once the secret channel produces a result and that result is made public rather than being quietly passed over to the front channel, the front channel becomes redundant at best, a source of discontent and protest at worst.

Analytical Conclusions

The Madrid Peace Conference and the Palestinian-Israeli bilateral track that followed it were negotiations in which the media was seen by both sides as a strategic partner in order to persuade their own followers that they were "giving nothing away" and defending their core interests while also conducting a global public relations exercise by showing that they were negotiating.

Owing to their conflicting end goals, the delegations spent considerable time locked on the normally preliminary issues of overarching framework, representation, and negotiation agenda. In the end, they only succeeded in exchanging mutually unacceptable competing drafts on the interim arrangements of Palestinian self-rule. In order to get beyond this conceptual debate on the nature of self-government, they would have needed either a stronger mandate to negotiate from their respective leaders or a more activist and skilled third-party intervener or both. Neither condition was present at any time for the Washington track, despite changes of party and government administration in both Israel and the United States. We see here more clearly the linkages between factors explored in the sections of the chapter: the negotiation agenda appears problematic in the front channel, at least in part, because of wrangling over who is to be invited to the negotiation table. Without requisite closeness to top decision makers, negotiators ironically lack sufficient autonomy to achieve breakthroughs. Third-party interveners may succeed in getting the parties to the table, but this is certainly no guarantee that they will be able to negotiate effectively.

Although Likud tried to exclude both the PLO and the Israeli Labor Party from the peace process, it could not do so for long. The Oslo channel was very much a PLO-Labor project. The Washington bilateral talks enjoyed broader political participation on both sides, but this proceeded along irregular patterns; the Israelis switched leadership and parties midstream, while the nominally marginalized PLO increasingly asserted itself. The delegations in Washington were distanced from the key decision makers and were continually denied the broad mandate to negotiate that they needed to accomplish their goals. When the PLO and Labor were together in charge of the Washington talks, the existence of a separate back channel in Oslo prevented them from making positive use of the front channel, which remained a contentious and unsuccessful negotiating forum where the positions of each delegation only became more unyielding over time.

The United States' role was unsatisfactory to both sides; Palestinians yearned for a more activist stance that would confer leverage on them at the expense of the close Israel-United States relationship. The Shamir government balked at the mildly coercive measures enacted by the Bush administration. Although solicited by the Palestinians for the leverage it could exercise with the Israelis and the power and prestige associated with the world's remaining superpower, the United States disavowed any intention of becoming an active mediator during the Bush administration. This lack of a *mutually accepted* mediator contributed to the track's failure. After the transition to the Clinton administration, there was a qualitative change in the U.S. diplomatic presence in the Palestinian-Israeli bilateral track. Yet the United States' new activism did not succeed. By meeting separately with each delegation, the United States made itself a proxy negotiator for the absent party rather than a true mediator simultaneously exercising leverage and creating value for all. In this second phase of the Washington track, the intermediary approach used by the United States only intensified the adversarial dynamics.

The Washington process, when initiated, was the sole Palestinian-Israeli negotiation process, with the exception of the failed informal sessions in Washington and the secret meeting between Ashrawi, al-Husseini, Peres, and Sneh that had no concrete outcome. At the commencement of the Washington talks, there were no direct lines of communication between Palestinian and Israeli decision makers. The Oslo negotiations were initiated and concluded along a separate channel, overlapping with the Washington track for nine months, presenting the decision makers ample opportunities to use both for strategic purposes. The Oslo channel took the top decision makers by surprise for several asymmetrical reasons. The Israelis were surprised at the moderation they heard from the PLO. The PLO was surprised to find itself across the table from Rabin's envoys and later perceived the opportunity to achieve recognition, to be the signers of an agreement rather than anonymous drafters.[71] Both sides pursued both channels until the back channel produced a viable framework agreement. The multiple channels available to the decision makers provided them with opportunities to test each others' intentions and the extent of the negotiators' proximity to decision makers. The flaws of the negotiations in Washington prevented that forum from becoming the place where the parties would sign the Declaration of Principles drafted in Oslo, which at one point was the only stated purpose of the Oslo channel.

The Madrid Peace Conference and the negotiations that emerged from it held valuable lessons for the Israelis, Palestinians, and Americans involved in the peace process, if anyone was trying to leverage such lessons for the monumental exercise in peacemaking upon which they had embarked. Procedural conflicts embittered the atmosphere when Israel tried to dictate the terms of participation and the proposals of autonomy. The United States implemented wholly ineffective third-party roles after the initial breakthrough of the Madrid Peace Conference. Publicity provided the parties with the benefit of legitimacy but hindered the creativity of the negotiators. The strategic manipulation of this channel by both Israel and the PLO, in attempts to steer each other in the direction of the back channel at Oslo, also undermined the work of the front channel delegations and set the tone for the secret back channel diplomacy that both sides' leaders would find so deceptively seductive for the remainder of the decade.

4

Negotiations in the Oslo Channel, 1993

Gnawing at us all was the paradox of the agreement's momentous importance—for our peoples, for the Middle East and perhaps the whole world—
and the clandestine way in which it had been sealed.

—URI SAVIR, Israeli envoy to the Oslo
back channel[1]

Getting to the Secret Oslo Channel

The secret negotiations conducted in various places in Norway began modestly
without any official involvement from the Israeli government. Collectively, these
discussions have come to be known to interested observers as the "Oslo channel." At their outset, there was little to suggest these talks would result in Israel
and the PLO recognizing each other after thirty years of armed conflict. At first,
two Israeli academics linked to the foreign ministry held exploratory discussions with PLO officials under Norwegian auspices. At all times, Oslo remained
a secret channel of negotiation and underwent several transformations until it
became the main channel of diplomacy for both parties' top decision makers.
Ultimately, it resulted in an agreement to divide issues between interim and final
status negotiations, an agreement to divide Palestinian territory and authority
over it in chronologically spaced stages conferring limited but gradually expanding spheres of civil authority and territorial jurisdiction. The Oslo channel ultimately eclipsed the Washington track when the parties determined that they
would *conclude* an accord directly with each other in the Oslo channel and work
toward mutual recognition between Israel and the PLO, rather than hand off
their work for completion by the front channel negotiators in Washington. The
"architecture" of parallel front and back channels came to characterize much of

the rest of Palestinian-Israeli peacemaking. What began as a coincidence soon became a strategic choice and would ultimately result in important trade-offs, impressively detailed agreements, and unfortunately, progressively less imple-mentation of their terms.

Oslo's Two Phases

The Oslo channel is often regarded as one single negotiation process. In reality, it consisted of two conflict-management phases that must be distinguished from one another even though the phases proceeded sequentially.[2] The first phase was a quasi–Track II effort in which only one side, the Palestinians, was officially represented and empowered to make negotiated commitments, while the Israeli side was represented by two academics with strong connections to Yossi Beilin, who hoped to persuade his foreign minister, and later, the prime minister, to invest diplomatic resources in the Oslo channel—not entirely Track II, nor a fully official back channel. The first phase may be more accurately characterized as a "Track II and a half" effort that became a back channel.

During this first phase, the Israelis present at Oslo disavowed any decision-making authority. The second phase of the Oslo channel involved "upgrading" the Israeli participants to the Oslo talks to officials directly authorized by the prime minister. This is not to demean in any way the critical foundation laid by professor Yair Hirschfeld and Dr. Ron Pundik for their pioneering exploratory talks with their PLO counterparts. However, once both sets of delegates were fully and officially empowered, the track became a full back channel negotia-tion; it worked in parallel with an existing front channel negotiation process (the Madrid track) while its existence was kept secret from the front channel negotiators.

The Oslo channel resulted from a convergence of international political circumstances, internal political considerations for both the Palestinians and Israelis, and their respective actions to find a suitable negotiating partner on the other side. Although systemic considerations supply some of the reasons for the use of a negotiation strategy involving a parallel secret channel, I look to the peace process and negotiations themselves for other explanations for the use of the secret channel. The analytic categories for case comparison are used to organize the case data.

Converging Efforts

Diverse initiatives contributed to creation of the direct PLO-Israel negotiation channel in Norway. The three sides of this triangular relationship were formed by the following aspects:

- PLO efforts to negotiate directly with Israeli officials of both Labor and Likud and prevent the creation of a so-called alternative leadership that Israel had been promoting since the beginning of the 1967 military occupation of the West Bank and Gaza
- The work of progressive factions within the Israeli Labor Party and the Israeli peace movement calling for direct talks with the PLO
- Offers of assistance by third parties that both the PLO and the Israelis trusted, such as the Norwegian and Dutch Labor Parties

In the following sections of this chapter, I consider each of these aspects and how the parties took advantage of them.

Yossi Beilin and the Norway Connection

The earliest direct secret Israel-PLO contacts were detailed in chapter 2. These took place in New York and London in 1985, followed by 1986 talks in Brussels and Paris, the Amirav-Nusseibeh (Likud-PLO) document of principles in 1987, and a series of secret Israel-PLO encounters in Paris in 1988. Besides these recently revealed official secret negotiations, several quiet, nonofficial dialogues were taking place among Palestinian and Israeli public figures during that period. Yossi Beilin, a Labor Party member of the Knesset and Israel's deputy foreign minister after June 1992, knew about and participated in some of the nonofficial dialogues and knew about some of the direct contacts through his boss, Shimon Peres.

The Israeli leg of the Israel-Norway-PLO Oslo "triangle" began with Yossi Beilin. Beilin had developed a relationship with Norwegian sociologist Terje Rød Larsen, then director of the Institute of Applied Social Science in Oslo (FAFO),[3] and Norwegian deputy foreign minister Jan Egeland of the Norway Labor Party before their electoral victory in 1992.[4] As an activist in the Labor Party, Beilin had founded the Mashov Caucus, a progressive faction that worked to build party consensus on diverse social issues in order to move the party to the Left. Through Mashov, Beilin met an Israeli academic named Yair Hirschfeld who brought with him an extensive network of informal affiliations with Palestinian leaders in East Jerusalem and the West Bank, including Jerusalem leader Faisal al-Husseini and Dr. Hanan Ashrawi.[5] As leader of the Mashov Caucus, Beilin initiated and attended several unpublicized dialogues with Palestinian leaders even while he was serving first as cabinet secretary and then as deputy finance minister in the Israeli national unity coalition government.[6]

In early 1989, the former Dutch foreign minister Max van der Stoel proposed to Shimon Peres that he open a back channel with PLO officials in Holland. Peres declined the invitation. However, Beilin was interested and traveled to the Hague in July 1989 in order for Van der Stoel to conduct "proximity" talks, shuttling between the hotel rooms of Beilin and two PLO officials, Abd Allah Hourani and Afif Safiyeh. Van der Stoel's efforts resulted in a draft joint statement of principles for peace negotiations that Van der Stoel planned to take to the two sides' leadership for approval, ostensibly presenting it as his own document while counting on the complicit input of both sides to facilitate acceptance. When the PLO leadership wanted to negotiate further revisions, Beilin felt he could not continue and the initiative eventually collapsed.[7]

In March 1990, Shimon Peres, as finance minister, decided to risk withdrawing the Labor Party from the national unity coalition government, thereby dissolving it in order to call for new elections in which he hoped to form a Labor-led government. Because of defections by the religious parties Peres was courting, the effort failed completely; Likud not only won, it formed a government without the need to enter into a coalition with Labor.[8]

With the Labor Party out of the Israeli government, Beilin, as a member of the Knesset, continued his efforts to pave the way for a peace process. He made contacts with Palestinian leaders in 1990 and 1991, including Dr. Sari Nusseibeh (a prominent academic and PLO affiliate from Jerusalem), Faisal al-Husseini, and others.[9] Beilin's purpose in these contacts was to draft a protocol that would guide negotiations between the Palestinians and the Israeli Labor Party and left-wing parties if and when they managed to form a future Israeli government. The meetings culminated in a plenary on August 5, 1990, at which a relatively progressive document was indeed approved.[10] This negotiating protocol and the growing strength of Israeli-Palestinian relationships upon which it rested were immediately overshadowed by the Iraqi invasion of Kuwait and the consequences that flowed therefrom.

Upon the conclusion of the Persian Gulf War, James Baker spent much of 1991 conducting his shuttle diplomacy in preparation for the Madrid Peace Conference, as discussed in chapter 3.

Beilin and Hirschfeld, with the financing of European development agencies, set up an NGO called the Economic Cooperation Foundation (ECF) in 1991, which employed Hirschfeld and his former student Dr. Ron Pundik full time on peace issues and provided Beilin a way to continue his work through individuals who were neither Labor Party officials nor government employees, thus achieving the expression of official ideas through nonofficial people. While Shamir's government conducted the Madrid conference with its bilateral and multilateral tracks, the Mashov Caucus served as a progressive vanguard of the Labor Party while out of power. Beilin pushed the party to adopt positions in favor of eliminating the legal prohibition on meetings with the PLO and, ultimately, negotiating with the PLO directly, as soon as the party should return to power.[11]

In January and August 1992, (before and after Rabin's election) the PLO itself, through Abu Alaa and Arafat's aide Bassam Abu Sharif, asked the Norwegian government to take the initiative of facilitating direct Israel-PLO negotiations. The Norwegian government conveyed this message to the Israeli ambassador in Norway, who apparently rejected it without any consultation with the political leadership in Jerusalem and Tel Aviv.[12]

As I discussed in the previous chapter, the first phase of the Madrid peace process had two titular sponsors, the United States and the Soviet Union. The Madrid Peace Conference was not the only front channel diplomatic conference launched by the sponsors. It fell to the new government in Moscow (then called the Commonwealth of Independent States—the CIS) to structure a conference on various negotiation issues that would be addressed by multilateral working groups rather than in bilateral negotiations.[13] The CIS set up a conference in Moscow at which the "multilateral" talks were launched in January 1992. A multilateral steering committee was also set up to monitor the progress of the working groups.

In the early 1990s, the Norwegian think tank FAFO undertook extensive research on the living conditions in Gaza. As director of FAFO, Terje Rød Larsen came into contact with both Palestinians and Israelis in the course of the field research, and he began to understand the fundamentals of the Palestinian-Israel

conflict and the shortcomings of the Madrid conference and its ensuing negotiations. He began to believe that FAFO itself could serve as "the perfect venue
for a secret Israeli-Palestinian meeting."[14] Some of their data were used for the
multilateral working group on refugees that emerged from the Moscow conference.[15] On May 29, 1992, Larsen met with Yossi Beilin and openly proposed that
FAFO be used as the conduit for a supplementary channel of secret negotiation between Labor and the PLO, stating, "we can provide you with a venue . . .
before the elections, after the elections, whether you remain in the opposition or
return to power."[16] Larsen made the same proposal to Faisal al-Husseini. Beilin
put Larsen in touch with Hirschfeld, who already had his network of contacts
among Palestinians.

Larsen's wife, Mona Juul, was the director of the office of deputy foreign
minister Jan Egeland, and in that capacity had received a PLO delegation to Norway headed by Abu Alaa in January 1992 (mentioned previously). Abu Alaa gave
Juul and Larsen the impression that he would be willing and able to negotiate
directly with the Israelis, given the proper forum.[17] The FAFO-Labor-PLO triangle was forming.

The only missing ingredient, it seemed, was Labor's return to power. This
condition, once it was realized, did not automatically set in motion a parallel peace process between Israel and the PLO because of the internal divisions
within the new cabinet, principally the rivalry between Rabin and Peres.

PLO contacts with the Israeli Labor Party were not the only channels being
pursued. Abu Mazen hints at stranger encounters than the Oslo channel. Before
the June 1992 electoral defeat of the Likud Party, a PLO envoy met in March
and April with a senior Israeli intelligence official who claimed he had briefed
the Israeli cabinet (and thus Shamir) on these contacts. The PLO also made contact with one of Likud's most ideologically extreme leaders, former general and
defense minister Ariel Sharon, the architect of the Israeli invasion of Lebanon
in 1982 and the failed military alliance with the Maronite Christian Phalan-
gist Party there. The purpose of these secret meetings was to convey to Likud
and Sharon that Abu Mazen desired direct negotiations between the PLO and
Israel.[18] Also in April, there were several secret meetings between a Palestinian
notable from the West Bank city of Nablus with ties to the PLO, Said Kanaan; and
two Israeli figures, the first military governor of the West Bank general (retired)
Shlomo Gazit; and Yossi Genosar, a high official with Shin Bet, the Israeli

counterintelligence and internal security service. The purpose of these meetings was to explore Palestinian support for the Labor Party, to get clarification on the Labor Party platform, and to suggest ways to expedite progress in the stalled Washington negotiations.[19]

The June 23, 1992, elections in Israel brought to power a Labor-dominated government with a solid propeace process mandate, which sidelined the PLO's efforts to court Likud. Shimon Peres and Yitzhak Rabin, longtime Labor Party rivals, formed a new government that enjoyed not only broad popular support but also enjoyed the approval of the outgoing Bush and incoming Clinton administrations in the United States. The light sanctions that Bush and Baker had imposed on Israel gave way to renewed support for Israel.

Rabin worked hard to reduce the extent of Shimon Peres's influence in the new government, retaining for himself the defense minister and prime minister portfolios. Peres, even though he was offered the cabinet position of minister of foreign affairs, was excluded from managing Israeli-United States relations and, more critically, was prevented from supervising the bilateral Palestinian-Israeli track. Rabin himself took charge of the Palestinian-Israeli track, assigning Peres the supervision of the lower-profile multilateral negotiations.[20]

To the consternation of both the Palestinian and Israeli delegations in Washington, the Rabin government did not modify its strategy in Washington either in terms of negotiators or their negotiating mandate. The Washington track continued as it had before the election.

On September 9, Jan Egeland visited Israel to meet with Beilin, who was now deputy minister of foreign affairs in the new government, especially to revisit the idea of conducting a secret channel of negotiations through Oslo. Egeland indicated that Norwegian foreign minister Thorvald Stoltenberg (replaced by Johan Jørgen Holst in April 1993) stood behind the FAFO proposal to host the secret channel and would provide both political and financial support. There was no disagreement between Beilin and Egeland on the need for a parallel track. Beilin wanted to recreate the negotiations that had led to the Peres-Hussein London Agreement of 1987, in which he had participated. His desire was to negotiate an accord in secret with the PLO and then "lay the completed work on the negotiating table without the existence of the track ever being known. To the world it would then seem that all the problems had been solved by official negotiation while the truth would be very different."[21] The negotiation would be with the PLO, even though the signing and implementation was supposed to fall to the local Palestinian leadership. Yossi Beilin's nascent conception of the back channel did not include structuring it as an independent forum for negotiation and decision making. As discussed in earlier chapters, the PLO did in fact entertain the idea of parallel secret channels and at various times proposed them as the principal channels.

To proceed, Beilin needed the open support of Peres. It proved impossible to even ask for this because in early September, Rabin had prohibited Peres from even meeting with al-Husseini to discuss the Washington talks. Beilin felt he could not ask Peres to sanction the Oslo meeting and also felt he could not go alone and hide the channel from him. With Rabin prohibiting activities that were much less daring than a secret channel in Oslo, Beilin felt compelled to deputize Hirschfeld to go to Oslo in his stead while he would feed Hirschfeld information on substantive problems of the Washington talks.[22] At the end of September 1992, the talks in Washington completed another round and were expected to be on hold until the outcome of the U.S. elections.

Hanan Ashrawi's Suggestion

While Beilin was exploring the options of a back channel through the Norwegians, the Palestinians were also looking for ways to make progress. Pundik and others point, not to Beilin, but rather to Hanan Ashrawi as the author of the Oslo channel because she first suggested the meeting that would blossom into the Oslo channel. While she was still spokeswoman for the Palestinian talks in Washington, Ashrawi met with Hirschfeld and Pundik at her home in Ramallah on November 30, 1992.

At that meeting, she made two radical suggestions.[23] First, despite (or perhaps because of) her prominent role as spokesperson for the talks in Washington, she suggested that a secret three-way working group be set up in Washington, involving the United States, the PLO, and Israeli high-level officials to work in parallel with the official track. Pundik and Hirschfeld promised to suggest the idea to Beilin. Second, she proposed that Hirschfeld go to London while a meeting of the Multilateral Talks Steering Committee was to take place. While there, Hirschfeld could meet with the PLO official secretly overseeing the (non-PLO) Palestinian delegation to the multilateral negotiations. That official was Ahmed Qurei (Abu Alaa), then the PLO's director general of economic affairs and planning.[24]

Although not a prominent PLO official at that time, Abu Alaa was already known to Beilin and Hirschfeld through a progressive paper he wrote that advocated regional economic integration and joint development projects among Palestine, Israel, and neighboring states.[25] Ashrawi's suggestion directly set in motion the encounter that would lead to the series of negotiation sessions in Norway held between the PLO and Israel (the Oslo channel).[26]

The Multilateral Talks Steering Committee was scheduled to meet in London on December 4, 1992. Hirschfeld traveled to London regarding a Track II initiative funded by the Swiss government, which brought together Israelis and Palestinians to discuss the issue of water use, the subject of one of the multilateral working groups.[27] Israel's legal ban on meetings with the PLO was still in effect (the "Law of Association"), and Hirschfeld was not entirely sure that he should meet with Abu Alaa.[28] Only journalists and academics attending conferences were exempt from the anti-PLO legislation and the three year prison sentence it prescribed,[29] an exception that provided the Norwegians with an idea to camouflage the Oslo channel.

The London Encounter

Beilin arrived in London heading the Israeli delegation to the multilaterals. Abu Alaa arrived in London to supervise the Palestinian participation in the working groups. Larsen was there on other business. Once Hirschfeld decided to meet with Abu Alaa, Terje Rød Larsen arranged the logistics of the Hirschfeld-Abu Alaa encounter in London. The Norwegian government, through Larsen, offered to host further meetings in Norway if all went well.[30] Hirschfeld recalled informing Beilin about meeting the PLO leader on the same day.[31] The Hirschfeld-Abu Alaa encounter resulted in both sides realizing that there was a new opportunity for direct Israel-PLO talks.

Hirschfeld presented himself to his counterparts as an academic with only tenuous connections to the Israeli leadership, but the Palestinians who met with him (Abu Alaa and Afif Safiyeh, the PLO representative in London) were present in their full official capacity, with the authorization and knowledge of the Executive Committee of the PLO.[32]

Yasir Arafat assigned one of his closest confidants, Mahmoud Abbas (also known by his patronymic, Abu Mazen) with the tasks of overseeing the London meeting and recommending any follow-up. His assessment of the London meeting was that Hirschfeld "could not have acted on his own initiative, that he must have received authorization from . . . Peres and Beilin, that he had been sent to sound us out and that this faction in the Israeli cabinet wanted to open a channel other than the Washington channel."[33]

At that point, the PLO was ready to participate officially and at a senior level in any eventual Oslo encounter, sidelining Palestinian leaders such as Faisal al-Husseini from the occupied territories. For the initial contacts in London and the first five rounds of Oslo meetings, the PLO was engaging in what was basically a quasi–Track II effort that Beilin, on the Israeli side, hoped would transform itself into a full back channel negotiation. Paradoxically, the Israeli cabinet was not even informed of the London meeting, except insofar as Beilin helped to set it in motion and asked his colleague from their NGO, Yair Hirschfeld, to stand in for him. Beilin observes that "it is possible that had [the PLO] known I was the only government official aware of the [initial Oslo] negotiations they would not have invested as much as they did."[34]

Larsen then issued the fateful invitation to a meeting in Norway that would be the first of the Oslo back channel sessions. He invited Beilin's two associates Hirschfeld and Pundik, as well as three senior PLO officials, Ahmed Qurei (Abu Alaa), Maher al-Kurd (later replaced by Mohamed Abu Koush), and Hassan Asfour (who was then the secretary of the Negotiations Committee of the PLO and was overseeing every detail of the Washington track) to Oslo in January 1993 for the purpose of drafting a document of principles that, it was hoped, would serve to set out the guidelines by which the parties would proceed to manage their relationship and resolve their conflicts.

The Norwegians' stated purpose was not to create a fully operational parallel negotiation track. They did not initially plan to "circumvent" the talks in Washington, but rather to "circumvent some of the political obstacles which prevented direct and open negotiations between Israel and the PLO, with a view to injecting the results of the 'back channel' into the 'front channel.'"[35]

The Oslo Channel, Phase I

In this section I discuss progress made in the first phase of the Oslo channel, during which there was official PLO representation but no corresponding official

Israeli presence. Initial Israeli participation, though not official, benefited from the input and guidance of Yossi Beilin, and eventually of both foreign minister Shimon Peres and prime minister Yitzhak Rabin.[36] It is nevertheless true that, from the Israeli perspective, the Oslo channel was a freelance operation run by Beilin that only gradually became imbued with the full authority of the government of Israel.[37]

On January 19, 1993, the Israeli Knesset repealed the "Law of Association" that had made it a crime for Israelis to meet with any PLO official. The first Israeli-Palestinian encounter within the new legal framework took place the next day in Norway.

On January 20, the five Israelis and Palestinians arrived in Oslo and were taken to Sarpsborg, a two-hour drive south of Oslo, and treated to a presentation by FAFO on economic conditions in Gaza. The delegates eagerly started their own talks directly afterward and agreed broadly on an initial Israeli withdrawal from Gaza, (the so-called Gaza-first concept, previously a nonstarter from the PLO point of view). The idea of Palestinian self-government in Gaza first had been circulating among Israelis, Palestinians, and the Arab states since 1949 when the Palestinians declared an All-Palestine Government in Gaza, then controlled by Egypt. It was later brought up in the context of Camp David autonomy talks, and Peres credits himself with having proposed the concept to a reluctant al-Sadat.[38] Furthermore, they agreed on the need to facilitate a "mini Marshall Plan" for international aid and investment in Palestinian territories, as well as on the need to promote economic cooperation between the Palestinians and Israelis.

The Palestinians worked from a ten-point draft declaration prepared by Abu Mazen. His draft integrated the interim/permanent status distinction, but it conceived Palestinian authority as extending to all the pre-1967 territory during the interim stage, with spheres of authority to be negotiated.[39] Abu Mazen also sought the creation of a joint "Israeli-Palestinian Committee" to address "common issues and disputes," with final recourse to an ad hoc arbitral tribunal composed of U.S., Russian, Egyptian, Jordanian, Palestinian, and Israeli members.

The Israeli and Palestinian back channel envoys began discussions on the components of a draft declaration of principles for Israeli-Palestinian peace negotiations during their second encounter in Norway (February 11 and 12, 1993). They argued about the extent of Palestinian self-government jurisdiction, and the Israelis argued that during the interim stage, Palestinian rule could not extend to the entire West Bank and Gaza because such an arrangement would necessitate dealing with the settlements and Jerusalem, which they wanted to consign to a final status arrangement to be separately negotiated. Hirschfeld insisted that Palestinian self-rule would commence in Gaza and gradually extend to the West Bank but not East Jerusalem.

Between the second and third rounds, the seriousness of the Palestinian side having been demonstrated, Yossi Beilin felt that it was time to seek "the legitimization of the process."[40] He decided to present the draft documents to Foreign Minister Peres, informing him for the first time of the existence of the Oslo channel. Peres himself informed Rabin about the channel, evidently arguing that the Oslo channel at least had the merit of providing low-risk intelligence on the PLO without formal Israeli commitment.[41] Rabin seemed unimpressed but did not attempt to quash the effort. At minimum, he did not want Oslo to replace the Washington talks. The official track in Washington had been frozen by Palestinian nonparticipation because of Prime Minister Rabin's expulsion of 415 alleged HAMAS members to a no-man's-land in Lebanon on December 17, 1992, following the killings of Israeli soldiers by HAMAS and Palestinian civilians by the IDF.

Hoping to save face before an incoming new U.S. administration, Rabin made further Israeli participation in Oslo contingent upon a resumption of the Washington talks.[42] To persuade the Palestinians to go back to the table in Washington, Rabin authorized Peres to get involved with the bilateral track that Rabin had jealously kept away from his Labor Party rival. Peres and Ephraim Sneh on the Israeli side met with Faisal al-Husseini and Hanan Ashrawi on the Palestinian side four times in secret, but they were unable to obtain a Palestinian commitment to return to Washington in light of the expulsions.[43]

At this point, the highest Israeli and Palestinian decision makers knew that they indeed had two structurally parallel (and not simply alternative) tracks available to them, one secretly proceeding in Oslo and the other openly "proceeding" in Washington. This awareness of separate, parallel *negotiation* channels (as opposed to simply exploratory talks among people with varying levels of authority) led both sides to marginalize several other *additional* channels, some of which operated under the direction of Prime Minister Rabin himself, according to statements by the principal architects of the secret channel on both sides.

Mohamed Heikel reports that "no fewer than nine different channels ran through Cairo, where aides to Mubarak were highly active arranging meetings. David Kimche, undersecretary of the Israeli Foreign Ministry and former director of Mossad, was in charge of one of these channels."[44]

Finally made aware that two negotiation channels were available to them, decision makers were now in a position to use them both strategically through manipulation of the information, the negotiators, and their instructions in the respective channels.

By this third round (March 20 and 21, 1993), the negotiators had produced a draft declaration of principles for approval of each side's leadership. The pace of progress was nothing short of stunning compared to the talks in Washington, which they agreed were to be resumed as Rabin's condition for continuing Israeli participation at Oslo. Thorvald Stoltenberg renounced his position as Norwegian foreign minister to assume a UN appointment to address the conflict in the former Yugoslavia. He was replaced by the equally supportive Johan Jørgen Holst in early April.

In the fourth round (April 30, 1993), the parties discussed the PLO's move to slow progress in the Washington talks to allow the Israeli side to consider the draft declaration more broadly and to find a mechanism for having the United States adopt any agreement from Oslo as its own. The Israelis emphasized that the Oslo channel was designed to provide input into Washington, not replace Washington, a move perceived by the Palestinians as Israeli intransigence, drawing attention to the possibility of completing and signing the draft declaration in the Oslo channel. The Gaza-plus-Jericho concept was brought up again by the Palestinians during this round, meaning the gradual implementation of autonomy both in Gaza and in a foothold on the West Bank. This idea extended the "Gaza-first" concept and tested the Israeli's seriousness regarding withdrawal of forces from the West Bank. The Washington talks had by this time resumed.[45]

The fifth round (May 8 and 9, 1993) was spent reviewing Israeli progress in building internal consensus on the draft declaration, but the Israeli side indicated that its own status was not yet "official." Hirschfeld and Pundik, though they now enjoyed the backing of Rabin and Peres, were still isolated from Israeli decision making at the policy level. They were instructed to avoid discussing the draft declaration of principles and, ironically, to once again emphasize the Washington track's preeminence. The Israelis conveyed Rabin's satisfaction that the PLO had demonstrated its commitment to the Oslo channel by unilaterally slowing down progress in the Washington talks and indicated that Rabin would shift his attention from Israel-Syria negotiations back to the Israel-Palestinian track.

Abu Alaa had conceded in Oslo that Palestinian interim self-rule would not include East Jerusalem, a concession at variance with long-standing Palestinian policy on the status of the occupied territories and wholly inconsistent with the Palestinian demands in the Washington track, as discussed in the previous chapter. But he needed to know that his concession was being taken seriously and that it would be reciprocated. Abu Alaa demanded more concrete assurances about Israeli investment of political and diplomatic capital in the Oslo channel. Abu Alaa voiced his concerns to Terje Rød Larsen, who communicated them to the Israeli leadership.[46]

Upon the conclusion of the fifth round, the Israeli delegates felt they could not return to Oslo without discussing the draft declaration, which had been put on hold while Rabin and Peres reviewed it. The draft was extensive and reached far beyond the meager accomplishments of the Israeli and Palestinian negotiators in the Washington talks, who had failed to even agree on what they were negotiating. Significantly, the draft declaration integrated an incremental approach, provided for East Jerusalemites to participate as candidates and voters in Palestinian elections, and divided the peace process into interim and permanent stages. The permanent stage would include Jerusalem's political status, Palestinian refugees, sovereignty, borders, and security arrangements. The territory over which the Palestinians would exercise authority in the interim period was not specified in the draft.[47]

The Oslo Channel: Phase II

During the second phase of the Oslo channel, the Israeli delegation added two government officials to their delegation in response to Palestinian demands for more Israeli commitment to Oslo and corresponding to Peres and Rabin's desire to at least complement the Washington talks with the Oslo channel. This second phase of Oslo is therefore characterized by parity in the official status of both the Palestinian and Israeli delegations, although there continued to be internal and cross-party jockeying to determine which channel would predominate.

In the second phase, the negotiations in Oslo also became more serious and focused on problem solving and survived several crises and negotiator brinksmanship. The new Israeli arrivals came with the consent, knowledge, and trust of Prime Minister Rabin and an official mandate to represent the State of Israel in the Oslo negotiations with the PLO. But their first duty was to assess, for Rabin, the benefits of continuing the channel.[48]

It would be an error to dismiss the first phase (rounds one to five) of the Oslo channel as an academic exercise. Equally, the significance of "upgrading" the Oslo channel should not be underestimated. Had Oslo failed or leaked during the second phase, the Israeli government would no longer have been able to portray the Oslo channel as a simple conversation devoid of political commitment; hence deniability in the second phase was possible but no longer *plausible*. In contrast, during the first phase of Oslo, Israel's deniability was both possible and plausible, given the absence of officially empowered negotiators. The upgrading of the Israeli delegation was the direct product of Israeli decision making at the highest levels and therefore reflected a major policy shift to use a second channel (Oslo) to work toward an accord (and not simply for exploratory talks).

After the fifth round, the Oslo channel was no longer a project of Yossi Beilin's NGO, about which Shimon Peres happened to be informed. Consequently, a meeting between Israeli and PLO officials implicitly carried with it the element of de facto political recognition, with consequent political uncertainties and possible costs for both sides. Although there had been prior secret negotiations between Israel and the PLO, the purpose was now decidedly more concrete for *both* parties; the conclusion of a preliminary accord and not simply the discussion of Israeli MIAs in Lebanon as cover for exploratory talks, as had been the case before. (See chapter 2 for details of the secret talks between 1985 and 1988.)

The first official approved by Peres and Rabin to attend the sixth round in Oslo was Uri Savir, newly appointed director general of the foreign ministry. Savir's presence signaled Rabin's approval of the channel in his capacity as prime minister. Savir arrived in Oslo on May 20, 1993, acutely aware of the historical significance of his involvement. He brought with him two sets of conditions for Israeli support for the back channel: a procedural set and a substantive set. The procedural conditions, he attributes to Yitzhak Rabin: total secrecy regarding Oslo and resumption of the talks in Washington. To Shimon Peres he attributes the substantive conditions: continued PLO agreement to exclude Jerusalem from interim arrangements, the possibility of starting Palestinian autonomy in Gaza (the "Gaza-first" concept), and a Palestinian pledge to negotiate everything within a bilateral framework rather than pursue other avenues of dispute resolution, such as international arbitration and third-party mediation.[49]

Savir attended the sixth round of the Oslo channel on May 20, 1993, and set out the conditions imposed by his superiors. The Palestinians contacted Tunis and acknowledged some of the Israeli interests underlying these conditions (without entirely conceding the points), while they brought up the demand for Jericho in conjunction with an initial handover of Gaza. The atmosphere in the Oslo channel was one of intense contention over the substance combined with equally intense relationship building and trust building. Once inducted and accepted into the Oslo clique, Savir recommended to Peres and Rabin that the negotiations continue in Oslo.[50] The PLO was anxious for Savir to move forward on the draft so that it could be passed on to the Washington delegations. However, the Israeli side was not prepared to return to Oslo until a resumption of the Washington talks.[51]

At a meeting with Peres on June 6, 1993, Prime Minister Rabin abruptly changed his mind about the Oslo channel and ordered all work on it postponed until the resumption of the Washington talks. On the following day, Rabin sent an official letter to Peres outlining his objections to the Oslo channel and his suspicion that the PLO was trying to sideline its own moderates in the Washington delegation.[52] The Palestinian Washington delegation, on orders from Tunis, had recently refused to meet with the American peace team to avoid having to deal with American bridging proposals. The Palestinian Washington delegation continued to insist on concessions Israel was not willing to make.[53] Arafat's intent with these moves was to signal to Rabin that Oslo was the preferred forum, but it has been surmised that Rabin misinterpreted the signal, nearly derailing the only channel with the potential to produce an initial accord.[54]

Peres and his staff worked on a written response to Rabin's letter in which they emphasized the relative moderation of the PLO envoys in Oslo and underlined the PLO's agreement to restart the Washington talks, thus pointing out to Rabin the true import of Tunis's actions regarding the Washington talks. Rabin relented at a meeting with Peres on June 10, 1993.[55]

The next and seventh Oslo round (June 14 and 15, 1993) coincided with the resumption of talks in Washington (the ninth round of the Washington bilaterals). The eighth Oslo round took place from June 25 to 27, 1993. Both the seventh and eighth Oslo rounds introduced new negotiation dynamics caused by the arrival of an Israeli attorney, Joel Singer, who entered the Oslo channel as a legal consultant to the Israeli Ministry of Foreign Affairs.[56] These two rounds were marked by intense, interrogatory-style questioning of the Palestinians by Singer. Among the many questions he put to the Palestinians, Singer inquired whether the PLO would be willing to resort to secret agreements (secret texts) or secret exchanges of letters in the course of negotiating their agreements.[57] Singer came aboard with an initial sense that the existing Oslo draft declaration of principals did not meet Israeli interests in numerous regards. He redrafted the declaration to respond to Israeli interests and to take into account the answers to the questions he posed to the Palestinian delegation at Oslo, almost alienating the PLO from the Oslo channel.

Singer brought to the negotiations the idea that the Oslo channel should produce an agreement of mutual recognition. This was so the PLO would be more than a mere working group serving the Washington track. Singer hoped the PLO would actually assume responsibility for controlling dissident factions in the occupied territories and for preventing outbreaks of anti-Israeli violence, and he recognized that the PLO would only play such a role if it were the signatory of any accord and Israel's acknowledged negotiation partner. At first, neither Rabin nor Peres agreed to this, but Rabin gave his consent for Singer to bring it up in Oslo as a private initiative.[58]

At that time, Ephraim Sneh, a member of the Knesset and former military governor in the occupied territories, was meeting informally with Nabil Shaath, then the PLO representative in Cairo. This new potential "channel" caused some confusion, and Abu Alaa suspected that Israel was trying to open several channels to find the shortest path to an agreement signed by the delegations in Washington, which he feared would then be sidelined by Israeli negotiations with Jordan and Syria, both of which were being taken very seriously by Rabin.[59] Within two months' time, with progress and risks both accumulating rapidly, the envoys in Oslo mutually agreed to keep up Israeli contacts with Shaath because they deflected attention from the Oslo channel.[60]

During the eighth Oslo round, Singer formally presented a new draft declaration of principles to the Palestinians; this draft provoked a crisis as the Palestinians wondered what had become of the understandings previously reached with the Israeli academics Hirschfeld and Pundik. Abu Alaa countered with Arafat's own set of questions for the Israeli delegation. Almost as an inducement, Singer held out the mutual recognition issue, which corresponded exceedingly well with the PLO's own reasons for participating in the Oslo channel. The PLO's interest in drafting an agreement merely for the signature of the Washington delegation was declining, and the possibility of playing a central role as a newly indispensable partner that had long been scorned was enticing.[61]

The ninth round was held from July 4 to 6 in Gresheim, north of Oslo, and Singer submitted a new draft declaration of principles including gradual conferral of autonomy to Gaza and later to Jericho. An interim agreement would be negotiated afterward to work out the extension of autonomy to other areas of the West Bank. Key differences remained over the mention of Jerusalem and its Palestinian residents, demands for arbitration provisions, and displaced Palestinians, among other issues. However, both sides felt that progress was being made, and trust and confidence were being strengthened at both an interpersonal level as well as regarding mutual political perceptions. Abu Mazen reports that the Palestinians felt the PLO was being recognized as the key partner, despite the continued Israeli insistence on plugging final results into Washington.[62] Uri Savir commented that the Palestinians at first balked at the new draft and characterized it as a step backward. The delegates pushed on and incorporated Palestinian objections into the draft for further consultation.

The tenth round took place on July 11 and marked another turning point. Abu Alaa arrived with a new draft incorporating several new amendments to the "Gresheim draft," among them the concept of territorial links between Gaza and the West Bank. The Israelis protested what they termed "new demands."[63] On that day, Norwegian foreign minister Holst was visiting Arafat in Tunis, under the guise of an official visit to that country. Holst then stepped away from the facilitative role Norway had previously assumed and took on the role of active mediator, conveying to Arafat the risk involved in insisting on his new demands. Holst is credited with coming up with the concept of "safe passage" in lieu of extraterritorial corridors and with convincing Arafat to accept this compromise.[64]

While the Norwegians were assuming a newly active intermediary role during July 1993, Peres became persuaded that it was now in Israel's interest to recognize the PLO and permit the arrival of Arafat in Gaza to begin assuming the administration of the territory. Before the next round of the Oslo channel, Holst and his team met with both the PLO and the Israelis to build confidence: they provided assurances, urged flexibility and commitment to the process, and conveyed messages about each side's interests and priorities to the other side.[65]

The eleventh round in Oslo took place July 24 to 26, 1993. The Palestinians arrived with their own new draft that incorporated new substantive demands, including negotiated (rather than unilateral) Israeli military redeployments, a large Palestinian police force, and others.[66] The Palestinians expressed concern that the sponsors of the official Madrid process—meaning the United States and Russia—would be happy if the Oslo channel failed to produce an agreement.[67] Pledges that Arafat had made to the Norwegians since the last round were kept, thus eliminating some areas of disagreement. But the Palestinians were still concerned about the balance between what could be agreed upon in the text of the draft declaration and what needed to be deferred until the interim and permanent status negotiations.[68]

The parties went over the Israeli draft clause by clause to confirm agreements reached and see if further discussion was merited on the remaining issues. Savir and Singer themselves brought up Israeli concerns about security issues and limiting the powers of the Palestinian council, but this only "soured the atmosphere of the talks."[69] The specific issues for which there remained substantial disagreement included the wording concerning the implementation of UN Security Council Resolutions 242 and 338, whether or not the final status issues should be named in the text (the Palestinians wanted Jerusalem as well as the other issues mentioned), the extent of the area around Jericho to be part of the initial Israeli withdrawal, whether or not the Palestinian refugees would be mentioned as a subject for regional coordination, and the wording on the extent of participation or exclusion of the East Jerusalemites from Palestinian elections, among others.[70] The negotiators recall sixteen outstanding areas of disagreement.[71] Thus the crisis in the Oslo channel had another important effect. It had brought an important issue—previously kept aside by Rabin and Peres—directly onto the table for discussion.

On July 26, the crisis came to a head. There seems to have been a mix of acrimony and brinksmanship in the atmosphere. Abu Alaa announced his intention to resign as negotiator and withdraw from the Oslo talks. Savir and Hirschfeld eulogized the Oslo channel as another lost opportunity for both Palestinians and Israelis. The Palestinians began packing their luggage. Uri Savir, sensing that the time had come for drastic measures, approached Abu Alaa privately at the suggestion of Terje Rød Larsen. Savir asked him to consider getting Palestinian concessions on eight of the sixteen issues on which Israel felt it could be flexible. He also held out to Abu Alaa the seven conditions that would most likely cause Israel to recognize the PLO publicly, although this was still a private initiative of Joel Singer's making. The Norwegians were appointed to be the intermediaries on this move to break the deadlock. Savir appealed for a yes or no answer, hoping to avoid further bargaining. Abu Alaa accepted Savir's proposal and committed himself to persuade Arafat to "split the difference" on the outstanding disagreements and accept the Israeli conditions for recognition.[72]

With their private meeting, confidence in the Oslo channel was restored; but it had been badly shaken as each side felt that the end was in sight and sought to maximize its own advantages and minimize losses. The Palestinians sought clarity about the endgame, the final status and issues linked to it, whereas the Israelis preferred to defer decision making on most critical issues by consigning them to the permanent status talks while also insisting that the terms of the initial agreement not prejudice in any way the outcome of the final status. In other words, they sought to decouple the interim negotiations from the permanent status negotiations, precisely the opposite of the PLO's interests and traditional policies.

As if to prove that one channel of secret negotiation does not preclude the existence of other secret channels between the same parties at the same time, Rabin and Arafat communicated with each other via an exchange of letters. At the end of July and beginning of August, without informing his closest advisors—including the Israeli officials working on Oslo (Peres, Beilin, Savir, and Gil)—Rabin sent a letter to Arafat through the health minister, Haim Ramon, who had a link to the PLO through Dr. Ahmed al-Tibi, a Palestinian citizen of Israel. Rabin sought to outline the Israeli perspective on limiting interim Palestinian jurisdiction both in geographic and functional terms, reserving for Israel rights of "hot pursuit" and IDF intervention in the autonomous territories, and to remove settlements from the scope of Palestinian jurisdiction. Arafat's letter to Rabin conceded Israeli control of settlements, consented to the exclusion of Jerusalem from interim self-rule, and conditioned all of this on a mutual recognition agreement.

Abu Mazen was Ahmed al-Tibi's interlocutor in Tunis for this exchange of letters. While meeting with al-Tibi, Abu Mazen announced his intention to step down from his supervisory role for the Oslo channel and as head of the PLO negotiations committee, and he threatened to cancel Palestinian participation in the Washington talks. Al-Tibi evidently repeated the remarks to Ramon while he was conveying the letter from Arafat to Rabin. According to Abu Mazen, these remarks convinced Rabin of the possibility that his government might collapse if the Washington talks were cancelled. Abu Mazen claims that the Israelis were more flexible in the Oslo channel after hearing of his remarks.[73]

As an example of the use of a third-party intermediary to establish back channel contacts, Peres approached Egyptian president Hosni Mubarak and asked him to use his good offices to persuade Arafat to set aside the search for more Israeli concessions and to make the necessary decisions.[74]

The parties' political context offered two compelling reasons for both parties to return to Oslo. Beilin recalls that the "dominant sensation [in the Oslo steering committee] was that of time running out."[75] The PLO was concerned that Rabin's preference for an accord with Syria would sideline Palestinian arrangements. Indeed, in August it seemed that progress was being made on the Israeli-Syrian negotiations. Secretary of State Warren Christopher served as conduit for an exchange of messages between Syrian president Hafez al-Asad and Prime Minister Rabin on August 3 and 4. In these exchanges, the parties accepted the concept of full Israeli withdrawal from Golan Heights in exchange for full normalization of relations from Syria, predicated on an extended implementation timetable and acceptable security arrangements.[76]

The Israelis used PLO concerns about an impending deal with Syria as a tactic to push the PLO back into the Oslo channel on Israeli terms. Rabin and Peres preferred to conduct one deal at a time, believing it would be difficult to "sell" two peace agreements involving concessions of territory to the Israeli public, not to mention the political opposition.[77]

The second contextual factor worked directly against the Rabin government's interests and against the process as a whole. Rabin and Peres were concerned that their governing coalition could weaken because a corruption inquiry had just resulted in the indictment of Aryeh Deri, leader of Shas (a Sephardic religious party) and Rabin's interior minister.[78] Deri was obliged to resign from the cabinet by judicial order, and it was feared his party would leave the government coalition as a result.

No Israeli government takes the loss of any of its coalition partners lightly. Because individual parties often fail to command a majority in the Knesset, no party can form a government on its own; this in turn increases the importance of small parties who can join or defect from coalitions. Relatively small numbers of votes in the cabinet and the Knesset are often sufficient to derail or legitimize policy changes. Upon the departure of Shas, the Labor-Meretz coalition would become a minority cabinet, unable to command a Knesset majority without the assistance of parties outside of the coalition—the Israeli Arab parties.[79] Deri survived until the conclusion of the Oslo channel, but his indictment prevented him from casting his cabinet vote in favor of the Oslo Accords.[80]

Norwegian foreign minister Holst explicitly offered Beilin his services as a proactive mediator to reverse the apparent breakdown in the Oslo channel. The Norwegians began looking for ways to restart the talks. The last round had ended without any agreement on a date to resume talks in Oslo. In August, the Norwegians set up an informal encounter between Abu Alaa and Yair Hirschfeld. Together they reduced the issues in dispute from over twenty to about three that concerned Palestinian institutions in Jerusalem and security responsibilities, and both parties agreed to resume negotiations in Oslo.[81] This was accomplished, not by coming to agreement on all outstanding issues, but by jointly deciding that several disputes did not need to be resolved early and could be postponed until the negotiation of arrangements for the handover of Jericho and Gaza.[82]

The Norwegians proposed a new date for the resumption of talks. The twelfth round was convened on August 13, 1993. The Israelis would not accept the Palestinian reformulations of the seven Israeli conditions for mutual recognition, so this issue was also deferred until after the conclusion of the declaration. Despite the small number of outstanding issues remaining to be negotiated, the Palestinians could not get authority to either make further concessions or to accept proposals that bridged the gaps between the two sides, and the round closed on August 15.[83]

Shimon Peres was previously scheduled to make an official state visit to Sweden and Norway on August 17. The Israelis decided to take advantage of Peres's trip by proposing that he meet with Holst in Stockholm so that Holst could mediate between the parties and resolve the outstanding disputes over the draft declaration. Holst placed the calls to Arafat's office in Tunisia where Abu Mazen, Yasir Abd Rabbuh (who had led the Palestinian participation in the United States-PLO dialogue), Abu Alaa, and Hassan Asfour had gathered for this round of telephone diplomacy. Peres, Joel Singer, and Avi Gil (Peres's chief of staff) were on the other end of the line in Stockholm. Holst acted as the intermediary in a marathon of nine phone conferences between the Israeli and Palestinian leadership that lasted the entire night and continued into the next day.[84] Thanks in part to the presence of decision makers such as Peres and Arafat that night, only one issue remained open; Peres delegated it to Uri Savir, who was immediately dispatched to Norway from Israel, along with Hirschfeld and Pundik.[85] Abu Alaa and Hassan Asfour immediately flew to Norway from Tunis to meet the Israelis.

In the evening of August 19, Savir and Abu Alaa worked out the last issue pending in the draft declaration: when the five-year interim period would begin and end. The Israeli withdrawal from Gaza and Jericho would mark the initiation of the countdown and the final status talks were to be *concluded* (not begun) no later than five years after that initial withdrawal.[86]

Yasir Arafat still wanted a legal expert to go over the declaration of principles. The Egyptian government produced one instantly: Taher al-Shash, an Egyptian diplomat and lawyer who worked on the Camp David Accords and assisted the Palestinian delegation in Washington. Al-Shash was summoned to go to Oslo the morning of August 19. In giving his conditional approval of the text to Arafat, he noted that its main defects were the political concessions made in the negotiations, not the legal language of the text itself, although he doubted the PLO could have done any better.[87]

Near midnight on August 19, 1993, Holst arranged a clandestine ceremony for the initialing of the document on the same table that Norway had used to sign a secession agreement from Sweden in 1905. Abu Alaa and Hassan Asfour initialed the document for the PLO while Singer and Savir initialed it for the Israeli government as Egeland, Gil, Hirschfeld, Holst, Juul, Larsen, Peres, Pundik, and al-Shash looked on.

The Declaration of Principles on Interim Self-Government Arrangements, as it was titled, was now approved by high-level policy makers on both sides. A breakthrough was made, but three things still needed to take place: the agreement had to be officially signed, then ratified, and finally implemented. All of this hinged on the question of *who* would sign on behalf of the Palestinians. And this question was tied to the mutual recognition issue.

Shortly after the initialing, Yitzhak Rabin contacted Yossi Beilin on August 22, wanting to know if the initialed declaration included any clause in which the PLO renounced terrorism. Beilin informed him that only the drafted mutual recognition documents explicitly did so and the declaration of principles did not. Rabin ordered him to "see what can be done" about getting such a commitment and to contact the Norwegians. Neither Holst nor Beilin thought that it would be feasible for the PLO to renounce the use of force without being openly recognized.[88]

In the meantime, the United States, which had been aware of but seemingly indifferent to the Oslo channel, was informed of the agreement. Peres, recalling his abortive 1987 ploy to get U.S. sponsorship of an Israeli-Jordanian initiative (see chapter 2), tried to convince Secretary Christopher to present the agreement to the world as an American achievement. Although Christopher declined to do so, the United States was fully supportive and began making preparations for a signing ceremony of historic proportions to take place at the White House.

News of the Oslo back channel began leaking toward the end of August, and on August 30 the entire Israeli cabinet and top security officials were presented with the initialed declaration of principles. Rabin presented it as an agreement that would be signed by the Washington delegation, not mentioning the role of the PLO. Several of those present openly expressed substantive concerns while wondering why they were excluded from this momentous policy shift. The IDF chief of staff Ehud Barak expressed several reservations about future security. However, it was Eliyakim Rubinstein who, as both secretary of the cabinet and the chief of the Israeli delegation in Washington, had been doubly excluded. Peres spent much time with him trying to persuade him not to resign from government and to assuage his sense of betrayal.[89]

On the same day, but again without the knowledge of the cabinet, Uri Savir and Abu Alaa returned to Oslo to work out the mutual recognition issue. As they were unable to completely resolve their differences, Foreign Minister Holst continued to play an active intermediary role. Without this agreement, the Israelis feared that the PLO would not go forward with the declaration of principles.[90] On September 3, Peres and Holst once again conducted a round of telephone diplomacy to Tunis. Savir and Abu Alaa continued their talks in Paris September 9 and 10 at the suggestion of Holst and Mubarak.

The Israelis, Palestinians, and Norwegians (led by Foreign Minister Holst) reconvened in Paris. In Tunis, Arafat convened the PLO's Executive Committee while Rabin and Peres were monitoring events from Israel. During another twenty-two-hour session, the delegations dealt with PLO recognition of Israel ("unconditionally" versus "within secure and recognized borders"); a commitment from the PLO to end the intifada, renounce the use of force, and to discipline Palestinians who resort to violence; and rescinding of clauses in the Palestinian National Charter that contradicted the recognition of Israel.

The Palestinians also sought Israeli assurances regarding a freeze on Jewish settlements in the occupied territories and preservation of the Palestinian institutions in Jerusalem. Rabin and Peres decided to convene the cabinet to ratify an agreement, if there was one, at 5:00 p.m. (Jerusalem time—it would be 4:00 p.m. in Paris), creating the pressure of a deadline. Holst asked Arafat to take responsibility for decision making alone—without seeking consensus in the Executive Committee. Most of the disputed language was resolved in Israel's favor.[91] There was no document constituting an agreement, as had been previously planned. Mutual recognition was embodied in an exchange of letters: one from Arafat to Rabin incorporating the Palestinian concessions, and one from Rabin simply recognizing the PLO as negotiating partner on behalf of the Palestinians. In a side letter to Holst, Arafat committed himself to call for an end to the intifada in his public statements. A fourth letter, which was to be kept secret, was also drafted: this letter, addressed to Holst from Peres, committed Israel to the preservation of Palestinian institutions in Jerusalem. It was dated October 11, 1993, and therefore subsequent to the official signing of the Declaration of Principles in order to protect it from cabinet and Knesset ratification or public scrutiny.[92]

In any case, the declaration was unanimously approved, with only two ministers abstaining, including Aryeh Deri of Shas who supported the declaration but was on the verge of resigning from government.[93] The Israeli cabinet also approved the letter exchange except for the Peres-Holst letter (of which they knew nothing). This act conferred Israeli recognition of the PLO—with whom it had been at war for three decades—without so much as a public or parliamentary debate.

Holst once again undertook a mission of shuttle diplomacy. He flew to Tunis on Thursday, September 9, where he expected to pick up Arafat's signed copy and fly on to Jerusalem to witness Rabin's signing of the reply letter. Holst was delayed by the deliberations of the PLO Executive Committee, some of whose members were troubled by the highly asymmetrical concessions reflected in the mutual recognition letters. Nevertheless, both Arafat and Rabin signed their letters for Holst.[94] With this exchange of letters, President Clinton removed prohibitions on

United States-PLO contact on September 10, noting that the PLO's commitments to Israel formed the basis for a renewed dialogue. This facilitated the arrival of Arafat in Washington for the signing ceremony.

On the morning of the signing ceremony, September 13, 1993, Arafat let it be known that he was leaving Washington unless the wording in the preamble of the Declaration of Principles was changed from "Palestinian delegation" to "PLO." The Americans and Israelis at first refused to make this last change. Once they relented, the negotiations that began in Norway on January 20, 1993, had reached their endpoint. Abu Mazen and Shimon Peres signed the Declaration of Principles, while President Clinton nudged Yitzhak Rabin and Yasir Arafat together for one of the most publicized handshakes in history. The historic signing ceremony did not in any way signify the end of a negotiated peace process but, more modestly, made the world witness to a simple framework agreement to negotiate the modalities in the exchange of territory for peace in one of the century's most enduring conflicts.

Oslo's Outcome

Once the Oslo channel produced the Declaration of Principles and the mutual recognition discussions, the Washington Palestinian-Israeli track instantly became redundant because nothing even remotely similar was happening there in terms of progress.

After 1993, Israelis and Palestinians entered new, uncharted territory: negotiated coexistence with a gradual disengagement of Israel from its military control over the territories and lives of the Palestinians. The Oslo Accords were not peace treaties; they were agreements to continue negotiating, first on the comparatively easy interim issues and later on the relatively more complex permanent status issues. The formal signing of the Declaration of Principles heralded the initiation of the interim phase of Palestinian-Israeli relations.

During the interim phase, from 1993 to 1998 and beyond, Palestinian-Israeli diplomacy functioned in several ways. First, the parties began negotiating the operational details of Israeli withdrawal, Palestinian administrative powers, elections, and numerous other issues. Second, some of these issues were negotiated both in front channel negotiations and in back channel negotiations. Third, secret negotiations took place in order to accelerate the final status phase. Fourth, the permanent status talks commenced officially in the front channel, but this was little more than a ceremonial event. The parties never resumed front channel permanent status talks throughout the interim period, which expired on May 4, 1999.

Mobilized opposition to the peace process emerged among both secular nationalists and religious movements in both Israel and Palestine, demonstrating sharp polarization of each side's supporters and opponents. Their exclusion from the process had been instrumental in its success up to that point. Indeed, few if any informed observers or participants believed that any agreement—especially one embodying mutual recognition between Israel and the PLO—would have been possible in front channels. Certainly the failure of the Washington track to do so by August 1993 seemed to support this argument. But from this point onward, the parties would come to trust back channels to a great extent, deepening their working relationships in secret, exploring solutions to the problems of implementation. This implied the ongoing denial of knowledge of the peace process to the internal opposition on each side.

Analysis

In the following analytical categories, the key case data are discussed. These categories are interrelated; they interact with each other. For example, any degree of secrecy implies some exclusion of subparties. The inclusion and exclusion of subparties helps determine who sits at the negotiation table, how close the negotiator is to the decision makers, and the degree of autonomy the negotiator has. The intervention of third parties may be problematic in some regards, leading the parties carefully to manage the involvement of such third parties. The existence of multiple channels may mean that different issues are discussed in different channels.

As noted in chapter 1, each of the cases will be analyzed according to the following analytical framework. In the following sections, direct comparisons are made between how each of these factors was manifest in the Oslo channel and the Washington track.

- Issues negotiated
- Secrecy and publicity
- Exclusion and inclusion of subparties

- Proximity of negotiators to decision makers
- Autonomy of the negotiators
- Third parties: presence and role
- Strategic use of front and back channels

Issues Negotiated

As mentioned in the last chapter, the delegations in the Washington talks brought negotiation positions to the table that were based on incompatible concepts of Palestinian autonomy. The Israeli delegation in Washington held fast to the key assumption of the previous Likud government: that Palestinian self-government could only have functional attributes and no territorial sovereignty.[95] As mentioned in the previous chapter, the Israeli and Palestinian delegations in Madrid never reached agreement on what they were there to negotiate. At all times, they differed on the goals of the interim stage. The Palestinian delegation in Washington sought assurances that the permanent status would lead to statehood and all the implications that flow from that goal, while the Israelis insisted on autonomous interim arrangements, without any territorial basis, that would not prejudice their preferred final outcome for the occupied territory. As Yossi Beilin has observed, "in Washington the Palestinians had rejected this concept; in Oslo, they accepted it, in that they agreed—*at variance with* their positions in Washington—that Jerusalem, the settlements and Israel's military security zones would be left outside the scope of autonomy."[96]

Beilin overstates the case: the Palestinian delegation in Oslo accepted an incremental approach but did not concede that the final outcome would in any way be diminished. They simply accepted the Israeli time preference to defer negotiations on it. Beilin also overlooks the fact that the Israeli delegation in Oslo, in both phases, proceeded on the assumption that Palestinian self-government would have some dimension of territoriality and that this territory would progressively increase during the interim phase of the peace process. The Israeli delegation in Washington had no such conception of Palestinian autonomy.

Issues being negotiated were treated much differently in the Oslo channel. First of all, the main activity the two delegations worked on in both phases was the drafting of a declaration of principles, a framework to guide further negotiations. They worked jointly on revising the drafts of this document. A declaration of principles is by no means a final peace accord but something much more modest in scope. The parties spent much time in Oslo deciding on broad principles that would guide them on *how* to resolve disputed issues, but that did not resolve the issues themselves. Such a document amounts to setting the ground rules for subsequent negotiations. They also agreed to divide negotiated issues into two piles: one pile of "interim" issues and a second pile of "permanent status" issues. This protected the parties from having such issues "predetermined" to the benefit of one side only. This was in fact the substance of the agreement they were making in Oslo. Technical aspects of the interim issues were not decided in Oslo.

The Camp David Accords have provisions for Palestinian autonomy and divide its envisioned peace process into two phases: a transitional period during which interim measures were to be taken and a final phase in which full peace would be attained. All outstanding issues would be resolved and the political status of the Palestinians finally settled. All those who tried to revive the Camp David Accords at some point were faced with question of linkage: is the final status linked to the interim phase? If so, how? Is one legally dependent on the other? Do concessions in the interim phase prejudice one's preferred outcomes, rights, or interests in the permanent status negotiations? American political figures such as special envoy Sol Linowitz and Secretaries of State Shultz, Baker, and Christopher all faced this issue when involving themselves in the Palestinian-Israeli conflict.

In the Washington track, the Palestinians found themselves on the opposite end of the spectrum from the Israelis who, even when agreeable to negotiations, sought to reduce the strength of linkage between interim and final phases. Although their preferences were opposed, the motivations for both sides were similar: to minimize their potential losses and concessions in the final phase. In this sense, each used the linkage issue to minimize the uncertainty of outcome for their side. No party wants its goals in the permanent status talks to be prejudiced by whatever happens (or doesn't happen) during the interim stage. For Israel, this meant not committing to any permanent stage outcome for the Palestinians, regardless of how much progress was made in the interim stage. For the Palestinians, the opposite preference holds: they sought assurances that the West Bank and Gaza would be the accepted endgame, regardless of how little they gained in the interim stage and despite any setbacks along the way. If, for example, at the conclusion of the interim stage the Palestinians were to exercise effective sovereignty over only 40 percent of the West Bank and the Gaza Strip, they did not want the state to be limited to that figure.

By insisting that relevant UN Security Council Resolutions 242 (1967) and 338 (1973) were not applicable to the interim phases, the Israelis in the Washington track wanted to minimize any "painful" early concessions—painful in terms of security interests, as well as domestic political concerns. The Palestinian delegation insisted on the linkage because it implicitly predetermined the outcome of the final status: a Palestinian state on all the territory of Mandate Palestine that was not under Israeli control from 1949 to 1967. The Palestinian delegation in Washington was faithfully following PLO guidance and long-standing policy that explicitly sought to specify the destination in advance of the journey.

The Oslo channel modified these dynamics in certain ways. Whereas the Washington track had not resolved this dispute between the delegations, the Oslo channel moved quickly toward a pragmatic compromise whereby the negotiation principles such as UN Security Council Resolution 242 were invoked by both parties, but no explicit final outcome was sketched out in advance. In other words, Oslo provided linkage, but it did not specify to *what* the interim stage was linked. Although the Oslo declaration of principles did not explicitly commit Israel to withdrawal from all of the pre-1967 Palestinian territories, it accomplished something the drafts in Washington did not: it provided an initial *territorial* foundation for the establishment of Palestinian authority and sovereignty. As mentioned, the dimension of territorial sovereignty was a Palestinian desideratum in the Madrid track, but it was never conceded by the Israeli delegation.

Oslo embodied the incrementalist approach to managing issues in peace negotiations. The parties would start with small confidence-building measures: limited withdrawal of occupying forces, gradual transfer of civil and police powers, and limited self-government while consigning the defined set of final status issues (on return of occupied territory, settlements, the return of Palestinian refugees, and other final status items) to another negotiation process entirely, which was not scheduled to officially begin until 1996.

The issue of Jerusalem and its Palestinian residents became the hallmark of the incrementalist approach. At Oslo the PLO wanted some mention of Jerusalem in the drafts or some demonstration of its connection to the permanent status and the Palestinian desire to establish a capital there. The Israelis consistently opposed this. On the subject of elections, however, some provision had to be made for the Palestinians of East Jerusalem. This was done by adding an annex to the Declaration of Principles, whose first article permits those residents to "participate in the elections process, according to an agreement between the two sides" that had not yet been negotiated.[97]

With such creative terminology, the parties avoided deciding whether residents could run in or simply vote in the elections and set up a future negotiation over the issue.

The final version of the Declaration of Principles set forth the agreement to provide an initial Israeli withdrawal from Gaza and Jericho, endowing the PLO with a future territorial base in Gaza and with a foothold on the West Bank. It thus assured a starting point for Palestinian self-rule while also providing for future negotiations on five (later six) spheres of civil authority that would be assumed simultaneously with the first Israeli withdrawal (from Gaza and Jericho).[98] The annex on withdrawal from Gaza and Jericho stipulated that the parties would quickly negotiate another agreement that would resolve the size of the Jericho area subject to the Israeli withdrawal (much disputed in the later rounds of the Oslo channel), the timetable of withdrawal, and the establishment of the "safe passage" routes between Gaza and the West Bank that Johan Jørgen Holst had persuaded Arafat to accept in lieu of extraterritorial linkages between the otherwise sundered West Bank and Gaza.[99] Limited powers were to be immediately transferred to the Palestinians upon the initial withdrawal even though the Palestinian National Authority (PNA) had not yet been structured.

The negotiations over the Declaration provided for a future negotiation to conclude a comprehensive Interim Agreement, which would specify the structure of the PNA and the modalities for transferring power to it. Many issues disputed in the Oslo channel were left to the negotiations on the Interim Agreement.[100] Once the PNA was inaugurated (called a "council" in the Declaration of Principles), Israeli military units would be withdrawn and the military government (misnamed the Civil Administration) would be "dissolved."[101]

Additionally, the Declaration of Principles enumerated broad areas of Palestinian-Israeli cooperation in economic affairs and social development as well as areas of regional development under the auspices of the G-7 countries. These clauses were general enough to require the establishment of ongoing negotiation committees to specify details of implementation.[102] Another clause established the Joint Israeli-Palestinian Liaison Committee that would handle coordination and implementation of the declaration.[103]

The fact that the PLO itself was the negotiating partner for Israel in the Oslo channel brought up an issue that was never even remotely considered in the Washington track: mutual recognition between the state of Israel and the PLO as the political representative of the Palestinian people. The way Oslo was concluded made this inevitable, despite the initial Israeli preference that Oslo would simply produce an agreement to be executed by the Washington delegations. Indeed, the PLO participation in Oslo was, to a great extent, predicated on the PLO's goal of being the sole Palestinian signatory and implementing party, not simply the negotiating partner.[104]

This issue certainly could never have been on the negotiating table in Washington, despite occasional appeals by the Palestinian delegation to the U.S. hosts to recognize and reopen the dialogue with the PLO. In the Oslo channel as well, recognition was not initially "on the table"; and when it came up, it was as Joel Singer's private initiative. Uri Savir held it out as an inducement to Abu Alaa at the July crisis in the Oslo channel. Nevertheless, it took on a life of its own separate from talks on the Declaration of Principles. Thus separated, it provided both parties with leverage. The PLO wanted recognition, and Israel realized that recognition was the price of having the Declaration of Principles and getting an explicit renunciation on the use of force from the PLO. Recognition became a macro-level negotiation issue and the entirety of the declaration of principles depended on successful resolution of the issue. The somewhat transparent exclusion of the PLO from the Washington talks, and the fact that those talks were fruitless in terms of outcome, meant that such a critical issue could not have been brought to the table there, much less negotiated successfully. Given the dynamics of the parties and their complementary goals, the issue had to emerge somewhere, and the only place for it to be negotiated was in the direct back channel.

For the Palestinians, the universe of issues is the same in each "channel"; the difference between the channels reflected different approaches to handling the issues, as well as different solutions to the issues in contention. The Palestinian delegation in Washington enjoyed a historic first opportunity to gain global recognition for the Palestinian national cause, hence its preoccupation with representation of that cause and a rights-based orientation to counter the long denial of those rights. In Oslo, the PLO was a pragmatic political player, consumed by the goal of returning to the occupied territories and establishing itself as the legitimate Palestinian government recognized by Israel. The Israeli delegations in each channel reflected vastly different approaches to the political future of the occupied territories, as previously discussed.

Oslo enjoyed an agreed goal for the negotiations, which always eluded the delegations in Washington. With this agreed goal, the negotiators in the Oslo back channel were able to consider solutions that the Washington negotiators could not, such as recognition of the PLO and nonprejudicial deferral of permanent status issues.

The Role of Secrecy and Publicity

Secrecy. For Norway, as well as the PLO and Israel, secrecy was a strategic, desired condition of the talks. Johan Jørgen Holst, foreign minister of Norway at the time of the conclusion of the Oslo channel, explained that "the negotiations were conducted in secrecy in order to prevent opposition from blocking progress before the potential success had been demonstrated."[105]

What was the extent of secrecy? The U.S. State Department was informed early on, but it appeared to take no notice of the Oslo channel while it invested the prestige of the United States in the Washington talks. The Egyptian government was not only aware but, like Norway, helped the channel by playing an occasional intermediary role. The Egyptians were also aware of other Israel-PLO contacts.

A key aspect of structuring a back channel is to have a front channel that performs its work without any awareness of any other negotiations so that it conducts its negotiations as if it were the *only existing channel*, thereby making it responsive to the tactical and strategic directives of the top decision makers who are aware of all channels. The Oslo channel was successfully kept secret from the negotiators in the Washington talks on both delegations, although members of the Palestinian delegation—including legal advisor to the delegation Camille Mansour and Hanan Ashrawi, the spokesperson—both claimed to have deduced the existence of a secret channel operating in parallel with their efforts.[106] Hanan Ashrawi, as explained earlier in this chapter, inadvertently contributed to its initiation.

At the highest level of PLO policy making, the Oslo channel was gradually revealed to the PLO Executive Committee, which represented all the member political and military groups within the PLO, but not to other representative bodies such as the PNC or the executive councils of the parties that make up the PLO. Abu Mazen and Arafat did not reveal the existence of the Oslo channel to their own political group, Fatah, and Abu Mazen only hinted at his optimism in July 1993 meetings of the Revolutionary Council and the Central Committee, two high-level policy-making bodies of the Fatah leadership.[107] The small circle of Arafat advisors—Abd Rabbuh, Abu Mazen, Abu Alaa, and a few others—were the mirror image of the small circle of Israeli political figures who were aware of the channel within the government's cabinet (in addition to the two academics from ECF, Hirschfeld and Pundik).

The Israeli military command as well as the heads of three intelligence agencies were denied knowledge of the back channel.[108] Finally, Labor's coalition partners, Meretz and Shas, were not informed and neither were any of the ministers in the Rabin cabinet (except Peres and Beilin, of course).

It hardly needs to be said that the Israeli and Palestinian public were kept in the dark about the Oslo channel, including the Israeli settlers' organizations and the Palestinian religious nationalist groups, and they will be further discussed regarding the exclusion of subparties.

Shimon Peres is an Israeli statesman with much experience in secret diplomacy. He was present at the secret summit meeting in which the French, British, and Israeli governments decided to invade Egypt in 1956 (the Sèvres Protocol).[109] He helped build up the armed forces of Israel by negotiating secret arms sales from France[110] and was instrumental in developing the Dimona nuclear reactor for Israel, also built with French assistance in great secrecy.[111] In April 1987 he activated Israel's long-standing secret channel with Jordan in an attempt to fulfill his ambition of getting Jordan to assume the leadership role in Palestinian autonomy. A political figure with his experience clearly understood the value of preserving certain state actions under the cover of secrecy. His experience and instincts in this regard guided him to oversee the Oslo channel, and his exclusion from oversight of the Washington talks facilitated his exploration of alternatives.

When Peres attended the secret ceremony for the Oslo Declaration, he declined to initial it himself. Instead, he directed Singer and Savir to initial it on behalf of the Israeli government "because the agreement had not yet been submitted to the cabinet for approval. It had to remain 'deniable' in case, God forbid, the need to deny it should still arise."[112] Peres seemed to be assuming that by not attaching his name to it, the negotiations could still be dismissed as a freelance operation rather than a political action of the state. This conclusion is somewhat questionable given the high-level Norwegian, Palestinian, and Israeli involvement by that time.

Various key players have unequivocally stated that secrecy was a requirement for the Oslo channel. Savir and Abu Alaa noted that secrecy protected the negotiation process and helped the negotiators learn to trust each other as individuals and as political adversaries.[113] They make very clear that the publicity surrounding the Madrid track was a major disincentive to creative bargaining because of the dynamic that results when people negotiate in front of audiences with an interest in the outcome, principals and constituents. This dynamic is intensified in negotiations concerning a violent conflict.

Early in the second phase of the Oslo channel when it was contemplated that any agreement reached there would be signed in the Washington talks, Joel Singer asked the Palestinians what they thought about using secret agreements, secret letters, or letters to a third party to supplement any open agreement, as had been done in the Egypt-Israel peace process.[114] This in fact was done to close the negotiations over mutual recognition: the Peres letter to Holst on the preservation of Palestinian institutions in Jerusalem, such as the Orient House, an NGO that had long served as the PLO's quasi headquarters in Jerusalem and had many times been closed, blocked, and occupied by Israeli troops. The Oslo channel not only was conducted with procedural secrecy, but it also produced secret understandings.

Secrecy permeated every aspect of the Oslo process and permitted the decision makers to proceed without risking the interference of their advisors, coalition partners, political opponents, and domestic constituencies. It provided protection for the negotiators so that they could experiment with new ideas for managing the peace process and bridging the gaps in their respective positions, and permitted concessions to be made without immediate loss of face. It also protected them from the manipulation of third parties and internal domestic constituencies. Finally, secrecy insulated the negotiators from the events on the ground—violence, provocations, and other negative developments to which front channel negotiators would feel obligated to respond, usually by stopping the negotiations.

Publicity. Despite his long experience with secret diplomacy, Peres (as well as Hirschfeld and Abu Alaa) had at least a basic understanding of the importance of marketing peace arrangements to constituencies, which necessarily involves publicity. In his public statements, Peres occasionally would indicate that progress on the Israeli-Palestinian track was closer than people thought, leaving most observers of the problematic Washington track perplexed. At some point, Abu Mazen believed his optimistic assessments were putting the Oslo negotiators at risk of being discovered, and he passed a message to Peres asking him to moderate his public statements. Peres demurred, citing the need to prepare the public.[115] Peres's intentions were impeccable, but the measures taken were wholly inadequate, piquing curiosity rather than causing a shift in public opinion.

The Holst-Peres trip to the United States for the purpose of informing Warren Christopher and the resulting American plan to host a signing ceremony were partly for the purpose of converting the gains of the Oslo channel into a public commitment to peace by having a global audience. It was also part of Peres's plan to obtain American financial support for redeployment and to begin building diplomatic and economic support for the Palestinians. Ultimately, these were insufficient moves to build a domestic public consensus for the peace arrangements embodied in the Oslo Accord.[116]

Uri Savir has criticized both parties' failure to take any concrete steps toward reconciliation between ordinary Palestinians and Israelis, as part of a larger "peace propaganda plan" that was raised in the first phase of the Oslo channel but ultimately neglected in the second, fully official phase. Savir considers this omission to be a cause of the lack of public support for the peace process and the rising popularity of rejectionists, although he recently affirmed that the "detachment from public opinion" of BCN, while it prevents the parties from adequately preparing the public, is outweighed by the advantage that with BCN "we don't have to create such tremendous expectations" about a future peace deal (as in the Israel-Syria negotiations), and public opposition to potential concessions cannot be mobilized, thereby enabling negotiators to do their work.[117] Although this may have initially held true, Savir's observation became dangerously obsolete very quickly. Opposition became very mobilized in fact and drove his party out of office in Israel, which led to the assassination of Prime Minister Rabin and the start-up of suicide bombings from HAMAS. Back channel negotiators still face the dilemma of persuading fickle or hostile constituencies that the negotiations were conducted in their interest. Public signing ceremonies are just the first step of this process.

Exclusion and Inclusion of Subparties

Both parties sought to marginalize subparties within the Israeli government and within the PLO, not to mention parties who are not part of the governing structure of either: opposition parties (Likud, HAMAS, PFLP), settlers groups (YESHA), Palestinian refugees, dissident factions from the PLO (Abu Nidal, Abul Abbas).

On the Israeli and Palestinian sides, there is ample evidence that to some extent, different channels corresponded to different decision makers and negotiators within the same subgroup because of political and personal rivalry on the Israeli side and internal friction among PLO officials on the Palestinian side, as well as Arafat's patrimonial decision-making style, which results in the elevation or demotion of different negotiators according to political expediency.[118] Oslo was essentially a project of Abu Mazen and (eventually) Shimon Peres and not an initiative of more senior officials such as Faruq Qaddumi (then the most senior PLO official below Arafat) or Yitzhak Rabin. Rabin's efforts to exclude Peres, a member of his own cabinet and the minister of foreign affairs, from supervision of the bilateral Madrid track also played a role in encouraging Peres to explore other options, especially in light of Madrid's problematic handling of both the substance and process of negotiation. Rabin attempted to cut Peres out of the bilateral Palestinian-Israel peace talks and the Israel-Syria and Israel-Jordanian talks, leaving him supervision of the multilateral talks only. Abu Mazen had the advantage of being involved in both Washington and Oslo channels.

The Oslo channel was Shimon Peres's second major secret effort at a peace settlement concerning the West Bank and Gaza. The first was his London Agreement of April 11, 1987, negotiated in secret with King Hussein, at which he hoped to set in motion an international peace conference that would confer legitimacy on a joint Israeli-Jordanian solution in the West Bank and Gaza. It will be recalled that, as part of a "unity" government, Peres had no monopoly on decision making, even as foreign minister. In fact, Peres's exclusion of Yitzhak Shamir led to the latter's efforts to undermine the initiative. Despite their key role in Israeli decision making, the main excluded subparty throughout the negotiations with Hussein had been the prime minister and other cabinet members. The Peres-Hussein plan called for George Shultz to adopt and "sell" the plan back to Shamir and Hussein, which he ultimately found impossible to do (as detailed in chapter

2), primarily because his government's coalition structure determined that the policy decision could not be made by Shamir.

At the initiation of the Oslo channel (the first meeting in London and subsequent meetings in Norway), it appears that the highest levels of political decision making were not aware of events. Abu Mazen reported little to Arafat pending the determination of the Norwegian government's official involvement and the confirmation that the Israeli leadership was backing this channel. Similarly, Beilin did not initially inform Peres about the existence of the Oslo channel and certainly did not inform Rabin. Only gradually was the Oslo channel revealed to Peres, who later revealed it to Rabin.

From that point, other cabinet ministers, the military, political coalition partners, and of course, political parties in the opposition were deliberately excluded from the circle of those who knew about Oslo. The strategy of secrecy was broadened to exclude not only external actors but internal bureaucratic ones as well, and even high-level staff members in the PLO and the Israeli government. This exclusion was to prevent insiders from overburdening the process with concerns (legitimate or not) pertaining to their bureaucratic or political interests and to prevent others from mobilizing Israelis opposed to peace arrangements and provoking a political crisis by accusing the government of betraying the national interest.

Exclusion is both a cause and effect of secrecy. To keep something secret, knowledge of that thing is prevented from spreading to others. Secrecy and exclusion were instrumental in delaying but not eliminating internal crises that arose when the Oslo Accords were revealed. When the Oslo Accords became public, Binyamin Netanyahu led the opposition charge against Rabin in the Knesset and warned Rabin that future generations of Israelis would "settle the historic account" with him.[119]

Proximity of Decision Makers, Autonomy of Negotiators

Although the Oslo channel was not directly initiated by Peres, he quickly took "ownership" of it. Decision making—getting the Israeli government to take responsibility for the Oslo channel—was of great concern to Peres throughout the existence of the channel, and once the channel's existence was brought to his attention, he successfully persuaded Prime Minister Rabin to adopt the channel as his own (by the third round of Oslo negotiations) while shutting out the foreign ministry, the prime minister's aides, and his cabinet colleagues. He had learned from his 1987 experience that he needed at least the prime minister to be amenable to his plan.

To maintain his authority within the Oslo channel that he had no part in establishing, Rabin sent Joel Singer, an envoy he personally trusted, to the Oslo encounters when it was upgraded to fully official status.[120] In the second phase of the Oslo channel, therefore, the link between the negotiators and key decision makers was extremely direct, with no bureaucratic intermediaries at all to impede communication.

As a consequence of Peres and Rabin becoming gradually aware of and committed to the Oslo channel, the Israeli negotiators were upgraded to official status; Uri Savir, the director general of the foreign ministry, was first sent in the sixth round and was later joined by Joel Singer in the seventh round. The locus of Israeli decision making moved much closer to Oslo than to Washington. As for Hirschfeld and Pundik, the initial Israeli delegates to the Oslo channel, they saw their negotiating autonomy decline precipitously as their work bore fruit. As negotiators, they had an inherent obsolescence. They were necessary to open the channel, but their level of authority and proximity to Israeli decision making were insufficient to keep the Palestinians interested and thus insufficient to keep the channel open and operating.

Arafat too was apparently unaware of the existence of the Oslo channel at its initiation, according to one Arab confidant, and was not informed until after the first meeting had concluded.[121] His initial point of information was one of his closest and highest ranking aides, Mahmoud Abbas (Abu Mazen).

Abu Mazen was at that point not entirely certain that the government of Norway was supporting Larsen, who had informally helped to bring together Abu Alaa and Yair Hirschfeld. Abu Mazen was uncertain about the extent of Israeli commitment as well. Still, as the main PLO advocate of direct contacts with the Israeli political parties, in or out of power, and as the main advocate of interim (as opposed to comprehensive) solutions, he was highly interested.

He quickly understood the potential of Oslo and reported to Arafat, obtaining his approval for the talks. Few PLO officials in the Executive Committee found out about Oslo, while the larger PLO Central Committee and the PNC were sidelined. Despite his initial distance from Oslo, Arafat quickly became the central point of decision making for the Palestinian delegation at Oslo, and Abu Alaa returned to Tunis with his delegation to consult and debrief with Arafat and an intimate circle of aides after each Oslo encounter.[122]

The PLO and Israeli government excluded large categories of constituencies from knowledge of the Oslo channel and severely limited the access of their highest officials and staff (and as mentioned, kept it a secret from their front channel negotiators). Both parties' negotiators in Oslo enjoyed a highly direct connection and instant communication with the highest policy and decision makers within their side, and both were directly overseen by an official just below the cabinet rank (or its equivalent, in the case of the PLO): Beilin and Abu Mazen. The individual negotiators enjoyed a high level of confidence from their leaders.

Both Oslo delegations had similar and high levels of negotiating flexibility flowing from several factors, including the absence of bureaucratic or external actors asserting their demands and calling for constraints on bargaining behavior; the confidence their leaders had in them; the negotiators' proximity and access to the decision makers; and no doubt, their own skill as negotiators, on which each side has complimented (and criticized) the other.[123]

Their broad negotiation mandate stands in contrast to the highly constrained negotiation mandate of both delegations in Washington. The people sitting at the negotiation table in Washington were, on the Palestinian side, residents of the occupied territories, not PLO officials. This made their mandate highly circumscribed, and indeed, they openly sought PLO guidance until they felt they were being manipulated by Arafat. Besides advocating for the restoration of legitimate national rights for the Palestinians, the delegation served to represent the Palestinian plight before the world in a way that had never been done before. Their accomplishments were stronger in terms of representation than in terms of actual negotiation. This is especially true given the Shamir government's negotiation guidelines to its delegation, which remained the same under Rabin.

On the Israeli side, the chief of the delegation, Eliyakim Rubinstein, was a civil servant who had worked with numerous governments without regard to the party in power. Without any new policy guidance, he felt (understandably) that he had no mandate to do anything differently under Rabin than he had done under Shamir. This alone is enough to explain why the talks went nowhere.

At Oslo, the people and the process were different. Without the press, the Palestinians had one less audience to worry about on a daily basis. They were not concerned with the immediate effects on public opinion or press relations. Both delegations at Oslo made skillful use of brainstorming and early on had decided to permit any issue to be brought to the table and any concession to be retractable, especially in the first phase. These considerations helped them create common work agendas that they were committed to making progress on. These simple, businesslike, and process-oriented tasks were never accomplished in Washington.

The proximity and involvement of the decision makers to their negotiators at Oslo is certainly one factor that facilitated their ability to take steps beyond the bounds of political rhetoric and negotiate what they felt could be pragmatic arrangements. The PLO delegation arrived at Oslo actually *proposing* (as opposed to shunning) an interim solution with an initial territorial basis in Gaza, something that was not on the table at the Washington talks.[124] Hirschfeld and Pundik also worked with a great deal of flexibility, drafting the initial DoP that explicitly mentioned Jerusalem as a problem to be *negotiated* as opposed to claimed in its entirety at the outset. In their case, however, they were not close to the Israeli prime minister. However, once Savir and Singer were inducted into the Oslo channel, they worked with a broad mandate that included recognition of the PLO (under the right circumstances for Israel).

Presence and Role of Third Parties

As is widely understood, a third-party intervener such as the United States, with power and resources of its own, intervenes because of its interests in the conflict or because of its closeness to one of the conflict parties. The leverage it counts on with its ally and the other party to the conflict is due to the resulting triangular dynamic in which one party seeks to get closer to the intervener at the expense of the ally by making concessions to the intervener, while the ally may make concessions to preserve the relationship with the intervener. The role of power in mediation is the subject of several works in the literature, most recently a collection by Zartman and Rubin.[125]

The quality of Norway's role in the Oslo channel is captured in Uri Savir's recollection of his first trip to Oslo during the sixth round. After one attempt to break the ice between Savir and the Palestinians, Terje Rød Larsen "decided to leave us. . . . 'If you can't get along on your own, call me.'"[126] The Norwegian role was primarily one of facilitating appropriate logistics with due attention paid to secrecy, isolation, safety, and comfort. However, at key moments, the Norwegians, especially Terje Rød Larsen and Mona Juul, would intervene in a subtle manner in order to suggest compromise language or concepts or to clarify communication. Terje Rød Larsen was "appointed the liaison between Tunis and Jerusalem" by Savir and Abu Alaa.[127] They received briefings from each delegation at the start and end of each round, and they passed messages from one party to the other between rounds.[128] Norway also did not try to be a diplomatic advocate for either side asymmetrically, as the United States often did. This is a remarkably different model of third-party intervention than the one played by the United States in the Washington talks, which vacillated between passivity and imposition of proposals.

In Holst's words, Norway had "no special interests of her own to promote or defend"; had the confidence of both sides; a long tradition of quiet commitment to international peace; and the resources to underwrite the involvement of a small, interdisciplinary team of facilitators that hosted the Israeli and Palestinian negotiators. Their intervention was limited to "providing the logistical arrangements and communicating between the rounds, since there were no direct phone links between Israel and the PLO in Tunis."[129] Jan Egeland termed Norway's third-party role as one of "multiparty facilitation rather than mediation . . . the Palestinians and Israelis were uniquely qualified for and motivated to doing the actual negotiations by themselves."[130]

But the Norwegian role did not remain limited to providing quiet counsel and discreet Scandinavian country mansions for the talks. Norway's foreign minister Holst visited Tunisia and Israel in July 1993 for the purpose of speaking directly with Arafat and Peres in order to build their confidence as they approached agreement and recognition. Holst condemned the "interventionist propensities of third party mediators," whose past actions in the Arab-Israeli conflict "may also have contributed to past failures," a thinly veiled reference to the United States. Among other things, Holst reassured the respective leaderships that their own negotiators were not diluting the interests of their respective sides in the intimate, isolated Oslo negotiations.[131] In the final rounds of Oslo, Holst's active intermediation was pivotal in getting compromise proposals accepted and in encouraging timely decision making.

All of these assertions notwithstanding, the role Norway played was not confined to simple facilitation but took on many of the aspects of active mediation at several points in the Oslo channel, especially to manage crises and to build the confidence of both PLO and Israeli leadership.

Curiously, the United States was briefed about Oslo on several occasions and seemed to take little or no interest in the existence and work of the Oslo channel. This may have been because of the State Department's unwarranted belief in its own centrality to the Washington talks or because of an institutional blindness regarding the positive roles other states could play in the Middle East.[132] Hassan Asfour believed the United States' disinterest in Oslo can be attributed to its belief that the PLO was only "a temporary organization after the Gulf War."[133] All parties knew that the 1987 Peres-Hussein back channel attempt at concluding a framework accord on the Palestinian territories was derailed when the United States found it could not support an initiative that the Israeli cabinet was not united behind.[134] The United States may have wished to avoid confronting an analogous internal competition between Peres and Rabin, though it was less pronounced than the gap between Shamir and Peres in 1987.

The "official" Israeli negotiators at Oslo, Joel Singer and Uri Savir, did nothing to update the United States about the Oslo channel. This was only done at the commencement and conclusion of the Oslo channel. Savir states that Yitzhak Rabin's conditions for sending him to continue the Oslo process were ongoing secrecy and the absence of substantive intervention by any third parties.[135] The historic Israeli aversion to international intervention in the Arab-Israeli peace process was usually translated into a desire to exclude the UN and the Soviets from substantive roles. Behind this aversion lay the perception that the UN and the Soviets were traditionally pro-Arab in their political alignments and that their intervention would involve Israeli concessions. Given the United States' abiding interest in the peace process, interest which ebbed and flowed and took different forms according to U.S. presidential dispositions but which never disappeared in any U.S. administration, Israel no doubt wished to avoid having to make concessions to the one party who could credibly demand such a concession in return for its commitment of diplomatic and military support.

At the procedural level, I find additional reasons for Israeli aversion to third-party involvement, although Savir's analytical insights in this regard were made after the Oslo experience and subsequent negotiations. Savir makes quite clear that parties in conflict cannot develop "the creativity, the trust, the mutual understanding of interests with a third party present."[136] Savir believes that relying on a third party to pressure one's adversary is a tactic that may ultimately backfire, and he reserves his most strident criticism for the United States as mediator.[137] Abu Alaa recalls only half-jokingly, "we tried many times to involve the Americans, but fortunately they didn't take [Oslo] seriously." Abu Alaa also depicts third parties as interested in an accord for their own political purposes, rather than for facilitating the mutual learning between the adversaries—learning about tactics, strategies, true interests and concerns.[138]

On the PLO side, I find a historic longing to find support or at least empathy in Washington to get the United States to deliver Israeli concessions, just as the early Zionists sought the support of first the Ottoman and later the British government and finally, the Hashemites—a powerful party who could wring or make concessions on behalf of, or in spite of, the Palestinians.[139] One factor that contributed to PLO support for the Oslo channel was precisely the realization that the United States was not going to deliver Israeli concessions. Once the PLO understood the limits of U.S. leverage with the Israelis, Arafat opted for direct talks with the support of the Norwegians to negotiate an accord.

Certainly Norway and Israel have expressed reservations about an activist U.S. role in the Israeli-Palestinian peace process. Israel had little interest in a Russian role either. The PLO was precluded from having a direct bilateral relationship with the United States for the duration of the Washington talks and until the Oslo channel had concluded. As the weaker party, the PLO welcomed the reopening of the United States-PLO dialogue at the conclusion of the Oslo channel.

More important perhaps than the identity of the third-party intervener is the quality of intervention. Norwegian facilitation (with sporadic mediation as needed) was much better matched to the political needs of both parties in the Oslo channel than the U.S. role in the Washington talks. The back channel did therefore protect the Israelis and the PLO against pressures from the United States.

Syria is a third party without an intermediary role but with the potential to disrupt the progress of the Israeli-Palestinian track. Rabin's chief of staff, Eitan Haber (who knew little about the Oslo channel), argues that direct and open Israel-PLO negotiations at the time of the Washington talks would have made the Palestinians vulnerable to pressure from the Syrian government, which may have preferred a deal of its own with Israel before any Palestinian-Israeli accord.[140] At different times Rabin also seems to have preferred the Israeli-Syrian track with its relative lack of complexity compared to the Israeli-Palestinian negotiations. Oslo permitted the PLO to neutralize any pressure and interference the Syrians might have exerted, had they known about Oslo.

Strategic Use of Multiple Negotiation Channels

The secret channel was useful for facilitating communication, reducing uncertainty and information asymmetry, and signaling preferences, whereas the front channel was instrumental in protecting the secret channel and provided a practical motivation (lack of progress) to open the secret channel. To gain these advantages, the parties needed to have *multiple* channels. They had to conduct negotiations in two channels simultaneously.

The Oslo channel was established during a five-month lull in the Madrid negotiations, between its eighth and ninth rounds, and therefore began in parallel with the later phase of the Madrid track.

Egyptian observer Mohamed Heikel wrote that at least "nine different secret [PLO-Israel] channels ran through Cairo" at the time the Oslo channel was being started up, although little is known about the extent and purpose of these contacts.[141] By one account, senior Israeli academics and former military commanders met with PLO security officials and academics in London and Rome in October 1992 under the auspices of an academic conference on regional security in the Middle East.[142] They explored aspects of security cooperation under an eventual accord for Palestinian self-government. However, this dialogue had no participation or input from the Israeli government, although its results appear to have filtered back to the delegations in Washington.[143]

In addition to the talks in Washington and Oslo, the Norwegians and even the Egyptian government served as occasional intermediaries carrying messages to the PLO and Israeli leaders; some direct bilateral links existed as well, such as the relationship between al-Tibi and Ramon. All were made use of at different times, and in order to avoid confusion, there was some discussion at the beginning of the Oslo channel regarding the need to limit channels and focus efforts and commitments in one channel alone—the Oslo channel.[144]

Because the Madrid and Oslo tracks coexisted in time, there can be no doubt that they represented the parties with opportunities for strategic use. One of the first opportunities for such strategic use arose over the issue of East Jerusalem. Was it to be included in an eventual area of Palestinian self-rule during the interim period or not? While the PLO was conceding this point in the Oslo channel, it issued parallel but contrary instructions to the delegation in Washington. The first result was confusion: which channel was conveying the real PLO position? Was there a single PLO position? After the confusion, the signal was interpreted correctly; the Israelis could expect moderation only in the channel where the PLO was directly present: Oslo.

In the previous chapter, I have noted that the effect of the Oslo channel, once it was revealed, was to put an end to the talks proceeding in Washington, especially because the agreement from Oslo was not going to be passed over to the Washington delegations for final negotiations and execution. Rather, the Washington talks were bypassed altogether, alienating many of its participants on both sides.

With the PLO effectively guiding the Palestinian delegation in Washington anyway, the question must be asked: why bother with a direct parallel and secret channel between Israel and the PLO? Part of the answer is found in the qualitative differences between the negotiations at Washington and Oslo, elements such as the flexibility of the negotiators and their proximity to decision makers. Other factors behind the multiple channels are discussed here and include the domestic political concerns (for Israel) and the need for legitimacy and a central role (for the PLO).

Domestic political concerns for the Israelis help explain their aversion to the PLO, but for Rabin, the need to survive politically meant producing results on the peace process; and at some point, Rabin's best option for satisfying Israeli policy interests—controlling terrorism, managing the intifada, gaining legitimacy among the other Arab governments, and opening up new export and capital markets—was to reach an agreement with the PLO and bring the PLO back to the occupied territories to undertake the responsibilities toward Israel that the self-governing entity would assume. In short, Rabin needed a negotiation partner that could deliver the concessions for Israeli security and for Labor Party political survival. An agreement with the Washington delegation would not accomplish this and was too remote in any case. Ultimately, and perhaps paradoxically, Rabin's choice for the Oslo channel was consistent with older Zionist/Israeli policies of shunning local Palestinian interlocutors and seeking outsiders (the Emir Faysal, King Hussein in Jordan, Sadat in Egypt, and finally, the exiled PLO leadership) to "deliver" the Palestinians. Upon return to the occupied territories,

the PLO would have to control internal dissidents and manage religious nationalists and paramilitary groups while negotiating the terms of the interim agreements and the final status. By the time Oslo was signed, Palestinians in the West
Bank and Gaza often considered the PLO leadership in Tunis and elsewhere to
be the "external" leadership: people who did not live with the effects of the Israeli
occupation.[145]

The lure of being seen as a legitimate actor by the Israeli and U.S. governments helped motivate the PLO to seek a central, direct role via the back channel. Shunned by the United States and Israel, in conflict with regional players
such as Syria and Jordan, the PLO was suffering a severe financial crisis when
the Oslo channel opened. It desperately wanted to get the United States' support
after political isolation drove it to align with Iraq prior to the Persian Gulf War.
New legitimacy would pave the way for becoming the sole representative of the
Palestinian people's national aspirations. Neither party could accomplish these
goals through the Washington negotiations.

Multiple channels existed at the time that the Oslo channel was conducted,
and there were efforts to reduce the scope of such channels while simultaneously
making selective use of them to clarify intentions and facilitate communications
at the highest levels of decision making. The two parallel negotiation channels,
Washington and Oslo, served as opportunities to signal intentions and preferences about which channel to use most seriously and to issue preferences and
other information from one side to another, even though the original function of
this parallel dynamic was to send finalized drafts from the secret channel to the
front channel. Joel Singer, alluding to the complex sets of reasons that can motivate the use of multiple channels and changing purposes for them, noted that "if
life were simple, content being negotiated in secret could be finished in the front
channel. But life is not simple."[146] The Washington talks served to protect the Oslo
channel by deflecting attention from it. The existence of parallel channels was in
these several dimensions a useful part of the peace process for both parties.

Additional Aspects of the Oslo Channel

The secrecy and seclusion of the Oslo talks, skillful facilitation by the Norwegians, and the time to live together for brief but intense periods permitted some

Oslo negotiators to build personal friendships (such as the one between Abu Alaa and Uri Savir, for example). Although they did not erase their respective national identities in creating a personal relationship with a delegate from the other side, they succeeded in distancing themselves from the stereotypes each had of the other. Both Abu Alaa and Uri Savir mention that *trust building* was one of the chief benefits of the Oslo channel, at both interpersonal and political levels.[147]

Uri Savir believes that trust cannot be built with third parties present and that, in the absence of trust between parties, negotiation creativity cannot be exercised. "When you sit down with your counterpart and want to test a creative idea, and if it's not secret and not based on an element of trust, your counterpart will run to his boss and say 'I sense there is some flexibility on the other side' for leverage, and the idea is dead."[148]

Some back channel negotiators mention another motivation for pursuing back channel negotiations. They seek to reduce the *uncertainties* inherent not only in negotiation outcomes but also uncertainties *about what they know about their adversaries.* Abu Alaa states that at Oslo "we learned what's serious and what's not, what is true and what is not true with the Israelis. And . . . they know the same for us . . . we are open books for each other. We know their tactics and strategies, and they know the same for us."[149] Similarly, Uri Savir notes that "part of secret negotiations is really to try and learn . . . what is real, what is fake, where the real sensitivities are, the real issues are."[150] Abu Alaa believes that "the most important thing in secret negotiations is to educate, to teach the other side about your real concerns. And to listen to him about his real concerns."[151]

Both Savir and Peres noted the intelligence value of secret negotiations. Peres used this argument to convince Rabin to support the Oslo channel. Savir argues that Israel does not have the expertise on the Arab world it claims to have and that the intelligence community would learn a lot about the "sensitivities" of the Arab world by considering Israel's secret negotiators as a resource.[152]

The lack of information on the preferences and concerns of the other side is a key weakness in negotiations of any kind, and BCN is one mechanism for reducing a perceived information deficit. Reducing this deficit assists parties in formulating proposals that are calculated to be accepted by the adversaries while also tacitly conveying to the other side where one might be flexible and depart from a stated demand or long-held position.

Lessons Learned and Not Learned from the Oslo Channel

The Oslo channel and its outcome dramatically transformed the political land-scape of the Middle East by moving the parties away from declared mutual rejection to becoming publicly acknowledged partners in the search for negotiated solutions. The Oslo process was in many ways the result of more than five years of secret encounters between Israel and the PLO. It was also the result of the convergence of multiple links between the parties and several motivating factors.

Concessions were made by both parties on the issues by making trade-offs among the issues and against time (by deferring issues to future negotiation stages). The way the issues were discussed was qualitatively different and far more effective than what was happening in Washington. At Oslo, the parties quickly established a common work agenda.

The Oslo channel only gradually took on the characteristics of a fully official secret back channel because the top policy makers on the Israeli side were at first not fully aware or committed to it, which meant that it was in essence a freelance operation that later assumed the mantle of the state's authority.

The channel was successfully kept secret from the negotiators in the front channel, as well as the subparties, constituents, and bureaucratic insiders. At first, it was even kept secret from top Israeli and Palestinian policy makers. The secrecy protected the back channel negotiators from pressures that all the excluded parties could have exerted on the Oslo channel. The major interested third party, the United States, played no role in the creation and conduct of the back channel in Oslo. The United States did, however, assist in converting the secret channel into a public agreement, and reactivated United States-PLO relations.

The existence of multiple channels operating simultaneously presented interesting opportunities for tacit communication between the principals—Rabin and Arafat. The Oslo channel was itself supplemented by additional confidence building contacts that were made by confidants, as well as by Norway and Egypt. The multiple channels also enabled both parties to simultaneously hold different negotiating positions for strategic purposes.

Although it was not necessarily apparent at the time, it is my contention that there would have been no breakthrough accord had there not been multiple channels of substantive negotiations, i.e., both Madrid and Oslo operating together (as opposed to exploratory talks or other nonbargaining contacts). This is because the multiplicity of channels permitted both parties to manage significant uncertainties: by having two channels, the decision makers on each side communicated through close colleagues and through tacit signaling (by manipulating their own positions in each channel). They reduced their exposure to subparties: they could both point to the Washington track as evidence of talks, but there were no real concessions to justify in public. There were no major preconditions to comply with (except the resumption of the Washington talks). The Oslo talks were protected from interference by the United States or the Arab League, and there were no internal parties to negotiate in advance on the terms and conditions of an eventual bilateral agreement. The existence of both channels provided a deniable way to gather information on real preferences without the risk of public failure.

It is also my contention that the secret channel produced the breakthrough precisely because it was kept secret. *The secrecy permitted the negotiation to be conducted without the interference of obstructive third parties, disruptive internal subparties, before whom tough concessions could not be made.*

BCN permits the parties to align the factors that facilitate successful outcomes in negotiations not burdened by mutual rejection.

When BCN becomes institutionalized, however, excluded parties can begin to surmise the existence of secret channels and come to expect them, thereby reducing their impact and usefulness. The audience effect mentioned in the social psychology literature reasserts itself again if negotiators, even back channel ones, are aware that their work will at some point be revealed, scrutinized, and possibly subject to a hostile ratification process.

The very secrecy of the Oslo channel permitted it (and those responsible for it) to become lightning rods for rejectionism. The efforts of the top decision makers to explain to all observers the full implications of the agreement were insufficient at best. The subsequent stage of negotiations after the Washington signing ceremony did not strengthen the parties' confidence in each other. The failure to anticipate and address the initial alienation with the accord led to strident opposition. The alienation was partly the result of the exclusion of subparties, but more important, it reflected serious ideological incompatibilities between, for example, the Likud Party and the Labor coalition in power in 1993, and on the Palestinian side, between the centrist parties of the PLO and secular Palestinian factions based in Lebanon and Syria (not to mention the Palestine-based Movement for Islamic Jihad and HAMAS).

The effects of these difficulties were amplified by the failure of both sides' leadership to encourage the growth of propeace constituencies and the failure to facilitate immediate economic and social benefits to the Palestinians under the emerging self-rule arrangement. Settler organizations and Islamic nationalist groups were understood to reject both their respective political leaders and the new official rhetoric of peace that cautiously emerged from the DoP.

Added to all of this were the enormous challenges of starting the new implementation negotiations in full view of opposition groups, civil society, inquisitive media channels, enemies of the peace process, and the international community. The negotiations conducted in the remainder of the interim period are the subject of chapter 5.

5

Negotiations During the Interim Phase, 1993 to 1998

We in Israel might not notice the riotous progress of the settlements, but any Palestinian can see it going on from his window, day and night. He will also notice the bypass roads, and the roads built, in turn, to bypass those roads, as we concrete over his homeland.

—YOSSI SARID[1]

The Interim and Permanent Status Negotiations

Following the signing ceremony held on September 13, 1993, Palestinians, Israelis, and other interested parties around the world began declaring their support, skepticism, or rejection of the newly revealed PLO-Israel peace process. Among the Palestinians, secular and religious nationalist movements aligned themselves either for or against the Oslo Accords and by extension, the Palestinian and Israeli leadership. Suicide bombings by HAMAS and Islamic Jihad against Israeli settlers, soldiers, and civilians continued, as well as killings of Palestinian civilians by settlers and Israeli troops. Officials of Fatah, Arafat's party within the PLO, were assassinated by elements of the extremist splinter faction Abu Nidal. Israeli settlers began organizing large protests against the Rabin government and incurred warnings from the political leadership. A no-confidence motion against Rabin was defeated in the Knesset on November 9, 1993. The PLO began intensive efforts to persuade HAMAS and secular nationalist opposition groups, including factions within Fateh, not to obstruct the emerging peace process. Israeli military authorities began planning for numerous contingencies, including the possibility of Israeli civil conflict and insubordination within the ranks of the Israel Defense Force (IDF).[2] Controversy arose over plans by the settlers'

131

main organization to establish their own armed units (although settlers are often heavily armed in any case).[3] In short, constituencies, subparties, and outside parties mobilized for or against the process, magnifying the importance of each step taken in the negotiations.

This chapter covers all the negotiations that took place during the interim phase of the peace process, which was to have ended by May 4, 1999, and during which negotiations for the permanent status were to have been completed. The last agreement reached during this time was little more than a renegotiation of aspects of the main 1995 Interim Agreement, and it was left unimplemented by Israel's government at the time, which soon after lost a vote of confidence and lost power in late May 1999.

Overview

During the interim period (1993 to 1995), Israel and the PLO negotiated six major agreements leading up to the landmark September 28, 1995, Interim Agreement that required the Israelis to make more significant withdrawals of their military forces and to dismantle their military government, while requiring the Palestinians to begin assuming civil and police responsibilities and to participate in joint Palestinian-Israeli security patrols against Palestinian militants. Of these six, five were negotiated using both back and front channels.

The Declaration of Principles (DoP) signed on the White House lawn in September 1993 set out the general terms of Palestinian-Israeli cooperation and the gradual withdrawal of the Israeli military government and civil administration from parts of the West Bank and Gaza Strip. Two sets of complex negotiations were anticipated in the DoP in order to (1) implement the orderly transfer of power and territory to a new Palestinian government and (2) determine the final disposition of the occupied territory.

The Oslo Accords were negotiated to create a condition that *did not yet exist:* limited Palestinian autonomy. The DoP itself had very few implementation consequences, being limited to expressing the will of the parties to work with each other. The fact of direct PLO-Israel negotiations was the controversial dimension of the DoP. By contrast, the negotiations that followed Oslo not only had immediate and controversial effects on the substance, they were also extremely sensitive to daily, unfolding events. The parties' front channel negotiations were the subject of local and global scrutiny after Oslo. The media reported rumors of further back channels on occasion and leaked documents linked to them. The secret negotiations that followed Oslo awakened a wide spectrum of popular expectations spanning from rage and despair to exuberance and hope.

The Madrid and Oslo negotiation channels constituted a single negotiation "set." They are treated separately in the previous two chapters partly because they evolved separately: the highest-level policy makers did not initially design the back channels, especially on the Israeli side. Following Oslo, the parties deliberately constructed "sets" of negotiations that each contained a back channel and a front channel. The pattern that emerged post-Oslo was characterized by constant use of multiple channels of negotiation.

The DoP provided for a five-year transitional period starting with the initial Israeli withdrawal from Gaza and Jericho, during which only two further stages of negotiations were envisioned. The first stage was to result in a comprehensive interim agreement that spelled out the details and limits of Palestinian autonomy. One purpose of the first stage, aside from reaching agreement on the details of autonomy, was to build trust between the parties and establish cooperative working relationships in economic, military, and social affairs of interest to both sides. Upon this anticipated basis of trust and cooperation, the parties hoped to enter into a second stage of negotiations by the beginning of the third year of the transitional period and conclude a permanent status agreement in the remaining two years that settled the major issues they had deferred in the DoP.

In practice, the entire interim period was punctuated by political crises that eroded rather than built trust and that generated new interparty conflict. More negotiations were required to implement what had already been agreed to both in principle and in detail. These further negotiations resulted in numerous additional accords not anticipated in the DoP. Both front and back channels were used for negotiations on interim and permanent status negotiations.

Israeli and Palestinian negotiators in the 1993 Oslo channel vigorously negotiated over the categorization of disputed issues as either interim or permanent status. The Palestinians generally preferred immediate as opposed to deferred negotiation, whereas the Israelis sought to reserve as much as possible for an indeterminate final-status negotiation process.

The difficult unfolding of the peace process provided support for the argument that the very deferral of the permanent status issues permitted the Oslo channel to succeed, but it also exposed the entire Israeli-Palestinian peace process to the risk of collapse on numerous occasions. Sectors within the Israeli and Palestinian population claimed they had been betrayed by their own leaders during the interim period, not trusting a process based on incremental transfer of autonomy to the Palestinian side. The uncertainty of the eventual permanent status ironically permitted pessimists on both sides to consider those issues as having been predetermined *against* their own respective interests, further entrenching their opposition to the peace process.

The division of issues into interim and permanent status groupings was made according to the logic of resolving "easy" issues first. This failed to account for the linkages between issues. The *deferral of the permanent status issues* also complicated the *implementation of the interim issues* because some were organically linked to each other. The primary example of this concerned the timing and geographical extent of Israeli redeployment of its armed forces in the occupied territory.

Redeployment was an interim obligation for Israel whereas the fate of settlements was reserved for permanent status talks. But the interim redeployments were constrained above all by the security arrangements for Jewish settlements in the West Bank and Gaza. Redeployments were constantly constrained by the unwillingness of Israeli governments to confront the settlers, as well as the Israeli desire to provide them with IDF protection. The expansion of settlements, the new construction of bypass roads (which link the settlements to Israel and are built on private and public land claimed by Palestinians), and acts of violence by each side consistently eroded public confidence in the peace process.

Israeli politics, not inherently stable even in the absence of crisis, were agitated by the ebb and flow of the peace process. Symptomatic of this instability was the resurgence of the secular and religious right wing in Israel, which mirrored Palestinian secular and religious rejectionism of the peace process. Palestinian rejectionism was expressed along a spectrum that ranged from nonparticipation in the peace process to violent paramilitary actions against both Palestinians and Israelis.

For Israel, political stability reached a new nadir with the assassination of Prime Minister Rabin. The assassination of Rabin was followed by the failure of Shimon Peres's 1995 reelection bid, the triumph and then the fall of Likud and prime minister Binyamin Netanyahu, the return of Labor and the rise of

Barak in 1999, and Barak's steep decline between 2000 and 2001. According to one of the chief Israeli negotiators at Oslo and in the post-Oslo period, the turnover of Israeli governments also contributed to the needless renegotiation of previous agreements' clauses, mostly so that successive governments could claim they were implementing their very own agreement and not any (allegedly defective) agreement of the previous government. "A lion, entering new territory, marks it as his by pissing on it, in an effort to erase the scent of a lion who had previously been there. Arafat and the PLO could have the successive Israeli administrations 'buy-in' to the process formally. On the Israeli side, Netanyahu could then say (politically) 'we're not implementing Oslo, we're implementing Wye.' In the same manner, Barak could say: 'we're not implementing Wye, we're implementing Sharm el-Sheikh. [But] there was no need for any of these [subsequent] agreements."[4]

The Major Agreements

The multitude of agreements negotiated and signed during the interim period is symptomatic of varying degrees of good faith invested in the negotiations, real and imagined implementation failures, constant changes in negotiators, and constant accretion of issues to be negotiated. The basic interests of the parties continued to be fundamentally opposed on all issues of critical importance. Some of the early agreements arose from crises that occurred in the course of the transitional period. Others were significant stand-alone agreements that were later integrated into the Interim Agreement. The Hebron Accords of 1997 and the Wye River Memorandum were little more than renegotiations of issues that had already been thoroughly debated and agreed upon but had not been implemented. The chronology of the major agreements and associated negotiations in this case is summarized in table 4.

Negotiations continued intensively with the Barak government that replaced Netanyahu, and these are covered in the following chapter.

Negotiations and Channels

The DoP allotted the parties a three-month period in which to conclude the next agreement, which would set out the modalities of the initial withdrawal from the

Table 4. Major Agreements of the Interim Period, 1993 to 1998

Agreements	Dates of negotiation	Scope	BCN/FCN
1 Cairo Agreement, Feb. 9, 1994	Oct. 13, 1993 to Jan. 9, 1994	Security aspects of initial IDF withdrawal.	BCN/FCN
2 Israeli-Palestinian Security Agreement, Mar. 31, 1994	Mar. 6 to 31, 1994	Interim; limited to Hebron in aftermath of massacre at Ibrahimi Mosque.	BCN/FCN
3 Economic Agreement (Paris Protocol), Apr. 29, 1994	Nov. 1993 to Apr. 29, 1994	Interim; limited to economic issues.	FCN
4 Agreement on the Gaza Strip and Jericho Area, May 4, 1994 (incorporating both the Cairo Agreement and Paris Protocol)	Sept. 13, 1993 to May 4, 1994	Interim; initial Israeli withdrawal.	BCN/FCN
5 Agreement on the Preparatory Transfer of Powers and Responsibilities, Aug. 29, 1994	July 5, 1994 to Aug. 29, 1994	Interim; spheres of authority.	BCN/FCN
6 Interim Agreement on the West Bank and Gaza Strip ("Oslo II"), Sept. 28, 1995	Dec. 6, 1994 to Sept. 24, 1995	Interim; comprehensive.	BCN/FCN
7 Framework for the Conclusion of a Final Status Agreement (Stockholm or Beilin-Abu Mazen Agreement), Oct. 31, 1995	Sept. 1, 1994 to Oct. 31, 1995	Permanent; framework agreement.	BCN
8 Israel-PLO Permanent Status Negotiations [joint communiqué]	May 5 to 6, 1996	Permanent.	FCN
9 Hebron Protocol, Note for the Record, and Agreed Minute, Jan. 15, 1997	Aug. 1996–Jan. 15, 1997	Interim; implementation of Interim Agreement.	BCN/FCN
10 Wye River Memorandum, Oct. 23, 1998	Back channels from May to Oct. 1998 Summit Oct. 15 to 23, 1998	Interim; implementation of Interim Agreement.	BCN/FCN

Gaza Strip and Jericho. This new agreement also had to set out the structure of the Palestinian National Authority (PNA), as well as the training and deployment of Palestinian police officers (some of whom would come from the exiled military forces of parties belonging to the PLO—such as the Palestine Liberation Army, PLA) who would assume responsibility for public order upon the withdrawal of Israeli forces. Also, a joint security cooperation mechanism was created to deter Palestinian attacks on Israelis as was an arrangement for introducing Palestinian control and presence at the border crossings between Gaza and Egypt and between Jericho and Jordan, which were pending. The details of the "safe passage" for Palestinians between the West Bank and Gaza remained to be worked out.[5]

The first PLO-Israel negotiation meeting of the post-Oslo period took place at the Mayflower Hotel in Washington, D.C., on the same day as the signing of the Oslo Accord, September 13, 1993. Those present included the two Oslo delegations, as well as Shimon Peres, Yossi Beilin, and Abu Mazen. They set out the general plans for their next steps: appointing new negotiating teams and defining the issues for upcoming negotiations. Israeli negotiators complained that for several weeks after this, they heard nothing more from the Palestinian side, which was trying to build internal consensus on the accords, neutralize internal opposition, and work out the operational implications of the Declaration of Principles.[6]

Both the Israelis and the PLO were undergoing internal reassessments of what had been committed to and what needed to be done going forward. On the Palestinian side, new individuals were constantly being brought into the negotiations while existing negotiators were marginalized by PLO senior leadership. Similarly, on the Israeli side, the military staff, which was not consulted on the negotiation of the Oslo Accords, positioned themselves to assume a high-profile role in the coming negotiations.

Toward the Withdrawal from Gaza-Jericho

Negotiations on the details of the first post-Oslo issues began in October 1993 in Cairo and Taba. The Taba talks were extensively covered by the media. Joel Singer complained to Uri Savir that no actual negotiations were taking place, only "endless soapboxing."[7] The negotiators at Taba nevertheless took care not to replicate all the adverse conditions of the 1992/93 talks in Washington. For example, the heads of the delegations announced their intention to establish "a direct channel of communication." In addition, they established joint working groups on security and civilian matters, with smaller joint subgroups under these as well.[8] Another set of negotiations on economic cooperation was initiated in November in Paris. At the end of November, in al-Arish on the Egyptian Sinai coast, front channel Israeli and PLO delegations began negotiating the areas of authority to be transferred to the Palestinians.

As perhaps was to be expected, the PLO and Israel set up a parallel back channel right away. A separate set of negotiators began meeting in Rome and Geneva, negotiating and planning the security cooperation aspects of the Israeli-Palestinian peace process.[9] Most of the negotiators at Taba were kept in the dark about the Rome and Geneva talks. Hassan Asfour, one of the Palestinians from the Oslo channel, has revealed that he, Dr. Nabil Shaath, and General Abd al-Razak Yihye conducted these back channel negotiations with General Amnon Shahak (chief of staff of the IDF), Joel Singer, and an unnamed officer of the Shin Bet internal security force. This back channel was arranged by Egypt and spanned November and December 1993. They worked in parallel with the front channel negotiators, and indeed, some of them were simultaneously participating in the front channel negotiations.[10]

Toward the end of the year, after three and one-half months of both front and back channel negotiations, it was apparent to both sides that negotiations on the initial Israeli withdrawal would not be completed by the agreed deadline. In an effort to accelerate the talks, the top decision makers were brought in. Two summits were held, the first between Arafat and Peres (December 11, 1993) and the second between Arafat and Rabin on the deadline for the Gaza-Jericho agreement (Cairo, December 13). The impasse revolved around Israeli efforts to ascertain that Israeli security concerns would be paramount in the interim period, which meant the Palestinians had to incorporate the Israeli security concept in the self-government arrangements or persuade the Israelis to modify it.

The failure of the Arafat-Rabin summit led Rabin to reinsert Peres more fully into the post-Oslo negotiations so that he could take charge of the Israeli side of the Joint Liaison Committee (JLC) that was formally set up in the DoP.[11] The media channels knew of the JLC negotiations but were denied access to the negotiators themselves during December. The JLC called on the Norwegians to convene a meeting in Oslo in late December 1993. Top-level negotiators for both sides met in Oslo on December 20 and 21, including Yossi Sarid (then the environment minister), General Amnon Shahak, Yasir Abd Rabbuh (the PLO official who had previously led the United States-PLO dialogue), and Abu Alaa in the hope that solid progress by them could pave the way for a decisive summit between Arafat and Rabin.

Rabin explained his absence in terms of a desire for certainty in the negotiation's outcome: "There should be no meeting unless we know beforehand that the results are assured," he declared.[12] The second day of the Oslo session uncharacteristically included delegates from the United States, Russia, Egypt, the European Union. The JLC then continued negotiations in Versailles as guests of the French government on December 22 and 23, 1993, in the presence of only three Norwegians and without informing the media of its whereabouts.

This JLC channel continued working in Cairo on December 27, with the presence of Peres and Abu Mazen. The talks made progress, but Peres is reported to have lost his patience. After dictating a draft agreement embodying compromises in the details of the border passages, he abruptly departed Cairo with his delegation. Arafat proposed certain modifications to the extent of the Jericho area and the procedures for crossing from Jordan, which were in turn rejected by Peres and Rabin.[13]

The main delegations for the Gaza-Jericho agreement reconvened in Taba, Egypt, for intense negotiations from January 10 to 12 and January 18 to 20 and managed to narrow differences and resolve numerous outstanding details in dispute.[14]

The parties then reconvened in Oslo on January 20 for the funeral of Johan Jørgen Holst, the Norwegian foreign minister who had played such a key role in the original Oslo channel. At the funeral, Peres and Arafat held two meetings and authorized Joel Singer and Abu Alaa to remain behind in Oslo with new negotiation teams to jointly prepare a single draft of the agreement. Thus the reintegration of both Peres and Abu Alaa in the main Gaza-Jericho negotiations had taken place by the start of 1994. Further negotiations in this channel took place in Davos on joint security issues (January 28 to 30) and Cairo (February 1, 7 to 9, 1994). On February 7, Peres and Arafat met at the Egyptian foreign ministry to try to break deadlocks on the disputed details concerning control of Palestinian border crossings to Jordan and Egypt and exhorted their delegations to work around the clock if necessary to hammer out an agreement.

Before this round was over, however, Peres discovered that Israeli military officers attached to his negotiating delegation were quietly passing information on these proceedings to the Planning Branch of the IDF in Israel. His vigorous protests directly to Rabin secured his negotiating autonomy. At the same time, Peres asked the Egyptian foreign minister, Amr Musa, to intervene with Arafat and encourage him to concede that only Israel would control the border crossings between Gaza and Egypt. As the delegations continued to dispute the details, it took a private encounter between only Savir and Abu Alaa to finally break the impasse on the issue of controlling border crossings and to agree on some measure of joint control at the crossings. A dispute arose over control of key roads in Gaza and Jericho. The Israeli position on this issue was revealed late in the process and aroused the ire of the Palestinian negotiators. Arafat conceded to the Israelis on this issue but had difficulty persuading the Palestinian delegation. Peres insisted on initialing these understandings, but Abu Alaa refused to initial the maps delineating Israeli authority on key roads.

It took President Mubarak's intervention with Arafat to get Abu Alaa to initial the maps at a ceremony hosted by the Egyptians on February 9.[15] The "Cairo Agreement," as it was called, was made public without the controversial maps, a pattern that would be repeated in future Palestinian-Israeli accords. Because the maps graphically demonstrated the degree of accommodation each side had shown, we should not be too surprised that leaders who feared their own internal opponents (sometimes just as much as they feared "the other side") would hide the maps annexed to peace agreements.

Although significant in itself, the Cairo Agreement did not cover all the issues included in the larger Gaza-Jericho negotiations. The delegations passed their work back to the negotiating committees working on the rest of the Gaza-Jericho Agreement, who resumed work in Taba on February 14 and in Cairo from February 21 to 23. The parties reported making progress in these talks, and the IDF began planning its Gaza redeployment, a historic moment in the narrative of Palestinian-Israeli conflict.[16] This new momentum of the peace process faced its first severe test before the end of February 1994.

Hebron: The First Security Crisis

Baruch Goldstein was a resident of Kiryat Arba, a militant Jewish settlement built provocatively just outside the Palestinian city of Khalil (Hebron). He was formerly a U.S. spokesman of the Israeli Kach party, which openly advocates expulsion of Palestinians by violent means. Early in the morning of February 25, 1994, he put on his IDF uniform and with his weapon proceeded to the Ibrahimi Mosque/Tomb of the Patriarchs, holy to Muslims and Jews. While Muslim worshippers were observing dawn prayers there, Goldstein opened fire on them, killing twenty-nine people before being killed himself. In response to the massacre, Arafat suspended Palestinian participation in the negotiations.

Goldstein's massacre succeeded in dramatically altering the negotiation agenda and greatly eroding the parties' fragile trust in each other and in the peace process. Palestinian protests over the killings resulted in IDF curfews, shootings, and more deaths.[17]

The PLO recalled its delegates from all the different negotiation venues. Israel decided to send a delegation to Tunis on March 6 to convince Arafat (who had not yet made his return to Palestine) to send back the negotiators and drop his preconditions for their resumption. These preconditions included the removal of settlers who had invaded Palestinian homes in Old Khalil (the center of Hebron), the disarming of all settlers, and international protection for Palestinians. The United States and Norway also sent their representatives to Tunis to intervene. The U.S. Department of State coordinator on the peace process, Dennis Ross, threatened a U.S. veto on a UN Security Council Resolution condemning the massacre unless the PLO returned to the negotiation table.

Terje Rød Larsen stayed on in Tunis to mediate a solution on security measures for the protection of Palestinians in Hebron. Rabin and Peres decided to remove the small group of extremist Jewish settlers from the midst of Old Hebron, where they were constantly provoking the Arab residents and calling on the IDF to defend them afterward. The United States conditionally and reluctantly cast its Security Council vote in favor of the UN Security Council Resolution 904 (1994) on March 18, which denounced the massacre and called for disarming the settlers and for a temporary international protection force in Hebron.

A second Israeli delegation left for Tunis led by Savir and Shahak on March 20 and, without revealing the plans to remove the settlers, convinced Arafat to simultaneously pursue negotiations on new security arrangements in Hebron as well as the Gaza-Jericho Agreement. While this delegation was in Tunis, Rabin abandoned the plan for removal of the settlers within Hebron.[18] His reluctance to move against the militant fringe of the settlers would have regrettable consequences for the peace process, for his political party, and for him.

From March 23 to 31, Israel and the PLO continued negotiations in Cairo on security arrangements for the Hebronites. They signed an agreement that permitted the introduction of a "temporary international presence in Hebron" (the TIPH) to protect the Palestinians there, composed of 160 Norwegians, Danes, and Italians. The agreement committed the parties to resume the Gaza-Jericho negotiations on an accelerated schedule and to follow up the next agreement with discussions on expanding the areas of authority to be transferred to the Palestinians. Israel agreed to shorten the anticipated initial withdrawal schedule.[19] Negotiations resumed in Cairo. In early April, Israeli soldiers began leaving their bases in Jericho and Gaza. By mid-April, the parties reached agreement on the composition of and logistical arrangements for the Palestinian police that would enter Gaza and Jericho. Change was in the air.

Summits for Gaza-Jericho

Abu Alaa, who had assumed the leadership of the newly formed development agency Palestinian Economic Council for Development and Reconstruction (PECDAR) and his counterpart, Israeli finance minister Avraham Shochat, were appointed to lead their respective delegations through a sequence of negotiating sessions that took place in France. At the end of April, they completed their work on an Israeli-Palestinian economic agreement that covered customs rates, movement of agricultural and industrial goods, tourism, the establishment of a Palestinian Monetary Authority, taxation cooperation, insurance, and the details of Palestinian labor rights in Israel. The agreement became an annex to the later Gaza-Jericho Agreement and was therefore subordinated to that accord's security arrangements.[20]

A breakthrough in the Gaza-Jericho negotiations was announced on April 28; enough issues had been settled that the parties could declare they had a tentative agreement in hand. A summit was to be convened on May 4 in order for the highest-level decision makers to resolve the remaining disputes on the security arrangements and territorial extent of the Jericho area. Both the Israeli cabinet and the PLO Executive Committee approved the tentative accord on May 1. The delegations continued working until another summit in President Mubarak's office on the night of May 3 into May 4, 1994. As with the Oslo Declaration of Principles, disagreements continued until the moment of signature in the Cairo

Auditorium on May 4, when Arafat refused to initial certain appended maps on the argument that some issues still remained to be negotiated. Despite another episode of eleventh-hour brinksmanship by Arafat, the agreement was finalized, thus paving the way for the first *negotiated* Israeli withdrawal from parts of the West Bank and Gaza, the initial transfer of governing power to the Palestinians, and the return of Yasir Arafat to the land he dreamed of governing.

The May 4, 1994, signing in Cairo of the "Agreement on the Gaza Strip and the Jericho Area" officially initiated the five-year interim period during which the parties were to finalize a full interim agreement and to commence, no later than the third year, negotiations on a the permanent status agreement. The groundwork had already been laid for the pursuit of these two different negotiations processes simultaneously. Palestinian police officers began assuming the posts abandoned by the Israelis and joint patrols were organized under the terms of the agreement. The IDF completed its initial withdrawal from Gaza and Jericho within three weeks, by May 25, 1994. Change was no longer in the air; it was now "on the ground," as both Palestinians and Israelis are fond of saying.

Arrival of Arafat, Empowerment of Palestinian National Authority

At the end of June, Nabil Shaath and General Shahak continued bilateral negotiations on the scope of Palestinian self-rule and coordination for the arrival of PLO chairman Arafat so that he could assume leadership of the PNA. Arafat returned to Gaza on July 1, 1994, and during his three-day visit, he appealed directly to both secular and religious opposition groups to cooperate with him in negotiating the dismantlement of the Israeli occupation. In Israel demonstrators protested against Arafat's arrival, and some carried placards portraying Rabin as a traitor. The Rabin government faced and defeated further no-confidence motions on July 4. After continuing his journey to Jericho, Arafat met with Rabin for meetings July 6 and 7 and inaugurated the next stage of negotiations on expanding the PNA's powers.

On July 11, Palestinian and Israeli front channel delegations led by Nabil Shaath (a PLO official who within the PNA began assuming responsibilities like those of a foreign minister) and General Danny Rothschild (who headed the IDF's policy-planning branch), respectively, convened open negotiations on early empowerment, Israeli redeployment, Palestinian elections, and expansion of the

Palestinian autonomous area; they set up new working groups and subcommittees to structure the negotiations. On a separate track, negotiations resumed to complete the unfinished business from the Gaza-Jericho Agreement.

Rabin decided to postpone the opening of safe passage routes between Gaza and Jericho in August and accused the PNA of not taking enough action against HAMAS for its attacks against Israeli civilians and soldiers. The ability of rejectionists to derail a peace effort depends in part upon the willingness of the negotiating parties to react to the provocations of those determined to delegitimize the negotiations, thus enabling the rejectionists to exercise an effective veto and rendering the actions of the parties reactive rather than proactive. At the same time, there is a tension between the need to proceed with negotiations despite provocation and the parties' unwillingness to be attacked or victimized while they are conducting negotiations. This general description could apply to either side in this case.

The delay in opening the safe passage routes was one of the first indications that the accords were often ambiguous enough for each side to interpret them to its own advantage and to condition its own compliance with its perception of its counterpart's willingness to comply. The basis for the Palestinian-Israeli peace arrangements could not be considered land for peace, but rather "security cooperation in exchange for limited autonomy."

Peres involved himself in the Cairo negotiations on the expansion of the PNA's areas of jurisdiction, and a partial agreement was concluded by August 18. The draft was initialed on August 24 and the final version, the Agreement on the Preparatory Transfer of Powers and Responsibilities, was signed in Gaza by Shaath and Rothschild on August 29, 1994.

Elections and Redeployment of the IDF

The PNA began to assume self-government responsibilities in the areas under its jurisdiction while preparing for new negotiations on Palestinian elections that would be linked to Israeli military withdrawal from the major cities of the West Bank and Gaza. These negotiations began on October 3, 1994, and were conducted by Saeb Eraqat, minister of local affairs of the PNA (and one of the Palestinian delegates to the Madrid Peace Conference) and General Rothschild.[21] Abu Mazen participated on the Palestinian side when negotiations were held outside of Israel and the occupied territories. Agenda items included the size of the legislative council to be elected, whether or not separate government branches could be formed, and whether or not secular and religious opposition groups could participate in the Palestinian elections.

At the end of November 1994, the issue of IDF withdrawal in advance of the Palestinian elections had not been resolved, with Prime Minister Rabin proposing that a three-day, temporary withdrawal take place only for conducting the elections. For opposite reasons, both the IDF and the Palestinians rejected this approach. The negotiations on the elections became part of a larger set of negotiations on the full Interim Agreement that had been anticipated in the DoP and after November were addressed in both front and back channels.

Back and Front Channels for the Interim Agreement

From the conclusion of the Gaza-Jericho Agreement in May 1994, more than a year passed before the full Interim Agreement was signed. In that year, negotiations were held on the transfer of power to the PNA and continued with the focus on elections and the related military withdrawal from Palestinian cities. In December 1994, Israeli and PLO delegations began meeting in Cairo to negotiate the full interim agreement.

A highly complex system of negotiations evolved in the making of the interim agreement. At the highest level were periodic summits between Arafat and Rabin or Peres. At the next level below them, the JLC was tasked with implementation and dispute resolution responsibilities. The JLC became a critical negotiation forum on several occasions and was led by Shimon Peres on the Israeli side and Abu Mazen (later replaced by Nabil Shaath) on the Palestinian side. Formal negotiation teams were organized around the main interim issues of the elections, the Israeli redeployment, and the transfer of powers to the PNA. The Palestinian negotiators reported directly to the Higher Committee on Negotiations, a PLO body kept separate from the PNA, thus formalizing the PLO's separate existence and management of the peace process. Three additional joint Israeli-Palestinian coordination committees were set up to address civil affairs, security cooperation, and economic cooperation. On the Palestinian side, these negotiators reported to the PNA executive cabinet rather than to the organs of the PLO. All the Israeli negotiators reported to Uri Savir, the director general of the Israeli foreign minister and the chief Israeli negotiator, who answered to Peres and Rabin.

The Nobel Peace Prize was conferred upon Arafat, Rabin, and Peres in Oslo on December 9, 1994, and the three held a four-day-long summit immediately after in Stockholm. Their meetings only highlighted the differences between the two sides on the elections/withdrawal issues. Israel felt compelled to delay its withdrawal until it felt security arrangements were in place and proposed delaying the Palestinian elections for one year, while the PLO insisted on the planned withdrawal. Because open negotiations had failed to resolve this problem, Peres and Arafat jointly decided to have the JLC provide the cover for a back channel that would be led by Savir and Abu Alaa.[22]

The back channel began operation on January 4, 1995. Israeli participants included Joel Singer, Uri Savir, and two IDF generals while the Palestinians sent Abu Alaa, Hassan Asfour, Hassan Abu Libdeh, and Abd al-Razak Yihye, thus mixing new members and veterans of Oslo. These delegations met at the Yamit Hotel in Tel Aviv for two months, without the knowledge of the public, the media, or the front channel negotiators. One of the most innovative outcomes of this back channel was the Palestinian proposal to create joint Palestinian-Israeli security forces in parts of the West Bank and Gaza, in order to create temporary joint responsibility for security and to change the mutually negative perceptions of Israelis and Palestinians.[23]

In January, Rabin began authorizing the confiscation of Palestinian lands to build roads from Jewish settlements in the West Bank directly to Israel so that settlers could bypass Palestinian population centers. A bomb attack against Israelis carried out by Islamic Jihad resulted in Israel imposing a sanction known as "closure" on the Palestinian territories: the total prevention of movement of people, vehicles, and goods. A Rabin-Arafat summit on February 9 highlighted mutually incompatible demands: Israel demanded that the PNA succeed where the IDF and Israeli internal security forces had failed, to prevent terror attacks by cracking down on the PNA's internal opposition as a minimum condition for Israel to continue negotiating the Israeli interim withdrawal. Arafat demanded an end to the closure and the harsh economic effects it had on Palestinians, citing it as a cause of militancy. Despite these setbacks, lower-level talks resulted in agreement on the construction of a commercial seaport in Gaza in February 1995.

A March summit between Arafat and Peres was needed to make progress on the issue of creating Gaza-West Bank "safe passages" and setting limits on the expansion of settlements and the confiscation of land. Israel also agreed to permit limited numbers of Palestinian workers to return to their jobs in Israel. Savir claims that the progress made at the Peres-Arafat summit was largely due to the bargaining completed in the back channel at the Yamit Hotel.[24] The closure remained in place, however, and renewed anti-Israel attacks took place, resulting in further Israeli calls for a PNA crackdown on HAMAS and Jihad. Israeli confiscations of Palestinian land for new highways and roads linking settlements to Israel continued despite the Arafat-Peres understandings.

Rabin persisted in this policy and personally authorized the confiscation of 134 acres of land in East Jerusalem for the construction of new Jewish settlements in April, declaring that the pledge to halt settlements did not apply to Jerusalem. By the end of April, Prime Minister Rabin and the IDF made unilateral announcements of decisions to redeploy Israeli forces from Hebron, Nablus, Ramallah, Tulkarm, and Bethlehem back to bases in Israel. Rabin did not announce a timetable for the redeployments. In May, right-wing opponents of Rabin in an unlikely alliance with Arab members of the Knesset threatened to bring down the government with a no-confidence vote. Rabin temporarily suspended the confiscation of the Jerusalem land to regain the confidence of the Arab legislators, thus preempting the parliamentary measure.

Resistance to the peace process was becoming intense among both Israelis and Palestinians. Doubts arose about the ability of the parties to negotiate a complex interim agreement, much less begin a permanent status negotiation. The population on both sides was not content with the slow pace and elusive gains of the process. Yossi Beilin believed the Interim Agreement might be skipped altogether and that the parties should proceed to the permanent status negotiations.[25]

In May 1995, the parties decided that negotiations on several different interim issues had to proceed in parallel to reach the deadline of July 1. Three sets of open negotiations were set up: in one set of negotiations, the parties worked on the Palestinian elections, while in a second, they worked on the IDF redeployment and the expansion of spheres of self-rule for the Palestinians. The third set was a high-level channel: it consisted of direct negotiation sessions between Arafat and Peres.

This structure did not produce an agreement by the July 1 deadline, and a new structure was put in place, comprising one comprehensive set of negotiations made up of twenty subcommittees supplemented by intensive high-level summits between Arafat and Peres. Peres conceived of the summit level channel to be little more than a cover for a back channel between Abu Alaa and Uri Savir. The back channel met throughout June and focused on details of the interim security arrangements. The back channel continued from where the January talks at the Yamit Hotel had left off.

Also beginning in May, several back channel sessions on the security arrangements were held in Turin, Italy, courtesy of the Italian government and the Fiat company, which provided a private jet to bring the delegations to Italy as well as the facilities for the talks. The parties continued in the back channel in Israel after news about the Italy meetings leaked to the press. Despite severe disagreements on the details of the Israeli withdrawal and the subsequent security arrangements, Abu Alaa and Uri Savir continued to meet in the back channel throughout June, at times without their colleagues. On July 1, Peres and Arafat met to bridge the remaining gaps in the work accomplished in the back channel. The PLO conceded that Israel would retain "overriding" responsibility for security for the interim period in parts of the West Bank in return for Israeli compliance with a firm schedule of redeployments and transfer of territory to Palestinian control.[26]

Peres and Arafat announced on July 4 that they had reached agreement on a two-year phased withdrawal and appointed Abu Alaa and Uri Savir to continue negotiating the details. This arrangement would entail subdividing the West Bank and Gaza into three areas: Areas A, B, and C. Only Area A would be under the full sovereignty of the PNA; in Area B, civil governance responsibilities would be transferred to the PNA with the Israeli and joint patrols handling security. The largest subdivision included all the territory in which little or no Palestinian control could be exercised: Area C. This included Israeli settlements, military bases, and border areas with Jordan and Israel proper as well as other Palestinian territory appropriated for Israeli purposes. In essence, Area C was a continuation of the status quo of the occupation. Palestinian villages, roads, ancestral lands, communal and private land for agriculture, undeveloped land, and important water and other natural resources were also left in the Area C category.

After this announcement the parties decided to remove the talks from the scrutiny of each sides' opposition. Nevertheless, Israeli right-wing protesters located the site of the back channel negotiations at a hotel in the Israeli coastal town of Zichron Yaacov. These negotiation sessions had brought together 150 delegates in four subcommittees operating simultaneously on portions of the draft interim agreement. Talks were moved to two remote locations in order to avoid the scrutiny of Israeli protestors: Ayn Jidi on the Dead Sea shore and the Taba resort in Egypt. Talks were temporarily halted by a Palestinian suicide bombing in Tel Aviv on July 24.

The parties moved negotiations to the Israeli resort Eilat, on the Red Sea, on August 1, 1995. By this time, both sides were integrating into the front channel negotiations all the understandings they had reached in the back channels dealing with interim agreement issues. A preliminary interim agreement was reached by August 11 in Eilat and was initialed by the chief negotiators in the back channels: Abu Alaa and Uri Savir. Together, Areas A and B would include seven major Palestinian cities and 450 villages and refugee camps but initially would amount to less than 30 percent of the West Bank. East Jerusalem was excluded from this arrangement, being reserved as an issue for the permanent status talks. The geographic scope of the interim agreement had to be graphically represented in a series of maps. Israel, the party withdrawing its forces, reserved the right to draft the maps indicating the lines of withdrawal and only revealed the maps to the Palestinian negotiators on September 4. The maps themselves became the subject of intense bargaining throughout September because they provided for isolated enclaves of Palestinian control. At one negotiation session, Peres presented revised maps to Arafat, who walked out of the meeting declaring that the maps depicted a "fig leaf" for the continuation of the occupation.

The comprehensive Interim Agreement was finally initialed on September 24, 1995, even as Israel imposed another closure on the West Bank. The Interim Agreement was signed at a White House ceremony by Arafat and Rabin on September 28. Twenty-six appended maps that detailed the scope of the initial redeployment were initialed behind closed doors. The previous partial agreements on elections, expansion of spheres of authority, and economic cooperation were integrated into the complete agreement.[27] The preamble recommitted the parties to commencing permanent status talks no later than May 4, 1996.

The entire peace process had become known in the international media simply as "Oslo," and this latest agreement became known as "Oslo II," despite having little to do with Norway. The reference was to the secrecy of some of the negotiations that contributed to the agreement and the perception that a new breakthrough had been achieved on the details (as opposed to only the principles) of interim coexistence.

The Palestinian elections provided for in the agreement envisioned the creation of a "Palestinian Council" with legislative powers and incorporating an executive authority. This was to be the body responsible for assuming the different spheres of authority relinquished by the Israeli military government and Civil Administration in Areas A and B of Palestinian territory for the duration of the transitional period.

Implementation on the structured area withdrawal arrangements began on time one month after the signing ceremony. A key provision of the interim agreement concerned the future Israeli withdrawals and transfer of territory to the PNA. Significantly, the agreement set forth a specific timetable for four Israeli redeployments from Palestinian territories: the first redeployment was to be from the major Palestinian population centers ("cities, towns, villages, refugee camps and hamlets")[28] in the West Bank only to facilitate the elections of the president and Palestinian Legislative Council. This was to commence within ten days of the signing of the Interim Agreement and be completed by December 1995. The three additional "further redeployments of Israeli military forces" (Interim Agreement, Ch. 2, Art. X, ¶2) were to take place at six-month intervals after the inauguration of the Palestinian Legislative Council.[29] The location and extent of these three further redeployments (or FRDs, as they came to be known) were not set forth in either the Interim Agreement or its voluminous annexes and appendices, although a map detailing the first redeployment was included.[30] Security cooperation between Israelis and Palestinians, including joint patrols in the West Bank and Gaza, also began pursuant to the agreement. The failure of the parties to negotiate the scope of the FRDs early on, and the failure of Israel to fully implement the FRDs once they were negotiated, would become a causal factor in the breakdown of trust that led up to the complete suspension of the peace process.

At the time of the signing of the Interim Agreement, the PLO (ostensibly with Israel's approval) was encouraging HAMAS to transform itself into a political party and participate in the upcoming electoral process. The HAMAS movement was apparently split between leaders in the West Bank/Gaza and those in the Diaspora, with the latter resisting accommodation with the PNA and refusing to participate in the elections. Within Israel, opposition to the interim agreement had been building throughout the period of negotiation and was evident in demonstrations by settler groups and right-wing parties. Posters of Yitzhak Rabin were circulated in which he was depicted wearing a Nazi uniform. The Likud Party refused to distance itself from this rising tide of rejectionism and, indeed, seemed to take political advantage of this rejection of negotiated settlement in order to increase its own chances of returning to power.

The official cars of Prime Minister Rabin and another of his ministers were attacked by Israeli mobs in the month following the signing of the Interim Agreement. Some of the Israeli negotiators recognized that they had failed to build popular Israeli support for the peace process, as a counterweight to the religious and secular Right. In response to this need, Israeli supporters of the peace process organized a major peace rally on November 4, 1995, in Kings of Israel Square in Tel Aviv. Rabin and Peres, the old Labor Party rivals and now partners in the peace process with the Palestinians, appeared together on the stage singing peace hymns. It marked a turning point for Rabin. He had started his military career as one of David Ben-Gurion's up-and-coming military officers, had been the armed forces chief of staff during the June 1967 War, and become defense minister and prime minister. In 1948, he had used force to expel the civilian population of Ramleh and Lydd, and had formulated the "break bones" policy during the first intifada.[31] The dedicated man of war had now embraced the mission of peace: "Today I believe there is a chance for peace. A good chance. We must take advantage of it for the sake of those who are standing here and for the sake of those who are not standing here. And they are many among our people."[32]

While leaving the rally, Rabin was assassinated by an Israeli law student and member of a settler group that advocated violence against Arabs and opposed to Palestinian autonomy. The assassin, Yigal Allon, shocked Israel's leaders into the recognition that peacemaking was a dangerous undertaking fraught with real dangers from within one's own ranks. Shimon Peres, as acting prime minister, formed a new cabinet in the turbulent days that followed the assassination.

The joint Steering and Monitoring Committee met frequently during the Peres government to negotiate the details and resolve differences in the implementation plans. The Palestinian elections were held on schedule on January 20, 1996, despite the nonparticipation of two secular parties (the Democratic Front for the Liberation of Palestine and the Popular Front for the Liberation of Palestine, DFLP and PFLP) and two religious movements (Islamic Jihad and HAMAS).

Palestinian suicide bombers carried out several attacks at the end of February and beginning of March 1996 following Israel's controversial assassination of an alleged HAMAS bomb maker Yihye Ayyash, also known as "the Engineer." The suicide bombings provoked further right-wing demonstrations against the Peres government in Israel and severely eroded Peres's base of electoral support.

In April 1996, facing an election in May in which small parties would exercise great leverage and trying to manage rumors concerning secret negotiations on the permanent status, Shimon Peres declared that any final settlement would be subject to a public referendum in Israel. By conceding this final veto to the electorate, he hoped to extract both negotiation leverage and political advantage.

The referendum offer was an implicit bargain: he wanted a public mandate to continue the peace process under the tutelage of the Labor Party while gaining votes at the expense of the Likud leader Binyamin Netanyahu, in exchange for reducing the electorate's lack of input into the negotiations processes. In essence, Peres was proposing a strategy for the reduction of the electorate's uncertainty in the outcome of the peace process.

During the same month, two startling revelations were made. First, Yossi Beilin and Abu Mazen admitted having conducted secret talks in order to draft a framework agreement on the *permanent status issues*. Details of the draft agreement had already leaked to the press in February. Beilin and Abu Mazen were operating the so-called Stockholm channel, discussed in the following section of this chapter. Second, settler leaders and PNA officials revealed that they had held ten meetings since June 1995 to discuss possible coexistence arrangements in the permanent status.

The Stockholm Back Channel: Modeling the Endgame

The permanent and interim phases exerted influence on each other. Some on each side feared that the interim arrangements would necessarily predetermine or limit (according to one's preferences for the outcome) the outcome of the permanent settlement. Others believed that the interim stage was too indeterminate, that little trust building could be accomplished in this stage because it was vulnerable to spoilers and because it did not necessarily represent a dramatic change for the Palestinians' living conditions. Yossi Beilin, the Israel's chief proponent of the Oslo back channel, was of the latter camp.

In October 1993, Yossi Beilin attended a meeting of the multilateral talks that were launched at the Madrid Peace Conference two years earlier. Because Tunisia was the host, Beilin decided to take advantage of being there to meet with Yasir Arafat. During a private moment with Arafat, Beilin proposed setting up a nonbinding Israeli-Palestinian dialogue on the permanent status issues in order to demonstrate progress and build public support for the peace process before difficulties arose in the interim stage. Arafat agreed with Beilin on the need for such a dialogue and named Abu Mazen as the likely interlocutor. Beilin notes that he did not inform Peres about this proposal on the assumption that Peres would feel obliged to discuss it with Rabin, and that Rabin in turn would quash the effort.[33]

Beilin did not have to wait long for the interim period crises he feared would undermine support for the peace process among both Palestinians and Israelis. Under the auspices of the Jaffee Center for Strategic Studies at Tel Aviv University and the Economic Cooperation Foundation (the ECF, Beilin's own nonprofit think tank), Beilin organized a series of seminars on aspects of the permanent status issues to "bypass negotiations and look to the end of the process, rather than planning Israel's opening gambits."[34] These seminars took place between April 1994 and May 1995.[35]

Participants believed they were simply conducting an academic exercise that could contribute to the formal, official permanent status talks scheduled to begin in May 1996 and were unaware of Beilin's intention to use the work of the seminars as ideas for his own quasi back channel. Beilin was also looking ahead to the next elections. He believed that his back channel could advance work on the permanent status so that when the formal opening of talks took place, a framework agreement could be almost immediately announced. This would prevent Likud from using a campaign strategy that invoked the fear that Labor would concede all to the PLO.[36] Subsequent events proved Beilin all too prescient.

Starting on September 1, 1994, Beilin sent Yair Hirschfeld and Ron Pundik to Stockholm, where the Swedish government had agreed to host the new back channel. The Palestinian side was also represented by two academics, Ahmed

Khalidi and Hussein Agha. Meetings in Sweden proceeded on a monthly basis. During 1995, Abu Mazen and Yossi Beilin supervised the work of the Stockholm channel, as it came to be known, and the two "supervisors" met in Jerusalem to discuss the progress being made in this effort. The Stockholm channel of 1994 and 1995 was a hybrid of Track II and back channel negotiations. The participation of nonofficials was characteristic of Track II efforts, whereas the supervision of officials such as Abu Mazen and Beilin was more characteristic of a back channel arrangement. Neither Beilin nor Abu Mazen had played a central role in the post-Oslo interim negotiations, and their exclusion brought them together to consider the permanent status issues. The ECF continued to sponsor seminars and debates to generate ideas for the talks between the academics. In June 1995, Faisal al-Husseini joined the Stockholm talks. Nominally a minister in the PNA, al-Husseini was the embodiment of the PLO claim on East Jerusalem as the rightful capital of Palestine and held the PNA ministerial portfolio on East Jerusalem, where he operated a Palestinian political organization known as Orient House. In July 1995, Beilin assumed his new post as minister of economics and planning but changed nothing in the conduct of the Stockholm channel, although his ability to travel abroad without raising eyebrows was curtailed.

From July to October 1995, the academics and political figures who worked with them negotiated the final provisions of the draft Framework for the Conclusion of a Final Status Agreement Between Israel and the Palestine Liberation Organization. At the end of October, the academics reached agreement among themselves and decided to present the final document to their principals, Beilin and Abu Mazen. On October 31, the two sides met in Tel Aviv, and Beilin and Abu Mazen proposed adjustments to the document regarding the few items on which there was disagreement. Once the changes were accepted by the academics, thirteen months of back channel negotiations supplemented by university seminars came to an end. Beilin recorded in his memoirs that "what was deferred in Oslo was the grist of Stockholm." Once the draft was finalized it became "something to be recommended to the higher political echelons . . . Arafat . . . Rabin and Peres."[37] The Stockholm channel participants believed realistically that their document would not be adopted in its entirety by either side, but that at least it might eliminate years of fruitless bargaining. Beilin hoped it could actually be unveiled on the day of the deadline for the initiation of permanent status talks, May 4, 1996, only four days after it was finalized.

Somewhat less realistically, Beilin believed that if Labor were to win the October 1996 elections, the agreement could actually be signed by both parties. Abu Mazen set out to persuade Arafat that the draft was a solid basis for negotiations, and Beilin made plans to show it to Peres and then to Rabin upon his return from an official trip to Washington. While attending an event in his honor at the Israeli consulate in New York, Beilin learned that Rabin had been assassinated. Upon his return, Beilin presented the document to Peres, who was just learning of this channel two years after it was conceived. No move was made to use the document as the formal basis for the permanent status negotiations. Peres first faced an uphill battle against Palestinian and Israeli rejectionists of the peace process and could not prevail at the polls.

The essential terms of the Beilin-Abu Mazen framework agreement demonstrate the impossibility of a negotiated solution without significant concessions from both sides. They also demonstrate remarkable creativity while protecting the core interests of each nation.[38] The back channel nature of the Stockholm channel provided both the opportunity to explore the concessions made and the creativity needed to bridge the gaps. The document provided for the following:

- Israeli recognition of the state of Palestine to be established in most of the West Bank and Gaza by May 5, 1999.
- An extraterritorial passageway between the West Bank and Gaza.
- A three-stage Israeli troop withdrawal to be completed by May 4, 2000.
- A residual Israeli armed force in the Jordan Valley comprising three battalions, three air-defense units, and three early-warning stations, with joint patrols in the Jordan Valley. These measures are to continue until November 2007 but only until Israel concludes peace treaties with other states in the region.
- The deployment of an international observer force in Palestine.
- Unification of Jerusalem under the Joint Higher Municipal Council and two subcouncils to govern Palestinian and Israeli areas; an expansion of the municipal borders of Jerusalem to include Palestinian villages and Israeli settlements; the establishment of two capitals ("al-Quds" and "Yerushalayim") within the undivided city, each under its own sovereignty; the Old City of Jerusalem would enjoy a special status, with the respective submunicipalities governing the affairs of citizens of Palestine and Israel who

reside within the walls; extraterritorial jurisdiction for Palestine on the Haram al-Sharif.

- Right of return of the Palestinian refugees to the state of Palestine, Israel to acknowledge the "suffering caused to the Palestinian people . . . and their right to compensation and rehabilitation for moral and material losses"; some refugees can enter Israel under family reunification provisions (Article VII, ¶2).

Rabin's untimely death just a few days after the finalization of the Stockholm document; the adamant opposition to the peace process of right-wing Israelis and religious Palestinian groups; and Peres's electoral defeat meant that this creative, daring draft was not to be adopted by official, front channel negotiators, although some of its ideas would return in the 2003 Geneva Accord (also a quasi–Track II/back channel effort that is discussed further in chapter 6).

The permanent status talks commenced officially in the front channel at Taba, Egypt, on May 5, 1996, in accordance with the schedule set out in the DoP and the Interim Agreement and on the eve of Israeli elections. There was no evidence that the negotiators considered the Stockholm channel document as a starting point or even as input to their work. With the Israeli elections being held at the end of the month on May 29, the initial meetings did little more than discuss the structure of the negotiation process, including setting up a steering committee and naming working groups. Notably, the joint communiqué released stated that "the steering negotiation group will meet periodically, both formally and informally,"[39] an oblique reference to further use of back channels. Savir notes that he and Abu Alaa agreed that the permanent status talks, if they proceeded, would have to be supplemented by their now institutionalized back channel format.[40]

As Yossi Beilin feared, the events in the interim stage had and would continue to have a profoundly negative effect on the permanent status talks. After the Taba opening sessions, permanent status talks ended abruptly and did not resume until after the defeat of the incoming Likud government.

Likud: Rejectionist Rhetoric and Back Channels

The Israeli elections were held on May 29, 1996. A wave of both Palestinian and Israeli rejectionism of the peace process helped propel the Likud candidate,

Binyamin Netanyahu, to victory. Netanyahu formed a government in coalition with other, smaller right-wing parties and was inaugurated on June 18, 1996. There was little movement on the Palestinian-Israeli peace process until Netanyahu announced the formation of Israeli negotiation teams to address outstanding interim implementation issues in August. The reactivation of the high-level Steering and Monitoring Committee was delayed, but the other joint liaison committees also began work in August.

Nearly from its inauguration, the dual channel approach was adopted by the new government: Netanyahu appointed his personal attorney, Isaac Molho, to be his special envoy to Yasir Arafat, the PNA, and the PLO. Molho was not a formal member of any of Israel's negotiation teams, committees, or working groups but was explicitly instructed by Netanyahu to set up a secret channel with Arafat.[41]

The Interim Agreement signed by the PLO and the previous Israeli government provided for the IDF's "further redeployments" (FRDs) from seven Palestinian cities. The redeployment from Hebron was to take place in accordance with a detailed provision of the Interim Agreement[42] on March 28, 1996, under Shimon Peres's caretaker government. Peres suspended redeployment until after the elections because of suicide bombings in Israel. The Netanyahu government took no action to withdraw either, guaranteeing that the parties would renegotiate the circumstances of withdrawal from Hebron. Later in June, Netanyahu declared invalid the once-secret side letter to Norwegian prime minister Holst from Shimon Peres that accompanied the Oslo Accords and in which Israel committed itself to preserving Palestinian institutions in Jerusalem.

Instead of implementing the Interim Agreement, the Netanyahu government proposed that the Palestinians accept a new arrangement on Hebron in which Israel would be free to strengthen the settlement in the midst of the city and avoid substantial redeployment. The issue quickly became the subject of international attention because of Kiryat Arba, the large militant settlement that had been built on Hebron land, and the small number of settlers that had occupied homes in the center of Old Hebron, necessitating the presence of large numbers of IDF troops in the middle of the town. Additionally, Israeli troops had closed the main road in Hebron, al-Shuhada Street, to Palestinian traffic. Israel wanted to retain sole control for security in Hebron and also wanted to place limits on the type of armament that Palestinian security forces could carry. Another point of contention was that Netanyahu's government sought the PLO's consent to give the Israeli security forces "hot pursuit" rights, that is, the ability to pursue Palestinians into Area A. A final point of contention was the ongoing detention of thousands of Palestinians in Israeli jails, a subject that negotiators had dealt with in prior agreements.

The Norwegian social scientist who had been so instrumental in the Oslo Accords, Terje Rød Larsen, had by then become UN special coordinator for the occupied territories and in this capacity facilitated two weeks of secret talks at the end of August between Netanyahu and Arafat's envoys. Larsen's goals were modest: simply to identify outstanding matters to be discussed in the Palestinian Israeli Steering and Monitoring Committee (PISMC). This negotiation group was headed by Saeb Eraqat and Lieutenant General Dan Shomron, but managed to meet only once before a crisis erupted in September.

The date for the first of three stipulated Israeli redeployments, September 7, 1996, came without Israel identifying regions from where it would remove troops and hand over security responsibility to the PNA. The closure continued while Netanyahu's new minister of infrastructure, the former general and defense minister who had presided over the disastrous 1982 invasion of Lebanon, Ariel Sharon, worked on plans to expand Israeli settlements in the West Bank (including East Jerusalem) and Gaza.

The September 24 opening and completion of a long-disputed tunnel underneath the Haram al-Sharif/Temple Mount became imbued with political significance when Netanyahu stated that his purpose was to assert Israeli dominance and sovereignty in East Jerusalem. This action (the "tunnel incident") ignited an already tense situation caused by the closures and lack of progress on the peace process. Intense protest and rioting by the Palestinians ensued for two days and spread throughout the West Bank and Gaza. Defense minister Yitzhak Mordechai authorized the use of live ammunition, tanks, and helicopter gunships to put down the clashes. Security cooperation between Israeli and Palestinian officers, a major component of the Interim Agreement, helped control the situation in parts of the West Bank and by keeping soldiers and civilians apart; but elsewhere, Palestinian police returned fire against the Israeli forces when the latter fired on Palestinian civilians, thus outlining the hard limits of security cooperation.

The United States government immediately prepared a two-day summit meeting in Washington while the clashes continued in the West Bank and Gaza. Netanyahu and Arafat met privately during the summit held October 1 and 2, but they made no breakthroughs. Their major achievement was to agree on holding further negotiations on all issues in dispute. This was hardly an accomplishment, considering that their new goal was to have more negotiations rather than fulfill past commitments. U.S. envoy Dennis Ross credits himself for the idea of the emergency summit and blames "Bibi" for its failure to produce any substantive goals, specifically, his complete unwillingness to make any concessions while at the summit. This was the prelude to a change of role for Ross; from that point on, he believed "was to become a full-time mediator."[43]

The parties reopened negotiations at Erez Checkpoint on the Gaza-Israel border on October 6 but decided to move their meetings to Eilat and Taba and close them to the media beginning October 14. U.S. envoy Dennis Ross acted as intermediary between Arafat and Netanyahu, conveying messages and proposals, while the high-level PISMC held its oversight meetings in Jerusalem and Tel Aviv. The delegations formed three subcommittees to address Hebron arrangements, security issues such as the closures, and economic issues. By the end of October, the parties decided to shift the center of negotiation to "back room talks": quiet third-party shuttle diplomacy exercised by Dennis Ross. The key sticking point tackled by Ross was Netanyahu's refusal to comply with the Interim Agreement provisions on withdrawal from Hebron as well as the FRDs.

Netanyahu accused the PNA of inciting the protests following the tunnel incident and therefore not complying with the Interim Agreement. For Israel, the Interim Agreement needed to be renegotiated to further improve security for settlers while thousands of houses and apartments were being constructed in the existing settlements. During the final three months of the year, minister of infrastructure Ariel Sharon announced the construction of several entirely new settlements even as this critical phase of negotiations was underway.

Major General Oren Shahor, who had been heading the Hebron talks for Israel, was removed by Netanyahu and accused of meeting privately with PNA officials, as well as passing information on the negotiations to former prime minister Shimon Peres of Labor in November 1997. This was a sign of political tension within the Netanyahu government and also demonstrated the extent that party politics permeate negotiation dynamics in Israel. Shahor's secret meetings with PNA officials during the period of negotiations indicate a quasi–back channel initiative undertaken by one of the official front channel negotiators.

In order to increase momentum in their negotiations, in mid-November the parties raised the level of authority in the Hebron talks by appointing IDF chief of staff General Shahak and the head of the PLO's Negotiation Affairs director-ate Abu Mazen to head their respective delegations on the Hebron redeployment issue. At the beginning of December, Palestinian and Israeli security officials established a hotline to enable them to communicate directly in emergencies.

At the end of November, Arafat himself met with several leaders of the settler movement to discuss cooperative actions as well as the possibility of joint busi-ness arrangements. These remarkable meetings were supposed to be kept secret, but they were reported in the Palestinian media and hinted at the potential for official Palestinian tolerance of the settlements within Palestinian territory in a future permanent arrangement between the PLO and Israel.

At the end of December 1996, Netanyahu's envoy to Arafat, Isaac Molho, met with Arafat and Saeb Eraqat after Netanyahu announced plans to restore large subsidies for settlers. President Clinton made a public statement criticiz-ing moves to expand the settlements and subsidize settlers. Netanyahu publicly rejected Clinton's remarks and vowed to strengthen the settlements. Clinton and Netanyahu's public exchange of remarks indicated a remarkable degree of ten-sion between the governments of the United States and Israel. Israel was sending a signal about the limits of its tolerance for pressure from the United States in the context of the peace process.

Despite this bilateral tension, by the end of December, the United States was visibly trying to act as mediator and made no effort to maintain a low profile.[44] U.S. ambassador to Israel Martin Indyk proposed a new document embodying agreements reached so far on the outstanding issues in dispute and proposing a timetable for Israel to comply with the redeployment commitments of the Interim Agreement. The timetable for withdrawal also drew a public rejection by Netanyahu. On December 24, 1996, and January 5, 1997, Arafat and Netanyahu held summit meetings at Erez Crossing in an attempt to close the remaining gaps on a new accord for Hebron.

As 1996 drew to a close, the political organization representing the settler movement, YESHA, announced the conditions under which it would end its sup-port for Netanyahu's government, despite months of regular meetings between Netanyahu and settler groups, as well as implementation of pro-settlement poli-cies. YESHA's conditions included the failure to complete construction of new settlements in East Jerusalem and Hebron, as well as the withdrawal of the IDF from parts of Area C (the scheduled redeployments anticipated in the Interim

Agreement). In other words, YESHA conditioned its further support for Netan-yahu on his noncompliance with the prior arrangements made with the Palestin-ians, and perhaps more damaging to Netanyahu, on his avoidance of any *new* negotiated agreements with the PLO. Although negotiators often point to limita-tions on their authority as a tactic to minimize their ability to make concessions, YESHA's limits encroached on Netanyahu's political survival.

The new accords included the Hebron Protocol, a Note for the Record sub-mitted by the United States, and an Agreed Minute; they gave Israel ten days to redeploy from 80 percent of Hebron (Area H1) into an Israeli-controlled sec-tor (H2) and to turn over to the PNA all civil governance responsibilities in the new, reduced Palestinian area of Hebron.[45] Joint mobile units were to operate from H2 and both sides would bear the same kinds of arms. Since Israeli legal experts had expressed the opinion that Israel's security forces could enter Area A if they wished, Israel no longer insisted on consent from the PNA for "hot pursuit" rights. Al-Shuhada Street and the Palestinian marketplace were to be reopened, and the United States committed itself to renovate the street through the U.S. Agency for International Development. The PNA would also have to consult the Israelis concerning construction of new Palestinian buildings from which Netanyahu feared the settlers could be attacked.

The Note for the Record, one of the documents within the accords on Hebron, set out what Dennis Ross saw as the unfulfilled obligations of the Interim Agree-ment and listed them as either items to be simply implemented or items subject to further negotiation, despite all of them having been negotiated and agreed previously. As to implementation, Israel was to carry out the long-delayed first stage of FRD during the first week of March 1997 (and thus trigger the time-table for the remaining two FRDs) and release Palestinian prisoners in accor-dance with Annex VII to the Interim Agreement. The PLO was to complete the revision of the Palestinian National Charter, prevent violent protest, fight ter-rorism, limit the number of Palestinian security forces, and keep official PNA offices only in areas agreed upon with Israel (to prevent the PNA from operat-ing in Jerusalem and supporting Palestinian claims there). The items for further negotiation included financial affairs, economic cooperation, the construction of the Gaza seaport and airport, and the safe passageways (that had not yet been opened), among others. Several joint subcommittees were set up to negotiate on one agenda item each and to work in parallel with each other. Both parties were also to resume the stalled permanent status talks within two months of imple-mentation of the Hebron Protocol (March 1997). In January 1997, Isaac Molho was appointed to head the Israeli permanent status delegation.

The lack of Israeli implementation of the FRDs continued to bedevil the peace process even after the Hebron Protocol was signed. In February, Israel's foreign minister David Levy asserted that the redeployments were unilateral Israeli decisions, not subject to negotiation or consultation with the Palestin-ians. This posture on the three remaining stages of troop withdrawal served to underline the fundamental difference between the PLO and the Netanyahu gov-ernment's strategic goals. The former insisted on the return of the entire West Bank and Gaza. Netanyahu, on the other hand, spoke in terms of retaining large portions of Palestinian territory in any permanent status arrangement, avoiding a return to the pre-June 1967 lines and preventing the emergence of a Palestinian state.[46] He therefore wished to avoid or at least delay the FRDs so as to minimize the transfer of territory to PNA control during the interim period.

The ink had barely dried on the Hebron Protocol when the Netanyahu gov-ernment announced on February 19 its intention to build 6,500 housing units on one of the last undeveloped tracts of land in East Jerusalem, known as Jabal Abu Ghunaym in Arabic and Har Homa in Hebrew. Within a month of the announce-ment, the site became the scene of daily protests and clashes between protesters and Israeli troops.

The controversy coincided with the Netanyahu cabinet's March 6 decision to limit its first phase of redeployment to an area comprising 9 percent of the West Bank, 7 percent of which was already under joint control (Area B). The new Area A would increase to approximately 9 percent of the West Bank. The areas to be transferred would be noncontiguous, and Israel would control major transporta-tion routes, territory adjacent to settlements, and other large strategic tracts, such as the corridor east of Jerusalem dividing the northern and southern halves of the West Bank. The PLO informed the Israeli government of its "nonacceptance" of this unilateral determination, and Israel indicated it would not turn over the territory if the PLO declined to accept it. The PLO suspended negotiations with Israel on March 9 because of Netanyahu's refusal to reverse the Har Homa settle-ment and the refusal to negotiate the redeployment map.

This suspension of acknowledged negotiations marked the commencement of an eighteen-month period in which there was little or no *discernible* progress on the implementation of the Interim Agreement. Third parties such as the United States and Egypt attempted to wrestle the parties back to the table without success.

In February and March, Arafat convened a meeting of the Palestinian secular and religious nationalist groups that had rejected the peace process in order to build consensus on the permanent status issues and to brief them on the FRD dispute. The PLO desired to reconstruct national unity and heal the rift among secular and religious nationalist groups in an effort to undermine the militant wings and violent actions of those groups. But doing so risked accusations by the Israeli government that the PLO was not doing enough to eradicate these organizations and to stop violence against Israelis.

In fact, Israel accused Arafat of encouraging terrorism by holding talks with the rejectionists. Arafat's crackdown on HAMAS and Jihad after a March 21 suicide bombing led the Israelis to suspend their participation in the dialogue with the PNA and only complicated the fragile Palestinian-Israeli consensus on the peace process. The Israeli government had spent political capital repudiating the Oslo Accords and the Interim Agreement, and it now found itself seeking a way to escape its commitments under those agreements (by then embodied in the Hebron Accords) in order to appease the religious and secular Right that had brought Netanyahu to power. Appeasing the religious Right meant that Israel would either delay or simply not implement its obligations under those agreements. But such a choice would encourage Palestinian protest and the conditions under which terrorism flourishes and paradoxically create new insecurity for Israelis.

In this dilemma, Netanyahu resorted to direct and secret negotiations with the PLO as a way of making progress with the Palestinians while presenting a public posture of implacable hostility toward them.

At the end of April and the beginning of May 1997, Yossi Beilin of Labor, at that moment a member of the Knesset opposition, met with Arafat to propose his own five-point plan for restarting talks and set off to Egypt and Jordan to build support for his plan, despite Netanyahu's denunciation of the Beilin initiatives. March 17, the date the Hebron Accords had set for resumption of the permanent status talks, passed without action because of the continuing controversy over Har Homa and the unimplemented FRD. Beilin, at that point, can be said to have been acting in a quasi–mediator role.

Egypt tried to assume the role of third-party intervener after the failure of a regional mission by Dennis Ross in May. Egyptian president Hosni Mubarak succeeded only in obtaining a one-day delay in the demolition of Palestinian homes at Jabal Abu Ghunaym/Har Homa and came away with no other gains. The U.S. Congress passed a resolution on June 10 calling on the Clinton administration to move the U.S. embassy to Jerusalem, a move resisted by all American governments since the occupation and annexation of East Jerusalem. Clashes between Palestinian protesters and Israeli forces grew in intensity throughout June while the Israeli press described Netanyahu's plans for a permanent settlement as "Allon plus." (The term "plus" referred to Israeli territorial gains, not Palestinian ones. The return of land to the Palestinians would be even less than anticipated in the 1968 Allon Plan for partition of the West Bank.)

The volatility of Israeli politics during the years of the peace process meant that no single Israeli party could determine the direction of the process and also that neither of the main parties would tolerate being excluded from the process. With this in mind, the PLO and the Labor Party (by this time headed by retired general and former IDF chief of staff Ehud Barak) set up a joint committee at the end of July to discuss negotiation positions.

In late July, Netanyahu called on American Jewish leaders to constrain the Clinton administration's attempts to pressure Israel on settlements and FRD compliance. Suicide bombs killed fourteen Israelis and wounded over 170 Israelis and Palestinians on July 30 in a Jerusalem market. After the bombings, negotiations were again suspended and Israel imposed an extremely severe closure within the Palestinian areas and between them and Israel, Jordan, and Egypt. U.S. initiatives in July and August focused on getting the Central Intelligence Agency involved in security cooperation between Israel and the PNA.

A new round of suicide bomb attacks on September 4 led to more closures and led Israel to declare that it would no longer be bound by any of its agreements with the PLO. Israel depicted the bombings as a PLO violation of the accords despite being actions committed by parties that were never a part of the PLO. U.S. secretary of state Madeleine Albright issued a straightforward call to Israel to refrain from provocative actions such as expansion or construction of settlements. Netanyahu, in response, pledged to continue settlement activity.

The United States persuaded both sides to attend high-level meetings in Washington in late October and early November to encourage the implementation of the

FRDs and discourage "unilateral" actions (creation of new settlements or expansion of existing ones). The Israeli cabinet at first would not give foreign minister David Levy a clear negotiating mandate for the Washington talks. When he finally obtained instructions, he found his authority to negotiate highly circumscribed. The Israeli delegation was empowered only to discuss the implementation issues pending from the Interim Agreement rather than the scope and timing of FRDs, which were precisely what the Palestinian team wanted to discuss during the Washington meetings from November 3 to 6, 1997. Predictably, no progress was made at these meetings. Netanyahu proposed eliminating the interim phase and jumping directly to the permanent status negotiations. The Palestinians wanted the full implementation and completion of the Interim Agreement provisions. The U.S. mediation team proposed doing both: going forward with implementation and renegotiation of the outstanding Interim Agreement provisions while conducting the permanent status negotiations in parallel to the implementation of the FRDs.

At the end of 1997, the Israeli government drew up two competing permanent status plans under which Israel would retain either 52 percent or 64 percent of the West Bank. The plans were proposed by Defense Minister Mordechai and Infrastructure Minister Sharon, respectively. Netanyahu refused to advance any proposals for FRDs to the PLO, preferring to only discuss another list of conditions with which he wanted the PLO to comply.

Clinton publicly called on Israel to redeploy from 10 percent to 15 percent of Area C just prior to his scheduled end-of-year meetings with Arafat and Netanyahu. The Netanyahu government announced a plan that contemplated a single 6 percent to 8 percent redeployment without indication of whether Area C or Area B would be involved. This proposal was too meager for the PLO and the United States but considered too generous by the Israeli settlers, who protested the fact that Netanyahu's government considering any redeployment at all.

Foreign Minister Levy did not enjoy great autonomy during his time under Netanyahu. He resigned as foreign minister in January 1998, before the end of his ministerial tenure. The Netanyahu cabinet, composed of coalition allies, imposed restrictions on the scope of redeployment, conditioning any redeployment at all on PLO compliance with a growing list of demands mostly concerned with fighting terrorism. At the same time, the Israeli cabinet approved ambitious new plans in 1998 to expand the settlements. The announcements coincided with the arrival of Dennis Ross in the region.

At the end of 1997, Clinton secretly proposed his own redeployment plan for the purpose of restarting the final status talks, entitled "The American Initiative for Reviving the Oslo Process, December 1997."[47] In place of the first two of the Interim Agreement's three FRDs, the U.S. proposal proposed three FRD mini stages, each tied to specific joint and unilateral Palestinian, Israeli, and U.S. actions on security issues, Israeli constraint on settlements, and land seizures for bypass roads and demolitions of Palestinian homes. The proposal envisioned direct U.S. mediation between Palestinians and Israelis in order to agree on the third and final FRD. The percentages of land to be transferred from Israeli to Palestinian (or joint) control were eventually carried over intact into the Wye River Memorandum, which is discussed in the following text.

Neither Arafat nor Netanyahu wholeheartedly accepted the Clinton proposals, even after they were modified in February meetings in Washington with Israeli and Palestinian envoys.

Quieter diplomatic initiatives directly between Israeli and PLO officials—back channel negotiations between Molho and Abu Mazen—followed the consultations with the Clinton administration, which by then was preoccupied with a crisis in the Persian Gulf and new air strikes against Iraq. The United States' position on the FRD was that the three ministages of the FRD would be contingent on the PLO taking anti-incitement and antiterrorism measures, annulling the Palestine National Charter, and extraditing Palestinian suspects to Israel, among other conditions. Under the March 1998 Clinton proposal, a total of 13.1 percent of the West Bank Area C would be covered by the FRD. Netanyahu continued to resist any pressure from the United States to predetermine the amount of territory transferred.

Back channel talks between the Israeli government and the PLO were continuing at this time. In March, settler-initiated violence toward Palestinians sparked riots in Hebron, and a bomb was planted outside the al-Aqsa Mosque in Jerusalem, wounding people as they left prayer services. In April, Netanyahu expressed a willingness to transfer 9 percent in this second FRD plus 2 percent to cover the first FRD that was never implemented, but he found Madeleine Albright firmly fixed on the 13.1 percent figure. This 13.1 percent referred only to the transfer of Area C territory (sole Israeli control) to the status of Area B and Area A (joint or sole Palestinian control, respectively). Furthermore, Albright held a press conference in which she directly accused Netanyahu of impeding progress on the Clinton proposal, which had been accepted by Arafat. She also asserted that, contrary to Netanyahu's declarations, the 13.1 percent transfer would not endanger Israel's security.

Albright publicly summoned the parties to a Washington summit scheduled for May 11, 1998. The condition for attendance was explicit acceptance of the 13.1 percent FRD and an immediate commencement of the final status talks at the May 11 meeting. Netanyahu actively resisted the pressure he was getting from the third party whose favor and support he most desired, and Clinton canceled the May 11 summit. Further meetings between Albright and Netanyahu resulted in no progress but prompted President Clinton to openly criticize delaying tactics without mentioning Netanyahu by name.

With no progress on either the FRD or on the implementation of less-controversial provisions of the Interim Agreement—as well as ongoing clashes between Palestinians and Israeli forces, suicide bombings, confiscations of land, demolitions of homes, expanding settlements, and the revocation of Jerusalem residency rights of East Jerusalem Palestinians who had U.S. residency—the peace process appeared to have died an agonizing death by mid-1998, for all intents and purposes. Behind the scenes, however, Isaac Molho and Abu Alaa, who had become the speaker of the Palestinian legislature (the Palestinian Legislative Council, or PLC) were holding meetings. While to the public it appeared that no negotiations were taking place, Molho and Abu Alaa had begun conducting back channel sessions. They discussed two modifications to the FRD proposal that might make it palatable enough to both parties so that it could be implemented. First was the creation of a fourth category of territory in the West Bank, Area D, which could be transferred to Palestinian control in little more than name. No housing development or security responsibilities for Palestinians were to be permitted in the new area. The second modification concerned a higher number for the overall FRD: 15 percent.

Between May and July, Netanyahu initiated secret talks with the leader of the opposition Labor Party chairman, Ehud Barak, to explore the eventuality of structuring of a Labor-Likud unity government and the strategies such a government would pursue in the negotiations with the PLO and Syria. Relations with the opposition did not improve despite this example of what might be called "internal back channel negotiation." Nevertheless, Netanyahu was correct to anticipate the need for support from the opposition because his natural constituencies and right-wing allies denied his cabinet any flexibility in the peace process.

In June, Netanyahu explored but eventually discarded the idea of subjecting the FRD to a national referendum. Although this would evidently cause significant delay, Netanyahu shared concerns similar to those of Shimon Peres when the latter offered to submit any permanent status agreement to referendum prior to losing the national elections. The underlying concern was to carve out negotiating "space" while appearing to minimize risks of such negotiation as perceived by the electorate and politically mobilized subgroups. Netanyahu was concerned, as was Peres before him, about losing the political support of the religious and settler groups. During the summer of 1998, the United States withdrew from its highly visible role in the FRD controversy and even declined to send Dennis Ross to the region at Israel's request. The idea of a new territorial category took on importance in the back channel as the parties began to bargain, not over whether to accept this modification, but over how much Palestinian control could be exerted under the new territorial classification.

Molho continued to meet secretly with Abu Alaa and Arafat while Abu Alaa held at least four meetings with Netanyahu in August 1998. The parties quietly informed the United States of having made progress, prompting a regional visit by Dennis Ross and an invitation to Arafat and Netanyahu to meet with Clinton on September 28. A 13 percent figure for the FRD was agreed upon, but the PLO's reciprocal obligations were not yet settled. Clinton scheduled further talks at the Wye River Plantation in Maryland later in the year. Ariel Sharon was given the job of chief negotiator for the upcoming Wye negotiations and was also named minister of foreign affairs. Settlement expansion proceeded aggressively in August and September, and settler violence so significantly increased throughout the West Bank that the IDF sent troops to halt settler attacks in Hebron.

During the Netanyahu years prior to the Wye summit, there had been no implementation of the Israeli FRD obligations under the Interim Agreement. The parties sent their delegations to the White House on October 15, 1998, for the opening ceremony of the Wye negotiations and then secluded themselves for nine days at the Wye Plantation under a media blackout that was leaky at best. Settler leaders arrived to meet with Israeli negotiators at Wye on the sidelines of the talks in spite of U.S. efforts to seclude the parties. Halfway through the summit, Netanyahu suspended his delegation's official involvement in the negotiations to protest a grenade attack at a bus stop in Israel. President Clinton and King Hussein of Jordan reentered the talks to apply pressure on both parties. On October 21, the Israeli delegation announced its intention to leave talks if Arafat did not accept Netanyahu's demands on Israeli security. In the absence of any U.S. support for his position, Netanyahu backed down from his threat to leave. An agreement, known as the Wye River Memorandum, was finally reached in the early morning of October 23, 1998.[48]

Upon the signing of the Wye River Memorandum, the United States, for the first time, choose to take an active part in the *implementation* of the agreement by committing the CIA to assist the Palestinian security forces with the prevention of terrorist actions and the prosecution of organizations that instigated them. The agreement provided for the formation of a Palestinian-United States security committee, as well as a Palestinian-Israeli security committee. Seven years earlier, in contrast, Secretary of State James Baker had convened the parties at the Madrid Peace Conference without getting the United States involved in the substance of the ensuing negotiations. Now President Clinton himself was acting as a mediator.

On the day the agreement was reached, Netanyahu overplayed his hand. In trying to appease domestic constituencies who would oppose the agreement, he informed Clinton that he would not attend the signing ceremony unless the United States freed convicted spy Jonathan Pollard, a civilian employee of the U.S. Navy who had sold military secrets to Israel. Clinton offered only to "review" the Pollard case.

The Wye River Memorandum obligated the parties to meet a set of requirements relating to the three FRD mini stages (which would substitute for the Interim Agreement's first two FRDs) and Palestinian security cooperation according to a twelve-week timetable. In return for concrete steps the Palestinians were to take against militants opposed to the peace process, Israel would fulfill the first two of the Interim Agreement's FRDs (in three mini stages) by turning over a total of 13 percent of the West Bank Area C to the Palestinians. One percent of this would be reclassified as Area A. The remaining 12 percent should have become Area B and was to include a 3 percent portion to be classified as "nature reserves" on which the Palestinians could not build or otherwise develop. Additionally, 14.2 percent of Area B was to become Area A.

Upon completion of the FRDs, the Palestinians hoped to control nearly 40 percent of the West Bank and govern most Palestinians living in the West Bank and Gaza. But the map would not provide a clean line of separation between

Palestinians and settlers, who were interspersed among the Palestinian areas. See table 5 for the Wye River Memorandum's renegotiated breakdown of the FRDs. The entire transfer of territory was to proceed in three stages and take no more than twelve weeks to accomplish. The PLO was also to publicly void portions of the Palestine National Charter and both parties pledged to resume permanent status negotiations immediately.[49]

Upon his return to Israel, Netanyahu delayed cabinet consideration of the Wye River Memorandum. The agreement was eventually approved by the Knesset and the Israeli cabinet but without the support of key coalition members. His government aggressively resumed settlement expansion, demolitions of Palestinian homes, and military confrontations with Palestinians whether civilians or militants. Arafat warned that he would declare the independent state of Palestine on May 4, 1999, when the interim arrangements were to expire. In November, immediately after the first stage of the territorial handover, Israel's foreign minister Ariel Sharon called upon Israelis to "grab" new land in the Palestinian territories because "whatever isn't seized will end up in their hands,"[50] provoking the creation of several new settlements in the West Bank.

The permanent status negotiations were not restarted despite one preliminary meeting between Sharon (who was busy trying to create new settlements)

Table 5. Agreed Further Redeployments (FRDs) from Wye River Memorandum, 1998

FRD from	Area C to B	Area B to A	Area C to A	Stage subtotal	Implemented?
Stage 1 (within 2 weeks of entry into force of agreement)	2%	7.1%	—	9.1%	Yes, 11/20/98
Stage 2 (between weeks 2 and 6)	5%	—	—	5%	No
Stage 3 (between weeks 6 and 12)	5%	7.1%	1%	13.1%	No
Category total	12%	14.2%	1%	27.2%	

Source: Wye River Memorandum Timetable

and Abu Mazen on November 18, 1998. Two days later, on November 20, 1998, Israel carried out the first of the three new mini FRDs. With the two remaining mini stages of the Wye FRD already delayed, Netanyahu formally declared a freeze on implementation of the Wye River Memorandum on December 2, 1998, and presented a list of demands that the PLO and PNA had to comply with to renew implementation.[51]

In contrast with Netanyahu's nonimplementation tactics, the PLO immediately began fulfilling its commitments under Wye. In the presence of President Clinton, the Palestine National Council convened in Gaza on December 14 to affirm a letter that revoked clauses of the National Charter that contradicted coexistence with Israel. Despite fulfilling this key condition for the second stage of the FRD, Netanyahu insisted he would not carry out any further FRD activity.

Stages 2 and 3 of the Wye River Memorandum's mini FRD provisions were not carried out during the Netanyahu government because of its unilateral noncompliance. They were renegotiated into three new mini stages in the later Sharm el-Sheikh Memorandum (PLO-Israel), concluded in Egypt on September 4, 1999. These new FRD measures were supposed to be implemented by Netanyahu's successor, prime minister Ehud Barak, by January 20, 2000, but this deadline too was honored in the breach.

The statements by Sharon and Netanyahu on noncompliance and exhortations to the settlers to seize Palestinian land and the statements by Arafat on unilateral declarations of a Palestinian state were at least partly designed for public consumption, to project a tough image to their constituents. On the Palestinian side, they reflected the PLO's understanding of the peace process as a negotiation that was to lead to an independent state of Palestine within the time frame fixed by the accords (May 1999). The failure of the negotiations did not, in the PLO perspective, qualify as sufficient reason to indefinitely defer the declaration of the state within the 1967 borders.

As for Israel, these moves were not enough to appease Netanyahu's right-wing supporters, who now quickly turned on him. The Knesset scheduled a vote on a no-confidence motion against the Netanyahu government for December 9, 1998, but postponed it until December 21, after the scheduled date of the second stage of the Wye FRD (December 18) and to accommodate President Clinton's visit to the region (December 12 to 15). On the day of the Knesset vote, Netanyahu preempted the no-confidence motion by signing a bill permitting early elections to take place on May 17, 1999, after the scheduled expiration date of the interim period (May 4, 1999).

The Clinton administration was by December 1998 fully preoccupied with the impeachment proceedings that led up to the U.S. Senate trial of the president. In December 1998, Saudi dissident Osama bin Laden resurfaced with an acknowledgement that he had "instigated" the August 1998 attacks on the U.S. Embassies in Tanzania and Kenya. Almost as soon as President Clinton had returned from his December trip to the Middle East, he ordered the controversial Operation Desert Fox against Iraq for that country's alleged interference with the UNSCOM inspection mission. On February 12, 1999, President Clinton's Senate impeachment trial resulted in his acquittal.

During the lame-duck remainder of the Netanyahu government, no progress was made on either the implementation of the Interim Agreement or the Wye River Memorandum, whose final deadline passed on January 29, 1999. On January 17, 1999, despite the impeachment proceedings, the United States invited the PLO and the Israelis to come to Washington to revive the implementation of the Wye River Memorandum. The PLO accepted right away, but Israel did not respond until Foreign Minister Sharon declined the invitation on January 24. As the Israeli commitment to the Wye River Memorandum's provisions faded away and the expiration date of the interim period (May 4, 1999) approached, Arafat began declaring that he would consider a unilateral declaration of sovereignty of the Palestinian state. In March he began a world tour to sound out the depth and breadth of international support for such a unilateral declaration in the absence of any negotiations with Israel on the terms of the permanent settlement.

As Arafat began his global diplomacy, the United States was leading NATO into an armed confrontation with Yugoslavia over its massive human rights abuses in Kosovo. "Operation Allied Force" began on March 24, 1999. Russia remained opposed to the NATO strike, and Israel gave Russia some diplomatic support for its stance, which helped to greatly alienate the U.S. government from Israel. In exchange for a decision to defer the unilateral declaration (which in any case had already been made in 1988), Palestinian negotiators Abu Mazen and Saeb Eraqat negotiated the text of an April 26, 1999, Letter of Assurances from President Clinton to President Arafat.[52] The letter affirmed Palestinian compliance and Israeli noncompliance of the Wye commitments and stated that "we support the aspirations of the Palestinian people to determine their own future on their own land."

Clinton urged reinvigorated permanent status negotiations and offered to help launch and facilitate them once a new Israeli government was in place. The Clinton letter mirrored a declaration from the European Union on the Middle East Peace Process, issued March 25, 1999, that reaffirmed "the continued and unqualified Palestinian right to self-determination, including the option of a state."[53] The PLO Central Council (PCC), with the documents from Clinton and the European Union in front of them, voted to delay a unilateral declaration of statehood until June 1999, when the Israeli elections had been completed.

In the aftermath of the Wye River Memorandum, the Israeli governing coalition began crumbling in the face of challenges from the center and right of Likud. Netanyahu dismissed Yitzhak Mordechai as defense minister in anticipation of Mordechai's bid to create a centrist political party that would challenge Netanyahu. Former IDF chief of staff and the chief negotiator of the Interim Agreement's FRD provisions, General Amnon Lipkin-Shahak, also called for an end to the Likud government. Both soldiers criticized the freeze on implementation of the Wye River Memorandum. On the right, prominent Likud Party members such as Yitzhak Shamir and Binyamin Begin (son of former prime minister Menachem Begin) defected in order to form their own smaller and more militant parties.

Despite Netanyahu's explicit commitments to President Clinton at the Wye summit on halting settlement expansion, approximately twenty-five new settlements were created between the end of the summit and the dissolution of the Netanyahu government. May 4, 1999, marked the official end of the interim period contemplated in the early accords, but no tangible progress toward peace had been achieved. Former defense minister Yitzhak Mordechai's newly formed Center Party and Binyamin Begin's Herut Party withdrew from the Israeli elections just one day before the May 18 ballot, but this could not stop former IDF chief of staff Ehud Barak from winning with 56.1 percent of the popular vote. By June 7, a new Israeli parliament was sworn in; but it would not be until July 6 that Prime Minister elect Barak succeeded in forming his seven-party coalition government, without Likud. Ariel Sharon had pulled out of coalition talks with Barak claiming that Barak would not be sufficiently committed to settlements.

Netanyahu did nothing to advance the peace process while he also failed to make a qualitative change to Israel's security. In choosing not to implement the existent Interim Agreement, Netanyahu was obliged to renegotiate their outstanding provisions. Although this gained him some tactical points regarding

PLO concessions on security cooperation, the simple act of negotiation and the simple commitment to comply with the Hebron and Wye Accords cost Netanyahu the support of the settlers and the right-wing political groups that formed the core of his coalition. This simply slowed the interim peace process to a crawl, and because security cooperation was a critical component of the interim peace process, he damaged Israel's security and inflamed militancy on both sides.

The logical consequence of this was to completely undermine the premise of the entire peace process. There was little or no trust left for permanent status talks to begin. Neither party was able to proceed with the permanent status talks, in large part because of the implementation failures at the interim stage. Netanyahu claimed to have introduced the concept of "reciprocity" in both the Hebron and Wye Accords and cited this repeatedly as one of the most significant changes he introduced to the peace process. His interpretation of reciprocity, however, was a constructed one that twisted the actual meaning of the word. Molho accuses the Clinton administration of failing to understand the Netanyahu conception of reciprocity when it urged Israel to carry out its obligations under the Wye River Memorandum. "Israel didn't have to comply with any of the agreement as long as the Palestinians didn't comply with a part of it. Everyone understood this. Absolutely." [54]

The PLO began the phase of the peace process that coincided with the Netanyahu government with an attempt to build consensus in favor of the peace process among the most entrenched Palestinian rejectionists by negotiating with them. The PLO and the PNA attempted to fulfill two roles: one as Israel's security enforcer and the other as a political movement leading its constituency to statehood. The inherent contradictions of these roles cost the Palestinian leadership popular support and helped to dampen any remaining popular enthusiasm for the peace process among Palestinians after the failures of the Netanyahu years. Israeli noncompliance, expansion of settlements, and incitement further weakened both Palestinian and Israeli public support for a negotiated resolution of the conflict. Arafat's pledge to unilaterally declare a Palestinian state in the aftermath of the Wye River Memorandum raised unrealistic expectations among Palestinians while needlessly causing concern among Israelis.

The back channel the parties used in the Netanyahu years helped them manage their constituencies, the interested third parties, and internal opponents. It also helped them create workable compromise language in their agreements, even if they accomplished nothing more than the reformulation of previously agreed items. Netanyahu's decision to suspend compliance weakens the link between BCN and implementation of outcomes. His government could only negotiate effectively in secret. Once negotiations were revealed, his political power base crumbled despite his attempts to downplay, condition, and "spin" the mutual commitments under the Wye River Memorandum—which, after all, was little more than a renegotiation of a renegotiation.

Analysis

As noted in chapter 1, the comparison of front and back channels requires an analytical framework. In the following sections, direct comparisons are made for each of the following analytical factors in the front and back channels for the interim period that began in 1994 and was to have ended by 1999.

- Issues negotiated
- Secrecy and publicity
- Exclusion and inclusion of subparties
- Proximity of negotiators to decision makers
- Autonomy of the negotiators
- Third parties: presence and role
- Strategic use of front and back channels

Issues Negotiated

Formal negotiation agenda items (the subjects of a negotiation to resolve a dispute or craft a deal) can be defined as "issues" that negotiators agree to include on their agenda, set aside for later, or avoid altogether. The negotiations in the post-Oslo period covered a vast amount of issues, ranging from troop withdrawals to tax collection. The division of issues was formally determined in the DoP. Everything but Jerusalem, Palestinian refugees, borders, and settlements was subject to negotiation in the interim talks. All these topics reserved for the permanent status talks cast their shadow on the more mundane interim status negotiations. Of these, the issues of borders and settlements cast the longest shadow on the interim negotiations. The drafters of the DoP, in their recognition of the difficulty of the permanent status issues, perhaps did not pay enough attention to the *issue linkages*. A completely clean division between interim and permanent status issues was not possible.

The Israeli settlements in the West Bank and Gaza proved to be a difficult problem throughout the peace process. Israeli governments began permitting several settlements to expand in capacity, geographical extent, and population despite the DoP commitment to maintain the status quo in the occupied territories during the interim period. The discontinuity between the accords and reality would eventually cause a shift in the parties' negotiation agenda. Some of the settlements were areas of frequent tension precisely because they were set up in the midst of or adjacent to important Palestinian population centers, such as East Jerusalem and Hebron, Ramallah, Nablus, and other Palestinian population centers. Israel felt that large numbers of troops would be required to safeguard settlers in such places.

Thus, the presence of the settlers had a direct and negative impact on the cornerstone of the Interim Agreement—the further redeployments. The inability to entirely separate the effect of the permanent status issues from the interim issues is mentioned here because this interaction among the issues affected the decision to work on certain issues in back channels.

The Oslo and Madrid peace negotiations greatly differed from each other in terms of solutions proposed to the same sets of issues. The post-Oslo period encompassed both interim and permanent status negotiations.

Interim negotiations. In the negotiation of the Interim Agreement, the Hebron Accords, and the Wye River Memorandum, the amount of territorial control ceded to the Palestinians, the security arrangements, and the timetable of Israeli redeployments were among the most difficult issues faced. These topics were on the agenda of both front and back channels. The solutions, however temporary or unfulfilled, were found in the *back* channels.

Permanent status negotiations. In the five years under review here, front channel negotiations on the permanent status issues were only inaugurated but never actually conducted. The back channel Stockholm document negotiated by the Israeli and Palestinian academics working under Yossi Beilin and Abu Mazen were nevertheless engaged in very daring scenario building in order to find acceptable trade-offs among the issues, each parties' prioritization of the issues, and across the table between the parties. The lack of a front channel does

not permit any comparative conclusions about what might have been different in the front channel. The Stockholm document was on the very margins of
back channel diplomacy because the extent of negotiation authority is extremely
ambiguous, especially on the Israeli side, with Beilin operating in a freelance
capacity and not reporting to Rabin or Peres, even as he held a high-level government post. On the Palestinian side, Abu Mazen acted with the knowledge and
authority of Yasir Arafat, although probably not with the approval of PLO bodies
overseeing negotiations. There was an element of "freelancing" on the Palestinian side as well.

Counterfactually, and using knowledge from the front channel permanent-
status negotiations that were conducted after the period of this study, we can
surmise that, had there been a front channel on the permanent status issues in
1995–96, it very likely would have resembled the Palestinian-Israeli negotiations that followed the Madrid Peace Conference in 1991–93, with diametrically
opposed opening positions on each final status issue and even procedural disputes that prevent substantive exchanges. And this scenario was likely whether a
Labor or a Likud government governed from 1996 to 1999.

The Palestinian and Israeli negotiators cast light on the reasons why something might be discussed in a back channel while it is kept off the agenda or set
aside in the front channel. Isaac Molho believes that "if some issue in the back
channel is revealed to the public, the decision makers have to express their views
on it. This complicates the negotiations. So issues are kept off the table in the
front channel in order to not have to make public statements that later bind the
decision maker."[55] Hassan Asfour, PLO official and negotiator present in Oslo
and back channel negotiations throughout the post-Oslo period and now a minister in the PNA, stated that the issues were the same in both the front channel
and the back channel. After this remark, however, he noted that each party had
taboo issues that could not be discussed in front of the media.[56]

However, neither Molho nor Asfour are referring to the problems or issues
that first bring the parties together, but rather to the *different possible solutions*
that might be agreed upon to resolve the problem. There can be little doubt that
potential solutions that might be construed as concessions by parties or observers
are more likely to be discussed in a back channel than in a front channel if both
are available.

The Role of Secrecy and Publicity

It is relatively easy to see why the parties chose secrecy for the Oslo negotiations. The lack of recognition and long-standing mutual demonization made it extremely difficult for the Israelis to admit they were talking to the PLO. The PLO, despite having declared its willingness to do so long before Oslo, still found the political costs of talking to the Israelis to be very high. After the breakthrough of Oslo and the mutual recognition letters, the parties were much freer (in terms of political risk) to openly negotiate with each other. Because there were no legal impediments to meeting with each other, the answer must lie in procedural and substantive concerns. These are summed up by Hassan Asfour, a PLO official involved in the back channels from the beginning. "Secrecy is used," he said to "protect the process."[57]

The Oslo process also involved a small measure of making secret agreements, not just conducting secret negotiations. One of the first reminders that Oslo had entailed not only procedural secrecy but also secret agreements came in June 1994 during the interim period. At that time, Shimon Peres publicly acknowledged that he had written a secret letter to Norwegian foreign minister Holst as part of the Oslo Accords, providing assurances to the PLO that Israel would not close down Palestinian institutions in Jerusalem. Peres's purpose in postdating the secret letter was to avoid making it subject to cabinet and Knesset approval. Yasir Arafat had earlier revealed the existence of the commitment in a provocative speech given at a mosque in South Africa. Netanyahu, when he took office, repudiated the Peres letter and set out to remove Palestinian institutions from Jerusalem and prevent Palestinian political activity in the city. The issue of secret documents did not seriously arise again until the Wye River Memorandum was signed, although little has been offered to support the contention that there were secret undertakings, other than the "letters of assurance" provided by the United States to each side.

The degree of publicity that Palestinian and Israeli negotiators faced in the post-Oslo period was unprecedented. Mobilized constituencies, rejectionists, supporters, regional and global players all carefully monitored events to see the impact on their respective interests and aspirations. Expectations and suspicions were raised in the aftermath of Oslo. On the Israeli side, both Labor and Likud governments felt obligated to remove negotiations from the view of the settlers and the right.

In the chronology of negotiations from the end of 1993 to the end of 1998, we find that the parties returned more and more to back channels. This pattern culminated in 1998 with the preparation for the Wye summit being conducted by BCN, even while most observers believed the peace process was at worst dead or at best dormant.

Netanyahu's chief negotiator, Isaac Molho, understood the need to have a front and back channel operating simultaneously, not only to divert attention from the back channel, but to protect the leadership from having to take public positions from which it would be difficult to make needed concessions.[58] Despite Molho's insight, the Netanyahu years were characterized by a measure of negotiation intransigence that cannot solely be attributed to Israeli posturing for the sake of remaining in power. Nevertheless, the intentions and good faith of the negotiators and decision makers are not subject to analysis here. Our focus is on why the parties used secret back channels.

A certain feeling of optimism can be sensed from some of the back channel negotiators. Abu Alaa believes that only in the back channel negotiations can parties truly discover each others' underlying interests and priorities, and that this knowledge greatly facilitates agreement. "The most important thing in the secret negotiations is to educate, to teach the other side about your real concerns. And to listen to him about his real concerns."[59]

Uri Savir, reflecting on the use of several back channels to draft portions of the Interim Agreement, argues that secrecy is needed to model ideas without them being considered concessions. "It's only in a secret surrounding with both parties trust[ing] the secrecy that the best ideas can be tested. And without jointly testing ideas, a good agreement is actually impossible."[60]

Savir's argument echoes and supports that of Hassan Abu Libdeh, one of the PLO negotiators involved in the back channels leading to the Interim Agreement and later the president of the Palestinian Bureau of Statistics. Abu Libdeh believes that back channels are useful to test out innovative ideas while minimizing the risk of having to commit oneself to the idea or the risk of being accused of having made an unnecessary concession: "Of course, in the back channels, there have always been very daring ideas floating around— ideas that are initiated on the table and then sometimes one team or both teams would go back to their leaders to convince them of these things. Back channel activities are much more entrepreneurial. [They] cannot produce the final agreement because at some stage, you have to bring in the experts. . . . Whenever there was a back channel, most of the time [it is] used for modeling."[61]

During Netanyahu's tenure as prime minister of Israel, a period lasting nearly twenty months passed without any apparent negotiation activity. Yet during that time, some of the worst days of Palestinian-Israeli relations, Abu Alaa held at least thirteen secret face-to-face meetings with Netanyahu himself, as well as with Ariel Sharon and Netanyahu's chief back channel negotiator, Isaac Molho.[62] Secrecy was firmly embedded in the negotiation practices of both sides, even as one of them (Netanyahu) was publicly declaring that he would not negotiate with the other side.

Molho met with Saeb Eraqat, Abu Alaa, and Arafat himself numerous times in secret to negotiate the terms of the Hebron Accords and to prepare for the Wye Plantation summit in 1998.[63] The back channel negotiator during the Netanyahu years had a different vision of the utility of secrecy; it is used to help maintain two postures: an adversarial one in public and a more collaborative one in secret. When the Netanyahu government took over, Isaac Molho, Netanyahu's personal attorney, was asked to undertake a mission on behalf of the Likud government: secretly convey to Yasir Arafat that "[o]ur public statements [against the PLO, the peace process, and the prior agreements] had a strategic and tactical purpose. More important than the public statement is the importance of the messenger. I was sent there to reach agreement. The Palestinians learned that my presence was an indication of seriousness on Netanyahu's part."[64]

Dr. Saeb Eraqat, who played a leading role in front and back channels, interim and permanent status negotiations throughout the peace process, distinguishes between what he termed "off-media" negotiations and back channel negotiations. He openly recognizes the value of holding negotiations out of the range of the news media, because "the pressure of the media kills the negotiations." However, he also believes that the Israelis use the real back channels to get undue concessions out of the Palestinians. "They would go to negotiate [in secret] with Abu Alaa if they didn't like what they heard [from me in front channel negotiations]. My negotiations are one item, one price," he recounted with fervor.[65] In his perspective, negotiations with the Israelis in the Netanyahu years were an attempt by Israel to "dictate terms," not to negotiate. From Eraqat's perspective, we can speak of parties "channel shopping": trying to obtain the terms most favorable to themselves in whichever channel provides those terms.

While comparing the progress of the front channel interim agreement talks in Cairo and his own 1995 Stockholm back channel, Yossi Beilin writes about the effect that publicity had on the interim agreement negotiations and the negotiator behaviors in that environment: "at a certain stage these [interim] talks [in Cairo] had fallen victim to the Washington syndrome: media hype, predetermined positions, confrontation in the conference hall and inconclusive stalemate, presaging neither disintegration nor progress. It was clear that this could not be allowed to continue and another secret negotiating track was initiated forthwith, headed by Uri Savir and Abu Alaa, which made progress."[66]

Not surprisingly, then, we find that negotiators increasingly used back channels throughout the interim period, whether they were addressing interim or permanent status issues. They were using them *simultaneously with* front channels to negotiate the Interim Agreement. The were used *in sequence with* (followed by) front channels, as was the case in the preparation for the Wye Plantation summit. Similarly, they were used when a *front channel did not yet exist,* as in the Stockholm channel, which began its work long before the commencement of the formal permanent status negotiations.

Exclusion and Inclusion of Subparties

The exclusion and inclusion of subparties in the negotiations process exerted unexpected effects in this case, as excluded Palestinians helped determine what would happen in the Israeli elections. The scrutiny of the excluded rejectionists was a constant motivation for further use of back channels.

Subparties of the PLO and the Israeli government immediately registered their presence as the post-Oslo stage began. The inclusion and exclusion of subparties exerted an influence on the selection of negotiators and, on the Israeli side, determined who the decision makers would be. In their ongoing jockeying for access to power, Israeli political parties that are marginalized in one government are not static. They seek access to power by aligning themselves with each other in order to exert more influence on policy in the following elections or cabinet reshuffle. Or like Barak and Beilin while the Labor Party was out of government, they get in touch with the Palestinian leadership anyway.

The Executive Committee of the PLO was the first contentious internal forum that Arafat faced. Six of eighteen members resigned rather than legitimize the Oslo Accords. Those who had been intimately involved in the Oslo channel and close to the center of PLO decision making were rebuffed. Savir claims that Yasir Arafat relieved Abu Mazen and Abu Alaa of their responsibilities regarding contacts with the Israelis, ostensibly to diminish their highly public profile.[67] If so, this could not have lasted very long, given the prominent negotiation roles played by both of them during the interim phase.

At the beginning of 1994, a delegation of Palestinians from the West Bank and Gaza flew to Tunis for four days of meetings with Yasir Arafat to demand changes in the PLO's leadership. The delegation was led by Dr. Haydar Abd al-Shafi, the former head of the Palestinian delegation to the talks in Washington and one of the founding members of the PLO.[68] Throughout the interim period, Abd al-Shafi proposed alternative models of political leadership, especially regarding the conduct of the peace process.[69] Groups such as these have not been able to more effectively participate in Palestinian decision making or peace negotiations. It is revealing that Yitzhak Shamir expressed his preference for dealing with Abd al-Shafi rather than Arafat, characterizing the former as "an extremist, but an honest man."[70] This is certainly not because Shamir expected a more moderate negotiation stance from Abd al-Shafi, but more likely it is because the difficulty of reaching agreement with the local Palestinian leaders suited Shamir's use of negotiations as a delay tactic.

The most difficult challenge that faced the PNA in terms of parties excluded from the peace process concerned the rise of Palestinian political organizations solidly rooted in religious nationalism: HAMAS and the Movement for Islamic Jihad. HAMAS is a complex organization, partly a social-service network that provided for the basic needs of a population living under a hostile military occupation and without a functioning government. At the same time, HAMAS and Jihad reject a model of Palestinian emergence into sovereignty based on secular nationalism and do not accept the existence of Israel. They mobilize their constituencies by appealing to religious principles and religious identity, in contrast with the other groups under the PLO umbrella, most of whom were originally organized according to ideologies of liberation on the left side of the political spectrum. As rejectionists of the PLO-Israel negotiations, militant wings of both HAMAS and Jihad organized paramilitary operations and terror attacks against Israeli military installations and settlers. When they exceeded these limits and targeted Israeli civilians within Israeli population centers they succeeded in damaging and nearly reversing the peace process.

A great deal of PLO-Israel negotiation resources were dedicated to the containment and deterrence of the military wings of these organizations and exposed the PNA to ongoing pressure to suppress these movements on its own and in cooperation with Israel. According to the narratives of the early Oslo encounters, the PLO encouraged Israel to believe it had a choice between recognizing the PLO and confronting a growing Islamic fundamentalist "threat" among Palestinians. Indeed, one of Israel's rationales for recognizing the PLO in the Oslo channel was that such recognition would empower the PLO not only to be to be the sole representative of the Palestinians, thus marginalizing the Islamic groups, but also to require the PLO to repress them as potential threats to its monopoly on political power. The PNA attempted several strategies for dealing with its internal religious opposition, ranging from embracing them as partners in the struggle against the occupation to imprisonment of their leaders and members suspected of military activity against Israel. During the Rabin/Peres years, there was some attempt by Israel to distinguish between the PNA and rejectionist militants; but during the Netanyahu years, no measure taken by the PNA was sufficient, and blame for Palestinian terror attacks was regularly placed on the PNA, which only served to undermine the Palestinian struggle against violence and turn even moderate Palestinians into militants.

The structure of this relationship, in which rejectionists were excluded from political participation, not to mention the decision making in the peace process, permitted them to exercise strong negative influence on the peace process. If Israelis could be made to feel insecure while coexistence was being negotiated, then the entire premise for the peace process could easily be questioned, not only by the secular and religious right-wing parties in Israel, from which this could be expected, but by the population in general and undecided voters in particular. This is a clear link between marginalized Palestinian parties and the determination of Israeli decision makers. The link between the settlers excluded from negotiations and the Israeli armed forces had the same effect on Palestinians. Palestinians facing checkpoints, closures, harassment, assaults, land seizures, and killings at the hands of settlers and the IDF itself could hardly be expected to validate the peace process, even if they could breath freer air in their major population centers.

Israeli domestic groups also mobilized demonstrations and other political activity to oppose the peace process. Uri Savir condemns Israeli political parties that support the settlers, including the National Religious Party and the secular Likud Party (especially the party chairman in 1993, Binyamin Netanyahu) for sowing "the seeds of violence" in the post-Oslo period.[71] Openly violent groups like Kach, which was linked to the Hebron massacre, were involved in the killing of Palestinian civilians in those years.

Israel's most important bureaucratic players who had been excluded from Oslo took center stage in the post-Oslo period: the military itself. Major General Amnon Lipkin-Shahak, at the time the deputy chief of staff under General Ehud Barak, was named the new head of the Israeli delegation post-Oslo, and continued to have negotiation duties in the Netanyahu government. Two other generals, Uzi Dayan (nephew of Moshe Dayan) and Danny Rothschild, joined Joel Singer ("the sole remnant of the original Oslo Club")[72] to negotiate the Interim Agreement under Rabin.

Ironically, Yossi Beilin, as well as his associates from the Economic Cooperation Foundation, Dr. Hirschfeld and Dr. Pundik, were sidelined by Peres in the negotiations for the Interim Agreement.[73]

By contrast, Major General Ehud Barak, the IDF chief of staff under Rabin, resigned from the military at the end of 1994 and on January 1, 1995, entered deeper into Rabin's inner circle by becoming one of his special advisors, thus bringing him one step closer to government and party leadership, both of which he would eventually assume.

At the first Rabin-Arafat session in Cairo on October 6, 1993, the presence of local (not Tunis/Diaspora) Palestinian figures was noticed, including Hanan Ashrawi, Faisal al-Husseini, and Jerusalemite Ziyad Abu Zayyad. In the coming years, all three would later have cabinet positions in the PNA; but at that time, Ashrawi and al-Husseini were fresh from the experience of having participated in the futile front channel in Washington. Their presence as negotiators in Cairo seems to have been symbolic, because the PLO was busy trying to obtain the loyalty of its internal factions and perhaps make some symbolic reparation to the front channel negotiators, and in any case, they were not part of future negotiation teams. The Washington delegation had even drafted a plan for staffing post-DoP negotiation committees, but the names the PLO proposed to fill the positions "appeared to be either politically motivated to deliver factional representation or rewards for earlier favors" rather than meeting professional or technical expertise criteria.[74]

The Israeli delegation to the first working session in Cairo also included three figures who had been completely kept in the dark about the Oslo channel: Eitan Haber, Rabin's chef de cabinet; Shimon Sheves, director of the prime minister's office; and Jacques Neria, Rabin's foreign policy advisor. Eitan Haber had a long and close relationship with Rabin, having served on his staff when he was defense minister under Yitzhak Shamir. Haber was also the official who set up Rabin's secret contacts with Palestinian mayors prior to the intifada, discussed in chapter 2.[75]

Given the immediate exclusion of some of the most important figures behind the Oslo Accords from the interim negotiations, it is hardly surprising to find that some of these figures were active in the Stockholm back channels addressing the permanent status. As we saw in the Oslo case, chapter 5, the exclusion of high-level bureaucratic insiders sometimes motivates them to support activities that are at variance with the declared, official policies and channels.

At the level of subparties, however, the Palestinian attempts to find an option for including rejectionists and persuading them to join, or at least not to impede the peace process, appears to have yielded some results in the period studied here. Security cooperation greatly assisted in reducing violence against Israelis. The Israelis in the Rabin/Peres years appear to have rejected any accommodation with their own rejectionists because they felt strong enough to govern without them. Netanyahu was himself one of the rejectionists, and yet he found himself constrained by the same political realities that faced his predecessors.

To save face and not openly abandon some of the claims made during election campaigns, both Rabin and Netanyahu used back channels to continue negotiations with the Palestinians. In the Netanyahu years, back channels replaced or preceded rather than supplemented open negotiations, whereas in the prior governments, they were used to supplement open channels. In Netanyahu's case, his government included parties that were more Rightist than his own Likud Party. The net effect of Netanyahu's back channel diplomacy was the concentration of negotiation and decision-making authority by exclusion of subparties, even within his own cabinet.

In the post-Oslo period, the Palestinian side did not change in terms of leadership, although negotiators were themselves moved around from front to back channels or out of the negotiations altogether. The Palestinian subparties excluded from negotiations were themselves one of the motivations to use back channels because they rejected the compromises implied by negotiation. The Israeli experience suggests a stronger idea: excluded parties, once they are in power, seek to engage in the negotiations processes from which they have been excluded. They were originally excluded because of their rejectionism, but when they assumed the responsibilities of government, they resorted to back channels to minimize the risk of being accused of betraying principle.

Proximity of Decision Makers, Autonomy of Negotiators

In this section, we will discuss both proximity of negotiators to their decision makers, and the comparative autonomy of front and back channel negotiators to see what the links are between these two topics and how strong such a link may be.

During the first two and one-half years of the Netanyahu government, there was a widespread perception that little was being accomplished in the peace process, or worse, that it was being reversed. In fact, the back channel negotiators were highly active. Isaac Molho recalled that "Netanyahu asked me to make a secret mission to Arafat right after the Netanyahu's election to convey that Netanyahu meant business and would not suspend relations between Israel and the Palestinians. Netanyahu took on the DoP, and my mission was to convey the message that he would not break the commitments of the previous government. . . . Our public statements [in contrast] had a strategic/tactical purpose."[76]

Molho stated, "I probably have more face time with Arafat than any other Israeli. We had meetings in Gaza, Jericho, Nablus, Hebron, all of them in Arafat's offices. I was in constant communication with Arafat and the Palestinians despite the darkest days of our relationship with them."[77] Molho was the quintessential outsider in government. He had never held public office or served the government. He was not part of the military bureaucracy in Israel or the intelligence services and, by his own admission, knew nothing about Middle East political negotiations. Yet he was chosen by Netanyahu to be his secret envoy to the PLO. Indeed, one of the reasons Netanyahu trusted Molho was the latter's distance from government.

This, Molho explained, was a factor contributing to the broad negotiating mandate he enjoyed as a back channel negotiator: "When the leaders trusts you a lot, you have lots of room to maneuver. I was not a strategic decision maker. I was entrusted to get tactical results. I asked Bibi [Netanyahu], 'Where do you want to go? I'll take you there.' There is a division between the strategic and the tactical [dimensions of political negotiations]. You have lots of freedom to negotiate if you are not involved in the strategic decision making and have the trust of the decision maker."[78]

Molho's negotiating flexibility was remarkable compared to the limits that were put on Foreign Minister Levy and later on Defense Minister Mordechai, both of whom grappled with the FRD issue in front channels while Molho was addressing it in the back channel. Mordechai was dismissed and Levy quit the cabinet.

On the Palestinian side, a similar dynamic was observable. The principal back channel negotiators included Abu Alaa, Hassan Asfour, and Hassan Abu Libdeh, as well as Abu Mazen. Of these four men, three were among the top five decision makers within the inner circles of the PLO. The only person missing was top aide Yasir Abd Rabbuh (and Yasir Arafat himself). Abd Rabbuh was often part of front channel negotiations. But all reported to Abu Mazen and Yasir Arafat. In the Palestinian case, the back channel negotiators were themselves part of the decision making mechanism, and so their proximity to decision making was great.[79]

Joel Singer summed this up by stating that back channel negotiations "allow you to bypass difficulties, by establishing a channel behind or next to an open negotiation channel. It is another, smaller, higher-level channel with more authority to negotiate and maneuver so that more difficult and sensitive problems can be handled in a manner less subject to peer pressure. Secret negotiations have more qualified participants by virtue of their rank and negotiating mandate and therefore [have] the ability to be flexible."[80]

Presence and Role of Third Parties

The United States' role in hosting the public ceremony of the Oslo Accords signified the beginning of new American involvement in the Israeli-Palestinian peace process. Having been excluded from the channel in which real negotiations were being conducted even while it sponsored futile talks in Washington, the United States reasserted itself. Uri Savir recalled that "our working contacts with the American peace team became almost daily."[81] At the same time, the Norwegians who had set up the Oslo channel remained very active in the post-Oslo stage. At times, it appears that the various third parties, including Egypt, Jordan, Sweden, and others were vying for the attention of the parties, nearly competing with each other for influence.

This was not always well received by the parties. At the beginning of Secretary of State Warren Christopher's December 1993 visit to Israel and during the crisis negotiations after the Hebron massacre, Israel asked the Americans and Norwegians, respectively, to refrain from getting involved in the substantive details of the negotiations.[82] Nevertheless, officials from the United States and Norway continued to carry messages between the parties on numerous occasions.

As the peace process continued into the Netanyahu years, the United States as well as the member states and institutions of the European Union became increasingly involved in the Israeli-Palestinian peace process. The European Union designated a Spanish diplomat, Miguel Moratinos, to be its special envoy to the Middle East peace process, a role similar to that of Dennis Ross, the U.S. State Department "coordinator." The role of their respective special envoys to the peace process grew as both Israelis and Palestinians competed for the influence of the third parties and sought to have the third parties legitimize their positions and use third parties to exert their influence on the other side.

Dennis Ross and King Hussein of Jordan played significant intermediary roles after the summit held on January 5, 1997, enabling the parties to finalize a written agreement in the predawn hours of January 15 with the participation of Netanyahu and Arafat. King Hussein contributed a compromise plan regarding dates for Israel's FRDs. Netanyahu preferred to either avoid setting dates for further deployments or to defer the completion date of the redeployments until the conclusion of the permanent status talks. Arafat preferred early redeployments in order to exert PNA jurisdiction over the maximum amount of West Bank and Gaza territory as early as possible, in advance of the permanent status settlement. Jordan, the United States, and the European Union favored the Palestinian time preference, while letting Israel determine the geographical extent and location of these FRDs. Implicit in both parties' negotiation postures is the assumption that the extent of the PNA's territorial reach prior to the permanent status accord would greatly influence, if not completely predetermine, the final territorial demarcation.

The presence of Dennis Ross and the inclusion of his Note for the Record in the Hebron Accords signaled that both Israel and the PLO desired to leverage the United States' presence in the peace process. Israel took pains to interpret the Note for the Record as the United States' approval of Israel's ability to unilaterally halt negotiations on either interim or final status issues if it felt that the PLO were not complying with any of its commitments, thus practically ensuring further negotiations would be needed to achieve full compliance by the parties.[83] The PLO, for its part, insisted on the Note for the Record precisely to minimize the chances of Israeli noncompliance, to establish linkage between the different negotiation processes, and to make the United States a witness to the entire process. This combination amounted to the Palestinian desire to avoid renegotiation of agreed-upon issues. The parties agreed to include the United States' Note for the Record for reasons that were not only asymmetrical but also incompatible. Dennis Ross sent letters of assurance to both Israel and the PLO dated January 15, 1997. The existence of the letters was announced, but their content was kept secret. Israel leaked its letter to the press within the first two days after the Hebron Protocol. The intervention of the third party, although not unproblematic from the perspective of either the PLO or Israel, was nevertheless accepted for the usual reason that parties accept a mediator that is openly favorable to one side only. The disfavored party (Palestine) hoped that the mediator (the United States) would use its influence to get the favored party (Israel) to make concessions, whereas the favored party wants to maintain that status. As noted, the United States was not the only third party present in the Hebron negotiations. The European Union's Council of Ministers also provided a letter to President Arafat as part of the new Hebron Accords. The letter was reportedly approved by both the United States and Israel, ostensibly because they perceived it to serve their respective interests. The Israeli side asked that the letter be kept secret. The letter addresses Arafat as "President" (he had won the internationally vetted elections in the West Bank and Gaza of 1996), refers to the Madrid and Oslo frameworks, and finally, commits the European Union to use "all its political and moral weight to ensure that all the provisions in the agreements reached will be fully implemented on the basis of reciprocity."[84] The reference to "reciprocity" served Netanyahu's interests, whereas the engagement of the European Union in supervising compliance was a Palestinian desideratum. Arafat referred to the letter at a joint press conference with the Dutch prime and foreign ministers at the Hague two weeks after the Hebron Protocol was signed, thus making it public.

President Clinton and Secretary of State Albright became even more directly involved in the Palestinian-Israeli negotiation impasse after the failed Washington summit of November 1997. As the third parties grew increasingly active during the Netanyahu years, the use of back channels *appeared* to recede somewhat. However, when communication between the PLO and the Netanyahu government seemed to be completely interrupted, the third parties seemed helpless to intercede. Neither the Palestinian nor Israeli back channel negotiators during the Netanyahu years give significant credit to U.S. State Department envoy Dennis Ross during their period of intense back channel negotiations.[85] Dennis Ross, nevertheless, gives himself at least some of the credit for the progress made in the back channels.[86]   Perhaps because of a desire to sideline the interests and peculiarities of the third party, back channels once again became the preferred modus operandi. The back channel, however, was prelude to further third-party involvement to provide the cover for concessions and to wring concessions from the other side, as the Wye River talks demonstrated. They excluded the United States from their back channel mostly because the third party was not perceived as having anything to contribute during those talks. When the moment arrived to actually sign an official agreement, the third parties were again needed, either to save face while making concessions or to exert pressure on the other party.

The Netanyahu government's political downfall, which began in earnest just after signing the Wye River Memorandum, demonstrated to many observers that there were significant limits to what even a powerful and engaged third party can do in an international conflict resolution role. When the Barak government took over from Likud, the tolerance for U.S. intervention was much more selective and reflected a realization that back channel, direct contacts had been more effective in particular moments of the peace process over last decade.

This case continues to provide support for the concept that back channels are used by parties as part of their strategies for managing third-party involvement in their negotiations. The desire for third-party intervention need not be uniform at all points during a negotiation. A party that is aware of this will seek to limit or expand that intervention according to the perceived benefits of either action. The back channel is in this sense useful to contain the third party, either because a party fears being manipulated into giving concessions or because a party fears that the third party is more likely to promote its own or the adversary's interests. Although the third-party role still presents a somewhat murky picture for the interim phase with numerous third parties playing constantly shifting roles, it seems very clear that the United States played little or no role in the back channels, while it played an ever more assertive role in front channels and summits.

Strategic Use of Multiple Negotiation Channels

Earlier we saw that throughout the interim period, the PLO and Israel used multiple channels of negotiation: both front and back channels together. We also saw that back channels are used to negotiate difficult issues and to test controversial solutions to those issues even while front channels are being used. Thus, one of the drivers of multiple channels is the existence of subsets of issues that the negotiators prefer not to manage by conventional, front channel means. Negotiators in the post-Oslo period believed that multiple channels were *needed* as part of their system of negotiation. As Molho explained it: "I was not familiar with Middle East negotiations at first. Terje [Larsen] explained . . . to me [that] you have to have a front channel in order to have a back channel. Efficiency is secrecy. Back channels, if used alone, will be revealed. Business negotiations do not attract public attention. Political negotiations do. . . . It is helpful to have heads of delegations know about each other's negotiations and coordinate with each other."[87]

In the analyses using the variables discussed above, there is ample evidence of multiple negotiation channels being used. The way in which this multiplicity is manifested can also be analyzed; back channels were used *simultaneously, sequentially,* or *as substitutes* for front channels.

It is especially clear that during the post-Oslo period, the top decision makers deliberately planned the back channels on interim issues to be simultaneous and sequential with front channels. On the Israeli side, the top negotiators and decision makers claim to have known nothing about the Stockholm channel. In his memoirs, Uri Savir went so far as to claim (inaccurately) that no agreement had been reached there. Although it is technically true that no agreement was signed, a final draft suitable for presentation to the decision makers for further negotiation was in fact completed. Peres took pains to claim that no Israeli minister authorized the Stockholm channel.[88] Beilin also claimed to have informed Peres only after the document was finalized.[89]

The back channels used for the Interim Agreement differed from those used in the Hebron and Wye Accords; the strategic purposes were different, as mentioned in the previous subsections. Yet the back and front channels for the interim accords were complementary projects deliberately employed by the parties' top decision makers, who used multiple channels for purposes as divergent as "channel shopping" and trust building.

Some Systems Aspects of the Interim and Permanent Status Negotiations

Several aspects of this complex web of negotiations should be analyzed for their interactivity; the peace process became a "system" over time. Some contextual aspects of the interim period also point to "feedback" effects: phenomena that cause the factors from which they arise. Considering the peace process negotiations as a system allows us to perceive how several important dysfunctions arose over time. We can begin to discern the unintended consequences of BCN.

Subordination of agreements and the security paradox. Given the numerous accords that were negotiated in this period, another aspect worth noting is the prioritization of the different agreements reached. Earlier, we noted that one of the first post-Oslo agreements to be reached concerned Israeli-Palestinian economic cooperation. This agreement became an annex to the Gaza-Jericho Agreement, but its provisions were not to supersede the security aspects of the interim arrangements, which would predominate. This prioritization had serious consequences for the interim period. As security for Palestinians and Israelis deteriorated, Israel unilaterally imposed "closures" of the entire West Bank and Gaza on security grounds, with devastating economic effects on Palestinians, who considered it as collective punishment. This resulted in further erosion of public confidence in the peace process and created conditions that facilitated militancy and rejectionism.

The subordination of all negotiation issues to questions of security permitted spoilers to have veto on the entire process—on the entire project of interim coexistence—simply by eroding security. For the rejectionist, this is an easy call to make. Their actions erode the support of the other side's moderates for the peace process, and without that support, the consensus for peace is threatened.

This subordination and prioritization is an important contextual factor for the Palestinian-Israeli peace process. Necessitated by the multiplicity of channels and complexity of the accords, not to mention the overarching Israeli interest in security arrangements, the overall effect, paradoxically, has been to diminish the security for Israelis and Palestinians alike.

Feedback loops: audiences and back channels. Just as the subordination of all things to security has a paradoxical effect on the security situation, other factors examined in this section operate together: the presence of audiences, for example, drives negotiators to harden their positions. Parties use back channels to manage this dilemma. We have seen what happens when agreements negotiated in the back channel come to light. For example, prior to the May 4, 1995, signing ceremony for the full Interim Agreement, a third party—Egypt—was at work facilitating negotiations removed from the media. After the back channel negotiations ended and the full agreement was drafted, Egypt hosted the very public signing agreement, which the parties understood would be closely watched, particularly by those whose interests were not represented or who opposed the peace process. Arafat's well-publicized balking at the signing of the maps and the consequent interruption of the ceremony received broad media coverage. Uri Savir interpreted this as evidence that Arafat "wanted to show his constituents that he was fighting for their interests, against a broadside of international pressure, and was prepared to embarrass his partners in order to protect their rights."[90] Although Savir's interpretation may suffer from some measure of partisanship, it nevertheless points to the audience effect on negotiations: *an effect with potential impact even when the public is presented with a fait accompli that was negotiated in a back channel.*

The use of a back channel can indeed postpone public response to secret negotiations while they remain secret. *Ultimately, that response emerges,* and when it does, it may be characterized by suspicion and resentment. Some of the negotiators' behaviors are made in anticipation of this reaction, leading to a systemic structure, a feedback loop: concern about audiences and publicity drives negotiators to use back channels. When the agreements come to light, the negotiators fear the rejection of the public. They act in ways calculated to restore confidence of their own constituents, which erodes the trust of their adversaries. Constituents resent the concessions that have been made, and they lose trust in their leadership and the peace process. Without this trust, negotiators will feel the need to negotiate in the back channel for their next interaction. And so, actions have unintended consequences that cause the parties to deepen their reliance on a mechanism that, while calculated to facilitate agreement in the present, casts a shadow on the future.

Incompatible goals and the failure of incrementalism. The fundamental goals of the parties continued to be opposed throughout the interim period. All of the negotiations took place under the shadow of the occupation. Indeed, two purposes of all this negotiation were the mitigation of the administrative and military burden on Israel and the partial rollback of the occupation. Israel became increasingly concerned about its own security and increasingly demanding that the PNA do more to prevent attacks against Israel. The resulting pressure on the PNA compromised Arafat's standing among Palestinians and led to fractures within the PLO, undermining Arafat's ability to control dissidents. Such Israeli military responses within the West Bank and Gaza provided further motivation for militant opposition to compromise and cooperation with Israel. Israel moved toward consensus on the need to separate Palestinians from Israelis, but the interim agreements failed to sustain the working relationship necessary for effective compromise on the final status issues.

The interim agreements also left in place or exacerbated numerous problems for the Palestinians, including military checkpoints between the different areas of the West Bank and Gaza, prevention of movement between the West Bank and Gaza, limitations on entry into Jerusalem, revocation of East Jerusalem residency cards for Palestinians, expansion of the settlements and the construction of bypass roads to carry traffic to Israel from the Israeli settlements in the West Bank and Gaza, and the continued presence of the IDF near Palestinian population centers. The economic isolation of Palestinian territory, severely exacerbated by recurrent closures, further contributed to growing Palestinian disillusionment with the peace process. Finally, key provisions of the interim agreements were renegotiated by successive Israeli governments as the formula of "land for peace" quickly degenerated and was reconstructed as "limited autonomy for security cooperation and limited separation."

During the Netanyahu years, the back channel negotiations started out as a way to find creative compromises while appeasing an inflamed antipeace electorate in Israel, but they evolved into a substitute for both implementation of the Interim Agreement and the permanent status negotiations. The incompatibility of each side's goals, in combination with Netanyahu's double posture of negotiating while denying the legitimacy of negotiations, ultimately reduced the back channel to little more than a delaying mechanism. Israeli and Palestinian negotiators spent years conducting front and back channel negotiations efforts that were only partially implemented, if at all.

The Results of the Interim Phase

During the interim phase, the PLO and the three successive governments in Israel concluded a series of agreements culminating in the Interim Agreement (and the various renegotiations of its provisions). They also began exploring the contours of a permanent settlement. For both interim and permanent status talks, they used front and back channels. At first, the parties deliberately invoked the success of the 1993 Oslo channel to construct back channels during the post-Oslo period. Agreement was reached on the most difficult *interim* challenges only by explicitly using back channels. The understandings reached in back channels were plugged into front channel negotiations that were conducted simultaneously or sequentially with the back channels.

The agreements and channels of negotiation analyzed in this chapter were characteristic of an incremental approach to a negotiated peace process. The common hope for both parties was that progress in the negotiation and implementation of the interim accords would facilitate agreement on the permanent status issues. *In most of the negotiations of the interim period, BCN is highly correlated with reaching agreement.* But that is not the whole story, of course.

The actual implementation of these agreements, a necessarily open and public activity, proved far more challenging. The Oslo Accords of 1993 required the parties only to refrain from taking certain unilateral actions and, more importantly, set out basic guidelines (the negotiating "framework" in the lexicon of negotiation experts) for further negotiation, thereby minimizing the need for operational implementation plans. In contrast, all interim accords involved positive acts of implementation. Difficulties in implementation of the Interim Agreement caused damage to the fragile working relationship needed to build a solid partnership for peace. This made it much more difficult to conclude a viable permanent status agreement. In this sense, Yossi Beilin's fears that drove him to open the Stockholm channel proved to be well founded.

Back channels used for the permanent status issues during the interim period are somewhat more difficult to evaluate. Although they did not produce anything like the expectation and momentum (much less signed accords) of the Oslo negotiations of 1993, BCN created a model for a permanent settlement and helped sectors within each party build interpersonal trust. The Beilin-Abu Mazen

Framework Agreement was an early sign that permitted optimism. It served more as an exercise in modeling possible contours of the permanent settlement than an agreement itself. In this sense it was both more and less substantial than the DoP, which was an official agreement but did not model anything at all and said very little in terms of specific actions the parties should or should not undertake.

Some of the broad contours of a permanent settlement indicated in the Beilin-Abu Mazen Stockholm agreement reappeared later in the Camp David summit held during July 2000 (discussed in the next chapter) and in the Clinton proposals of January 2001, demonstrating at minimum that a permanent status agreement could be reached, though at great cost to the preferred positions of the parties. Both sides pointed to unacceptable political costs, existing commitments and nonnegotiable principles that precluded agreement on the permanent status issues. In this sense, the Stockholm channel proved useful for the exercise of crafting a model agreement, and possibly even preparing mobilized constituencies for the sacrifices involved by putting taboo issues on the agenda to be negotiated and compromised on in some form.

Despite the deliberate and successful use of BCN to conclude (but not always implement) agreements over the course of the five years reviewed here, a critical appraisal is necessary.

If the interim agreements and the channels used to achieve them are evaluated by the narrow criterion of whether or not they created the trust and confidence necessary to move to the permanent status issues, *they must collectively be considered a failure.* The continued erosion of Palestinian self-determination claims, renewed protests, and the Israeli military response to the protests in 2000 and 2001 demonstrated the extent to which the interim phase and its aftermath failed to achieve their overall strategic goal of transforming a conflictual relationship to a cooperative one.

BCN was a fundamental element in the successful conclusion of interim accords, given the distance between the negotiating positions of the parties. The characteristics of BCN are such that a party is able to present an agreement as a fait accompli. Over time, however, subparties, constituencies, and opposition groups came to expect back channels, and some mobilized to oppose secret agreements and multiple negotiation channels from which they were excluded.

At the conclusion of the period being researched, as well as in the two years that followed, BCN had not resulted in any permanent status agreements. As permanent-status back channels and their possible terms and conditions came to light, the short-term effect was uniformly negative. Few if any configurations of the permanent status could possibly please all the interested subparties and constituencies. It remained to be seen whether or not the mere discussion of the previously undiscussable had prepared the way for broader acceptance of a permanent status agreement. The continued reliance on BCN was useful for reaching agreements that committed the parties to a negotiated peace process and challenged their fundamental assumptions about each other.

The very usefulness of BCN as a tool for making agreements in principle and modeling possible scenarios of implementation reached its limit when the agreements had practical aspects that needed to be operationalized. The very exclusion of spoilers and other subparties that made the conclusion of such agreements possible became a severe liability as constituencies mobilized to prevent what they feared and perceived to be further concessions on the ground.

The simple comparison of the Madrid negotiations and the Oslo channel leads to the optimistic conclusion that back channels are indispensable for breakthroughs. A longer view of the peace process reveals a far more problematic diplomatic landscape. Back channels exacerbate and even cause some of the very problems for which decision makers use them, completing their transformation from being an action taken as a consequence of something to becoming a cause of that very thing.

6

Endgame or Endless Game?

Permanent Status and Crisis Negotiations, 1999 to 2008

We had to maintain a delicate balance between secrecy of the content and
the need to consolidate public opinion that would support the results of the
negotiations.

—GILEAD SHER[1]

Overview of the Endgame

By May 1999, the interim phase of the Palestinian-Israeli peace process was officially over. Both Interim and Permanent Status Agreements should have been
reached, but only an Interim Agreement had been signed. The Interim Agreement, signed on September 28, 1995, should also have been completely implemented long before the end of this period. Instead, the Interim Agreement was
only partially implemented, much delayed, and sorely tested.

The core trade-off in that lengthy agreement was the staged redeployment of
the Israel Defense Force from the West Bank and Gaza, in exchange for Palestinian cooperation on security matters, including joint Palestinian-Israeli patrols
and prevention of acts of terrorism. The scope and timing of those withdrawals
(the "further redeployments," or FRDs) were heavily renegotiated by Israel after
the Interim Agreement was signed. New extended timetables for the FRDs had
been mediated by the United States and memorialized in two different agreements, first the Wye River Memorandum (see chapter 5) and later in the Sharm
el-Sheikh Memorandum, discussed in this chapter, following. Nevertheless, the
FRDs were still only partially implemented by late 1999, four years later.

Also as recounted in chapter 5, *permanent status* negotiation issues had
been explored in a deep back channel in Stockholm in 1995 just prior to Israeli

198

prime minister Yitzhak Rabin's assassination, but then they were left aside in the political climate that followed his death and throughout the years that Binyamin Netanyahu was prime minister of Israel. Netanyahu spent his premiership trying to disown the peace process begun by his predecessors but then found himself frantically renegotiating the Interim Agreement, which in the end he failed to implement.

Netanyahu—responsible for so much antipeace process rhetoric and delays—had himself fallen out of favor with his own coalition partners on the extreme right. Netanyahu also succeeded in alienating the U.S. administration of president Bill Clinton. The United States under Clinton had invested ever increasing amounts of political capital in the peace process but without realizing significant political dividends. Clinton's Middle East peace team worked hard during the Netanyahu years to provide some forward momentum for the commitments made under the 1995 Interim Agreement.

This chapter provides an analysis of the three kinds of substantive negotiations that took place from 1999 onward: interim status, permanent status, and the several crisis management negotiations. In continuation of the pattern established throughout this study, both front and back channels were in use.

During the period covered in this chapter, negotiations were renewed between the PLO and Israel's Labor government under Prime Minister Ehud Barak and his One Israel coalition, which incorporated interim and permanent status negotiations, a high-stakes Camp David summit sponsored by the United States, and tantalizing follow-on negotiations that came very close to reaching agreement on the permanent status.

The unique nature of the permanent status issues inclined the parties to approach the permanent status negotiations differently: on each issue, Israel holds all or most of the cards as a result of the 1967 War and its consequent policies regarding the occupied territories. Israel occupied all of the West Bank and Gaza, including East Jerusalem; Palestinian refugees have long been prevented from returning to what is now Israel; the major Israeli settlements in the West Bank (and at the time, Gaza) were being expanded and connected to Israel, not dismantled. Given this massive asymmetry between the parties, the Israelis appeared to be making incremental concessions that did not violate the spirit of Barak's electoral victory promises, while the Palestinians essentially were asking for the reversal of the occupation. Neither party believed that the opening positions of the other were their bottom-line preferences and that concessions would be made *by the other side*. These large gaps in the negotiation positions would elude resolution by even the most skillful and persuasive mediator. From the Palestinian perspective, Israel, as the party with all the cards, needed to make substantial concessionary moves. And the PLO's recognition of Israel, signifying that there is no claim to recreate pre-1948 Palestine, is seen as the maximal prior concession that should be reciprocated by the recognition of a Palestinian state on all of Gaza and the West Bank, including East Jerusalem.

The lack of any permanent status agreement, and thus the overall failure of the peace process by 2001, seemed only to empower antipeace process militancy on both sides: Israel's settlers and right-wing parties and Palestinian rejectionist groups. The resurgence of the Israeli Right also led to an electoral victory by former general Ariel Sharon, leading the Likud Party, in 2000. The second part of this chapter thus covers the negotiations that took place after the onset the "al-Aqsa Intifada": a violent confrontation that had several different manifestations. The initial confrontations pitted Israeli forces against civilian Palestinian protests at key checkpoints and other areas of friction. These quickly escalated into confrontations between IDF and religious and secular armed Palestinian groups such as the Qassam Brigades, rejectionist elements of the PLO's main party, Fatah, and other militants. The violence culminated in an attempt by Israel to dismantle the institutions of the Palestinian National Authority (PNA) by assassinations, destruction of ministries, and wholesale detentions of PNA officials and PLC legislators. Paying the price for all of this were thousands of Palestinian civilians killed and wounded by IDF incursions and assassinations. No less tragic were the killings of Israeli civilians who were victims of suicide bombings.

The tragic unraveling of the peace process is thus also analyzed here, although meaningful negotiations were rare after 2001. Enormous bilateral and international diplomatic resources were expended on crisis management, the pursuit of ceasefires, and humanitarian access for Palestinians victimized by the renewed fighting and economic devastation of sanctions and closures imposed by Israel.

Prime Minister Sharon explored tentative back channels to President Arafat through his son Omri Sharon, but he ultimately embarked on a unilateral disengagement plan that included the erection of a barrier within the West Bank, carving out large swaths of it for settlements and separating West Bank Palestinians from their homes, fields, schools, and neighbors. This was coupled with the removal of all Israeli settlements in the Gaza Strip. Ultimately, Sharon openly threatened to assassinate Arafat and had him besieged in his Ramallah presidential compound. Yasir Arafat's death removed a key Israeli and U.S. objection to the resumption of negotiations, but Israeli governments failed to return to negotiations anyway, focusing instead on destabilizing the PNA internally while isolating it internationally. Occasionally, the Israelis would set out new conditions for the resumption of ceasefire talks.

U.S. diplomacy in the eight years of George W. Bush's presidency was singularly ineffective in moving the Israelis back toward the negotiation table. The Palestinians were fragmented enough so that the PNA could do little to stop secular and religious militants from taking up their armed struggle against Israel. Civilians on both sides died in large numbers: Palestinians from direct military attacks by the IDF and armed settlers, and Israelis by paramilitary attacks against soldiers within Palestine and suicide bomb attacks against civilians in Israel.

As this book was completed, serious armed conflict had erupted several times between armed forces loyal to Fatah and HAMAS, both of whom were trying to work out power-sharing arrangements as they tried to revitalize the PNA. Not least among their internal disputes was a vast divergence over the PLO's path of negotiation with Israel.

As of late 2010, the stalemated peace process could yet hold the seeds of an enlightened and just peace for both sides, but that prospect seemed remote as this book went into publication. The prevailing political climate in the region with the return of Binyamin Netanyahu as prime minister, the political fragmentation of the Palestinians, a major Israeli offensive in Gaza, the ongoing war in Afghanistan, the tensions between Israel and Hezbollah, the political standoff within Lebanon, and the United States and European Union's standoff with Iran over its nuclear enrichment programs seemed a far cry from the global and regional peace dividends that could have been realized had Palestinian-Israeli peace been achieved in the 1994 to 1999 timeframe originally set out in the Oslo Accords.

Negotiation Toward a Permanent Peace Agreement

In the months leading up to Ehud Barak's electoral victory in Israel, the United States took some steps to prepare for the renewal of the peace process. As Yasir

Arafat and the Palestinians grew frustrated with Netanyahu's inability to negotiate and implement agreements, May 4 approached—the official end-date of the interim period—and the Palestinian leadership repeated often and publicly that they would be actively considering a unilateral declaration of the state. Netanyahu in turn portrayed any unilateral declaration of the state of Palestine as an act of aggression that would result in seizure and annexation of large swaths of the West Bank and Gaza by the Israeli military.

U.S. diplomacy focused on getting Arafat and the Palestinians to back away from, or at least defer, the unilateral declaration. The Palestinian leadership hoped for a commitment from the United States to restarting the permanent status talks and support for Palestinian self-determination and requested a written instrument from Clinton.

In late April 1999, President Clinton sent what was meant to be a confidential letter of assurances to Yasir Arafat, in which Clinton confirmed Palestinian implementation of the interim arrangements and pledged the United States to "work actively for implementation by Israel." The letter recognized "how destructive settlement activities, land confiscations and house demolitions are to the pursuit of Palestinian-Israeli peace." Clinton exclaimed that "the Palestinian people should live free today, tomorrow and forever" and can "determine their own future on their own land," while also asking Arafat to "continue to rely on the peace process as the way to fulfill the aspirations of your people."[2]

In spite of, or perhaps because of, the contradictions inherent in Netanyahu's political stance—engagement in negotiations with the Palestinians, coupled with a reluctance to implement agreements he signed—Netanyahu could not sustain the governing coalition that brought him to power.

On May 17, 1999, former Israeli Army chief of staff Ehud Barak won the Israeli elections. In his victory speech at Rabin Square, he declared that his government would "move quickly toward a separation from the Palestinians by drawing four lines in the sand."[3] He pledged the following:

- To keep all of Jerusalem under Israeli sovereignty
- To never return to the pre-June 1967 borders
- To never tolerate any foreign forces west of the Jordan River
- To keep the majority of settlers in "Judea and Samaria" (the West Bank) in settlement blocs under Israeli sovereignty

As a basis for his strategic goal of negotiating a peace with the PLO, Barak had started by giving himself an extremely narrow margin of flexibility because these negotiation positions are essentially the polar opposite of those employed by moderate Palestinians seeking a two-state solution. The possibility of a permanent peace with the Palestinians would be seriously imperiled by such a wide gap in the positions of the parties and, in fact, did not recover from it. Barak also pledged to withdraw Israeli forces from Lebanon and conclude a peace agreement with Syria, further crowding his political-diplomatic agenda.

Barak was installed as prime minister on July 7, 1999, leading a broad seven-party coalition government. Cabinet positions were handed out to the amalgam of Left, center, and religious parties that could be cobbled together under Barak. Yossi Beilin, protégé of Shimon Peres and architect of the original Oslo talks, became the minister of justice. Peres, however, was not offered a strategic post and would remain sidelined from the peace process until it began falling apart. Barak immediately set out to commence negotiations on both the Syrian and Palestinian tracks. By this time, both sets of negotiations and Israel's implementation of the Wye River Memorandum commitments had been suspended since Netanyahu's call for early elections in January 1999.

The outstanding interim issues that had been renegotiated during more than three years of Netanyahu's government—but which awaited implementation—can be summarized briefly:

- The unfulfilled further redeployments (FRDs) of Israel Defense Forces from the West Bank and Gaza and thus the extension of the PNA's civil governance powers, security responsibilities, and territorial oversight into additional Palestinian areas
- The creation of two safe-passage routes, a northern and a southern route, between Gaza and the West Bank
- The construction of a much-needed commercial seaport and the opening of the Gaza Airport as well as other economic measures
- The release of Palestinian detainees held by Israel
- The dismantling of the new settlements started during Netanyahu's term and the freezing of further new settlement and expansion of existing settlements
- The commencement of the long-delayed permanent status negotiations

Renegotiation, Redux

One key to successful resumption of serious peace negotiations would have been to find the appropriate balance between the new political needs of the Barak government and the legitimate implementation needs of the PLO, all the while keeping the permanent status talks on their own track. Turning this key proved to be elusive.

Clinton received Barak at the White House and Camp David in mid-July, and the president told his Middle East peace envoy Dennis Ross that "Barak wanted to reach a permanent status agreement with the Palestinians much sooner than anyone suspected, by April 2000, he said—but to do so he wanted to defer his obligations under the Wye agreement as long as he could because the final Wye redeployments raised security questions for a number of Israeli settlements at a time when no one had any idea what a permanent status might look like."[4] But Barak was also seeking to squeeze leverage where there was none to be had. He essentially sought to dangle Israeli compliance with its Wye commitments in exchange for further Palestinian concessions on some of those very issues and, more troubling still, for Palestinian concessions on the permanent status issues—a dangerous game.

Gilead Sher, Barak's chief negotiator, rationalized Barak's reluctance to implement the remaining third stage of the second FRD thus: "Conceding additional territory without reaching an agreement on these core issues [boundaries, refugees, Jerusalem, water, security, which] would leave Israel without any assets to negotiate."[5] Sher was essentially saying that Israel had to refrain from implementing its agreed interim commitments to retain leverage for permanent status talks. This working assumption helped to undermine rather than build up the trust needed to engage in the permanent status talks.

Sher believed that, in the end, the Palestinians would only "relinquish their claim for Right of Return for Palestinian refugees to Israel" if it was bargained away against the territorial question.[6] But Barak's ploy to avoid the previously agreed upon Wye territorial (and other) concessions was seen as the last straw by the Palestinian leadership: they had only one thing to show for their adherence to the peace process—the signed commitments embodied in agreements such as the Wye River Memorandum—and precious little else. Arafat and his negotiation team insisted on complete or at least substantial implementation of the interim arrangements, *separate from any discussion of the permanent status negotiations.*

The Palestinians had been through more than three years of nearly fruitless negotiations with a government led by a declared opponent of peaceful coexistence. Domestically, their investment in the peace process had not resulted in a recognized state, settlements had increased, and the 1995 Interim Agreement had been only partly implemented and had improved the lives of some Palestinians but not nearly enough. The Israeli occupation continued in various guises, though on the margins of the major Palestinian cities. Corruption scandals within the PNA undermined the little popular confidence available for peace negotiations. Support for non-PLO parties was growing alarmingly. During their first summit, Barak also asked Clinton for a diminished U.S. presence in the peace process and an end to the CIA's role in Palestinian-Israeli security coordination, which had been created under the Wye River Memorandum and which had helped build capacity for Palestinian counterterrorism and preventive security. Despite the problematic strategies Barak was formulating, he impressed Clinton with his seriousness about moving forward simultaneously on three fronts: disengagement from the occupation zone in Lebanon, a full peace with Syria, and an "end to the conflict" with the Palestinians. It is unlikely that any U.S. president could have been persuaded to distance himself from such ambitious and homegrown peace initiatives for the Middle East. The president indicated that Secretary Albright would conduct a regional trip to support Arab and Israeli peace efforts in mid-August.

The Israelis and Palestinians began their meetings. Two summits between Arafat and Barak at Erez on July 11 and July 27 resulted in no agreements, but they established a new and refreshing pattern of high-level engagement. Barak put on the table his proposal to delay the remaining Wye FRD until a final status agreement could be reached. Arafat agreed only to let the front channel negotiators discuss Barak's positions: PNA minister of local government Saeb Eraqat and Barak's chief negotiator Gilead Sher were tasked to follow up the July 27 meeting and discuss the pending third stage of the second Wye FRD. Eraqat quickly suspended the negotiations and accused Israel of not wanting to carry out its commitments.

The U.S. Middle East peace team, seeking an opportunity for engagement, found it quickly in these first stumbling blocks to the negotiations. U.S. envoy Dennis Ross recalls that at the time, "if Saeb didn't hear something concrete that was of value to the Palestinians . . . he [Saeb Eraqat] would soon advise Arafat to demand implementation of Wye as written."[7] Eraqat and Sher and their respective teams continued negotiations through August 1999, but their positions remained frozen. According to Gilead Sher, the negotiations agenda was quite full and covered the range of outstanding Wye issues, as well as an Israeli position on how to link the permanent status negotiations to the interim issues.[8]

Dennis Ross's assessment of the encroaching stalemate was straightforward. The Palestinians, stung by the Netanyahu government's backpedaling, wanted to see Israeli compliance on the outstanding interim issues. Barak, impatient with the whole incrementalism of the process, was seeking to skip implementing these commitments and go right for a permanent status agreement. Ross's intermediation at that moment was designed to help the Barak team to see the shortsightedness of this strategy, and Ross went as far as setting up a secret meeting with the Israelis in Zurich to do it.[9] A high-level push from U.S. Secretary of State Albright and the U.S. peace team was still needed to bring the parties closer to agreement on the outstanding interim issues, which are reviewed in the following text.

Prisoners

With regard to the outstanding prisoner releases, Netanyahu had previously released 250 Palestinians (out of the 750 that had been agreed to) on November 20, 1998. Only 100 of the released had been "security detainees"; the rest were people charged with criminal offenses, which caused Arafat to accuse Netanyahu of being in violation of the letter and spirit of Wye. In front channel negotiations, Eraqat was thus seeking the release of another 400 to 650 out of 2,000 security detainees then being held, in order to comply with Wye, but the Israelis countered with figures even lower than Wye. The Interim Agreement and subsequent documents such as the Note for the Record of January 15, 1997, did not spell out the number of prisoners to be released, but rather set out the criteria for release and seemed to set up a mechanism that would require further negotiation to determine who would be released and when.[10]

Interestingly, the Egyptian government began playing a role reminiscent of Norway's mediation in 1993, facilitating quiet meetings between the negotiating teams with only minimal intervention in their discussions. Egyptian ambassador to Israel Muhammed Bassiouni provided his good offices and his ambassadorial residence for the negotiation teams, who conducted a series of negotiation sessions there during the last week of August 1999. Negotiations on the principles to guide a permanent status agreement appeared to be moving along in this venue until—by his own admission—Israeli negotiator Gilead Sher scuttled them. The Palestinians insisted on a secret high-level channel for Barak and Arafat, and a select group of negotiators to come together directly. At the same time, Egyptian president Hosni Mubarak had sent his top political advisor Osama el-Baz to mediate between Barak and Arafat.[11]

A secret negotiation channel began operating in coordination with the talks at Bassiouni's residence. These negotiations were led by Muhammed Dahlan, the PNA's director of preventive security in Gaza; and Yossi Genosar, Israel's former deputy director of Shin Bet, who had a long-standing role in clandestine contact with the PLO. According to one source close to the negotiators, it was in this channel that the eventual agreement was negotiated on September 4, 1999, with the help of Osama el-Baz, political advisor to President Mubarak.[12]

Further Redeployments of Israeli Troops from Palestinian Territory

It will be recalled that the 1995 Interim Agreement had set out a phased approach to reversing the Israeli military occupation, in a series of "further redeployments." The assassination of Rabin and the HAMAS terror bombings contributed to acting Prime Minister Peres's suspension of the first FRD. For the purpose of the FRDs, Palestinian territory was categorized as either Area A, B, or C.

In Area A, people and territory were to be fully under the PNA's security and civil authority. In Area B, there would be PNA civil authority but joint Israeli-Palestinian security responsibilities; Area C was solely under control of the Israeli military. The ostensible purpose of the phases was to gradually expand the civil and security responsibilities of the PNA while diminishing those of the IDF, by progressively expanding the amount of territory categorized as Area B and Area A. Each side attached great importance to the phases; Palestinians saw them as a necessary prelude to their claim to the entire West Bank and Gaza and, indeed, the only basis for interim self-government on the way to sovereignty, while Israelis saw them as the emerging outlines of the West Bank territory they would want to retain under a permanent status agreement. Thus a zero-sum perception about the future territorial map cast its shadow on the contemporary FRD issue.

As noted in the previous chapter, the Netanyahu negotiation team spent enormous political capital trying to *avoid* the FRDs. With pressure from the United States and the PLO's insistence on Israeli compliance, the Wye negotiations did finally result in implementation of the first FRD stage in November 1998, more than two years after the original due date of September 1996 had passed. Ultimately, the Wye River Memorandum permitted the Israelis to break down the two remaining stages into three smaller phases (see table 5 in chapter 5) covering 27.2 percent of the West Bank and Gaza.

Officially, the United States' position, articulated by Secretary of State Madeleine Albright to Barak's justice minister Yossi Beilin, was that the Wye FRD should be carried out as written unless the Palestinians explicitly agreed to adjust the schedule.[13] In response to the Palestinian team's insistence on concrete numbers of prisoners to be released, it appears that Sher tried to hold the detainee issue hostage to Palestinian concessions on the FRDs while, according to him, the Palestinians held the entire agreement hostage to Israeli concessions on the detainees.[14]

To the Red Sea: The Sharm el-Sheikh Memorandum

Madeleine Albright arrived in the Middle East with the U.S. peace team at the beginning of September 1999 and shuttled between Arafat and Barak to "receive assurances that made the final deal possible": an Israeli commitment to fully implement a 6.1 percent transfer of territory to the PNA's control by January 31, whether or not a framework agreement on the permanent status had been reached.[15] The high-level intermediation of Secretary Albright and President Mubarak, and the facilitation of the Egyptian ambassador to Israel, all worked together to achieve a new Palestinian-Israeli agreement. Although the method of persuasion—negotiation—was better than unilateral imposition, neglect, or violence, there was nothing really "new" in the new agreement. Most of the substance had been covered four years earlier in the Interim Agreement and then later in the Wye River Memorandum.

The first agreement between the PLO and Barak's government: the Sharm el-Sheikh Memorandum (a.k.a. Wye II) was signed by Arafat and Barak on September 4, 1999, with Secretary Albright, President Mubarak, and King Abdallah of Jordan signing as witnesses. The issues covered included items carried over from the Wye River Memorandum: the creation of Palestinian safe-passage routes between the West Bank and Gaza; percentages of land to be transferred to the PNA control under the FRD arrangements; the opening of the Gaza Seaport; prisoner releases; and the reopening of two areas in the Palestinian city of Hebron—the central al-Shuhada Street, which had been closed to Palestinians and open only to settlers, and the town's central market.

With regard to the FRDs, the new agreement set out three new deadlines for territorial transfer in order to satisfy the "Phase one and Phase two of the further redeployments" (Sharm el-Sheikh Memorandum, ¶2) from the Wye River Memorandum and the Interim Agreement. (See table 6.) As to the third FRD, the new agreement said nothing except that the "Third Further Redeployment Committee shall commence its activities not later than September 13, 1999" (Sharm el-Sheikh Memorandum, ¶1.e).

In Article 1, the Sharm el-Sheikh Memorandum set forth a more critical item: *a new set of target dates for permanent status negotiations.* The parties agreed to resume permanent status negotiations not later than September 13, 1999, and to reach a Framework Agreement on All Permanent Status Issues (FAPS) within five months of having started negotiations—by February 2000. They planned for a further period of seven months to negotiate a Comprehensive Agreement on All Permanent Status Issues (CAPS) before September 2000 at the

Table 6. Sharm el-Sheikh Memorandum:
The Renegotiated Three Mini-Stages of the Second FRD

	Agreed deadline	Percentage of territorial transfer	Date of implementation	Status (until breakdown of peace process)
1	Sept. 5, 1999	7% from Area C to Area B	Sept. 10, 1999	Completed
2	Nov. 15, 1999	2% from Area B to Area A, 3% from Area C to Area B	Israeli maps rejected by Arafat; Israel postpones. Implementation Jan. 5, 2000	Completed
3	Jan. 20, 2000	1% from Area C to Area A5.1% from Area B to Area A	Postponed by Barak Jan. 16, 2000; PNA insists and obtains participation in selection of areas.Implementation Mar. 21, 2000	Completed

latest. The Sharm el-Sheikh Memorandum takes note of the United States' offer to facilitate the permanent status talks.[16] Subsequently, Israel and the PLO would pursue direct and mediated, secret and open channels throughout this period of reenergized peace negotiations.

On the sixth anniversary of the signing of the Oslo Accords, September 13, 1999, Israeli foreign minister David Levy and secretary general of the PLO Executive Committee Abu Mazen declared the symbolic (re)opening of permanent status negotiations. But the permanent status negotiation teams had not yet been named by either side. The announcement seemed hollow: exactly three years earlier, in 1996, the PLO and Israel had announced their first launch of official permanent status negotiations. Ironically, at that time, they had already secretly negotiated a prototype FAPS: the Beilin-Abu Mazen document, (discussed in chapter 5). The Beilin-Abu Mazen (Stockholm) document could have served as a basis for new talks in 1999, despite its lack of endorsement by either Arafat or Peres at the time it was drafted. There is no indication that it was considered as input for new permanent status negotiations. Former Israeli negotiator Uri Savir believes that the public revelation of the Beilin-Abu Mazen document prevented it from becoming a useful instrument.

"Now on Beilin-Abu Mazen, clearly it was not an agreement, it was a superb intellectual exercise, and in a certain way . . . it was wasted because every good idea, once it is floated in the air it has very little survivability."[17]

As during the Netanyahu years, easy implementation of the FRDs continued to be elusive. The percentage of territory was not the only or even the most important issue complicating it. Rather, the contiguity of areas being turned over to Palestinian governance, as well as their natural resources, population, and actual Israeli presence were all complicating factors that affected the parties' preferences. Palestinian preferences tended toward increasing contiguity, extending PNA authority to more Palestinians, and removing visible vestiges of the Israeli occupation (troops, military facilities, check points, etc.). Israeli preferences included leaving Israeli settlements intact and prioritized security concerns generally.

Nevertheless, by October 5, the negotiation teams had concluded a subsidiary agreement to the Sharm el-Sheikh Memorandum concerning the Palestinian safe passage between Gaza and the West Bank, and the corridor opened officially on October 25, 1999.[18]

It is not too surprising that in a replay of the Netanyahu years, the second phase of the Sharm el-Sheikh FRD, scheduled for November 15, was postponed by Israel when Arafat protested the location of areas to be turned over. The PNA would insist on participation in the selection of areas to be turned over and eventually obtained some measure of participation. The salutary effect that the completed mini stages of the second FRDs *could have had* on the overall peace process might have been significant as it triggered increased PNA governance responsibilities, intensified security cooperation among Palestinian and Israeli forces and relief for the populations affected by the removal of the IDF. Counterbalancing this effect was the ongoing construction and expansion of Israeli settlements in the West Bank, the sealing and seizure of Palestinian land, and the Israeli insistence on deferring the third FRD by incorporating it into the permanent status talks.

In effect, these implementation successes, which should have built confidence among the parties in the process and in each other, were "too little, too late." The continuous renegotiation eroded mutual confidence in the process and among the negotiators. Despite the new agreement, negotiations would *still* be required for the release of security detainees, the northern safe-passage route, and the remaining FRDs. These outstanding interim issues plagued the start of the permanent status talks.

In late September 1999, Arafat named Yasir Abd Rabbuh as head of the permanent status team on the Palestinian side, while Eraqat was to continue pushing ahead on outstanding interim issues. Abu Mazen was to oversee both teams. Barak delayed naming members of his negotiating teams until the end of October when he named Oded Eran to head Israel's permanent and interim issue teams. They now had three months to reach a FAPS according to the Sharm el-Sheikh deadline. Meetings of the front channel teams intensified in frequency, alternating between Ramallah and Jerusalem.

On the eve of Madeleine Albright's arrival in Israel during a regional tour in December 1999, the PLO announced a suspension of final status talks because of ongoing settlement construction, but talks resumed at the team level and in occasional discreet summits between Arafat and Barak throughout December 1999 and through January and February 2000. The FRDs and security detainees took up much of the time and efforts that might have been dedicated to the permanent status talks.

While the Palestinian-Israeli negotiations were moving forward valiantly but slowly, Israel and the United States were also involved in negotiations with Syria. Although not the subject of this analysis, the Israel-Syria track drained attention from the Palestinian-Israeli talks. The Palestinian leadership expressed frustration that both prior implementation and forward-looking permanent status issues were sidelined by the focus on Syria. Nevertheless, the Israeli leadership believed the Palestinians would tolerate the delay in the hope that a Syria-Israel agreement would establish the June 4, 1967, lines as a precedent for their own territorial negotiations.[19] The Syrian-Israeli negotiations began with great promise of an historic, fast, and comprehensive accord as Ehud Barak, Hafez al-Asad, and Bill Clinton seemed fully engaged. As Barak moved forward, he immediately discovered opposition from his right-wing coalition partners and also from members of his own inner circle who believed in giving primacy to the Palestinian-Israeli track. Barak decided that he could not politically survive the peace deal he most desired (a deal with Syria), and he believed the Israeli public and political parties remained opposed to any return of the Golan Heights to Syria. Ariel Sharon steadily maligned Barak's efforts and mobilized popular opposition to them. The initiative withered on the vine. Within months, Hafez al-Asad had died and with him the immediate hopes for definitive end to the Syrian-Israeli dimension of the broader Middle East conflict.

Arafat and Barak established a pattern of periodic summits. Yossi Genosar hosted both men at his home on January 17, 2000, in a session in which Arafat proposed that the FRDs incorporate Palestinian areas adjacent to Jerusalem. Barak, for his part, repeated his belief in the futility of Israel carrying out the third full FRD.[20] Abu Mazen also hosted both leaders at his home that January.[21] Further summits followed but did not yield any breakthroughs on either the substance of their negotiations or their professional relationship.

The January FAPS deadline passed without any framework agreement, but the United States seemed sufficiently interested to invite Arafat to the White House on January 20 to urge him to continue negotiations toward the FAPS and to give Barak extensions of time. Barak and Arafat continued to hold private summits at that time, and in one of those, Arafat explicitly requested that Barak include three Palestinian villages near Jerusalem as part of the upcoming (February 15) third mini phase of the Sharm el-Sheikh FRD.[22] The villages were already part of Area B. Barak made no commitment in their face-to-face meeting but, according to Dennis Ross, showed some understanding for Arafat's request. However, Arafat learned of Barak's refusal to include them only through Israeli media, which only caused Palestinian resolve to stiffen.[23]

As the February 2000 deadline passed without the implementation of the outstanding FRD, the Palestinians suspended all front channel negotiations—although, as discussed in the following, back channel negotiations continued. February and most of March passed without perceptible movement on the most critical component of the peace process, the FAPS negotiations.

By March, the peace process appeared to be in peril. The U.S. peace team, led by Dennis Ross, took a renewed interest in getting the Palestinian-Israeli negotiations restarted after having neglected them in order to push forward the Israel-Syria negotiations, including a last-ditch Geneva summit between Clinton and al-Asad in March. The U.S. peace team was also hearing concerns from Barak's chief of staff and the head of Shin Bet that their prime minister was ignoring their warnings that the Palestinian "street" was in danger of resorting to mass protests and even violence because of the failures of the peace process. To restore momentum, Ross proposed to Barak that Israel cede control of at least one the three Palestinian villages near Jerusalem as part of the still-to-be-negotiated third FRD and that he give the Palestinians greater participation in choosing areas for the upcoming last mini phase of the Sharm el-Sheikh commitments. Lipkin-Shahak argues that the village transfer proposal was an Israeli idea to assuage the Palestinian's concern with being sidelined.[24] Ross also asked Yossi Genosar to try to persuade Barak. Genosar succeeded in getting Barak to concede all three villages, if the deal would be kept secret by the Palestinians: two of the villages would be transferred to Palestinian control on April 23 and the third on May 23, the new target date for the third mini phase of the FRD. June 23 would be the new target date for the FAPS. Mohammed Dahlan asked Ross if President Clinton could give an assurance that Barak would actually implement his own proposal, and Barak consented to President Clinton giving Arafat assurance on the transfer of the villages.[25]

Arafat and Barak met privately on March 7, and Arafat publicly hosted Barak and his entourage in Ramallah the next day so that Arafat, Barak, and Ross could announce the end of the crisis and the resumption of negotiations.[26]

Later in March, Clinton called Arafat and verbally delivered the personal assurance on the village transfer, something he would have cause to regret.[27]

News of the transfer of the three villages leaked out, causing a large contingent of Barak's parliamentary coalition to threaten to move to the opposition.[28] Uri Savir noted that the village transfer, had it remained a back channel affair, would have been successfully implemented. The media's scrutiny of the villages issue exaggerated its importance and helped mobilize political opposition.[29] Barak capitulated to his internal spoilers, thereby giving them more veto power over the operational and technical aspects of the implementation of the Sharm el-Sheikh Memorandum. Their growing strength was being mustered for the purpose of preventing Israeli engagement with the permanent status negotiations. But Barak's political predicaments generated little empathy among the Palestinians who saw him increasingly hobbled in his efforts to carry out the interim commitments, and possibly incapable of delivering on the far more difficult permanent status issues.[30]

Two summit meetings between Arafat and Barak, one of them hosted by Egyptian president Hosni Mubarak on March 9, served only to urge the parties to resume negotiations. The U.S. peace team again intervened directly, hoping to restore momentum by bringing Palestinian and Israeli front channel FAPS negotiators to Washington, D.C., to resume FAPS negotiations away from the polarizing political climate in the region.

Intensifying the FAPS Negotiations: Toward a Final Summit

Palestinian and Israeli delegations led by Yasir Abd Rabbuh and Oded Eran, respectively, gathered at Bolling Air Force Base and undertook two rounds of permanent status talks lasting one week in March 2000 and an additional week in April. Omar Dajani, legal advisor for the Palestinian negotiation team, observed that Palestinian leaders had neglected serious internal preparation for permanent status issues during the Netanyahu years, and continued this neglect "until the Spring of 2000," and little could be expected from these rounds.[31] The first round began on March 21 but produced no texts or understandings, although the parties did exchange serious ideas regarding the permanent status.[32] More hopefully, the third stage of the second FRD was implemented by Israel during that first round. No further progress was reported for the round of Bolling talks that took place from April 6 to April 14, 2000. A third round took place at the Israeli resort town of Eilat on the Red Sea from April 30 to May 7, although it too ended in impasse. The Eilat sessions took place in an atmosphere made tense by the Israeli government's solicitation of construction bids on new housing units for a major Israeli settlement in East Jerusalem, Ma'ale Adumim.[33]

Ross joined the talks at Eilat, hoping to then quietly join parallel back channel talks that had been set up and were being led by Abu Alaa and Gilead Sher.[34] But even the back channel negotiators appeared to be reluctant to negotiate on any real substance. Believing he was protecting the back channel by boosting the functionality of the front channel, so that its own negotiators would take it seriously, Ross persuaded the Israelis to make a territorial offer and persuaded the Palestinians to negotiate on the basis of the Israeli proposal. When Oded Eran did so, however, the map he presented offered an initial 60 percent of the West Bank as part of the future state (growing over time to 80 percent). But contrary to Ross's expectations of further bargaining, the Palestinian negotiators simply walked out of the front channel negotiations, suspecting that their front channel negotiation was being undermined by efforts elsewhere: the back channel. Media rumors of better offers (up to 90 percent) being floated by Israel in back channel talks confirmed their fears of being a mere sideshow.[35] Ross scrambled to find what he called a "focal point" that would lend credibility to the front channel and draw attention away from the back channel so that front channel negotiators could explore further FAPS solutions, and he began several days of shuttle diplomacy between Eran on one hand, and Eraqat and Abd Rabbuh on the other.[36]

Dennis Ross believes that it was he who suggested to a reluctant Barak the need for a back channel to supplement the front channel talks on the permanent status, but that Barak "would not grant anyone on his side the mandate to offer serious ideas for shaping such a deal."[37] In taking credit for the FAPS back channel, Ross claims it began only in April 2000.[38] Other participants in the peace process give a different timeline for the opening of a back channel, however, and do not attribute it to Dennis Ross or the U.S. peace team. High-level, quiet talks had been already proceeding in parallel to the FAPS negotiations, led by Abu Mazen and Abu Alaa on the Palestinian side, with the Minister of Internal Security Shlomo Ben-Ami and senior Israeli negotiator and former IDF chief of staff Amnon Lipkin-Shahak, on the Israeli side.[39]

The FAPS back channel appears in fact to have been conceived in November 1999, when Arafat, Barak, and Clinton were in Oslo for the commemoration of the Nobel Peace Prize that had been previously conferred on Rabin, Peres, and

Arafat. While planning out the schedule of negotiations for the coming new year, a secret channel was built into their plans.[40] According to Palestinian sources, the permanent status back channel indeed began meeting in November 1999, and Yasir Abd Rabbuh revealed its existence the next month, although he characterized them as "talks away from the media spotlight . . . not secret talks." When Abu Mazen was subsequently interviewed about this, he too claimed that this back channel had never been "secret."[41]

Shlomo Ben-Ami and Abu Alaa held six rounds of these secret, or at least "quiet," FAPS talks starting in Oslo on November 4, 1999, and continued in parallel with the talks led by Oded Eran and Saeb Eraqat. Abu Alaa was replaced by Abu Mazen for an additional four back channel rounds.[42] Abu Mazen was then replaced again by Abu Alaa when the Swedish government offered its good offices to the PLO and Israel in April of 2000.[43] Although only two further back channel FAPS rounds were actually conducted in Sweden, this back channel has come to be known as the "Sweden channel" or "Stockholm channel."[44]

During the first set of negotiations in Sweden, an Israeli proposal on territory was floated: Palestinians would get back 76.6 percent of their territory, a further 10.1 percent would be classified as "security zones" controlled by Israel, and an additional 13.3 percent to be annexed outright to Israel. The proposal, although meant to be a starting point for discussions, had a negative impact on the Palestinian negotiators,[45] from whose perspective Israel had already claimed 78 percent of historical Palestine. They saw no reason to concede any part of the remaining 22 percent (the West Bank and Gaza, including East Jerusalem).

The Stockholm back channel's effectiveness was diminished by what some believed was bitter internal rivalry among the Palestinian top-level negotiators and concern among them that Arafat might not support the outcomes of the back channel. Ben-Ami blames Abu Mazen for exposing the back channel to the news media to undermine Abu Alaa.[46] Without the backing of Arafat, no Palestinian negotiator could tackle the permanent status issues with any authority or creativity.[47] Others believed that internal Israeli political party rivalries were working to undermine the back channel.[48] Still, it seemed to offer the only forum in which the negotiators could advance and explore arrangements and concessions that they simply could not mention, let alone negotiate, in front channel negotiations, where only tepid Israeli proposals had been made by Eran and where there appear to have been no Palestinian counterproposals made.

As the Stockholm channel had the potential for making progress on the FAPS, parties with an interest in undermining the peace process as a temporary tactic or long-term strategy would have an interest in undermining the back channel. Given the relative abundance of spoilers, internal opposition, and disaffected negotiators, it was almost inevitable that news of the Stockholm channel leaked to the press on May 14 and 15 while the negotiators were actually in Sweden, and as Dennis Ross arrived in Sweden to join the teams.[49]

Yasir Abd Rabbuh, somewhat surprisingly (because he was already on record for having spoken openly about the "quiet" parallel negotiations) immediately resigned as front channel FAPS negotiator when press reports appeared about the Stockholm channel. He claimed that the Israelis were manipulating the channels to see which one yielded more Palestinian concessions, and he believed his resignation would permit the back channel to be "the only one negotiating with Israel."[50]

While the FAPS negotiations were proceeding in front and back channels, Barak had committed himself (and President Clinton) to begin the transfer of the villages on April 23, 2000. But on April 11, Barak informed Dennis Ross that he wanted to delay until May 1. The Israeli attorney general, Eliyakim Rubinstein, the man who had headed the Israeli side of the Palestinian-Israeli talks at the Madrid Peace Conference and its follow-on talks in Washington, issued a legal opinion that the village transfer required parliamentary approval, not simply cabinet approval. Barak gambled his coalition's survival but succeeded in getting the Knesset to approve the transfer.[51]

Palestinian protests commemorating the 1948 al-nakba[52] also coincided with the back channel Stockholm talks and led to some violence in the West Bank and Gaza between protestors and IDF, and then between Palestinian police and IDF. Yossi Genosar had undertaken a direct mission from Barak to Arafat just prior to al-Nakba Day, asking him to work to prevent confrontation and violence so as to not call attention to and jeopardize the transfer of the villages.[53]

Observers disagree on whether or not Arafat had any control over the initiation of the violence and whether or not the PLO was seeking to derive any negotiating leverage from it—regardless of any ability to control it. As a sign of popular Palestinian frustration with the meager gains and spotty implementation of the peace process, and with no final agreement in sight, the al-Nakba Day protests and the confrontations with the IDF were a portent of much worse to come. Indeed, one Fatah activist indicated at the time that autonomous militia units were being organized to prepare for any Israeli reversals of the occupation, as an alternate means of resistance to the Israeli occupation. According to this source, the emerging resistance was beyond the control of the senior PLO/PNA leadership.[54]

Arafat was able to contain the spread of demonstrations and violent confrontations with the IDF and accomplished this, remarkably, in coordination with Israeli security officials.[55] Both sides' tendencies to resort to violence or to tolerate violence by their own militants would later become self-fulfilling prophecies: the peace process did not just have an expiration date, but a *self-destruct* date.

Despite the violence and the suspension of the village transfer, the back channel negotiators reconvened for another set of negotiations in Sweden on May 19, 2000, and worked to make progress on a sixth draft "nonpaper" that could serve as the basis for an eventual FAPS. On the issue of Palestinian refugees, the draft recognized the principle of recognition of their right of return but limited the implementation of that right to a symbolic number that could be admitted to Israel while the rest would either be compensated in place, repatriated to new host countries, or permitted to enter the new Palestine. The issue of the unimplemented prisoner releases was also folded into the draft FAPS and deferred until the negotiation of a Comprehensive Agreement on the Permanent Status (CAPS).[56]

In this dynamic environment, Barak decided to push the United States hard on plans for a summit. When Dennis Ross arrived in Israel from Sweden in mid-May, Barak informed him that he wanted Ross to help the negotiations along for one week, that he wanted to received Secretary of State Madeleine Albright in Israel the week after, and that a summit hosted by the United States should immediately follow.[57] Dennis Ross understood that Barak's urgency and logic were both flawed: "we had just begun a serious negotiation that was still, at best, conceptual . . . the issues were too hard, we did not have time to prepare the ground . . . and yet here he was with a two week timetable for an endgame summit. It was astonishingly unrealistic."[58]

Dennis Ross looked into the internal politics of each side; he found Abu Mazen disengaged from the negotiations—perhaps sidelined by Yasir Arafat. Barak's coalition partners in his own cabinet were learning critical information about the negotiations from Ross rather than from Barak. The ongoing weakening of Barak's cabinet coalition and a second round of violent confrontations between Palestinian demonstrators (protesting Israel's failure to release any Palestinian prisoners); the IDF caused Barak to not only cancel the transfer of the three Jerusalem villages but also to suspend transfer of tax revenues Israeli owed the PNA and to completely halt plans to release any prisoners—all actions that would be provocative to the Palestinian leadership. "Barak held to paradoxical position of not delivering on promises reaffirmed by the President [Clinton] while continuing to press for rapid movement to the endgame."[59]

In this environment and in the aftermath of his failures to move toward agreement with the ailing Syrian president, Hafez al-Assad, Barak decided to accelerate his planned unilateral withdrawal from Southern Lebanon at the end of May. The end of the Israeli occupation of Lebanon was hailed as a victory by the Lebanese Shi'ite movement Hezbollah, who believed the withdrawal to be the result of its uncompromising armed resistance to the occupation. The end of the occupation was also welcomed by the Israeli public, but the withdrawal was not linked to any regional or bilateral agreement (with either Lebanon or Syria) and left the state of belligerence on Israel's northern border dangerously unresolved. Nevertheless, operationally, the IDF evacuated and destroyed its positions in Lebanon in under twenty hours.[60] Palestinian and Israeli insiders have voiced concern that the unilateral withdrawal would only incite Palestinian militants who would attribute the Israeli withdrawal to the armed resistance of Hezbollah.

The redeployment from South Lebanon, some warned, would also invite unfavorable comparisons between an Israeli withdrawal under fire from Lebanon with a tedious, often renegotiated, and unimplemented Israeli withdrawal from Palestinian areas.[61]

In contrast with the IDF's lightning withdrawal from Lebanon, Barak's negotiations with the Palestinians had lasted for months and achieved precious little in terms of implementation. The Jerusalem suburbs had been offered and withdrawn; the outstanding prisoner releases, tax revenues, and the northern safe-passage route remained suspended. The third FRD, scheduled for June 23, did not seem likely: Arafat wanted it to result in a total of 91 percent of Palestinian territory under PNA control, whereas Barak did not wish to carry it out at all in order to use territorial offers as leverage to gain Palestinian concessions on Jerusalem and the refugee issues.[62]

The renewed burst of negotiations that began in early 2000—both open and secret—seemed to have run its course by the middle of the year. The fragility of both front and back channels had become very apparent by this point in the year: the failures to implement Wye and Sharm el-Sheikh agreements and the lack of progress on the FAPS diminished the trust of the negotiators themselves in the process, while front channel negotiators appeared increasingly unable to move forward without the relatively broader mandates that back channel negotiators tended to enjoy. And yet, the back channels were also failing to move toward either interim or permanent resolutions of the conflict.

In the back channel, Barak appeared reluctant to put out any Israeli proposals that included all the FAPS issues, fearing that the Palestinians would also play a positional bargaining game.[63] Arafat too was reluctant to vest the back channel with sufficient, clear negotiation authority.[64] Dennis Ross believed that his presence in Sweden, which remained secret, began moving the parties away from this stagnation because he urged the Israelis to present a more substantial territorial withdrawal than had been presented thus far. Ross also urged the Israelis to develop a proposal for the resolution of the Jerusalem issue, which Shlomo Ben-Ami was unwilling to do in the absence of an articulated position by Barak.[65] "Be careful with the issue of Jerusalem. Do not document positions. We cannot have drafted or written documents. Only notes and discussions," Barak warned his chief negotiator—hardly a broad mandate to find a solution.[66]

In spite of this lack of forward progress in either front or back channels, and the simultaneous erosion of internal political unity for each side, Barak was still anxious to move toward a tripartite summit that would hopefully result in the FAPS. Despite his serious misgivings about Barak's insistence on an accelerated summit, Dennis Ross told Arafat that "you will never have a better chance to do a final peace agreement than you have now with this Israeli government and with this [U.S.] President."[67] Arafat did not see the rush to the summit in the same way; the PLO continued to push for prior implementation of the outstanding interim issues and believed that the parties' positions should be far more closely aligned *before* going to the summit.

Dennis Ross's and others' narratives of the developments before the summit in June 2000 give the impression that the U.S. administration was initially very reluctant to proceed to a summit because Barak had failed to implement the interim commitments he had made and for which President Clinton had provided his assurances to Yasir Arafat.[68] Ross and other White House officials understood the risks of a failed effort for the U.S. presidency but failed to appreciate the risks for the region. Secretary of State Albright ultimately supported presidential sum-mitry as a historic obligation. However, the personal interventions of Clinton, Albright, Ross, and the U.S. peace team had not succeeded in improving any of the objective conditions for achieving a FAPS. There was no "ripe" moment: the parties did not perceive themselves to be in a "mutually hurting stalemate," nor had a "mutually enticing opportunity" yet been proposed.[69]

A brief encounter between President Clinton and Prime Minister Barak on June 1, 2000, on the sidelines of a United States-European Union summit in Lis-bon, Portugal, provided the president an opportunity to push Barak to implement the outstanding interim commitments that provided Arafat with grievances. It was also the moment for the president to push for more clarity on whether the respective positions of the parties were close enough to justify a summit.

Clinton deferred the summit decision, but he committed to getting Arafat to back off on his interim demands including the third FRD; Barak avoided commit-ting himself to any clarifications of his negotiating position. Subsequently, Mad-eleine Albright visited Barak in Israel and extracted a commitment from him to make some moves on the tax revenues, prisoners, and Jerusalem villages. He agreed to make some gestures only on the first two issues, prior to Arafat's planned trip to Washington on June 15. Barak also agreed reluctantly to a short burst of pre-summit negotiations in the United States. Ross reports that Barak "in effect, broke his prom-ises to us" and Arafat came to Washington with still nothing to show for the past year's worth of negotiations. Clinton tried to persuade Arafat to come to a summit anyway and offered to support a substantial FRD "if we could not produce a FAPS."[70] The due date of the third FRD, however, was only a week away. Arafat agreed to let the date slip in order to permit the United States to push for the FAPS.[71]

In the hopes of narrowing the wide negotiation gap, in June 2000 the United States invited the negotiating teams to Washington in order to help pave the way for a possible July summit. The negotiators flew in to Washington, D.C., and began parallel talks at both Andrews Air Force Base and at Bolling Air Force Base. Abu Alaa and Shlomo Ben-Ami went to Andrews AFB to continue work on FAPS issues, while Oded Eran and Saeb Eraqat went to Bolling to work on the interim issues. Sandy Berger, the national security advisor, echoed the president's concerns about Israeli noncompliance: he told the Israelis to reverse their withholding of tax revenues due to the PNA and to implement the third FRD as preconditions for the United States to convene a mediation summit.[72]

In a private dinner at Dennis Ross's home, Eraqat outlined a possible scenario for agreement: the Palestinians would be able to live with a FAPS arrangement in which they kept only 92 percent of West Bank territory in exchange for an equal area of land to expand the Gaza Strip. He expressed a vision of Jerusalem in which the Jewish settlements in East Jerusalem would simply be annexed to Israel, while Palestine would get the remaining Arab neighborhoods of East Jerusalem. A single municipality could provide services to both of the city's populations. On refugees, Eraqat proposed that the Israelis admit only a limited number back to Israel while admitting the principle of the right of return and providing financial compensation to the Palestinian Diaspora.

Separately, Shlomo Ben-Ami and Gilead Sher showed Ross a document that contained "sixteen assumptions"—ostensibly Israeli positions that the United States (as mediator) could advance and that would serve as a compromise between the preferences of each side on the outstanding issues. These were not official negotiation positions yet, but Ross wondered if they could become such. They had not been fully debated internally among the Israeli leadership and did not represent a formal internal consensus. Nor were they positions that had resulted from bargaining between the parties. They were, however, just intriguing enough to keep the U.S. peace team interested.

Taken together, the Israeli "sixteen assumptions" paper and Eraqat's articulation of a permanent settlement acceptable to the Palestinians permitted Ross to envision "the outlines of a deal on the core issues."[73]

The Israelis were still trying to convince Arafat about the futility of further preparatory negotiations and the utility of a summit. The mayor of Nablus in the West Bank, Ghassan Shakaa, hosted a meeting of top Israeli and Palestinian negotiators on June 25, 2000. In attendance were Gilead Sher and Shlomo Ben-Ami, Yasir Arafat, Abu Alaa, Abu Mazen, and Saeb Eraqat. The Palestinians insisted on the need to continue doing more fundamental negotiation before rushing to the summit, while the Israelis tried to make a case for an immediate summit and stated that they would negotiate an accord based on the Stockholm channel's nonpaper.[74]

Both Ross and Albright traveled to the region June 27 and 28, partly to "authenticate" the new concepts he had heard from Eraqat, Ben-Ami, and Sher, and to ascertain the support each enjoyed from their respective leaders, Arafat and Barak. Neither leader did so. Barak explicitly *disclaimed* an ability to approach the Palestinian position and distanced himself from the "sixteen assumptions" document of his own lead negotiators.[75] Albright also worked to persuade Arafat to come to a summit, despite his consistently expressed reservations.[76] He asked for two more weeks for pre-summit negotiations, although he did not make the outcome of such negotiations a precondition for his acquiescence to come to the summit. Arafat repeated his concerns to President Clinton after Albright's return to Washington.[77]

On July 1, Clinton called Barak to press him for some movement before Clinton made his summit decision, but he received only "fuzzy" noncommittal responses again on prisoners, the Jerusalem villages, the concept of a land swap, and possible scenarios regarding Jerusalem. Ross and Berger disagreed on how to interpret Barak's responses, with Berger saying that Barak had "stiffed" the president. Berger himself called Barak to get more clarity, but again the responses were cryptic, with Barak claiming that he had indicated "a lot of flexibility" to the president. Apparently, this was enough to mollify Berger. Ross asked U.S. ambassador Israel Martin Indyk to meet with Barak and restate the president's concerns. Again Barak demurred on the villages and offered to free thirty prisoners, but only when the summit convened.[78]

By July, the Clinton administration was fully advocating the summit idea to the Palestinians, asking (and getting) Palestinian concessions in advance of the summit. In contrast, the administration had gotten neither interim implementation nor clear indications of an endgame plan from Barak, despite direct requests from the president, the Secretary of State, the ambassador to Israel, the national security advisor, and the head of the U.S. peace team. Clinton himself had not yet fully embraced the summit and expressed doubts about the idea.

Paradoxically, on July 4, Albright, Ross, and Berger convened with the president for the Independence Day celebration at Camp David, and all three agreed to persuade Clinton of the feasibility of a summit. Clinton was still tentative, but he let himself be persuaded by the historical arguments and a call from Barak indicating that he was about to face a no-confidence vote in the Knesset. Clinton called and informed both Barak and Arafat of his decision to host the summit. Barak only agreed to "contemplate limited symbolic moves on both territorial swaps and the East Jerusalem neighborhoods . . . if at the end of the day these were the keys to an agreement." Clinton for his part "asked for nothing more" from Barak.[79] Perhaps cognizant that he had set himself up to fail in mediating one of contemporary history's most intractable conflicts, Clinton asked Ross, "this is the right thing to do, isn't it?" Ross recorded his "own feeling of dread."[80] The Camp David summit was set for July 11, 2001. Clinton needed to leave the United States to attend the G-8 summit by July 19.

Yasir Arafat, at that moment, was contemplating the coming September 13 anniversary date of the Oslo Accord, which would be the next obvious moment to make a unilateral declaration of the state of Palestine. Barak was watching his political coalition crumble and was busy making contingency plans with the IDF's chief of staff, Shaul Mofaz, for a reoccupation of the West Bank and Gaza should the PLO go forward with the unilateral declaration.[81]

Summit and Descent: Camp David

The summit at Camp David began on July 11, 2000, but the working delegations actually began meeting July 9 in Washington, D.C., at the Madison Hotel. Different visions of how to proceed had not yet been reconciled into an agreed summit process. At the Madison Hotel, some of the Israelis and Palestinians discussed using their May 2000 Stockholm talks and its resulting nonpaper as a starting point for Camp David. The Palestinians proposed that a comprehensive agreement (CAPS), rather than a framework agreement on the permanent status (FAPS), should be their goal for the summit.[82] Dennis Ross and the U.S. Middle East team prepared with President Clinton, who expressed interest in reaching an agreement in which the Palestinian state could be declared, with temporary borders involving Israeli withdrawal from only 75 percent of the West Bank[83]—a low aspiration point for a summit sponsored by the United States.

Various accounts of the Camp David summit have been published, and in its aftermath, the summit itself became the focus of polemics as the United States and Israel spent considerable political capital blaming the PLO and Arafat for its failure, ostensibly to bolster Barak's tenuous hold on government.[84]

On the first day at Camp David, President Clinton met separately with Arafat and then Barak. The U.S. team created an optimistic, informal atmosphere where they hoped the Palestinian and Israeli delegates would mingle easily with each other and with their U.S. hosts. Clinton tried to impose a media blackout, with information on the summit coming exclusively from a U.S. State Department daily briefing. In the secluded atmosphere of Camp David, the negotiators

and the mediator attempted to confront for the first time all of the most difficult issues that had prevented a Palestinian-Israeli permanent status accord from
being concluded. Both delegations were secluded from the daily pressures of their
respective citizens, political supporters and opponents, and from regional leaders
such as Egypt and Jordan.

From the start of the summit, Arafat appears to have begun a consistent
pattern of insisting on Palestinian sovereignty over East Jerusalem, or at least the
Haram al-Sharif/Temple Mount. President Clinton himself seems to have been
a quick study on the problems of sharing Jerusalem, and at one point jokingly
declared that he could become the "next mayor of Jerusalem," according to one
account.[85] Jerusalem appears to be the issue that helped assure the summit's failure, as will be explained in the following. Process-related errors permeated the
summit as well.

In contrast with the U.S. team's plan to first narrow the distance between
the two sides on the key issues by outlining "parameters" and then to interpose a
paper genuinely authored by the United States with solutions within the parameters, Barak preferred to "struggle . . . on old positions" for two days in order to
precipitate a crisis moment that he hoped would bring about serious negotiation
and commitment. Clinton's plan to present a U.S. "paper" was undermined by
Barak's insistence that it be vetted by his team and that it incorporate ideas from
an Israeli paper *before* it went to Arafat.[86] This effectively turned U.S. proposals into Israeli proposals. In contrast, Arafat accepted Clinton's process without
attaching conditions. Dennis Ross believed the United States lost control of the
summit process from the beginning, at the moment Clinton acceded to Barak's
game plan.[87]

The various accounts of Camp David convey a broad consensus about the
Jerusalem issue being the subject that President Clinton ended up dedicating the
most effort to, that the parties dedicated the least time to (prior to the summit),
and which consequently contributed to the collapse of the summit.[88]

On two issues, the Palestinians arrived at Camp David seeking the affirmation of a principle prior to the negotiation of its details. For example, regarding
the Palestinians' claim to the right of return for the refugees, the Palestinian delegation communicated that they wanted the right itself to be affirmed by Israel,
while the implementation could proceed with flexibility. If Israel acknowledged
the right of return *as a right,* enshrined in UN GA Resolution 194 (1948),[89] a

spectrum of solutions would be found, including the majority of refugees accepting either compensation, rehabilitation in their actual country of residence, or repatriation of some to Israel and most to the new Palestine. The territorial issue also was one on which a principle was sought by the Palestinians, whereas the Israelis seemed more concerned about the details of implementation to which a commitment would be made. At the core, the Israeli concern is demographic: there is a fear that an influx of Palestinian Arabs would upset the Jewish majority composition of the Israeli population and become a political force in the country.

The Palestinian side insisted on the "land for peace" formula enshrined in the peace process and in the diplomatic history of the conflict: UN Security Council Resolutions 242 (1967) and 338 (1973). If the Israelis accepted the June 4, 1967, lines separating the West Bank (including East Jerusalem and Gaza) from Israel, then the Palestinians would accept modifications to the line to accommodate Israeli security concerns and settlements.

The Israelis did not wish to acknowledge the principle on either issue, fearing that such acknowledgement would be tantamount to conceding on the implementation and that it would commit them in any future talks.[90] For the Palestinians, surrendering the principle was tantamount rewarding Israel for the impacts of its occupation. The U.S. team, including President Clinton, also rejected the Palestinian approach and expected the Palestinians to make concessions toward an elusive middle ground.[91]

The multiple incompatibilities of approaches yielded gradually to a working arrangement at Camp David that ended by focusing on implementation details. By July 13, two days into the summit, the United States had ready its working draft proposal (a so-called "nonpaper"). Clinton, at various points, asked for and received Israeli input into the U.S. drafts and subsequently sought Palestinian input. The Palestinians would sometimes get a hint from the Israeli delegation of the U.S. proposals before they were communicated to them, and the Palestinians felt that this showed prior coordination between the United States and Israel to the exclusion of the Palestinians.[92]

Surprisingly, the first U.S. nonpaper was immediately rejected by the Israelis. Barak's team got to see it first but rejected it despite its inclusion of language the Israelis had previously offered in the Stockholm nonpaper.[93] Dennis Ross would have preferred to configure the U.S. paper as a framework settlement and then use it to stimulate substantive discussions between the parties. The Israelis

insisted—and Clinton accepted—a major change in his summit strategy: eliminate the draft U.S. paper and offer a document that explicitly included the two
conflicting positions of the parties, annotated with I's and P's directly in the
document itself. The Palestinians, once they reviewed the "I's and P's" document,
wondered why the United States had abandoned its strategy and believed that
the Israelis had already influenced the U.S. paper.[94] President Clinton, in going
along with this more contentious approach, set aside and weakened one of his few
sources of leverage as mediator: control of the process and substantive input on
the disputed issues.

The system of three parallel working groups (security and borders, Jerusalem, and refugees) was put into operation.[95] As each group began its work, they
reported to President Clinton in person, who in turn asked each group to move
further, obtain greater flexibility, or make new assumptions that could push them
toward problem solving. He explicitly asked Arafat to permit Abu Alaa to make
concessions on territory (to accept that the Palestinians might not get either all of
the West Bank or be able to negotiate a swap for any annexed land).

The various subissues discussed in each committee were complicated, and
each group's work was interrelated. Despite the summit's ultimate close, the
parties made some significant progress over the course of the summit. At the
beginning, Israeli territorial proposals were simply about annexing outright 14
percent of the West Bank for the Israeli settlers, directly controlling for military purposes an additional 10 percent on the Jordan River for many years, and
leaving 76 percent of the West Bank to the Palestinians. Nothing was offered in
exchange for the annexation. Toward the end of the summit, the Israeli and U.S.
proposals had progressively reduced the annexation of the West Bank to 9 percent but in exchange for the equivalent of 1 percent that was to be constituted as
a secure land-crossing between Gaza and the West Bank or as land adjacent to
Gaza. The Palestinians were willing to commit to an exchange of territory on the
basis of equal percentages and equivalent value—again an important reference
to principles.

The issues that bedeviled the security and borders talks were control of the
borders with Egypt and Jordan, the control of airspace and Palestinian civil avia-
tion, the demilitarization of the Palestinian security forces, and the creation of
new Israeli early-warning stations and emergency troop deployment plans, forward deployments of heavy weapons, and access roads. Proposals for a U.S. or

multinational peacekeeping force, or even for a joint Israel-Jordan-Palestine security regime, held the possibility of reducing some of the Israeli claim to maintain
a military presence on the Jordan River; but ultimately, these issues were never
resolved, despite the presence and input of Central Intelligence director George
Tenet, who participated in the security committee's negotiations toward the end
of the summit.[96]

As the end of summit neared, on the matter of refugees, the Israelis were
entertaining the entry of only "several hundred" refugees to Israel for a "long
time." Israeli might accept "several thousand" if the refugees "stayed for a shorter
time,"[97] leaving the two sides very far apart on this issue of core importance to
both sides. The starting point for the Palestinians at Camp David was more likely
permanent repatriation for a number based on those offered by Israel in 1949
during the Lausanne Peace Conference (100,000 to 250,000), where there had
even been secret contacts between the refugees' leadership and the Israeli delegation.[98] Some Israeli negotiators tried to create a linkage between compensation
for the Palestinian refugees and compensation for Israelis who had left the Arab
and North African countries.[99]

On the matter of Jerusalem, considerable problems arose during the course
of the summit. All Palestinian Arabs had been expelled from West Jerusalem at
the time of Israel's creation, but the PLO's prior recognition of Israel meant that
the Palestinian delegation focused its claim on East Jerusalem so that it could
become the capital of Palestine. East Jerusalem was under Jordanian control
from 1948 until it was wrested by Israel in the 1967 War. The Palestinians' simple
claim to East Jerusalem, where Israel had built up considerable settlements, was
not accepted by either the United States or Israel, despite the Palestinians' non-
conditional offer to recognize Israel's sovereignty over both the Wailing Wall
(adjacent to the Haram al-Sharif/Temple Mount) and the Jewish Quarter of the
Old City in East Jerusalem. The Palestinians were ultimately willing to concede
some of the Jewish settlements in East Jerusalem to Israel as part of an overall
territorial settlement as well. But there was at first no coordinated response from
the Israelis, who arrived unprepared to make comprehensive proposals on the
city's destiny.

The Israelis added several positions during the course of Camp David: they
wanted to reserve a Jewish prayer space on the Haram al-Sharif/Temple Mount
and wanted to consolidate, under various guises, Israel's sovereignty at that holy

site, as well as to significantly expand Jerusalem's borders into the West Bank to accommodate Israeli settlements. As the summit wore on, the Israeli position of sovereignty would persist, softened by possible concessions of Palestinian "jurisdiction" and other soft-control formulas over the Haram al-Sharif/Temple Mount (the actual status quo), packaged with concessions to the Palestinians on the Arab villages near East Jerusalem (which the Palestinians believed the Israelis wouldn't want to annex anyway as they were Arab population centers). The internal Israeli deliberations on the issue took almost an entire day and night of the summit (July 17 and 18) and resulted in the "rapid hardening of the Israeli position."[100]

By the fifth day of the summit, Ross was thoroughly perplexed by Barak's reluctance to offer anything new, his reversal of prior exploratory positions, and his refusal to empower his own negotiators. But Barak only signaled a hard-line position.[101] Ross had even discovered that a smaller group consisting of Muhammed Dahlan, Shlomo Ben-Ami, Yossi Genosar, and Amnon Lipkin-Shahak had been meeting without informing their colleagues. Ross considered this a back channel within the summit that might be able to develop and lobby internally for real solutions.[102] But by the fifth day, the Israeli back channel negotiators had also been disempowered by Barak.

President Clinton exploded in rage at Abu Alaa during a working-group meeting and in front of his Israeli counterpart negotiators when Abu Alaa insisted the Israelis reduce the amount of territory they wanted to annex before he would make a counterproposal incorporating their security interests.[103] The president's outburst did not itself alter the stalemate of the summit, but it was not to be the last such display of executive temperament.

Ross proposed that the parties set aside the working groups (curiously, the summit structure did not include direct talks between Arafat and Barak because Barak refused the advice of his own advisors that such direct contact would contribute to the success of the summit).[104] Instead, he proposed that two negotiators from each side should work through the night of July 16 until they came up with a draft agreement to show to President Clinton, who promised to protect the negotiators from any fallout from their concessions by adopting their work as his own proposal.[105]

Before the negotiation vigil began, Dennis Ross gave the Israelis an advance confidential briefing on what President Clinton would propose if he were to issue a new U.S. paper, but he omitted to do the same with the Palestinians. After their all-night negotiating session, the Israelis felt they had exceeded their mandate, whereas the Palestinians thought negotiations should continue on the basis of what the Israelis had put on the table. The Israelis feared precisely this response, hoping for immediate Palestinian acquiescence on what they felt had been their best proposals.[106]

Clinton met with Arafat to berate him for not allowing his negotiators to go further, while Barak simultaneously sent a stark note to the president, rejecting what his own negotiators had offered during the night and alluding to "collective national suicide."[107] Arafat, for his part, sent a note to Clinton offering to let Clinton determine the annexation/swap ratio if he could deliver Palestinian sovereignty in East Jerusalem. Clinton communicated this opening to Barak, who refused to entertain even diluted layers of sovereignty for the Palestinians in East Jerusalem. This rejection came on the morning of the seventh day of the summit, after which Barak sequestered his entire team for thirteen hours of internal deliberations. When Clinton insisted that Barak's mysterious caucus come to an end, Barak emerged with a new position on Jerusalem that backpedaled on prior Israeli positions, and he asked Clinton to present the ideas as U.S. proposals. Clinton "blew up" at Barak.[108]

Ross came up with a set of hypothetical questions to pose to Arafat, to probe whether or not he would accept layered and limited sovereignty in East Jerusalem. Clinton posed these to Arafat on July 19, the morning of the eighth day of the summit, and Arafat rejected them, not wishing to "transform Israeli occupation . . . into Israeli sovereignty."[109] Dennis Ross then went to inform the negotiators that the president was ready to close the summit, hoping to jolt them into action.[110] He outlined his ambitious layered solution on Jerusalem to the "back channel" negotiators at Camp David (Amnon Lipkin-Shahak, Yossi Genosar, Shlomo Ben-Ami, Muhammed Rashid, and Muhammed Dahlan), and both sides went to brief their leaders. He gave them two hours to produce a response. Although these senior negotiators seemed interested, no response was forthcoming from either delegation.

Clinton tried again to issue a more comprehensive proposal authored by the United States, hoping to move the parties forward. Under Clinton's second proposal, only 9 percent of the West Bank would be annexed, in exchange for 1 percent; on the Jordan River, 15 percent to 20 percent would continue to be occupied by the Israeli military; and regarding Jerusalem, the PLO would exercise limited authority over selected parts of East Jerusalem.[111]

In Ross's version of events, this second proposal by Clinton was actually an Israeli package confidentially communicated to Clinton by Barak, which Clinton then presented to Arafat as a U.S. proposal. Ross's version on Jerusalem also had Barak conceding both the Muslim and Christian quarters of the Old City to Palestinian sovereign rule, while the inner neighborhoods of Arab East Jerusalem would stay under Israeli sovereignty but Palestine would get control of zoning, planning, and other critical municipal powers. The Palestinians would have "custody" of the Haram.[112] Clinton asked Arafat to accept the proposal as the "basis to conclude a deal."

During the night of July 19, the Palestinians explored the newest proposal and posed a number of questions, seeking to build internal consensus for it. Dennis Ross and Madeleine Albright were not awakened for these discussions as Sandy Berger was controlling a restricted flow of information back to the Palestinian delegation. As the next day began, the Palestinians asked that the summit be adjourned for two weeks. Sandy Berger insisted that the Palestinians give an immediate yes or no answer to the new proposal, and in the absence of further clarifications, the answer was negative.[113] Despite the process problems and confusion among the U.S. team, with Albright and the chief U.S. peace mediator having been cut out of the deliberations, the U.S. team decided to focus the blame on Arafat, who was personally rebuked first by Clinton and then by Albright. Barak spoke about new confrontation with the Palestinians.[114]

Clinton had to leave Camp David on Thursday for a G-8 summit in Japan, and he had contemplated ending the Camp David summit because of the elusiveness of any agreement. As Clinton prepared to leave, the U.S. team heard from various negotiators who wanted the process to continue. The Israeli team nevertheless was instructed by Barak to prepare for to depart from Camp David.[115]

Hassan Asfour upbraided Ross for failing to engage the Palestinians on their requests to clarify the latest proposal and offered a partial agreement deferring Jerusalem. With a certain degree of confusion, the U.S. team proposed that everyone stay on to continue negotiations in the president's absence. Arafat authorized his team to participate in both formal and informal talks, whereas Barak again wanted the Palestinians to simply acquiesce to something less than what Clinton had left on the table; he would not authorize any meetings at all. Barak's top negotiators sought out their Palestinian counterparts on their own initiative.[116]

The summit continued with Madeleine Albright and George Tenet playing intermediary roles. In Clinton's absence and at the request of the Israelis, the Palestinians presented a map of the West Bank that reflected their own preferences. As was the case with nearly all else at the summit, once proposed it was immediately rejected by the other side. While Clinton was at the G-8 summit, little negotiation seemed to take place at all until the day of his return. With George Tenet chairing the security talks, a new Israeli concession on Jerusalem was offered: a presidential compound for Arafat within the Muslim Quarter of the Old City. Barak openly said that he could no longer hold out the offer Clinton had made on his behalf regarding Jerusalem.

On Sunday, July 23, Clinton returned to take an active part in the mediation. Talks got down to the details of a future security regime between the parties, and regarding the territorial question, the Israelis finally adopted the proposal Clinton had made before leaving to attend the G-8 summit (which Dennis Ross says was Barak's own proposal) to annex 9 percent in exchange for 1 percent; but the continued lack of progress on Jerusalem seems to have impeded progress on the other issues. The U.S. peace team explored whether or not the parties could accept a partial accord—setting aside Jerusalem—as the outcome of the Camp David summit, but there was no longer any enthusiasm for this possibility from either side.

Instead of excluding Jerusalem from an agreement, one last effort was dedicated to that issue alone. A final session mediated by Clinton on the Jerusalem issue offered a glimmer of hope, but it was too late: the Israelis proposed allowing Palestinian sovereignty on one or two of the "inner" districts of Arab East Jerusalem and a "limited" sovereignty in others. A "special regime" would cover the Muslim, Christian, and Armenian quarters of the Old City, while the Palestinian government compound in the Old City would enjoy the same extraterritorial sovereign status of a foreign embassy. Security in the Old City would be conducted jointly while the Palestinians would be entrusted with the "custodianship" of (not sovereignty over) the Haram al-Sharif/Temple Mount. A Palestinian security force would be in place there. In exchange, the Israelis continued to assert a reserved site on the plaza of the mosques for Jewish prayers. Arafat rejected these proposals as well.[117] In a brief letter to Clinton, Arafat was quoted as having written, "the suggestions I have heard do not take us in the direction I find acceptable."[118]

For Clinton, Barak, and Arafat, it had become clear that the summit was coming to a close without an agreement. As the negotiators packed their luggage to return to the Middle East, the media begin reporting on the failure of the summit. At the heart of the media's messages were leaks from Barak's team that totally blamed the failure on Yasir Arafat.[119]

For the parties to have succeeded at Camp David, significant prior work would have had to be accomplished in both front and back channel negotiations. The front channel negotiations would have been the forum in which the specific details of the problems were clarified for all sides. The back channel negotiations would have been the protected forum in which the parties explored the most creative and daring ways to resolve those problems. As recounted previously, this did not happen, either prior to or during the summit. One of the key characteristics of back channels is that the negotiators tend to be closer to the decision makers and thus should be able to take advantage of greater room for maneuver. After the May 2000 Stockholm talks, back channel negotiators were disempowered by their respective leaders. In contrast with his praise for Abu Alaa's constructive and creative leadership in the Stockholm back channel, Ben-Ami thought Abu Alaa was "against the process" of the Camp David summit. Abu Alaa's leadership in the more discreet Taba talks, discussed below, is offered as evidence that back channels were a more serious and congenial negotiation venue.[120]

The United States and Sweden were engaged in encouraging direct talks, seeking to create more credibility for the back channel, and the United States was generally encouraging the parties. But the actual zone of possible agreement on the permanent status issues, taken as a whole, was extremely narrow, and the negotiators could not find it, let alone widen it, during the summit. Even U.S. diplomats have argued that more systematic use of back channel negotiations, coupled with more effective public diplomacy, would have been necessary for Camp David to have succeeded.[121]

Better mediator preparation would have involved identifying the extremely narrow range within which agreement may have been possible, rather than trying to improvise it during the summit. The various shifts in the summit process, which responded to Barak's preferences from the outset, introduced more contentious dynamics that clearly did not facilitate agreement, including his alleged refusal to meet directly with Arafat during the summit. Robert Malley, part of the U.S. peace team, argues that as mediator, the United States "lacked a sense of direction coming in, a coherent plan once there, and a fallback position coming out."[122] Ben-Ami, in noting that both territory and security issues were resolvable whereas the refugee and Jerusalem issues less so, criticized Barak's bargaining method of starting with low offers and slowly improving them: "Barak's negotiating tactics were a standing invitation to keep the pressure on the Israelis and never say 'yes' to what Barak liked to call his 'generous proposals.'"[123]

Summit failure aside, the very fact that the difficult permanent status issues had finally been put on the table and discussed openly was itself a small but important sign of progress that at least some of the negotiators recognized.

Upon returning to the region, Saeb Eraqat and Gilead Sher engaged in their own somewhat isolated back channel negotiations. According to Sher, the back channel was authorized by Barak and also included Ben-Ami and Dahlan. Throughout July, August, and September, this group essentially continued the working-group discussions from Camp David and until late August, kept Dennis Ross and the United States out of the discussions.[124] At the same time, Eraqat and Oded Eran continued working-level negotiations on the still-outstanding interim issues of prisoners and redeployments, as did Dahlan and Ben-Ami on day-to-day security cooperation.

When Ross and the U.S. peace team were reintegrated into the negotiations, they proposed a new summit by November 15.[125] In close coordination with Egypt, the United States got involved again in the details of a draft agreement, hoping that the Egyptians would table new proposals to Arafat and pressure him to accept new compromises.[126]

With the upcoming UN General Assembly Millennium Summit meeting convening in September, both sides prepared for the possibility of sessions mediated by the United States in New York. Barak spent time publicly disparaging Arafat in New York. Madeleine Albright met with Arafat in New York and heard a new proposal from Arafat on Jerusalem that came closer to the prior Israeli proposals at Camp David: the Haram al-Sharif/Temple Mount would come under the sovereignty of the Organization of the Islamic Conference, which would entrust it to its Jerusalem Committee (headed by Morocco), and which, in turn, would guarantee freedom of worship to all religions at the holy site. Albright reportedly ignored the concession implied therein and enraged Arafat, who had heard her refer to the holy site as the "temple."[127] George Tenet, meeting with Arafat in New York, also took the trouble to "shoot down" the OIC proposal. Dennis Ross went between the Israeli and Palestinian delegations to see if he could get agreement on a new comprehensive package. He did not reveal the same details to both sides, but he hoped to make them converge toward his proposals and relied on the Egyptians to pressure Arafat on an alternative to Palestinian sovereignty in East Jerusalem.[128] Ultimately, no negotiation sessions were held in New York, and nothing but a chance meeting between Arafat and Barak took place while they waited for an elevator at the UN Secretariat.

In late September, the U.S. peace team was attempting to put together a U.S. position paper on all the permanent status issues so that Clinton could present the parties with a new comprehensive proposal. Gilead Sher and Saeb Eraqat called Ross to request that he invite the two sides back to Washington for another round mediated by the United States. Prior to their arrival on September 26, Arafat paid a visit to Barak at his home in an effort to build the personal relationship that had been missing between the two leaders. Ross put the Israeli and Palestinian teams at the Ritz-Carlton Hotel in Pentagon City and notes the seriousness with which they approached their discussions, lauding even the Palestinians for making proposals that met Israeli needs. The meetings ended on September 28 on a high note, with Ross indicating the contours of the United States' eventual proposal, building on the parties' talks.[129] The United States' proposal, however, was to be sidelined for several months by a series of new and deadly events.

The Beginning of the End: Sharon, Violence, and the Crisis Management Negotiations

While the negotiators were sequestered in Pentagon City, Ariel Sharon announced plans to visit the Haram al-Sharif/Temple Mount on September 28, 2000, in the presence of a massive police force. Eraqat asked Ross to intervene directly with Sharon to stop his visit. Ross thought such a request would backfire. But Ross did intervene with Shlomo Ben-Ami, who was foreign minister and minister for internal security, to ask him to "limit or block the visit." Ben-Ami prevented Sharon from entering the mosques but permitted the visit. The visit was seen as highly provocative in the region, but it appeared not to have a negative effect on the negotiators. However, Palestinian demonstrations resulted in stone throwing against the Israeli police at the Haram on the next day, Friday, September 29. That day there were no joint Palestinian-Israeli security patrols (they had been cancelled the day before when a Palestinian officer shot his Israeli officer colleague), and the wounding of the Israeli police commander on the scene (knocked unconscious by a stone) led to the escalation of the use of force. Live ammunition resulted in the killing of five Palestinians at the Haram, and protests spread throughout Gaza and the West Bank. All were met with the IDF's use of "overwhelming force."[130] This was the start of what become known as the Intifada II, or the al-Aqsa Intifada, named for the mosque at the Haram al-Sharif and Sharon's visit there.

The al-Aqsa Intifada has been thoroughly explored in numerous mainstream and alternative media outlets. Presented is a tragic panorama of Palestinian civilian protesters being killed by the IDF, while the military wings of various Palestinian factions, including Fatah and HAMAS, started campaigns of suicide bombings aimed at Israeli civilians. A full retelling of the tragic dimensions of the al-Aqsa Intifada is far beyond the scope of this text. The death toll grew while images of the violence were captured and transmitted to global audiences. The Israeli government tried to hold Arafat accountable for all of the protest and militant activity, believing he could control it at will. The United States claimed it was trying to convince the Israelis to not use live ammunition on civilians, while demanding that Arafat deploy the Palestinian security forces to prevent protesters from reaching IDF checkpoints. But the level of Palestinian-Israeli violence was the worst in years and only escalated.

The violence delegitimized the peace process and refocused the United States and other third parties on crisis management, rather than the comprehensive settlement that lingered just beyond the reach of the parties on the eve of the outbreak of the violence. Protests spread to Israel's Arab communities and towns in October, but these too were met with deadly force.

The Attempt to Arrange a Ceasefire Summit at Sharm el-Sheikh

While Madeleine Albright was on an official visit to France on October 3, she and President Chirac invited Arafat and Barak to a crisis management summit in Paris. Albright and Chirac hoped to draft a document that Arafat would sign at a summit hosted by Egyptian President Hosni Mubarak. Madeleine Albright proposed to Arafat and Barak that a ceasefire commission led by the United States, headed by George Tenet, could be used to deescalate the violence. Arafat wanted the commission to include European and Middle Eastern countries, as well as the UN, something Barak vehemently opposed.

Albright proposed a ceasefire implementation mechanism headed by Tenet and a separate commission of inquiry into the causes of the violence. In announcing the news to Chirac, with Arafat and Barak present, Albright announced that Clinton was extending a new invitation to the parties to come back to the United States to renew negotiations on October 10 in Washington. Albright also wanted Arafat and Barak to initial or sign the document in Paris before the signing ceremony in Egypt. In the absence of sufficient detail on the commission of inquiry proposal, Albright appears to have provoked a new crisis. Arafat refused even to initial the document and attempted to flee the U.S. embassy, while Barak initialed the agreement but refused to go to Egypt.[131]

The violence continued with increased savagery when two Israeli soldiers were lynched after entering the West Bank city of Ramallah. Barak responded by having helicopter gunships destroy Palestinian police stations, even though the Palestinian police had tried to stop the mob and protect the soldiers. The West Bank cities and Gaza were subject to a severe closure.[132]

Despite the new escalation, Egypt and the United States continued planning for a new summit and scheduled it for October 16. The Palestinians at Sharm accused the Egyptians and Americans of having negotiated the ceasefire document in advance with the Israelis. With the active mediation of Javier Solana and Bill Clinton, the parties agreed that Clinton would make a speech closing the summit and that the accord would consist of his speech, instead of any other document or text.[133] The speech's text outlined a return to the September 28 positions, the "unsealing" of Palestinian Area A and Gaza Airport, Israeli troop redeployments, and measures to calm the protests and reign in the newly resurgent militants from Fatah (the so-called Tanzim), among other measures. Clinton also announced that a commission of inquiry would be set up (Barak had relented), and finally, Clinton again held out the need to renew permanent status negotiations as the best path to address "the underlying roots of the Israeli-Palestinian conflict."[134] Arafat indicated to Clinton that he was ready to have another permanent status summit, and he wanted Clinton to meet with him and Barak in advance of a new summit.[135]

The violence subsided only temporarily and then intensified with a terrible familiarity: Palestinian protests turned violent, and the IDF sharpshooters responded by killing protesters, Palestinian police, and security officers. IDF also deployed tanks and helicopter gunships against the Palestinians. The Bush administration continued to view Arafat as the party responsible for the violence, which continued despite his post—Sharm el-Sheikh call for an end to Palestinian acts of violence.[136]

In desperation, Barak turned to Shimon Peres, whom he had completely sidelined from the peace process, and agreed to let him try to get a ceasefire implemented directly with Arafat. Their all-night session started November 1 and was to result in withdrawal of IDF tanks and the resumption of joint Palestinian-Israeli security coordination. The IDF did not completely comply, however, and further confrontations resulted. A planned joint announcement of the ceasefire from Arafat and Barak was undermined by an explosion in Jerusalem that claimed the lives of two Israeli civilians.[137]

On November 7, Election Day in the United States, Clinton announced that he had asked former Senator George Mitchell to chair the commission of inquiry, which was to include Javier Solana, the European Union's foreign policy chief; Suleyman Demirel, former president of Turkey; and Thorbjorn Jagland, the prime minister of Norway.[138] They were later joined by former U.S. senator Warren Rudman.[139]

Back to Bolling, Onward to Taba: The Final Clinton Push

Even as the violence intensified, Arafat was received by Clinton at the White House on November 9 to explore the feasibility of returning to negotiations on the permanent status issues. He explicitly accepted Clinton's newest parameters as "in the ballpark" of terms to which he could actually agree. The parameters were a territorial settlement in "the mid-'90s," including a "small swap": a security regime that included an international presence with a reduced Israeli force and deployment duration on the Jordan River, an ambitious proposal to let the Palestinians have the Arab parts of East Jerusalem and the Israelis to have the Jewish parts while each would control its respective holy sites at the Haram al-Sharif/Temple Mount. Regarding refugees, Clinton spoke of no actual return of refugees into Israel, only to the new state of Palestine and other solutions. Noting that the Clinton parameters were principles, not details of an agreement, Arafat still accepted them.[140]

Ehud Barak arrived at the White House on November 12, but he was much less willing to return to the negotiation table while the Palestinian violence continued. When asked if, like Arafat, he'd return to the negotiation table on the basis of the Clinton parameters, "Barak's response was a nonresponse," according to Dennis Ross. In place of accepting the Clinton parameters, Barak asked the United States to "get tough" on Arafat. At the Barak-Clinton meeting, Dennis Ross proposed that Barak permit a back channel negotiation to proceed between Arafat and Lipkin-Shahak to tackle ceasefire issues. After a two-week delay by Barak, this back channel immediately resulted in a dramatic lowering of violent incidents. In the background, a group of Palestinian and Israeli negotiators (the internal back channel during Camp David) continued to meet to prepare for a further permanent status summit.[141]

Ross's next action was to have a private encounter with Arafat in Morocco, at which Arafat again indicated that he could say yes to an agreement based on the Clinton parameters.[142] Dennis Ross reported Arafat's answer to Albright, to Indyk, and to Barak. The Israeli prime minister, who had already resigned and triggered new elections, asked the United States to bring the negotiators back to Bolling Air Force Base one more time on December 19, 2000.[143]

After five days of the Bolling negotiations, Clinton presented his newest and last articulation of his parameters (which came to be known as the "Clinton ideas") orally to both delegations on December 23, 2000. No document was issued by either the White House or State Department.[144] During the previous evening, Ross had given Dahlan a preview of Clinton's presentation; he outlined for Dahlan the parts of the "ideas" he thought the Palestinians would find most difficult to accept. At the White House the next day, Clinton read out his ideas, some of which included various options for the parties to negotiate over. Clinton asked that any objections the parties had or adjustments they would seek should take place within the contours of the options he described. Clinton asked for the negotiators to indicate a "yes" or "no" to the parameters within five days. He noted that the ideas would end with his administration; the incoming Bush administration would not adopt them as policy. Clinton left the delegations immediately after his presentation, and Dennis Ross remained to ensure that everyone had written down the ideas accurately.

The "Clinton ideas" covered numerous aspects of the conflict and what would be required to settle it. Essentials include the following:

- A territorial settlement returning 94 percent to 96 percent of the West Bank (and all of Gaza).
- Thirty-six-month period in which Israel would withdraw from the Jordan River Valley, while an international force would replace it; three Israeli early-warning stations in the West Bank; a constrained power of emergency deployment for Israeli forces into Palestinian territory
- Palestinian sovereignty over the Haram al-Sharif, Israeli sovereignty over the Western Wall "and the space sacred to Judaism of which it is a part" (or a close alternative to this option).
- Palestinian sovereignty in Arab neighborhoods and Israeli sovereignty in Jewish neighborhoods (settlements) in East Jerusalem.
- Regarding refugees, a shared narrative in which Israel accepts some responsibility for the refugees' displacement while Israel retains control over any return to Israel itself; all refugees would have a "right" to return to the new Palestine itself only (to be called either a "right of return to historic Palestine" or a "right of return to the homeland"); an international mechanism to be set up for compensation and assistance.[145]

On December 27, Barak obtained the "approval with reservations" of the Clinton ideas from his security cabinet. Dennis Ross has characterized the Israeli reservations as "within the parameters."[146] The Palestinian negotiators asked for but could not get additional clarifications from the U.S. team and did not provide a response by the deadline. At a subsequent White House meeting with Clinton on January 2 and 3, 2001, Arafat expressed reservations that Dennis Ross characterized as "outside of the parameters" and "deal killers": rejection of Israeli sovereignty of the Western Wall, and reservations about the refugee formula and the security arrangements.[147]

The intent of Arafat's request for clarifications was more innocuous than Ross's version. Arafat indicated that on some points in the security regime, he wanted to be able to negotiate for better terms; regarding refugees, he claimed to the president that an existing interim mechanism for refugees to return had not resulted in a single returnee coming to areas under Palestinian National Authority control. The text of the Arafat letter appears focused more on the pursuit of specificity than the presentation of objections.[148] Separately, the PLO Negotiation Affairs Department issued its own statement of reservations about the Clinton ideas that were framed mostly as items requiring clarification.[149]

Both Palestinians and Israelis clearly had their respective reservations. Gilead Sher was sent to Washington to meet with the U.S. peace team and explain the Israeli reservations, and he also received confirmation that Arafat had indeed *accepted* the Clinton ideas, in contrast with Ross's depiction. Eraqat explained that Arafat's questions emerged from the concern that outright acceptance of the Clinton ideas, in the absence of a signed agreement, could be perceived as renunciation of the international principles upon which the peace process was based.[150] Abu Alaa, for his part, explicitly declared that the Palestinians were not proceeding on the basis of the Clinton ideas because they did not incorporate Arafat's reservations and "don't offer our people their legitimate rights."[151]

The Clinton ideas represented a somewhat daring third-party proposition; they went far in meeting the expressed needs of each party, with some exceptions, but also provided the most comprehensive basis for a permanent status agreement ever proposed by the United States to the parties. The degree of declared acceptance of the ideas by both parties must be seen as conditional and equivocal at best. The Israelis made their acceptance conditional on Palestinian acceptance, while the latter were also uncomfortable with several of the Clinton formulations. At the very least, the Clinton ideas represented an attractive platform on which to negotiate further.

Clinton offered Arafat an immediate return to the region to meet with him and Barak during the final days of his presidency. Dennis Ross suggested that Clinton attach a condition to his offer, namely, that Arafat should authorize some negotiators to meet with Shimon Peres to "resolve everything."[152] This condition, had it been fulfilled, would have obviated any reason for Clinton's visit; not surprisingly, Arafat demurred.

Still, things did not end there. All the accumulated work in the preparatory negotiations, the Camp David summit, the follow-on talks and proposals, combined with the increasing urgency of the violent situation on the ground, the persistent rise of the Islamic opposition to the PLO, and the impending electoral contest Barak was about to face created a context of pressure combined with negotiation resources that pushed the parties to try yet again.

The parties themselves decided to move their negotiations to Gaza and held at least one session, led by Peres and Arafat on January 13, 2001. At a meeting between Ben-Ami and Arafat in Cairo, the two agreed to bring their negotiation teams back together on January 21, 2001, at the Egyptian resort town of Taba.[153]

The new Bush administration had just assumed office and was still flirting with a brand of isolationism from which it would soon depart, but it had in any case little interest in the Palestinian-Israeli peace process. The talks at Taba had little of the drama, glamour, or intrigue of a summit hosted by the president of the United States. The posturing and strategizing that parties undertake when third parties interpose themselves as mediators was replaced by a straightforward bilateral negotiation session between the Palestinians and Israelis.

Before the Taba talks started, Barak, who was trailing far behind opponent Ariel Sharon in polling, declared through the media that he wanted to end the Israeli occupation and Israeli rule "over another people" while also promising not to give up Israel's claim to sovereignty over the Temple Mount[154]—a statement of mixed signals and a significant departure from the Clinton ideas of December 23, 2000, that was probably meant to mollify the growing tide of political opposition to his candidacy.

The Taba encounter lasted from the evening of January 21 to the afternoon of January 27, interrupted by a two-day hiatus during which Barak withdrew the top negotiators who were also cabinet members, as a protest against the killing of two Israeli civilians. The negotiations continued in their absence, however.[155]

Analyses of the Taba negotiations, derived from memoirs and interviews with the negotiators themselves, offer some evidence that the negotiations made immediate progress and could have resulted in a permanent status agreement. Early on, each side reported to its respective leadership that there had been progress. The Israelis saw agreement possible on security and territory, while the Palestinians reported early progress on the refugee issue. Barak, despite permitting top negotiators to return to Taba, is reported not to have invested them with a clear mandate. Several did not return to Taba from the midweek break. The Palestinian delegation, however, continued to bring in staff experts, which signaled some seriousness of intent and optimism on the process.[156] Palestinian negotiators "would feel fully prepared only by the start of the Taba talks" after years of being disempowered and set up for internal rivalry by their own leadership.[157]

The Jerusalem issue apparently was not intensely negotiated until the fifth day, but some progress was reported on the sovereignty issue regarding all Jerusalem subissues except the Haram al-Sharif/Temple Mount. Thus the Israeli settlements around East Jerusalem would go to Israel (as part of a land swap—see the following), while most or all of the Arab neighborhoods inside of and adjacent to East Jerusalem would become sovereign Palestine. Agreement on the forms of separate municipal administration was also close. Israeli sovereignty over the Western Wall in exchange for Palestinian sovereignty over the Haram al-Sharif was contemplated, but ultimately the parties did not agree on this subissue. The possibility of recognizing international sovereignty at the Haram al-Sharif/Temple Mount was raised but not agreed to. One possible solution was to assign sovereignty over the site to the UN Security Council's five permanent members (China, France, Great Britain, Russian Federation, United States) plus Morocco, who in turn would entrust the "guardianship" of the sacred space to the Palestinians until a new agreement was reached.

Regarding territory, the sides are believed to have come extraordinarily close to agreement. For the Palestinians, the territorial question was always a matter of international legal principle as well as the more pragmatic concerns about territorial integrity and contiguity. For the Israelis, it was about the ability to retain a high percentage of the settlers in consolidated territorial "blocks" carved out from the West Bank, including East Jerusalem. At Taba, the Palestinians ceded to Israel no more than 3.6 percent of the West Bank (or 3.1 percent, depending on the version), while the Israelis wanted a minimum of 6 percent for annexation, plus another 2 percent in a lease arrangement. This is a relatively small gap of 2.4 percent (or 2.9 percent) on the territorial question—slightly more than 100 square kilometers. The land swap concept (Israel to offer the Palestinians Israeli territory contiguous with Palestine in exchange for the annexation) was accepted by both sides, but Taba did not produce agreement on either the amount or location of Israeli territory to be ceded to Palestine.[158]

Regarding the issue of Palestinian refugees, there is some speculation that at Taba, the Palestinians came close to accepting implementation of the right of return to the new Palestinian state only, accompanied by a compensation package, rehabilitation in current host countries, and resettlement in third countries. There is also speculation that Israeli would have accepted partial responsibility for the flight and forced displacement of the refugees in 1948, in exchange for

Israeli control over the actual numbers of returnees to Israel proper (twenty-five thousand proposed by the Israelis, forty thousand proposed by the Palestinians).[159] Intriguingly, the European Union's version of the Taba negotiations includes a provision for an additional land swap to Palestine of Israeli territory "over and above territories discussed in the territorial negotiations" to accommodate returning refugees.[160]

Taba had been scheduled to last approximately ten days, but on the sixth day, the talks were abruptly called off, without great fanfare and despite the profound progress made by the negotiators. The early ending of the process is attributed variously to Ehud Barak (who has declined to give any consistent reason for his decision) and Arafat's top negotiators, who have denied wanting to end it (although they apparently did not object to ending it either). Some analysts and observers believed that at least a framework agreement could have been concluded at Taba had the negotiators taken advantage of the remaining four days.[161]

The ending of the Taba talks without an agreement did not cause the violence in the region, but it did nothing to put an end to the downward spiral either. Sharon's imminent ascent to power implied that anything achieved at Taba would not have a chance with the new government. However, given all that came after, it is somewhat perplexing and tragic that the negotiators did not present the Israeli and Palestinian populations or the incoming U.S. and Israeli administrations with a jointly-agreed upon framework that—with some hard work in the implementation details—could have resulted in a permanent peace between the Palestinians and Israelis at some later point (at least after Sharon).

At the conclusion of Taba, Arafat acclaimed the work of the negotiators in an interview with Israel Channel 2 television: "We have to respect what they had achieved. . . . Not all what we are looking (for), not all what you are looking for, but it was a step forward and the most important thing (is) that we are insisting to continue."[162] Nothing of the scale and intensity of Taba would be attempted once Ariel Sharon won the Israeli elections and took power.

By that point in the peace process, the forces arrayed against a peace agreement were moving from the margins to the center of both Palestinian and Israeli politics, although popular support for a negotiated settlement had been strong until the al-Aqsa Intifada. The "spoilers" were able to take over government in Israel when Ariel Sharon won the Israeli elections on February 6, 2001, and this event would eventually be the outcome among the Palestinians too when HAMAS won legislative elections and formed a governing cabinet in 2006.

The peace process, which had its first tentative steps as far back as 1986 and which began in earnest in 1992, had suffered a terrible setback by late 2000 and, according to many observers, was completely dead by early 2001 at the very moment when the most promising negotiations were being held. The gains of the interim period for both sides were wiped away, and an ever mounting death toll of civilians ensured that popular support for peace continued to deteriorate in the post-Clinton era.

The shortcomings in the process and substance of Palestinian-Israeli peace-making had come full circle. The spoilers, costs, and uncertainties the parties had thought to manage by secret back channel negotiation had paradoxically only been *magnified* over the course of those negotiations, instead of being *mitigated*. During the period when Palestinians and Israelis needed maximum room for exploration and bargaining to reach the elusive permanent status agreement, they found themselves bound by severe political constraints on their ability to negotiate and implement a permanent status agreement with the other side.

Mediation on the Margins:
The Descent from Summitry to Crisis Management

Overview of the Mission(s) Impossible

At the start of the George W. Bush administration, the Palestinian-Israeli peace process essentially collapsed following Taba. Subsequent efforts in the Middle East by the United States under the Bush administration consisted of a series of creative, assertive, but ultimately futile crisis management initiatives that followed up on the October 2000 Sharm el-Sheikh summit.

The United States later helped foment a mini civil war among the Palestinians by bolstering the Palestinian National Authority's security forces and, in essence, rearming Fatah loyalists against HAMAS, but this effort too only led to HAMAS retaining control of Gaza, while Fatah and the PLO dissolved the HAMAS government in the West Bank. The two territorial pieces of the Palestinian's territorial basis for a state, as this book was published, were governed by rival factions rather than within a unified Palestinian governance framework.

The first of the policy actions initiated by the United States after Clinton's departure was the implementation of the Mitchell Committee, which had been anticipated in the Sharm al-Sheikh encounter. The following subsections review the negotiations, context, and limitations of each initiative.

Mitchell Committee

The Mitchell Committee, officially known as the Sharm el-Sheikh Fact-Finding Committee, began its work at the end of 2000, and its members undertook a regional visit on March 21, 2001. By April 30, 2001, the Mitchell Committee released its report, in which it did not endorse either side's accusations of bad faith against the other: "we have no basis to conclude that there was a deliberate plan by the PA to initiate a campaign of violence . . . or to conclude that there was a deliberate plan by the Government of Israel to respond with lethal force."[163] Nevertheless, the report held both sides responsible for the escalation of violence: "there is also no evidence on which to conclude that the PA made a consistent effort to contain the demonstrations and control the violence once it began; or that the GOI [government of Israel] made a consistent effort to use non-lethal means to control demonstrations of unarmed Palestinians. Amid rising anger, fear, and mistrust, each side assumed the worst about the other and acted accordingly." In great detail, the report presents the facts it discovered and each side's perceptions of the actions and motivations of the other side. Without taking a partisan stance, the authors urged each side to exert control over its military forces and civilians and to rebuild mutual trust in order to resume negotiations.

The report constructively set forth detailed steps that both sides needed to take immediately to rebuild the peace process. Excerpts from the recommendations follow:

The PA [PNA]should make clear through concrete action to Palestinians and Israelis alike that terrorism is reprehensible and unacceptable, and that the PA will make a 100 percent effort to prevent terrorist operations and to punish perpetrators . . .

The GOI should freeze all settlement activity, including the "natural growth" of existing settlements.

The GOI should ensure that the IDF adopt and enforce policies and procedures encouraging non-lethal responses to unarmed demonstrators . . .

The PA should prevent gunmen from using Palestinian populated areas to fire upon Israeli populated areas and IDF positions . . .

The GOI should lift closures, transfer to the PA all tax revenues owed, and permit Palestinians who had been employed in Israel to return to their jobs; and should ensure that security forces and settlers refrain from the destruction of homes and roads, as well as trees and other agricultural property in Palestinian areas . . .

Notwithstanding their sound and detailed recommendations, the committee's work had the feel of an arbitration process: both sides documented their positions and submitted them formally to the committee for its consideration, as if hoping for a "finding" favorable to their own side.

The committee did not serve as a focal point for both sides to come together and explore their perceptions and misperceptions, or to jointly work out a new path toward a ceasefire, much less a return to the negotiation table. This remained a mere exhortation to the parties. When the committee released its report to the public, the PLO declared its willingness to return to negotiations, but the offer was immediately dismissed by Prime Minister Sharon.[164]

Insightfully, the committee recommended that the parties *not condition their return to negotiations on the implementation of the report's recommendations*. They understood that the report's recommendations and negotiations could be mutually reinforcing, if undertaken. They also understood that pre-conditions demanded by either party would simply turn into excuses to delay a return to negotiation. Despite the United States' renewed interest in the region, negotiations were not restarted.

Tenet Mission: CIA Mediation for Security Coordination

As Madeleine Albright had anticipated at the Sharm el-Sheikh summit, one of the more promising ways to reduce the violence between Israelis and Palestinians was to attempt to restore the cooperation that had previously existed between the Israeli and Palestinian security forces. As recounted in chapter 5, the Interim

Agreement between the PLO and Israel had created a series of confidence-building and peace-building measures founded upon the gradual withdrawal of IDF and military administration from the West Bank and Gaza, in exchange for Palestinian security cooperation with Israel. The security cooperation had held tenuously, despite the long delays and renegotiations of the redeployments under Netanyahu and Barak. The violence after September 2000 showed the limits of security cooperation when Palestinian security forces refused to remain idle while their Israeli counterparts opened fire on Palestinian civilian protestors. Israel also believed that the Palestinian security forces were implicated in inciting the protests and were themselves a front for the secular militant factions. Thus the IDF began deliberately targeting Palestinian police and other security agencies, holding the Palestinian National Authority, and especially PNA president Yasir Arafat, responsible for the violence of militant groups.

Almost immediately after the Mitchell Committee's report, George Tenet, director of Central Intelligence (DCI) in the U.S. government, came to the region at the beginning of June 2001 to persuade the parties to create a "Joint Security Committee" composed of senior Israeli and Palestinian security officials and accompanied by U.S. intelligence officers. Tenet wanted to get the parties to commit themselves to specific ceasefire steps. It took the DCI nearly a week of intensive mediation to get an agreed-upon text. The "Tenet Plan" was full of highly specific actions and timelines for the parties' security forces to undertake in order to return to the operational status quo before the al-Aqsa Intifada erupted. The IDF was to take concrete steps to reduce the lethality of its operations while preventing settlers from attacking Palestinian civilians, and was to explicitly refrain from attacking Palestinian National Authority facilities. The PNA was to move proactively against Palestinian militants. Together, they were to create jointly agreed-upon procedures for managing "flashpoints," for creating buffer zones and no-demonstration zones. The agreement, which would take effect June 13, 2001, gave the parties one week to create an agreed timetable for IDF redeployment to the September 28, 2000, positions (the date of Sharon's visit to the al-Aqsa Mosque), to be followed within forty-eight hours by further significant redeployments and lifting of closures of the Palestinian territories.

The Tenet Plan, having been constructed through active mediation, and with its highly specific action steps, offered the parties a solid opportunity to achieve the deescalation that might facilitate a return to political negotiations.

However, both sides had reservations about the Tenet Plan. The Palestinian National Authority was reluctant to undertake massive arrests of militants. And the Sharon government resorted to preconditions: it refused to implement the Tenet Plan until an entire week had passed without any violent incidents at all. Given the ongoing IDF assassination missions, settler attacks on Palestinians, and the ongoing fragmentation among Palestinian political groups, the spiral of violence never slowed. The agreement itself did not commit the parties to return to political negotiations.

Sharon's refusal to engage with the Tenet Plan in the absence of a full week without incident not only contravened the spirit and letter of the Tenet Plan, but it also had the effect of *empowering* the Palestinian militant groups opposed to a ceasefire. The purported week-long window would be perceived by the militant groups as an opportunity to forestall any return to the negotiations process they opposed.

The Tenet Plan was eclipsed by the September 11, 2001, terrorist attacks on the United States, which provided the Bush administration an opportunity to radically reprioritize its foreign policy objectives. It would have been surprising to find any U.S. engagement at all in the Palestinian-Israeli issue in the aftermath of the events of 9/11. Nevertheless, Secretary of State Colin Powell attempted to keep the United States engaged. Powell assigned assistant secretary of state for Near East affairs William Burns and the new special assistant, retired Marine Corps general Anthony Zinni, to push ahead with efforts toward a ceasefire.[165] In the policy speech in which he announced Burns and Zinni's mission, Secretary Powell noted that ceasefire negotiations had to be tied to the resumption of political negotiations to end the conflict. Indeed, he made what might be considered a bold statement for a U.S. cabinet secretary: "for the sake of Palestinians and Israelis alike, the occupation must end. And it can only end with negotiations."[166]

General Zinni traveled to the region several times starting in late November 2001, but the violence continued to escalate despite Zinni's activation of the trilateral security committee envisioned in the Tenet Plan. With Palestinian suicide bombings escalating and the Sharon government targeting Palestinian militants, civilians, and Palestinian National Authority infrastructure, Zinni threatened to leave on December 9. On December 17, the Palestinian militant groups announced plans to stop attacks within Israel but not against IDF in the West Bank and Gaza. General Zinni's continued reliance on the security committee structure did not succeed in immediately deescalating the crisis. However, Yasir Arafat did begin moving more aggressively against insubordination and more vocally denounced Palestinian attacks on Israelis from any group. The PNA also undertook to close HAMAS offices and arrested hundreds of HAMAS members. Palestinian attacks dropped dramatically toward the end of 2001. The IDF nonetheless continued its assassination operations.

Sharon, Peres, Qurei, and Abbas Turn to Back Channels

Shimon Peres, who had been sidelined when his own party controlled government, ironically had become Israeli foreign minister under Ariel Sharon. As December 2001 drew to a close, Peres and Ahmed Qurei (Abu Alaa), Speaker of the Palestinian Legislative Council, resorted once again to the back channel negotiations that had brought them together in the Oslo channel in 1993. In this late 2001 back channel effort, they produced a "letter of understanding" in which Israel was to recognize Palestine within two months of the implementation of the Mitchell Committee and Tenet Plan obligations. Once it came to light, their efforts became known as the Peres-Qurei Peace Initiative.

In January 2002, Zinni returned to the region and again worked through the trilateral security committee to create momentum and pressure for deescalatory moves. Prime Minister Sharon sent his son Omri to meet Arafat on January 29 for the purpose of setting up a direct secret meeting between Sharon and Arafat's top officials. Direct meetings with Abu Alaa and Mahmoud Abbas (Abu Mazen) took place January 30, 2002. Sharon, Qurei, and Abbas are reported to have agreed to implement an interim peace plan over the course of seven years, building on the back channel negotiations that had been conducted by Peres and Qurei. These were the first contacts and meetings between Sharon and the Palestinian officials since Sharon took office in February 2001 and the direct result of the back channel contacts among Omri Sharon, Peres, Abu Alaa, and Abu Mazen. The interim peace plan concept—whatever its merits and drawbacks—did not last beyond February 2002, despite being openly repackaged and reproposed by the government of France. The French version proposed immediate Palestinian elections to shore up the Palestinian National Authority's popular legitimacy and immediate Israeli recognition of the Palestinian state, on the assumption that these twin moves would "trigger the psychological effect that could justify ending the

Intifada."[167] Instead, the cycle of violence seemed to become more entrenched. The more the Palestinian militant groups were repressed by either the Palestinian Preventive Security Force (PSF) or the IDF, the more they stepped up their attacks on Israeli military and civilian targets. In return, the IDF sought above all to attack the PNA and directed much of its major retaliatory actions against the PNA, as well as the militant groups.

Back channel negotiations, with their high-level, secret, and creative tendencies for problem solving, and which until this point had consistently contributed to breakthrough agreements and major conceptual explorations of difficult negotiation issues, were no longer effective. The exclusion upon which they were predicated meant that the parties who would need to implement any back channel understandings were often excluded from the process. Additionally, the back channel talks of late 2001 and early 2002 appeared to have been little more than opportunities for the parties to talk without actually changing confrontational and violent policies on the ground. The landscape for a return to political negotiation thus did not improve, despite the Sharon-Peres-Qurei-Abbas back channel contacts.

The Saudi Peace Plan and the Zinni Ceasefire Plan

A public multilateral initiative for Middle East peace was announced in February 2002 by Saudi crown prince Abdullah. The initiative, in essence, offered the recognition of Israel by the entire membership of the League of Arab States in exchange for Israel's withdrawal to its 1967 borders and a negotiated solution for the Palestinian refugees. Prince Abdullah officially launched the plan at the Fourteenth Ordinary Session of the Council of Arab States in Beirut, Lebanon, in March 2002. The entire League of Arab States unanimously signed on to the peace plan, and it was published as an official League document on March 28, 2002.

In contrast with this unprecedented Arab peace initiative, which the Sharon government took pains to ignore, the United States began distancing itself from Arafat and the PNA at Sharon's request, and Israel began focusing military efforts on further undermining Arafat. In March 2002, the IDF reinvaded much of the West Bank and laid siege to Arafat's presidential compound.

Zinni returned to actively mediate between the two sides for the last two weeks of March and produced several drafts of a highly detailed ceasefire action plan on March 25 and 26.[168] The Israelis insisted that Arafat sign it as a condition to be permitted to attend the Beirut summit of the Arab League. The Palestinians, for their part, wanted the ceasefire to commit the Israelis to return to the peace process. A suicide bomber attacked a family religious ceremony in the Israeli town of Netanya on March 27, and this precipitated a major new IDF incursion, Operation Defensive Shield. By March 29, the IDF began destroying the entire presidential compound except for an office where Arafat was trapped.

General Zinni pushed the Israelis for a robust Israeli withdrawal from Palestinian Area A that had previously been under full Palestinian control. The siege was not lifted until Secretary of State Powell personally visited Arafat in his compound in April, and then it resumed until May. Powell had visited the region not only to support Zinni's mission but also to gain Arafat's and Sharon's support for a major peace conference modeled after the Madrid Peace Conference of October 1991. In response to U.S. pressure, the PNA began an internal reform process aimed at spreading power and decision making horizontally within the PNA in order to make the PNA a more palatable negotiating partner for Israel. At the same time, the Israelis began moving toward a two-prong unilateral disengagement plan in which they did not envision any negotiations with the Palestinians.

Toward Unilateral Disengagement

Despite the ongoing military operations of the IDF within the West Bank and the escalatory suicide bombings, the Palestinians proceeded with a political reform plan that they hoped would restore both popular legitimacy and overcome U.S. and Israeli objections to the PNA and PLO as negotiating partners. The reform plans notwithstanding, the Bush administration openly called for Arafat to be removed from power in a speech by President Bush on June 24, 2002.[169] In his memorable speech, President Bush also declared support for both interim and permanent status negotiations when he stated that

> when the Palestinian people have new leaders, new institutions and new security arrangements with their neighbors, the United States of America will support the creation of a Palestinian state whose borders and certain aspects of its sovereignty will be provisional until resolved as part of a final settlement in the Middle East."

As we make progress towards security, Israel forces need to withdraw fully to positions they held prior to September 28, 2000. And consistent with the recommendations of the Mitchell Committee, Israeli settlement activity in the occupied territories must stop. . . . The Israeli occupation that began in 1967 will be ended through a settlement negotiated between the parties, based on U.N. Resolutions 242 and 338, with Israeli withdrawal to secure and recognized borders. We must also resolve questions concerning Jerusalem, the plight and future of Palestinian refugees."

Within the West Bank, Israel began building a barrier of concrete walls and wire fencing designed to carve out West Bank territory Israel sought to keep while blocking entry into Israel for any would-be militants planning attacks.[170] Within the Palestinian territories, the barrier cuts through private and community property, separating students from schools, farmers from harvests, and neighbor from neighbor.

Regarding Gaza, Israel began exploring various scenarios of disengagement, predicated upon the dismantlement of Israeli settlements within Gaza but accompanied by the complete encirclement of the Gaza Strip and its shared border with Egypt, its Mediterranean coastline, and its shared border with Israel. Through his defense minister Ben Eliezer, Sharon began floating his unilateral disengagement ideas to the Palestinians and other interested parties, including the Egyptian and U.S. governments at the beginning of August 2002. The consultations over the plan also included the possibility of Israeli withdrawals from West Bank cities such as Bethlehem. Negotiations over the extent and terms of the disengagement were not successful, however, and the IDF siege of the PNA's presidential compound continued.

The Road Map to Nowhere

In April 2002, UN Secretary-General Kofi Annan invited representatives from the EU, the Russian Federation, and the United States to form a "Quartet" that would act in unison to reinvigorate the peace process. On the sidelines of the September 2002 UN General Assembly meeting, the European Union revealed its "Road Map" plan that called for the recognition of the Palestinian state with provisional borders by 2003, to be followed up with negotiations toward a permanent arrangement by June 2005. The United Nations Security Council, meeting on September 24, 2002, passed a resolution condemning the IDF attacks on the presidential compound and the reoccupation of Palestinian cities.[171] At the same time, the United States was desperately trying to build up an international coalition in favor of the impending invasion and occupation of Iraq.

The United States began proposing its own rival "Road Map" in October 2002, followed up by consultations with Israel and the PNA, and pushed the Quartet to adopt the United States' plan in place of the European Union's version.

In early February 2003, Sharon and Qurei met to discuss an Israeli proposal for a ceasefire and renewed security cooperation, and the U.S. ambassador to Israel, Dan Kurtzer, hosted follow-up meetings between the two sides, without any breakthrough.

On the same day that the United States launched its war against Iraq ("Operation Iraqi Freedom") on March 19, 2003, Mahmoud Abbas was nominated by Yasir Arafat to become the prime minister of the Palestinian National Authority. On the same day as the new Abbas government was officially empowered, April 30, 2003, the United States formally presented the Road Map document to both sides, and despite the U.S. preoccupation with the war in Iraq, Colin Powell returned to the region to hold talks with Abbas and Sharon on the implementation of the Road Map.

The Road Map held out as an explicit goal the end of the Palestinian-Israeli conflict by the facilitation of the emergence of an "independent, democratic and viable Palestinian state."[172] The plan asks both parties for a series of specific, incremental steps that, much in the spirit of the Mitchell Committee's recommendations, would establish a more peaceful, secure, and just atmosphere for the conclusion of permanent status negotiations by 2005. In many ways it was a restatement of the previous obligations of the parties as set out in the Interim Agreement (security cooperation, clamping down on incitement and violence by either side against the other). But it also explicitly set out as implementation goals more specific and critical measures: an end to collective punishment measures by the Israelis (home demolitions, closures), a freeze on existing Israeli settlements, and the dismantling of new settlements established by the Sharon government, for example. The Palestinians were to undertake a comprehensive political reform (which they had already begun), including setting up a new constitution, creation of a new prime minister's office empowered to create a new cabinet government, setting up of an electoral commission, and "based on a free, multi-party process, Palestinians hold free, open, and fair elections."[173] Israel demanded as a precondition for the implementation of its Road Map obligations that Abbas take firm action against Palestinian militant groups. Abbas, however, signaled his intention to pursue dialogue with the Palestinian militant groups in order to stop attacks on Israel. Sharon's refusal to endorse or implement the Road Map left the U.S. secretary of state negotiating with the PNA on behalf of the Israelis. In direct talks in May 2003, Sharon offered Abbas a modest IDF withdrawal from Gaza and one West Bank city only if Abbas would take repressive action against the Palestinian militant groups. Abbas indicated that he would do so only within the framework of the Road Map, which Sharon was unwilling to do, thus undermining what was otherwise a very promising effort by the United States to demilitarize the conflict and return the parties to permanent status negotiations.

With nowhere else to turn, Abbas approached the two Islamic opposition groups, the Movement for Islamic Jihad (MIJ) and HAMAS, in late May 2003, both of which offered to stop attacks within Israel if Israel stopped attacks on MIJ and HAMAS—a *hudna* (truce).

Navigating with the Road Map

The Sharon cabinet voted on May 25, 2003, to approve the Road Map by a vote of twelve to seven, with four ministers abstaining, but then proceeded to attach fourteen "reservations" to the cabinet's acceptance.[174] These reservations were no mere technical demands for reciprocal implementation. Rather, they were extreme positions that the Sharon government wanted the Palestinians to concede in advance on many of the critical issues that should have been the subject of the permanent status negotiations. Thus the reservations called for the renunciation of the Palestinian right of return, the extinguishing of any Palestinian claims against Israel, the complete disarmament of the secular and Islamic militant groups, and the continuing deferral of any negotiation over the Israeli settlements in the West Bank and Gaza. One precondition even made demands on other Arab states, which would be required to condemn any Palestinian terrorism.

In June, Condoleezza Rice, at that time the U.S. national security advisor, traveled to the region to meet with Abbas and Sharon. Her visit coincided with a

three-month truce declared by MIJ and HAMAS, as well as two secular opposition parties, the Democratic Front for the Liberation of Palestine (DFLP) and
the Popular Front for the Liberation of Palestine (PFLP). The IDF also began a
small redeployment out of Gaza and selected areas of the West Bank, as security cooperation began to resume. Security officials conducted negotiations over
further redeployments. Just as things began looking hopeful, in August the IDF
conducted an assassination against an MIJ commander, and HAMAS responded
with a suicide attack in Jerusalem. The futility of reaching a modus operandi on
security arrangements with Israel and the internal opposition precipitated the
September 6 resignation of Abu Mazen as prime minister and his replacement
by Abu Alaa on September 10, 2003. The spiral of violence that had almost been
reversed was now resuming.

The 2003 Geneva Accord:
Back Channel–Track II Work on the Permanent Status

Just as the hopes for the peace process were fading, a remarkable back channel
development came to light. A group of high-level officials and former officials
from both sides had worked for two years on a comprehensive permanent status
agreement text, with the sponsorship of the Swiss government. It will be recalled
that in 1995, a similar effort had resulted in a "framework" agreement on the
permanent status issues that offered helpful guidelines for a more detailed negotiation. The earlier plan had been dubbed the Beilin-Abu Mazen Agreement, and
once again, Yossi Beilin led the initiative on the Israeli side, while for the Palestinians, the main protagonist was Yasir Abd Rabbuh, who had resigned from the
PLO's negotiation team in 2000 (ostensibly because he was opposed to the official
secret negotiations then taking place in Stockholm).

Beilin and Abd Rabbuh began with a small circle of adherents and progressively expanded the circle of people consulted on the substance of a draft permanent settlement. They hoped to then build up a broad public consensus once they
briefed their respective leaderships.[175]

The Geneva Accord sets out a complete model of a comprehensive agreement that builds on the Taba negotiations, the Clinton ideas and parameters,
and the Camp David negotiations—and in some aspects, exceeds their most daring propositions. Notably, the text commits the parties to a definitive end to the

conflict predicated on a two-stage withdrawal of the IDF over a total period of thirty months, and security to both sides provided by a "multinational force"—a proposition that had never gained broad acceptance in past negotiations. In Jerusalem, the Palestinian capital would encompass the Arab neighborhoods while the Israeli capital would encompass the Jewish neighborhoods (including settlements in East Jerusalem). In the Old City, the Haram al-Sharif and the Wailing Wall would come under Palestinian and Israeli sovereignty, respectively.

The Israeli concessions on Jerusalem, however, are traded off against an arrangement on the Palestinian refugees reminiscent of the Clinton ideas: a comprehensive aid package including compensation, repatriation to the new Palestine, rehabilitation in situ, or departure to new countries. West Bank territory annexed to Israel, including the East Jerusalem settlements, would be compensated on a one-to-one basis for additional territory in the southern half of the West Bank and around Gaza.[176]

Although the Geneva Accord began as a relatively intimate initiative, over time it incorporated more and more experts, political figures, and former negotiators from each side, ultimately bringing in a large number of civil society figures as well. The December 2003 "launch" of the Geneva Accord was in some respects the beginning of a new civil society movement that sought to "start with the end": by having carefully drafted a complete model agreement, all supporters of the initiative agreed on the end goal of the peace process and could concentrate on building two important sources of support. First, the Swiss government funded a major effort to translate and distribute the text of the accord and to follow it up with advocacy and education campaigns to broaden and deepen public support for it in Israel and Palestine. But the Geneva Accord also transformed itself from a quasi–back channel/Track II effort into the "Geneva Initiative," an organization committed to building support for a Geneva-like settlement among the respective political leadership on both sides, an effort that continues as this manuscript is being completed. The Geneva Accord is the most complete and detailed vision for the realization of the two-state solution to the Palestinian-Israeli conflict.

Kadima, HAMAS, Hezbollah: Dramatic Changes but No Peace

The immediate aftermath of the launch of the Geneva Initiative was disappointing, although it came as little surprise. Sharon condemned and dismissed the initiative while Arafat cautiously applauded, although it is not likely that either leader could have been entirely in the dark about the process that led up to it.

For all of 2004 and 2005, the peace process made little or no progress. While a dramatic unilateral disengagement finally was implemented in Gaza, the military encirclement of Gaza provided little pretext for an end to Gazan militancy. The November 2004 death of Arafat and Sharon's stroke-induced coma in January 2006 marked two endpoints of an era in which both sides regularly blamed each other's leaders for the moribund peace process. Sharon was replaced by Ehud Olmert, former Likud member and mayor of Jerusalem whose contributions to the rejuvenation of the peace process are not apparent as of this writing.[177]

The electoral and governmental reform undertaken by the Palestinians resulted, ironically, in an electoral victory for HAMAS in 2006, for which the PLO, the Israelis, and the United States were ill-prepared. That year was spent in tragic efforts to isolate the HAMAS-led government by applying further economic sanctions on the HAMAS-led Palestinian National Authority. HAMAS, facing isolation from the United States and the European Union, outright rejection by Israel, and tensions with PLO-affiliated parties, nevertheless proposed a ten-year truce, or *hudna,* with Israel. In rejecting the peace process, HAMAS was also critiquing the PLO and Fatah. During the following year, 2007, even greater tragedy occurred as PLO loyalists and HAMAS-aligned security forces battled each other in fratricidal violence. The concrete result of all of this was to stimulate stronger U.S. and Israeli support for an Abbas-led Palestinian government. Negotiations did not resume until Gaza had been essentially abandoned to HAMAS, however, and the United States launched a conference in Annapolis, Maryland in December 2007 that led to serious follow-on negotiations on the permanent status issues. As 2008 drew to a close, and as the Bush administration reached the end of its second term, no agreement was apparent. Ehud Olmert resigned under the pressure of corruption investigations and was replaced by his foreign minister, Tzipi Livni, while Mahmoud Abbas continued to lead the PNA as its president, at least in the West Bank. Binyamin Netanyahu won subsequent general elections on February 11, 2009. When he formed his government on March 31, 2009, he named Avigdor Lieberman, a Moldova-born émigré who heads the Yisrael Beiteinu Party as foreign minister and deputy prime minister. Lieberman is one of Israel's most outspoken opponents of the peace process.

In analyzing these post–Camp David years, the regional context also bears examining: no comprehensive breakthrough has yet been reached on the Israeli-Syrian track, although negotiations have continued in direct and mediated back channels. Lebanon's fractious political landscape is as enmeshed as ever with events south of the Lebanese border, as Hezbollah both maintains a fighting stance against Israel and also promotes its political agenda from within the Lebanese government.

Iran's support for Hezbollah in Lebanon helped fuel the border war in the summer of 2006, while Iran's support for Shiite politics in Iraq also posed a strategic counterpoint to the U.S. administration's military and political goals in the ongoing Iraq and Afghanistan conflicts. In these years we have also seen a failed E.U. diplomatic initiative that—had it been better structured—might have resolved or at least deescalated the tense standoff between Iran and the United States over Iran's uranium enrichment program, which has withstood layers of sanctions imposed by the United Nations and outright threats from the United States and Israel to use force to prevent Iran from developing the capacity to make nuclear weapons (which Iran itself disclaims any interest in).

In Gaza, a tenuous ceasefire between HAMAS and Israel broke down as the Israelis tightened the siege of Gaza and HAMAS militants launched rockets into Israel. Between December 27, 2008, and January 19, 2009, Operation Cast Lead, a massive invasion of Gaza, claimed the lives of approximately 1,300 civilians, wounded more than 5,000, and left "tens of thousands homeless."[178] The operation failed to dislodge HAMAS and did not end the rocket attacks from Gaza.

Certainly a strategic peace linkage could be drawn among Tehran, Gaza, Beirut, Tel Aviv, Damascus, Baghdad, and Kabul. Neither U.S. nor E.U. diplomacy currently bears the mark of a grand strategy that would make such linkages. The United States continues to avoid talking directly with Iran despite Iran's ability to influence various areas of U.S. interests in the region. A strategic peace initiative could dramatically alter the political landscape of the Middle East/South West Asia. This would require coordinated attempts to simultaneously achieve the following:

- A resolution of Israeli-Lebanese state of war and the settlement of the remaining territorial, security, and water disputes
- A transition away from sectarian politics in Lebanon

- A settlement of the Syrian-Israeli state of war and the settlement of its territorial and security disputes
- The enlistment of Iranian assistance in moving Afghanistan and Iraq away from conflict and toward building peace
- The international community's engagement and monitoring of a peaceful Iranian atomic energy program

If such initiatives were creatively tied to the resolution of the Palestinian-Israeli conflict and the implementation of the Arab League's plan for accepting Israel, the world would indeed be a different place—palpably more peaceful and better poised to meet the human development needs of populations long burdened by legacies of colonialism, state formation, military intervention, and intractable conflicts.

After assuming office in January 2009, President Barack Obama named George Mitchell as his special envoy for Middle East peace. Mitchell and his team conducted quiet shuttle diplomacy between Abbas and Netanyahu throughout 2009 and 2010, hoping to create the conditions for a renewal of either mediated or direct Palestinian-Israeli negotiations. On August 31, 2010, Abbas and Netanyahu came to Washington, D.C., to publicly launch renewed permanent status negotiations that are planned to conclude within one year. This book went to press amidst pledges of biweekly Palestinian-Israeli summits and U.S. support for the process. Although optimism is not high among either Palestinians or Israelis, the U.S. interest in a peace settlement is notable. The conditions are more challenging than ever. Gaza's extreme impoverishment, Palestinian political fragmentation with a HAMAS-led government in Gaza, and nearly half a million settlers in the West Bank and East Jerusalem will not make the negotiations easier. The dual tasks of reaching an optimal permanent peace for Israelis and Palestinians and building up popular support for such a peace deal, however imperfect, are more urgent than ever.

7

Back Channel Negotiation

Causes and Consequences

We never did anything to prepare public opinion [for peace].
—DENNIS ROSS[1]

This chapter synthesizes findings from a decade of research into the Palestinian-Israeli negotiations whose origins lie in the late 1980s and extends the analysis of the phenomenon of back channel negotiation.[2] I set out to ascertain why back channel negotiations are used, what other negotiation variables they interact with, and what overall effect they can have on one of the most complex kinds of negotiations: an international peace process.[3] In this chapter, back channel negotiation (BCN) is put into context as a category of negotiation behavior, a process choice with implications for the outcome of negotiations. Based on the historical analyses of the prior chapters and selected observations from other historical instances of BCN, I offer some conclusions that are hopefully useful for two audiences: scholars interested in the analysis of negotiation; and actual negotiators of interpersonal, organizational, domestic, or international conflicts.

As defined earlier in this book, back channel negotiations are negotiations conducted in *secret* between the parties to a dispute. The negotiators may be "official" or they may be a mixed group of official and nonofficial, a quasi–Track II effort characterized by secrecy. These negotiations may also operate in parallel with—or replace—acknowledged "front" channels of negotiation; they can be described as the "black markets" of negotiation, providing separate negotiation spaces where bargaining takes place *in the shadows*. When front channel negotiations fail they are sometimes eclipsed by successful back channel negotiations even though the same principals, conflicts, and sociopolitical contexts are involved.

261

This chapter offers answers to the questions that I posed at the beginning of the book: Why do decision makers deploy back channels and how do they function? What is the impact of BCN on international peace processes? The Palestinian-Israeli peace process, in which both back and front channels have consistently been used, provides the basis for comparing channels and offering tentative answers to these questions. Although BCN can facilitate breakthrough agreements, BCN can also damage peace process negotiations by exacerbating some of the difficult conditions and challenges that characterize them. In this chapter, I seek to extend our general knowledge of international negotiation and contribute to its theory and practice by exploring causes and consequences of back channels, and by synthesizing what we know from the dynamics of the Palestinian-Israeli peace process. In the second section of this chapter, I explain why leaders decide to use back channels to negotiate. Considerable attention is paid to the consequences of long-term reliance on secrecy. In the third section, I discuss some specific outcomes of the reliance on secrecy in the Palestinian-Israeli negotiations. In the fourth section, I present five hypotheses testable in other negotiation cases, both domestic and international. In the final sections, I explore the implications for negotiating peace processes.

A Missing Variable in the Study of Peace Processes

Throughout the years of the formal Palestinian-Israeli peace process that officially began in 1991 at the Madrid Peace Conference, the Palestine Liberation Organization (PLO) and Israel made slow progress toward peaceful coexistence while negotiating the terms that would lead to the establishment of the state of Palestine in the West Bank and Gaza, the so-called two-state solution that, it was hoped, would resolve the core Middle East conflict. Hopes were high until the mid-1990s and even the late 1990s, and optimistic analyses prevailed among academics and practitioners. Some claimed that their own Track II work had contributed to the success of the peace process.[4] Given the return to armed conflict and the hardening of the Israeli occupation, it seems that such hopes and claims may have been at the very least premature.

Many factors have contributed to the impasse of the peace process but the *process* of the negotiations themselves has received less scrutiny than it merits.

Exceptions to the lack of analytical scrutiny include articles by Palestinian and Israeli negotiators such as Omar Dajani, who served as senior legal advisor to the Palestinian negotiating team.[5] Many examinations of the peace process have consisted of autobiographical memoirs that tell an insider's story but also apportion blame and take credit at the expense of analysis.[6]

As has been made evident throughout this text, one of the unusual characteristics of Palestinian-Israeli negotiations is that they have nearly always taken place in *two channels:* normal, publicly acknowledged diplomatic negotiations; and a second, parallel, secret channel that top-level Palestinian and Israeli decision makers "own and operate."[7] In essence, this means that while negotiators are hard at work at their front channel negotiation table, both sides' leaders have agreed to send out a second set of negotiators whose existence is unknown to the public and, sometimes, even to the front channel negotiators. This second set of negotiators works secretly and may even bargain over the same issues, but they do so at a second negotiation table far removed from the front channel, protected from publicity, domestic constituencies, and third parties. The continued use of BCN would seem to indicate that negotiators and decision makers believe in its advantages.

The analyses of chapters 3, 4, and 5, as well as the narratives of the genesis of the peace process (chapter 2) and its demise (chapter 6) provide ample opportunity to compare the process and content of front channel and back channel negotiations. I proposed seven elements of negotiation to analyze throughout the Palestinian-Israeli peace process and explicitly structured chapters 3, 4, and 5 around them to compare how they were dealt with in back channels and front channels. The seven-element framework consisted of the following:

1. Issues negotiated
2. Extent of secrecy and publicity
3. Exclusion of subparties
4. Proximity of negotiators to decision makers
5. Negotiator autonomy
6. Presence and role of third parties
7. Strategic use of multiple channels (simultaneous or sequenced front and back channel negotiations)

A brief summary of these elements across the various years and phases of the peace process follows.

Issues Negotiated

Regarding the consideration of issues, it appears that front and back channels do not necessarily consider different issues. However, identical sets of issues are treated very differently in front and back channels. The process of negotiation and the solutions offered are what differ between front and back channels. Process choice and issues work together. The ability to model solutions without commitment to them and without the fear of arousing immediate internal opposition is a process characteristic that protects the negotiator's ability to be flexible on the issues in contention. In essence, the secrecy can foster problem-solving process choices. This protection is afforded only by the secrecy of back channels. The ability of the negotiators to offer and consider solutions outside the range of official political rhetoric meant for public or constituent consumption is far greater in the back channels. Such negotiators need to be empowered to reach agreements that deviate from the maximal demands and rhetoric. Such empowerment results from the negotiator's autonomy and proximity to the top decision makers. Secrecy, autonomy, and proximity to decision makers are considered further in the following.

Extent of Secrecy

Throughout the Palestinian-Israeli peace process, a back channel precedes or accompanies a front channel on the same issues, indicating systematic use of back channels to supplement front channels, as if they were inseparable in practice. The analytical element of secrecy appears in every instance where the parties are negotiating a major agreement, and in each of these instances, it was the channel in which concessions were initially made and creative options for difficult issues were considered.

In the words of Uri Savir, it is clear that negotiators and decision makers need secrecy to reach "tomorrow's consensus," in other words, to come to agreements that do not conform to the declared policies or popular expectations of their respective sides.[8] Negotiators and decision makers seem to validate the realist contention that, to be rational (at least in peacemaking), policy must be freed from the bonds of public opinion. This obviously has direct consequences of exclusion of subparties and third parties. But peacemaking goes far beyond the conclusion of an accord. The mobilization of populations and constituents in order to unify them against a perceived enemy is a task that is constantly undertaken by governments and nonstate actors such as insurgency movements. The tools for doing this are well known; adversaries demonize each other relentlessly and take advantage of all the psychological mechanisms available to discourage people from forming more positive (and often more accurate) images.[9] The effect is hard to undo and may in fact be too hard to undo as a precondition for peacemaking negotiations. Because the political costs may be high, policy makers have little choice: they must negotiate in secret, and they may even conduct a front channel to protect the work of the back channel.

Exclusion of Subparties

Over the decades of the Palestinian-Israeli peace process, including the last decade of its severe reversals, each side's leaders sought out individuals or subparties within "the other side" who could deliver concessions from that side while being politically acceptable to their adversary and still having the requisite authority among their own people to enforce the conditions of a settlement. The different Palestinian and Israeli nationalist parties, bureaucratic actors, and politicians are all highly focused on attaining their own national goals, and some mix this with religious motivations. The political spectrum among both Palestinians and Israelis is very broad, and not all groupings fit comfortably within either the PNA framework or the Israeli parliamentary government. Within each side are politically organized groups that reject accommodation with the enemy and denounce their own leadership for making even symbolic concessions to the other side.

From the perspective of Palestinian nationalism, this is a conflict in which the Palestinians are now negotiating for the creation of a state on the 22 percent that remains of Mandate Palestine (the West Bank, including East Jerusalem, and Gaza). Zionist narratives of the conflict do not concede this point; the Arabs of Palestine renounced their legitimate rights to a state within Mandatory Palestine when they rejected the UN partition plan. At minimum, for the Palestinians, this peace process must result in the very demands that Israelis have always considered maximal—sovereign statehood.

In this sense, there is little of substance for the Palestinian side to concede, hence their understanding that the incrementalism enshrined in Oslo would lead to the attainment of their "redline" demands on the permanent status issues, not to further erosion of their rights, living conditions, and territorial basis. The years between 1991 and 2001 were characterized by a negotiations process in which the Palestinians had accepted Israeli conditions for interim autonomy while each side reserved their respective positions on the permanent status. This condition held in the period from 2001 to 2009 as well, even though most negotiations concerned conflict deescalation rather than substantive peace process arrangements, with the exception of the Geneva Accord, which was negotiated in a secret Track II channel.

For both sides to come to this fundamental and asymmetrical understanding, large portions of their respective political, popular, and bureaucratic bases had to be completely sidelined by excluding them from the negotiation process that began at Oslo. After Oslo, the bureaucratic insiders returned to the negotiation table, and few were permitted into the back channels. Popular groups and political parties began a struggle to reach power, by electoral process in Israel and by popular mobilization in Palestine. Their exclusion was critical for the initial breakthrough, but it also motivated them to organize themselves to oppose the peace process and to influence the outcome of national elections and policies. As each stage of the peace process involved more aspects of implementation on the ground, these excluded groups, such as secular and religious nationalists on both sides, pressed harder against their own leadership to forestall any substantive concessions. This drove new negotiations into back channels, stimulating the cyclical nature of these processes.

Proximity of Decision Makers and Negotiator Autonomy

Although all the variables work together to some extent, two in particular are very entwined: the proximity of decision makers to negotiators seems very closely correlated to the degree of autonomy enjoyed by the negotiator. The cases supported this assumption by showing that back channel negotiators have far more access to top decision makers than do their front channel counterparts. Along with this proximity to the decision makers comes greater trust and authority, which translates to greater negotiating autonomy for the negotiator.

Whether at Oslo, in the pre-Wye back channels, or in the secret BCN encounters from 2000 to 2001 and beyond, BCN negotiators reported directly to top decision makers. This was the case even when the back channel started with some unofficial negotiators on one side, as in the 1995 Stockholm channel and the 2005 Geneva Initiative. Beilin would have submitted the 1995 draft directly to Rabin had the prime minister not been assassinated. He submitted it directly to interim prime minister Shimon Peres, but the suicide bombings, impending elections, and continued closures of the Palestinian territories created a hostile context for further negotiation.

The exception to this observation is when the front channel is a summit, in which case, the front channel has the same or higher-level negotiators than the back channel, as in the Wye Plantation summit of 1998 and the Camp David negotiations of 2000. In those instances of summitry, the top leaders themselves were present, thus outranking their BCN negotiators.

In front channel negotiations, negotiators do not necessarily enjoy privileged access to the decision makers for whom they work. In back channels, the distance between decision makers and front-line negotiators is greatly reduced, although this may be asymmetrical, as the unsuccessful 1992 HAMAS deportation channel showed, when the Israeli side was represented by the foreign minister and the Palestinians were represented by members of their non-PLO delegation in Washington.

The proximity of decision makers to the negotiators is an aspect of BCN that surpasses the simple definitions of classic secret diplomacy. Proximity to decision makers is part of the design of back channels and enables the back channel negotiators to obtain greater flexibility in negotiation and to get more direct input from the decision makers. The negotiators tend to be of higher bureaucratic rank in the back channel and therefore more able to credibly deviate from declared policy and stretch the limits of rhetoric. The back channel negotiators in the Palestinian-Israeli peace process shared the quality of virtually being personal envoys of the decision makers. This trust-based relationship translated into negotiating practices that demonstrated more flexibility at the negotiation table than their front channel counterparts.

For example, the 1998 trade-offs made on the issue of transfer of territory to the PNA and the concurrent Israeli "FRDs" were facilitated by the creation of "nature preserves" in certain parts of the West Bank and by mechanisms for joint security cooperation, as well as by international observers in Hebron and other measures that were not contemplated in front channels. The entire territorial dimension of the interim period was never entertained by the Israeli negotiators in the Washington talks, whereas it was an integral component of the Oslo talks.

Palestinian back channel negotiators invariably reported to Arafat himself on the Palestinian side, or to Abu Mazen who replaced him. Israeli back channel negotiators have reported directly to the prime minister, the foreign minister, or both.

Presence and Role of Third Parties

Mediators with power, resources, and interests tied to the parties in conflict are often instrumental in bringing parties to the table by the triadic leverage they exercise over their allies and the allies' adversaries.

Diplomatic practices in the Middle East and outside the region lend strength to the contention that third-party interveners can overstep the bounds of useful intervention, driving the parties to work outside of a mediated framework in which the mediator fails to mitigate or take advantage of power asymmetry between the parties or in which the mediator is simply ineffective. The mediator with the greatest leverage over the parties, the United States, was the least effective third party from 1991 to 1997. After coordinating the Madrid Peace Conference, the role of the United States as a third party declined steadily until the peace process was imperiled by the problems of implementing the Interim Agreement.

In contrast, the other third-party states that played an intermediary role—such as Norway, Egypt, and Sweden—have been associated with back channels. And those back channels were more effective for reaching agreements than bilateral or United States–sponsored front channels. Terje Larsen continued to advise back channel negotiators on both sides even when he became the UN special coordinator for the occupied territories. Even the chief BCN negotiator for Netanyahu credits Larsen with teaching him the value of BCN.[10] Mediators other than the United States tended to be better at facilitative skills, to have less globally encompassing political interests, and to have more flexibility in terms of adapting their mediation role as needed by the parties. They also seem to have had more explicit trust from the parties.

Third party interveners are typically accepted by weak parties in the hope they will reduce power asymmetries. Third parties are accepted even when "biased" precisely because they can (it is hoped) influence their "client" state. The PLO has long sought out the United States as a sponsor of its self-determination claims, while Israel is highly dependent on the United States' diplomatic, political, and military support. Despite these considerations, both the PLO and Israel have proven willing to conduct much of their bilateral diplomacy beyond the range of regional U.S. peace efforts. Even during times of strenuous U.S. engagement as third party, such as the Clinton-sponsored summits at Wye Plantation and Camp David, a tendency for far-reaching possibilities to be explored in back channels is present.

In any case, the engagement of third parties inevitably seems to complicate already complicated situations. Mediators are themselves constrained by the circumstances and sometimes limited in their ability to deploy the correct mediation activity at the right moment.[11]

Strategic Use of Multiple Channels: Front and Back Channel Negotiation

The simultaneous use of back and front channels is another feature that distinguishes BCN from classic secret diplomacy. There is a relationship between back channel-front channel "sets" and the agreements reached. In all but one instance, the existence of multiple channels is not only correlated with reaching agreement but cited by the negotiators themselves as a causal factor in reaching that agreement.

Negotiation along multiple channels encompasses the use of both secret and open channels of negotiation, as mentioned in the discussion of a BCN typology in chapter 1. Not only do multiple channels (front and back) exist, their interaction was made evident in the cases where I found ample use of back channels to complement front channels (Oslo/Washington talks, Interim Agreement BCN/FCN, CAPS front and back channels) or to substitute for them (Hebron Protocol, Geneva Accord). Back channels were also used to prepare for front channel negotiations (pre-Wye to prepare for Wye, CAPS/FAPS to prepare for Camp David). Additionally, completely parallel negotiation channels provide decision makers opportunities to tacitly communicate. They can, for example, "test" each other by gauging the reaction of a proposal in one channel before it is used in another.

Summary of Case Conclusions

The protective mantle of secrecy permits parties to explore creative solutions to vexing problems and disputes, and it also permits parties to exclude third parties and internal spoilers who seek to impose their own partisan interests onto the negotiations at the expense of the parties' ability to reach agreement. The back channel negotiators are invested with more of the requisite authority needed to make concessions and to craft bold solutions that are not contemplated by their front channel counterparts; the back channel negotiator often reports directly to the head of state or government, bypassing layers of bureaucracy that career diplomats face. Back channels are certainly qualitatively different than front channels. But more importantly, they are better structured to help the parties reach agreements, at least initially.

If the analysis stopped with the examination of the relationship between back channels and agreements reached, one might simply conclude that back channels are a useful policy choice. But the analysis must not end there: to be considered effective, agreements reached in violent conflicts must be implemented and result in positive changes for the parties. This is not what happened in the Palestinian-Israeli cases. Over time, the agreements reached needed to address ever more difficult interim and, finally, permanent status issues because they were negotiated on the incrementalist assumption that success on smaller issues would build interparty trust and facilitate agreement on the most critical issues.

Until the signing of the Interim Agreement, both parties could credibly point to partisan and joint gains. After the Interim Agreement, this changed. The Palestinians' most important gain, the FRDs of Israeli forces, was never fully implemented. Similarly, the Israelis' most important gain, security (and consequently security cooperation with Palestinian security forces) began a downward spiral and did not recover until after the period studied here. Each and every new agreement since that time (with the exception of the draft Beilin-Abu Mazen Agreement and the Geneva Accord, and very possibly the Taba understandings) was little more than a renegotiation of these two issues of withdrawal and security cooperation. Each side faced considerable internal political pressure to deliver on its issue. This pressure culminated in public rejection of the negotiation process, which constrained the decision makers further still, necessitating new back channels and agreements. As each new agreement surfaced, the political leadership of each side was denounced by its hard-line supporters and hard-line opposition for the secrecy and exclusion used to attain the new agreement.

With the negotiation of the Interim Agreement, there was a turning point at which the diplomatic solution to the problem of rejectionists and mobilized subparties—back channel negotiation—became a cause of new rejectionism and mobilization. Throughout the Palestinian-Israeli peace process and across all the channels, one finds a progressive failure to implement critical portions of the agreements reached.

The defining characteristics that made BCN so helpful in the early stages of the Palestinian-Israeli peace process turn into liabilities for the peace process in the following ways: the exclusion of third parties and internal subparties that was so essential to effective, direct bargaining becomes more difficult because they react to their exclusion by getting involved in the political process from which they were excluded. The internal spoilers reacted negatively against the agreements reached because they felt that the agreements were "betrayals" of their interests that went too far in accommodating "the enemy." The decision makers who were closely identified with the back channels then became the target of the spoilers, who sought to reduce leaders' political power or otherwise constrain peacemaking policies. In the case of Prime Minister Rabin, this cost him his life. All of these liabilities in turn hurt the ability of the parties to continue implementing past agreements or negotiating current issues and certainly damage the ability to negotiate in the future. In such straits, the parties find themselves choosing between negotiating in a hostile social context or resorting again to back channels.

The Palestinian and Israeli decision makers and negotiators, over the course of the period reviewed here, when faced with the decaying peace process, consistently chose to open further back channels, initiating a vicious cycle of new secrecy that led to more exclusion and alienation of subparties, who in turn continuously mobilized against the peace process and political leaders involved in it.

This, then, is the final irony of the Palestinian-Israeli peace process: the diplomatic method that permitted the parties to conclude their most important agreements—BCN—progressively exacerbated the conditions that led decision makers to choose it in the first place.

The implications of this paradox are that back channels generate further use of back channels, at least under the conditions of an incrementalist model of peacemaking in which subsequent agreements involve ever greater concessions and implementation involves making real changes on the ground. As implementation fails to take place on schedule or at all, as was the case throughout the period from 1995 to 2001, mutual mistrust arises again between the parties.

Rejectionists point to the failed implementation as evidence of bad faith, which justifies further, sometimes violent, rejectionism. These conditions of mistrust and rejectionism that first generated the need for back channels reassert themselves and overtake the fragile momentum of agreements reached, thus undermining the process. Not even more back channels are sufficient to revive the peace process. On the contrary, more secrecy may be counterproductive.

From this brief summary of the seven comparative elements, a number of insights begin to emerge that require further elaboration: the specific reasons for resorting to back channels and the potential negative consequences of reliance on them.

Managing the Uncertainties of the Peacemaking Process

Contributions to negotiation theory from the behavioral-decision analytical side of the field have spent considerable time examining how "real" people make decisions, and this has contributed to our understanding of how real people negotiate (which is, after all, a joint decision making event).[12] Insights include whether or not to engage in a negotiation at all, when to make concessions on which issues, perceptual distortions in the evaluation of options and offers, and at what point to make a commitment and reach agreement. Their primary contribution in this regard has been to document the systematic cognitive, perceptual, and choice errors human beings make in negotiation situations. They have also contributed significantly to our understanding of the reasons and circumstances for such mistakes. The formal models of game theoretic analysis, and early negotiation analyses to some extent, relied on the abstraction of the rational, self-interested, gain-seeking decision maker with full information and certainty to elaborate prescriptive advice. More recent work in negotiation analysis has challenged both schools of thought and seeks to balance the descriptive accuracy of the behavioralists with prescriptive validity that works for real people.[13] It is in this latter tradition that I seek to place this work: accurate description of a real and understudied negotiation behavior, coupled with an understanding of its consequences.

There has been relatively little systematic study of negotiation under conditions of secrecy or the use of parallel channels of negotiation. In the international negotiation and conflict resolution literature, Jeffrey Rubin discussed the possibility that third parties could make use of what he called "covert negotiations" to get international disputants to decommit from their threats to wage war.[14] Zartman and Berman wrote of several kinds of negotiation channels, including "back" channels, which they defined as secret meetings among high-ranking national leaders seeking to negotiate an agreement in parallel with front-line but lower-level diplomatic negotiations.[15] Iklé described secret diplomacy as a useful tool for reducing pressure from domestic groups.[16] Aharon Klieman has argued that Israel and other countries use back channels to effect dramatic offensive or defensive shifts in foreign policy strategy.[17] Louis Kriesberg described the use of "secret meetings" as a prenegotiation activity that can later lead to substantive negotiations.[18] Kriesberg also regarded back channels as particularly useful for both prenegotiation encounters and to help build support for an existing agreement.[19] Rubin, Pruitt, and Kim discussed "covert problem solving" that permits parties to reduce the problems that can arise from "overt bargaining," including *image loss* (the perception that a party is "weak or irresolute, and hence, willing to make extensive concessions").[20] Raiffa prescriptively advised parties to take advantage of "informal dialogues" to reduce the informational uncertainties of entering into negotiations.[21] In his contributions to negotiation theory, he also noted that subparties and even principals on either side of a negotiation table could set up their own parallel negotiations to supplement those being conducted by their own agents, although he did not examine either the causes or consequences of such moves.[22]

These researchers at least paid attention to the existence of parallel and even secret negotiations. Still, the question of secrecy itself calls for further explanation. Some insight may be found by looking at secrecy per se and also at its mirror image: publicity.

Secrecy is the sine qua non characteristic of all types of BCN. Sissela Bok, in her broad exploration of the ethics of secrecy in diverse human activities, defines secrets and secrecy as follows: "To keep a secret from someone, then, is to block information about it or evidence of it from reaching that person, and to do so *intentionally*: to prevent him from learning it, and thus from possessing it, or revealing it. The word 'secrecy' refers to the resulting *concealment*. It also refers to the methods used to conceal, such as codes or disguises or camouflage, and the practices of concealment, as in trade secrecy or professional confidentiality."[23]

Humanity's recourse to secrecy has both positive connotations (as in the protection of the private and the sacred) and negative ones (the dangerous and the shameful). "Secrecy can work in opposite directions, so as both to inhibit

and to support moral choice."[24] Bok writes that secrecy shields political decision makers from criticism and obscures their failures. Secrecy psychologically
distances decision makers from the effects and human implications of their
decisions, working through the mechanism of discrimination between insider
and outsider.[25]

Bok suggests that secrecy creates exclusion and conflict: "the *separation
between insider and outsider* is inherent in secrecy; and to think something secret
is already to envisage potential conflict between what insiders conceal and outsiders want to inspect or lay bare."[26]

In the conduct of political affairs, however, she notes the legitimate uses
of "administrative secrecy," as when a president decides to devalue a currency
or when a prosecutor conducts a criminal investigation; premature revelation
would undermine the policy action itself. "If administrators had to do everything
in the open, they might be forced to express only safe and uncontroversial views,
and thus to bypass creative or still tentative ideas."[27]

Secrecy in negotiation, though not the subject of Bok's work, can easily be
viewed through these lenses: secrecy in negotiation creates distance and exclusion, but it may also protect fragile and needed problem solving.

Secrecy and publicity are two sides of the same coin with regard to negotiation. Publicity is examined as the presence and impact of "audiences" in negotiation research. Several researchers have specifically explored the negative impact
that audiences can have on negotiators. The relevance of this research stems from
the fact that BCN is characterized by the *exclusion of certain audiences* from
knowledge of the negotiation. Audiences in negotiation can include the principals and the constituents, and even members of one's negotiating team, government cabinet, or bureaucracy, as well as the general public and third parties.
The critical characteristic is perceptual: it refers to the negotiator's sense of being
observed, evaluated, reviewed, subject to critique from the sidelines. Research on
audiences has focused on their capacity to undermine agreement because of the
gaps between what the audience expects or desires and what the principals and
their negotiators may hope to achieve.

Rubin and Brown wrote that "[t]he mere presence of an audience . . . motivates bargainers to seek positive, and avoid negative evaluation [from the audi-
ence], especially when the audience is salient to the bargainers"—in other words,
if the audience has some kind of authority over or impact on the negotiator.[28] This

audience effect thus can induce negotiators to use needlessly aggressive negotiation tactics and strategies against other negotiation parties—even though such actions are counterproductive to one's interests. An escalatory pattern emerges of mutually destructive negotiation moves.[29] In such circumstances, negotiators save face before their "audiences" by inciting and harming each other: "although concessions must be made in order to reach agreement, the act of concession-making is likely to be seen by the conceder, the opposing party and others as a sign of weakness that may invite exploitation."[30] Facing the dilemma of damaging across-the-table negotiations for fear of the impact from one's audience, negotiators sometimes seek an escape. They look for or create an appropriately discreet context, relationship, or other pretext with which to conduct productive and creative negotiations while protecting themselves from this audience effect. Clearly this audience effect can drive political decision makers to seek venues of negotiation such as BCN, which can and do at least temporarily protect negotiators from manipulation by their salient audiences.

It is also true however, that public scrutiny of negotiations can be strategically employed to enhance the commitment of parties to a negotiation process or to encourage them to implement agreements and enhance norms of compliance. Making negotiation commitments publicly can help parties develop images of themselves as virtuous or honorable. The principle of consistency may then come into effect when a negotiator's subsequent decisions favor actions that sustain this image, and thus, foster compliance with prior agreement.[31] Positive audience effects are useful for ritualizing signing ceremonies and demonstrating to the public the importance and finality of a negotiated agreement. Such variations of the audience impact on negotiation need not be discouraged, unlike the more destructive variations that encourage intransigence at the negotiation table.

In their now classic work on labor negotiations, Walton and McKersie described how intraorganizational negotiations that are distributional in nature sometimes motivate the lead negotiator to hide information about the progress of the negotiations from members of the negotiation team, and even principals, in order to manage their expectations and prevent them from undermining a possible agreement with the other side.[32] Such a negotiator realizes that valuable agreements may be attainable with the other party but that more militant and aggressive behaviors within one's delegation work against success. A tactic often used in such situations is known as "tacit communications": the lead negotiators

drop hints to each other that their expressed positional demands are more flexible than they appear.[33] But this too may be insufficient if the signal is too subtle.
Walton and McKersie also described "covert bargaining meetings" that take
place away from the main negotiation table as a tactic for clarifying real priorities
and making concessions away from the scrutiny of one's team and principals—a
variation on parallel secret negotiations.[34]

Although the focus of this book is on international peace negotiations, negotiation analysts will find that business, labor, and interpersonal negotiations are
also subject to the audience effect and therefore use similar strategies to deal with
it, including BCN. The New York City transit strike of December 2005 showed
that when overt negotiations are suspended, back channels are useful to provide
"public cover for each side to resume negotiations, even as a war of rhetoric . . .
rage[s] at news conferences and on picket lines."[35] Both union leaders and the
Metropolitan Transit Authority set out their conditions for a resumption of negotiations. Neither side could publicly comply with the other's demands. A back
channel opening by Roger Toussaint, the beleaguered leader of the Transport
Workers Union, through mediators led by Richard Curreri of the New York State
Public Employment Relations Board, to New York City mayor Michael Bloom-
berg, led to an immediate end to the strike and the sanctions imposed on the
strikers. It also led to a pledge by the principals to continue their negotiations in
secret after the work stoppage had been resolved.

In international negotiations, audiences are particularly critical elements:
they can transform themselves from interested observers into organized, violent
groups opposed to negotiations. "Spoilers" are a kind of particularly sophisti-
cated audience that can have a significant impact on peace processes. They are
stakeholder groups who, in many cases, are not even present at the negotiation
table, but who have decided that they have an interest in undermining the principal parties' ability to reach and implement agreements. They can derail negotiations and provoke a return to violence in international and intrastate conflicts.
Spoilers are not a static phenomenon: they can be created by mobilizing internal
constituencies or outside parties to take a stance against negotiation. Similarly, by
actively engaging with stakeholders, civil society, and other actors—even those
opposed to negotiated settlements—principal parties can prevent spoilers from
emerging or otherwise manage them. The ability of spoilers to both derail peace
processes and also to prevent the implementation of signed peace agreements has

been considered in depth by several researchers, including Stephen Stedman and Louis Kriesberg.[36]

Just as soldiers must fight in the "fog of war," peacemakers must negotiate through the "fog of peacemaking," confronting considerable *uncertainties* about numerous variables, including the goals, intentions, commitment, and unity of spoilers.[37] From the research on the Palestinian-Israeli peace process, four categories of uncertainty emerged that pose special dilemmas for potential peacemakers, and each alone can drive the use of back channels. They are: (1) uncertainty regarding the cost of entry into negotiations, (2) uncertainty regarding the emergence and actions of spoilers, (3) uncertainty about underlying interests and priorities of the parties, and (4) uncertainty concerning negotiation outcome. These four categories of uncertainty encompass much that is at risk in peacemaking, from a leaders' political survival to his or her actual *physical* survival. Secret, back channel negotiations are highly prized by those who practice them precisely because they offer enticing ways to manage these four categories of uncertainty. Taken together, they provide compelling explanations for the phenomenon of BCN. Each of the four is considered in turn here.

Reducing the Costs of Entry

Preconditions set by one or more parties prior to international peace negotiations can include demands for ceasefire, disarmament, withdrawal of forces or settlements, dropping of previously articulated substantive demands, democratization, or surrender of wartime leaders for prosecution. In many complex international conflicts, a significant barrier to conflict resolution can arise from the parties' mutual denials of legitimacy and withholding of recognition. These by definition can result in a refusal to negotiate, at least using front channels. Parties can be reluctant to publicly agree to negotiate with another party whose right to exist is denied, because to do so might be perceived by international audiences or the party itself as a de facto grant of legitimacy and, consequently, a concession.

The initial refusals of the rightist governments of El Salvador to negotiate with the leftist guerrilla group Farabundo Martí de Liberación Nacional (FMLN), of the Indonesian government to negotiate with rebels in Banda Aceh or Timor Leste, and of the royalist Moroccan government to negotiate with the separatist Sahrawi rebels are but a few examples of this endemic problem in international conflict. In other cases, a party will have made public demands that another party agree first to a ceasefire or even complete disarmament. To then engage in public negotiations is to risk the perception of having given up on such a stringent precondition. Such was the case in late 1998 and early 1999 when the governments of Serbia and the Federal Republic of Yugoslavia demanded ceasefires and eventually the total disarmament of the rebel Kosovo Liberation Army as a precondition to negotiations for Kosovar Albanian autonomy. The main precondition for the United Kingdom to negotiate with Sinn Fein was a ceasefire by the Irish Republican Army.

By not publicly acknowledging their negotiations, parties permit themselves to negotiate without demanding or making *any* prior concessions, thereby reducing the political costs associated with entering negotiation. The former royalist government of Nepal long refused to recognize the Maoist rebels as a legitimate member of the political opposition but also felt compelled to negotiate with them; therefore, they alternated military offensives with quiet diplomatic overtures to the Maoists.

Uncertainty is rampant in the prenegotiation phase of peace talks. Conditions are often too difficult to meet, and requirements can be unclear; one side may not clearly specify the actions required of the other side or the reciprocal steps that will be taken upon satisfaction of the demands. What will each party receive in exchange for laying down its arms? And parties making demands cannot be entirely sure that their preconditions will result in the desired changes on the part of their adversaries. Indeed, the party making the demand may not actually intend to negotiate at all, and their demands may, in fact, be designed to discourage peacemaking by making it too politically costly for the other side to even consider negotiation. Different factions within one side may hold several of these postures. And given the ambiguity and fragmentation of demands, responding parties are never certain when they have conceded enough to be accepted as legitimate representatives.

Historically, Palestinian and Israeli political leaders have conditioned negotiations with each other on the satisfaction of prior conditions. This pattern, evident throughout the history of the Zionist-Arab and Palestinian-Israeli conflict, was present at the beginning of the official peace process in 1991: Israel's main precondition was that the PLO and any Palestinians from East Jerusalem be excluded from the negotiation team—and initially, the non-PLO Palestinians were required to negotiate as part of the Jordanian government's delegation. The United States, sponsor of the process, acquiesced in this precondition.[38] The pattern continues now, despite what is now a long track record of negotiations. If existing negotiations stall, leaders often see this as an opportunity to make new demands as a condition for returning to the negotiation table.

This uncertainty is *virtually eliminated* by BCN, which enables parties to maintain an adversarial public posture while secretly seeking ways to deescalate the conflict. The PLO and Israel were, in fact, negotiating with each other—albeit in exploratory, tentative ways—even during the years when such contacts were officially outlawed by Israel and discouraged by some parties within the PLO. The earliest secret contacts between PLO officials and Israeli government officials took place in 1985 and were interspersed with periods of intense violence.[39] There were open declarations of war on the table between the parties, and yet they were secretly and directly exploring possible deescalatory moves and cooperative gestures not uncommon to enemies in war, including the return of the remains of fallen soldiers and eventual peace negotiation scenarios.

Staying Ahead of the Spoilers

A leader who must decide whether to negotiate is concerned about both internal and external spoilers—the parties who challenge each side in the dispute and who have an interest in maintaining the conflict's status quo. Nagging uncertainties about the possible actions of parties who are absent from the table but have interests in the outcome permeate every peace process negotiation. But negotiators fear not only their own internal spoilers; each must be aware of the constraints its adversary faces because its adversary may also have spoilers. And all parties need to be aware of and jointly manage the potential manipulation that comes from external third parties, even those who act as mediators.[40] The failed negotiations between the European Union and Iran between 2004 and 2006 about the implementation of Iran's plans to enrich uranium in order to develop civil nuclear power suffered from the spoiler intervention of the United States, in its role as a board member of the International Atomic Energy Agency (IAEA) and as a permanent member of the UN Security Council. Having no official ties with Iran, and being locked in competition with Iran over the political situation in Iraq, the United States pursued adversarial strategies from the sidelines, including several rounds of sanctions authorized by the United Nations. The United States also dismissed all Iranian offers and attempts at settlement that fell short of a unilateral surrender of the pursuit of enrichment. The United States openly declared support for a negotiated solution, but its actions assured that Iran could never say yes to any negotiation proposal. In the unlikely case that the European Union-Iran talks had made use of BCN, they would have protected themselves from such outside pressures.

Initially, at least, parties are better able to manage potential spoilers (whether they are subparties or potential third-party interveners) when the spoilers are kept in the dark about the existence of the negotiation table. The benefit here is one of the most critically important aspects of BCN: parties can make breakthrough agreements before subparties or third parties have a chance to mobilize against negotiation, agreement, or implementation of agreement. Secrecy, by definition, implies exclusion. BCN thus becomes a way to exclude spoilers from the process by keeping them ignorant of the negotiators' work, thereby reducing the likelihood they will mobilize quickly enough to derail negotiation or prevent implementation. By using BCN, negotiators seek to stay ahead of spoilers, and they can do so if they reach *and* implement agreements in advance of significant efforts to derail them. But staying ahead of spoilers is not the same as mobilizing constituents in favor of a negotiated agreement or policy shift. Creating positive public support may require sustained efforts separate from the management of spoilers. Such actions include gestures and statements of reconciliation including sharing truth narratives, official apologies, group dialogues, joint truth commissions, legal and financial compensations, expressions of empathy and recognition, and ending of oppressive relationships. Public support and elite conversion to sustained peacemaking are strengthened (but not guaranteed) by conciliatory actions. Nevertheless, their intrinsic importance to conflict reduction, as well as their value to fostering a climate in which peace negotiations succeed cannot be underestimated.[41]

Spoilers are not monoliths, nor are they static. Their power to disrupt negotiations can wax and wane. Actions taken to isolate them can sometimes intensify their commitment, while creatively engaging them—or even co-opting them—may prevent violence. In international negotiations, in contrast with interpersonal negotiations, parties occasionally create or at least strengthen their own spoilers as a tactic for reducing their own room for making concessions. For example, the former president of the Greek Cypriots, Tassos Papadopoulos, adopted this tactic by openly appealing to his population to vote *against* the Annan Plan, a negotiated reunification of the two halves of Cyprus in the referendum of April 24, 2004.

This, of course, only makes BCN even more compelling as a strategic negotiation choice because, not only does a party minimize the possibility of damage from its own spoilers, but it also reduces the other side's incentive to rely on spoilers to alter the zone of possible agreement. In the short run, and at crisis moments, denying spoilers any access to the negotiations may be the only way to reach agreements. As discussed below, however, dependence on secrecy may be problematic in the long term as spoilers become more proactive about preventing agreements from being implemented.

Spoilers sometimes are nothing more than elements of the population loosely organized against a particular initiative or against negotiation in general. In this sense, it is civil society itself that has the dual capability of either supporting peace or descending into "uncivil" society, without actually transforming itself into a political party or a coherent militant group.

Discovering Interests, Priorities, and Mandates

Parties are often unsure of how to prioritize their own needs and interests, assuming they understand them well to begin with. They inevitably lack information about the opposing party's preferences, strategies, and priorities. This "negotiation intelligence" is essential to making negotiation decisions: the other party's underlying interests; how that party would structure trade-offs, priorities, and reservation values; and how flexible the other side is regarding those interests—all are key pieces of data that influence the ebb and flow of negotiation. In the absence of data, parties sometimes waste a fair amount of negotiation time posturing in the hope that the other side's rejections will mark the broad outlines of its preferences.

Parties also announce maximal demands as an "anchoring" tactic to create the perception of a smaller zone of agreement, but their flexibility is often greater than they are willing or able to communicate, and as negotiations proceed, interests and priorities can shift in unpredictable ways.[42]

Decision makers can use BCN to reduce such informational uncertainty in several ways. With BCN, adversaries can explore in secret the realities underlying their public declarations and policies, and they can communicate about the possible contours of agreement without the need to publicly commit to those ideas. By preventing outside parties and even internal actors from knowing about a back channel negotiation, ideas that might be "nonstarters" in public (the other side refuses to discuss them) can at least be raised and considered in discreet settings. This enables the parties to explore entire agreements that meet at least some of their partisan *and* joint interests.

Practitioners and theorists alike have discussed the benefits of privately exploring solutions before publicly committing to them.[43] Back channel negotiations offer parties the freedom to consider multiple problems that may seem intractable in a more public forum but that, discussed in secret, may in fact be amenable to creative solutions.

Knowing the interests and priorities among them helps decision makers craft their negotiators' mandates: the scope of authority to be flexible, to explore creative solutions, to deviate from established policy. Top leaders tend to be closer to their back channel negotiators than they are to the front channel negotiators and can authorize more creativity and flexibility. President Richard Nixon, who had campaigned on "running foreign policy from the White House," was close to Henry Kissinger, his national security advisor, and gave him greater leeway to negotiate with the Soviets, Chinese, and North Vietnamese, among others, than he gave Secretary of State William Rogers, who was eventually replaced by Kissinger. In the Palestinian-Israeli peace process, all back channel negotiators have been close confidants of the top leaders, while front channels are populated by lower-ranking "line" diplomats, or at least by negotiators with little room for bargaining. Eliyakim Rubenstein, the leader of the Israeli delegation at the 1991 Madrid Peace Conference and the ensuing Israeli-Palestinian talks in Washington, D.C., notes that he and his delegation were severely constrained in their ability to negotiate regarding Palestinian self-determination, in contrast with what Israeli back channel negotiators were able to negotiate over in the Oslo channel.[44] Predictably, no agreement arose from the front channel Palestinian-Israeli negotiations, despite two years of efforts.[45]

This by no means implies that the front channel negotiators are less skilled, creative, or committed. The proximity to the decision maker and the authority to be flexible that flows from that proximity create a qualitatively different negotiation context that, at least in some circumstances, is more likely to lead to agreement.

Political decision makers and their close associates have the authority to reveal to their back channel counterparts the true interests of their side or to deviate from declared policy in order to reach agreement to their counterparts on the other side. The closer a negotiator is to a decision maker, the less likely he or she is to be bound by restrictive instructions. As noted, all Palestinian and Israeli BCN negotiators from 1993 to 2001, as analyzed in chapters 3 to 6, were closer to their respective top-level decision makers and enjoyed a higher level of autonomy than front channel negotiators.[46]

Finally, the simultaneous use of front and back channels enables parties to obtain additional information about the other side's priorities. By using two channels, a leader can float different proposals in each channel and see how each is received. Thus a decision maker gains a more nuanced image of the adversary's underlying interests, priorities, and flexibility. Parties sometimes take an inflexible stance in the front channel, hoping to encourage adversaries to negotiate more seriously and creatively in the back channel.

Managing the Uncertainty Regarding the Outcome

Diplomats, labor-management mediators, business leaders, and even local politicians all know that top-level decision makers are often reluctant to attend a high-level summit or even authorize negotiations among subordinates unless they feel confident that the outcome will be politically advantageous for them. They fear to associate with an effort that is likely to fail. In democratic systems, the aversion to risky, high-level negotiations can be especially evident before a scheduled election. The probability of success and the confidence of decision makers are not always perfectly matched. Overconfidence in a successful outcome can distort leaders' assessment of success. The Camp David summit for Palestinian and Israeli leaders in July 2000 suffered from the Prime Minister Barak's overconfidence in a successful outcome. The hope that Clinton could help close a permanent status agreement, coupled with Barak's misplaced confidence, overpowered Arafat's and Clinton's foreboding,[47] as recounted in detail in chapter 6. The summit's failure exacerbated a brewing political crisis for the Israeli government, despite attempts to put all of the blame on the Palestinians.

BCN permits international decision makers to get involved in negotiations without immediate risk to their prestige, popularity, reputation, or political office. Barak would not invest sufficient time or negotiation mandate in the back channels that the U.S. peace coordinator Dennis Ross and others felt could make progress in advance of a summit. Barak gambled the peace and his political coalition, and he lost both.

Uncertainty poses problems for any type of negotiation. However, the uncertainties associated with negotiations to end violent conflicts are particularly dangerous because the stakes are so high: political instability, war, political and physical survival. Under such circumstances, decision makers seeking to deescalate a crisis or to negotiate a more comprehensive agreement in a violent conflict find the back channel negotiation very attractive.

Reliance on BCN in Incrementalist Peace Negotiations

Back Channels Generate More Back Channels

Back channels and front channels, when paired in "sets," can generate feedback effects. Initially, this can be viewed as a positive, deliberate result of BCN, as when the product of back channels is finalized in front channels.

The critical early years of the peace process show how the parties' early reliance on back channels only created the need for further back channels and failed to peacefully resolve the conflict. BCN helped the parties reach many agreements on paper, but on the ground, they drifted further and further from a feasible peace settlement. Beginning in 1997 with the government of Prime Minister Netanyahu, the Israelis openly refused to implement the Interim Agreement. Even Netanyahu's renegotiations of the Interim Agreement (the Wye River Memorandum, mediated by President Clinton) were not implemented, to the chagrin of the Clinton administration.

Delayed Implementation: The Price of Entry

Despite their expected benefits, in the context of peace processes under conditions of incremental negotiations and slow or faulty implementation, back channel negotiations seem to have some potential negative repercussions.

The very ease of entry afforded by BCN provides an opportunity for parties to use it as a delaying mechanism while they seek to unilaterally attain their goals. Back channels then become a substitute for real negotiated change. The adversary is kept busy negotiating, but real progress is never contemplated. In this sense, BCN is no guarantee of good faith in negotiation. It does not shape the parties' intentions. It cannot be relied upon as a panacea. It may facilitate the achievement of breakthrough agreements, but alone it does nothing to assure the implementation of those agreements.

The reduction of entry costs, by deferring concessions to future negotiations, simply postpones such concessions, rather than eliminating them altogether. Whereas some peace negotiations may involve the specification of conditions to be fulfilled prior to entering talks, the Israeli-Palestinian case is one in which the preconditions or concessions a party requires prior to coming to the table were assigned to a future negotiation table. This necessarily creates uncertainties about the endgame—the final outcome of the negotiation process—because the parties' key demands, or the key issues of importance to all parties, are deferred to a negotiation separated from the interim issues, negotiations, and agreements. In chapters 3 to 6, I argued that the negotiators often underestimated the importance of the linkages between the permanent status issues (Jerusalem, settlers, borders, etc.) and the interim issues (elections, redeployments, security). These linkages were often an obstacle to interim progress (redeployment from Hebron, for example, was impeded by the presence of the small but militant Israeli settlement in the middle of Hebron).

Exacerbating Spoiler Mobilization

In the ideal case, the principal parties, if they reach agreement using BCN, are able to implement them *before* internal opponents and spoilers can mobilize against them because BCN has permitted the negotiators to do their work without the interference of the spoilers. Practice can deviate from the ideal case, however. As the operational aspects of implementing agreements (troop withdrawals, territorial return, elections, etc.) become more difficult to manage and more (politically) costly to explain to internal subparties—as they inherently do in incrementalist negotiations—political opponents and excluded subparties react by mobilizing to protest against concluded accords, anticipate further *secret* negotiations, and express their opposition to future negotiations, ultimately working to derail the process entirely. Thus, over the long run, BCN can end up having a negative effect on an incrementalist peace process.

BCN, ironically, can bring the parties back to the kind of spiral of violence and confrontation that is possible in all peace processes. Although these episodes can happen in any peace process, BCN is ostensibly used precisely to avoid them. The actions of the various rejectionist groups reacting to secret negotiations, and therefore their exclusion from the process, also feed back on each other and are used as justifications by their counterparts: Palestinian suicide bombings were cited as a pretext for repressive measures by the IDF and land seizures by the Israeli settlers. Every killing of a Palestinian civilian, demolition of a home, or land seizure by the IDF or settlers was cited as further justification for terrorist attacks by armed wings of HAMAS or MIJ. Failures of implementation and anti–peace process militancy are a potent mix of feedback effects. BCN alone will not manage spoilers for long. The changing political circumstances on both sides ultimately led BCN negotiators to exceed what their leaders were willing or able to implement. Whereas spoilers can react against front channel negotiations, the exclusion, secrecy, and implementation problems of BCN have the potential to magnify the spoiler problem.

Parties may also find it hard to fully explore solutions in secret without knowing if the other side is willing to commit to them. If agreement is not reached, one party may want to start anew while another may wish to start at the point where previous secret negotiations left off. Any leak of a back channel will expose leaders to their spoilers. Secrecy protects negotiators only while the negotiation is *kept* secret.

Those who have been excluded discover their exclusion and react against it. They then accuse their own leaders of collaboration with the enemy. They can be managed best when each side implements its commitments in good faith and demonstrates the political gains derived by such implementation to internal mainstream and militant factions, bureaucratic actors, and armed forces. Shifts in popular attitudes in favor of a peace process would be highly valuable and may both stimulate and be the result of good faith implementation. Unfortunately, the possibility of such critical shifts in mainstream support *becomes more remote* as a peace process unravels.

The exclusion that appears so critical to early BCN breakthroughs becomes a liability over time. The prescriptive implication of this finding is that somehow, decision makers need to protect negotiators from the audience effect even as they engage civil society, constituencies, internal opposition, and even full-fledged spoilers in an ongoing effort to persuade them of the wisdom of negotiated peace. Indeed, related research suggests that the closer civil society is to a peace process, the more sustainable the peace.[48]

From Data Gathering to Channel Shopping

Managing the informational uncertainties is also a complex task. Parties may find it hard to truly "model" solutions without commitment to them. If agreement is not reached, one party may want to start anew while another may wish to start at the point where previous negotiations left off. If trust is not present among the negotiators or if the parties intend to leak information to damage their counterparts, modeling of possible solutions involving concessions is highly risky because it exposes negotiators to their spoilers. The Palestinian-Israeli peace process was never immune from leaks to the press about either the existence of back channels or their content. Over time, this significantly eroded the creative potential of BCN, and by the time the May 2000 back channels were leaked, they were discredited at the very moment when they might have been extremely helpful for the pending summit led by the United States (see chapter 6).

Confusion can also be a problem when using multiple channels to negotiate. Whenever a party adopts two contrasting positions on the same issue—as is the case when front and back channels are used together—or willingly discusses a possibility in the back channel that it will not contemplate in the front channel, an astute decision maker on the other side is posed with the dilemma of trying to decide which channel (and position) should be taken more seriously. Parties face challenges discerning each other's intentions when back channels and front channels are used together.

When multiple channels are used to manage informational uncertainties, a party may determine that it prefers to negotiate in the channel where it believes it can exact the most gains: parties can therefore use BCN to "channel shop." They minimize risks associated with individual negotiators on the other side who seem less inclined to make concessions or who have less authority to do so by negotiating in alternative channels.[49] The tendency to channel shop could also become problematic when, for example, important front channel negotiators express a sense of betrayal (about their leaders) or indignation (about the manipulative adversary) once they learn about a back channel from which they were excluded.[50]

Dr. Saeb Eraqat, the head of the PLO's Negotiation Affairs department who negotiated in both front and back channels and on both interim and permanent status issues throughout the peace process, has distinguished between what he has termed "off media" negotiations and back channel negotiations. He openly recognizes the value of holding negotiations out of the range of the news media because "the pressure of the media kills the negotiations." However, he also believes that the Israelis use the real back channels to get undue concessions out of the Palestinians. "They would go to negotiate [in secret] with Abu Alaa if they didn't like what they heard [from me in front channel negotiations]."[51]

Decision makers too may needlessly multiply channels for their own purposes. Yasir Arafat, in authorizing multiple, simultaneous negotiation tracks, sometimes gave different instructions and mandates in each channel and constantly moved negotiators among different teams and channels. According to one insider, this led to "fierce competition" and "mutual suspicion among negotiators, each of whom sought to be the man who brought home the deal but feared being disparaged as weak or traitorous by his competitors. This predicament led some negotiators to prefer secret talks with the Israelis."[52] Israeli negotiators too faced similar dilemmas that lead them to prefer secret channels at different points in the peace process.

Unexpected Outcomes

Finally, because the decision makers tend to be closer to back channels than front channels (except for summits) and generally prefer not to be associated with a failed negotiation outcome, it becomes important for them to determine the credibility of any available channel. A party faced with the availability of multiple channels may legitimately wonder which channel corresponds to its own interests while also being aligned with the decision maker on the other side. Because decision makers rise and fall, either through succession, struggles, or elections, channels too may shift in salience, as the Stockholm channel did after the assassination of Yitzhak Rabin.

Because BCN permits the highest-level decision makers to be involved in negotiations that might otherwise endanger their popular standing, they are more vulnerable to being criticized for the substance of whatever agreement is finally reached. The parallel use of front and back channels demonstrates that front channels are less likely to result in agreement. However, agreements reached in the back channel may incorporate more daring stances and riskier concessions than may have been explored in the front channels because the leader is initially protected from public backlash during the negotiations. Most critically, when the agreement is eventually made public, the leader may find that the secrecy needed to negotiate prevented the parties from preparing constituents and internal sub-parties for an eventual agreement.

Both Palestinians and Israelis criticized their respective leaders for conceding "too much" in back channel negotiations from the Oslo Agreement of 1994 to the unacknowledged Stockholm document of 2003. The concessions involved in the Oslo Accords—the decision to confer mutual recognition and engage in a gradual peace process without a declared final outcome—involved such large deviations from the declared policies and preferences of each side that they could only have been made by the highest authorities.

In using BCN to mitigate each of the four uncertainties I described earlier, negotiators risked confronting hidden costs if the parties failed to build a general consensus in favor of the peace process even as they negotiated in secret. More critically, in regard to spoilers, costs can escalate to the point where they surpass and finally cancel out any achieved benefits, yielding not diminishing returns but negative returns and facilitating the parties' spiral toward renewed violent confrontation. Table 7 presents uncertainties being managed by BCN and the feedback effects generated by reliance on the method.

The difference between BCN and FCN in this regard can be simply stated: when using front channels only, parties reach agreements (or fail to reach them), audiences and constituents know about the negotiations and react to them as soon as the outcome of the negotiation is announced. When the parties use BCN—alone or in parallel with FCN—the process, content, and possibilities of the negotiations are all hidden, the leaders are protected, and the negotiations may explore riskier agreements. In practice, BCN has a paradoxical quality. It is needed to actually negotiate and get to agreement, but it may then exacerbate the very dilemmas facing peacemakers who rely only on front channels.

Table 7. Four Uncertainties, Four Feedback Effects

Four uncertainties addressed by BCN	*Negative consequences*
COST OF ENTRY: How to avoid or minimize need to meet preconditions demanded of other party?	DELAY TACTICS: Real concessions or necessary moves are deferred or cancelled because secrecy permits them to negotiate without committing to implementation.
INFORMATION, INTERESTS, AND PRIORITIES: What are the real preferences among the parties? What trade-offs and linkages are possible?	CHANNEL SHOPPING AND CONFUSION: Multiple positions can communicate inconsistency and internal division. Parties may opt to negotiate only in the channel that seems most likely to get them desired concessions.
SPOILERS: How can a party manage its own extremists, militants, and internal constituencies?	MOBILIZATION DUE TO EXCLUSION: After realizing that secrecy is being used to exclude them, spoilers mobilize faster than decision makers can implement agreements.
OUTCOME: How to manage constituent expectations and reduce the impact of a failed negotiation on the decision makers and leaders?	DISCONNECTION FROM POPULAR WILL: Leaders are exposed to failure or make concessions for which supporters are unprepared, which provokes them into mobilization.

Negotiation Theory and Back Channel Negotiations

Based on my analyses of Palestinian-Israeli negotiations and on observations of back channel negotiations used in other cases, I have developed several propositions about back channel negotiations when used in international conflicts.

1. *Back channel negotiations used in international conflicts will facilitate early breakthrough agreements.* The Oslo Accords, in which the PLO and Israel recognized each other and agreed to negotiate the terms of peaceful coexistence, are an example of such a breakthrough early in the peace process. They took everyone by surprise, including the Norwegian hosts and facilitators. The United States—long

involved in the Middle East—was completely left out despite having initiated a front channel process that operated in parallel with the Oslo negotiations.

2. *Constant reliance on back channels will yield diminishing returns in the form of more difficult implementation of existing agreements and more constraints on current and future negotiations, especially under conditions of incrementalism.* The tortuous history of the Interim Agreement, which required so many back channels to negotiate and then suffered more than four years of renegotiation under successive Israeli leaders more vulnerable to spoilers, demonstrates this proposition.

3. *Decision makers confront an "implementation dilemma" once they have signed an agreement that was negotiated using BCN.* They risk losing the trust of internal spoilers *if they do implement* an agreement from which internal parties were excluded, *and* they risk losing the trust of their negotiating partners/ adversaries *if they do not* implement an agreement. This proposition stems from the prior proposition concerning renegotiation. Spoilers such as the Israeli and Palestinian groups opposed to negotiated settlement, when they fail to be incorporated into the peace process and succeed in framing the peace process as a betrayal by national leaders, use their "rejectionism" as a source of leverage. If they can successfully put the leaders at risk of losing power, this proposition is validated. (See fig. 1.)

Whether or not the parties implement their commitments negotiated in a back channel, they may face erosion of confidence and trust from either internal subparties or from their adversary. To escape the implementation dilemma, the decision makers must adopt a dual strategy that protects the trust of the adversary while minimizing the opportunities for internal subparties to mobilize opposition. The parties must progressively reduce their dependence on BCN and design implementation stages in order to minimize loss of party cohesion and maximize the speed of creating positive changes "on the ground," such as demobilization and disarmament of armed forces, provision of security to vulnerable populations, provision of humanitarian assistance, economic development, resettlement, and other tangibles. The parties may have to make significant investments in efforts to strategically "market" agreements reached, and this could involve collaborative efforts to bolster each other's moderate supporters by reaching out to them. Consulting the potential spoilers in advance and giving them a veto (such as a referendum) over any concessions or possible agreements are potentially counterproductive measures that only empower spoiler behavior.

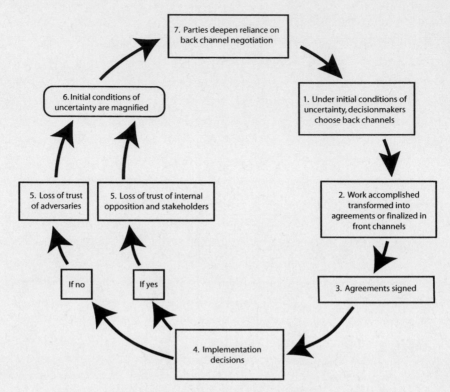

Figure 1. Back channel negotiation and the implementation dilemma.

4. *Back channels, if not managed carefully, thus generate and exacerbate the very conditions that led parties to use them, requiring further use of back channels.* If the negotiations tool meant to keep negotiators one step ahead of the spoilers only results in the empowerment of spoilers, then the parties are only more likely to rely on back channels, thus further neglecting the critical task of peacemaking: preparing their public for the eventuality of peace. This acts as a vicious cycle. The consistent pattern of back channel use by the PLO and Israel demonstrates that they understood proposition 1 (above) very well but did not foresee the consequences of ongoing reliance on BCN.

5. *Negotiations that rely on BCN proceed from breakthrough agreements to diminishing returns and, ultimately, to negative returns.* These are manifested in the form of failed implementations, constraints on future negotiations, renewed conflict, and loss of intraparty cohesion. Mutual recriminations, accusations of

bad faith, international and domestic constraints, and other classic factors do not explain the failure of the Palestinian-Israeli peace process. The most recent period of violence without meaningful negotiations is at least partially explained by the *process* variable of BCN and the complex dynamics that derived from it.

There is no lack of conflicts that have made use of secret back channels, including negotiations concerning the Iraqi Kurds, Armenia and Azerbaijan, the Cuban Missile Crisis, United States-Egypt contacts prior to the October 1973 War, and the United States-Soviet SALT I talks. More recently, secret parallel channels have been used to pursue negotiations regarding Kosovo, Burundi, Northern Ireland, and between Israel and Syria.

Negotiations characterized by secrecy will continue to be used to manage violent and intractable conflicts, while populations affected by war and civil society groups will increasingly play a role—for better or worse—in the resolution of those conflicts. Their clamor for inclusion is a signal that peacemakers can mold and shape public opinion in favor of peace, even in the wake of violent conflict.[53]

Implications for Negotiations and Peace Processes

By exploring all the Palestinian and Israeli front and back channels, it becomes apparent that there is an interlocking set of political uncertainties that motivates leaders to use both front and back channels together. It has been well understood that negotiations and decisions taking place under conditions of uncertainty offer interesting opportunities for heuristic thinking and systematic errors of judgment.[54] What I propose here is to disaggregate some of the uncertainties and show how they facilitate certain behaviors in international negotiations. Each uncertainty produces a political benefit that results from using secrecy. None of the benefits are absolute.

By hiding negotiations and decisions from internal opponents (those most likely to oppose peace talks), leaders hope to make deals and carry them out before any significant opposition can be organized. Indeed, there is a "package" of political benefits for the leader using back channel diplomacy.

But each beneficial effect of secret diplomacy has a direct, negative consequence. These consequences are what policy makers have failed to understand. By using secrecy, leaders get to agreements without creating a broad consensus in favor of their policies. But opponents of peace policies are neither idle nor blind. The excluded individuals and groups eventually mobilize *against* further negotiations faster than leaders can carry out negotiated commitments. Ultimately, the excluded parties damage and destroy peace processes by undermining the political power of their own leadership, whether by waging legislative battles or by resorting to violence to accomplish their aims. The stage is then set for renewed violent conflict that, ironically, is exacerbated by the very diplomacy that was intended to turn swords into ploughshares.

This synthesis in this chapter suggests several general concepts of policy-relevant implications. First of all, *BCN seems to have particular drawbacks for incrementalist peace processes* because of the ability of excluded parties to mobilize over time as the process continues without final resolution. Thus, for quick breakthroughs, the value of BCN is apparent. For long-term negotiations processes, caution is advised.

Reaching peace agreements with external parties will not resolve internal divisions within parties, even if those agreements are considered a breakthrough negotiated in a back channel. The international political events of the past decade give eloquent witness to the fact that internal divisions are difficult to manage during and after a peace process. BCN can be helpful early in the international conflict but can actually generate limitations as time goes on. The policy relevance of this observation is that there is really *no substitute for building a pro-peace consensus* among a party's supporters and detractors, what Dean Pruitt refers to as a "broad central coalition" ready to support resolution of conflict.[55] A government-sponsored peace rally in Tel Aviv was the site of the assassination of Prime Minister Rabin and signaled that the efforts to build a public consensus in the Palestinian-Israeli peace process were "too little, too late," as several negotiators have observed.[56] Joint efforts by the leaders to reach out to each party's mainstream should be part of the open efforts to build consensus on so critical a policy shift as that from war to peace.[57]

This is hard work for policy makers but presents itself as a critical task that policy makers cannot neglect whenever they engage in peace making, and especially if they feel compelled to use BCN. Front channels present more difficulties getting to the table, let alone getting to agreement, whereas back channels present more difficulties in the implementation of agreements. The solution is not to choose one over the other but to *combine early but diminishing use of secrecy with gradually increasing and public efforts to expand the central coalition* on each side. Joint Palestinian-Israeli public opinion research indicates that there are both great need and opportunities for Palestinian, Israeli, and international leaders to invest in reframing negotiation and political solutions as beneficial for their publics in order to broaden popular support and empower peacemaking.[58]

Finally, for BCN as for FCN, implementation of an agreement carries its own risks of damage to the internal consensus supporting conflict resolution. With that said, *the benefits of implementation of secret agreements seem to outweigh the costs.* It is early and rapid implementation rather than the simple existence of an agreement that presents spoilers with a fait accompli that they are hard pressed to undo. If the task of the leader is to deliver results to people and mute the criticisms of rejectionists, then slow or failed implementation of an agreement can only hurt the credibility of the leader or government that signed the agreement. As Uri Savir has noted, "this is the whole contradiction of peacemaking: In peacemaking, you break the consensus of today and you create tomorrow's consensus."[59] If a leader fails at implementation, then internal spoilers are strengthened on each side, the legitimacy of peacemaking is undermined, and support for peacemaking may decline. When Israel began to suspend implementation of the Interim Agreement and renegotiate its military withdrawals, a pattern of reciprocal suspension, blame, and escalation replaced the emerging norms of peacemaking that had been created by the Oslo Accords.

Implementation is always a challenge in peace processes, but the use of BCN in a peace process poses two related concerns: spoilers will work harder to discover negotiations and derail progress, and efforts to broaden the general support for peace may suffer simply because the reliance on secrecy can come at the expense of public consensus building.

BCN is in many ways the practice of "statecraft in the dark"[60] or what I have called "bargaining in the shadows." When international peace is at stake, policy makers and negotiators should have the clearest possible understanding of not only the benefits their negotiation process choices provide but also the impacts they can have on peacemaking efforts.

Notes | Bibliography | Index

Notes

1. Analyzing the Palestinian-Israeli Peace Process

1. Henry Kissinger, *Years of Upheaval* (Boston: Little, Brown, 1982), 115.

2. Louis Kriesberg, "Nature, Dynamics, and Phases of Intractability," in *Grasping the Nettle: Analyzing Cases of Intractable Conflict,* ed. Chester Crocker, Fen Osler Hampson, and Pamela Aall (Washington, D.C.: United States Institute of Peace, 2005).

3. These are just the most relevant bare facts. More detailed histories of the British Mandate period include David Fromkin, *A Peace to End All Peace* (New York: Avon, 1989), and the official history of the Mandate Government of Palestine, *A Survey of Palestine: Prepared December 1945 and January 1946 for the Information of the Anglo-American Committee of Inquiry,* 3 vols. (Washington, D.C.: 1946; reprint, Institute for Palestine Studies, 1991); Walid Khalidi, ed., *From Haven to Conquest: Readings in Zionism and the Palestine Problem Until 1948* (Washington, D.C.: Institute of Palestine Studies, 1991); Neil Caplan, *Futile Diplomacy,* vol. 1, *Early Arab-Zionist Negotiation Attempts* (London: F. Cass, 1983); Benny Morris, *Righteous Victims: A History of the Zionist-Arab Conflict, 1881–1999* (New York: Knopf, 1999). This is just a sampling.

4. Henry Kissinger, *White House Years* (Boston: Little, Brown, 1979), 138-39 (back channel with the Soviet Union), 258–80 (back channel with North Vietnam), 1292–98 (back channel with Egypt); Kissinger, *Years of Upheaval,* 503 (back channel with the PLO); and Henry Kissinger, *Years of Renewal* (New York: Simon and Schuster, 1999), 178 (back channel regarding the SALT talks), 778 (back channel with Cuba). All three volumes comprise a veritable collection of secret diplomatic initiatives.

5. See, for example, Thomas Schelling, *The Strategy of Conflict,* rev. ed. (Cambridge, Mass.: Harvard Univ. Press, 1980), 29–30; and Richard Walton and Robert McKersie, *A Behavioral Theory of Labor Relations,* rev. ed. (New York: McGraw-Hill, 1991).

6. Ronald Fisher, "The Potential Contribution of Training to Resolving International Conflict," *International Negotiation* 2, no. 3 (1997); Ronald Fisher, ed., *Paving the Way: Contributions of Interactive Conflict Resolution to Peacemaking* (Lanham, Md.: Lexington, 2005); Ronald Fisher, "Coordination Between Track Two and Track One Diplomacy in Successful Cases of Prenegotiation,"

International Negotiation 11, no. 1 (2006): 65–89; Ronald Fisher, "Interactive Conflict Resolution," in *Peacemaking in International Conflict: Methods and Techniques,* ed. I. William Zartman (Washington, D.C.: United States Institute of Peace, 2007); Herbert Kelman, "Informal Mediation by the Scholar/Practitioner," in *Mediation in International Relations: Multiple Approaches to Conflict Management,* ed. Jacob Bercovitch and Jeffrey Rubin (New York: St. Martin's, 1992); Harold Saunders, "Possibilities and Change: Another Way to Consider Unofficial Third Party Intervention," *Negotiation Journal* 11, no. 3 (1995).

7. Richard Holbrooke, *To End a War* (New York: Random House, 1998), 111; Kissinger, *White House Years,* 138–39.

8. Kissinger, *Years of Upheaval,* 351–69; Vernon Walters, *Silent Missions* (Garden City, N.Y.: Doubleday, 1978).

9. Anatoly Dobrynin, *In Confidence: Moscow's Ambassador to America's Six Cold War Presidents (1962–1986)* (New York: Random House, 1995); Kissinger, *Years of Upheaval;* Gerard Smith, *Doubletalk: The Story of SALT I* (New York: Univ. Press of America, 1985).

10. Donald Kagan, *On the Origins of War and the Preservation of Peace* (New York: Doubleday, 1995); Graham Allison, *Essence of Decision: Explaining the Cuban Missile Crisis* (New York: HarperCollins, 1971).

11. Gerard Libaridian (presentation at Program on Negotiation, Harvard Law School, Cambridge, Mass., February 25, 2000).

12. Uri Savir, "Roundtable Discussion: Strengths and Weaknesses of the Method" (paper presented at the conference "Back Channel Negotiations in the Arab-Israeli Conflict," Hebrew Univ., Jerusalem, May 4, 2000).

13. Ahmed Qurei (Abu Alaa), interview with the author, al-Bireh, Palestine, April 29, 2000.

14. Allister Sparks, "The Secret Revolution," *New Yorker,* April 11, 1994.

15. "I had repeatedly pledged that the United States would address the larger issue of peace between Arabs and Israelis after the crisis had been resolved." James Baker, "The Road to Madrid," in Chester Crocker, Fen Osler Hampson, and Pamela Aall, eds., *Herding Cats: Multiparty Mediation in a Complex World* (Washington, D.C.: United States Institute of Peace, 1999).

16. Anthony Wanis-St. John, *The Negotiations Between Palestinians and Israel: Short-Term Breakthrough or Long-Term Failure?* (Program on Negotiation Working Paper Series 95-4, Harvard Law School, Cambridge, Mass., 1995).

17. Aharon Klieman, *Statecraft in the Dark: Israel's Practice of Quiet Diplomacy* (Jerusalem: Jaffee Center for Strategic Studies, 1988).

18. See Camp David Accords, Framework for Peace in the Middle East (Egypt-Israel) and Framework for the Conclusion of a Peace Treaty Between Egypt and Israel (Egypt-Israel), September 17, 1978, reprinted in Institute for Palestine Studies, *The Palestinian-Israeli Peace Agreement: A Documentary Record,* rev. 2nd ed. (Washington, D.C.: IPS, 1993), 235–47.

19. See Declaration of Principles on Interim Self-Government Arrangements (Israel-PLO), September 13, 1993, Article V, ibid., 117–27.

2. The Search for Peace in the Palestinian-Israeli Conflict, 1973 to 1991

1. President Sadat's speech to the Israeli Knesset, Jerusalem, November 20, 1977, reprinted in Anwar el-Sadat, *In Search of Identity: An Autobiography* (New York: Harper and Row, 1978), appendix 5, 330–43.

2. For a comprehensive history of the earliest attempts to resolve the Arab-Zionist and Palestinian-Israeli conflicts, see Walid Khalidi, ed., *From Haven to Conquest;* Avi Shlaim, *The Politics of Partition: King Abdullah, the Zionists and Palestine 1921–1951* (Oxford: Oxford Univ. Press, 1998); George Antonius, *The Arab Awakening: The Story of the Arab National Movement* (Philadelphia: J. B. Lippincott, 1939); David Ben-Gurion, *My Talks with Arab Leaders* (New York: Third Press, 1973); and Caplan, *Futile Diplomacy,* vols. 1–4.

3. Caplan, *Futile Diplomacy,* vols. 1–4.

4. See Arab Summit Resolution, Rabat, October 28, 1974, reprinted in Mahdi Abdel Hadi, ed., *Documents on Palestine, Volume 1: From the Pre-Ottoman/Ottoman Period to the Prelude of the Madrid Middle East Conference* (Jerusalem: Palestinian Academic Society for the Study of International Affairs, 1997), document E26.

5. Kissinger, *Years of Upheaval,* 799–853.

6. Kissinger, *Years of Renewal,* 347–421.

7. These are the two UN Security Council resolutions that called for a ceasefire, termination of the state of war, withdrawal of Israel's military forces from occupied territories, and reciprocal recognitions of territorial sovereignty between the Arab states and Israel.

8. Later, the Reagan administration would add the condition that the PLO explicitly renounce terrorism.

9. Ambassador Vernon Walters, interview with the author, July 24, 2000. Also see Kissinger, *Years of Upheaval,* 626-29.

10. Prior to Carter, the U.S. presidency had been weakened by, inter alia, the weight of the Watergate political corruption scandal, the replacement of Vice President Spiro Agnew with Gerald Ford, political and military crises in South East Asia, and Richard Nixon's resignation and ultimate replacement by Gerald Ford.

11. William Quandt, *Peace Process: American Diplomacy and the Arab-Israeli Conflict since 1967* (Washington, D.C.: Brookings Institution, 1993).

12. Framework for the Conclusion of a Peace Treaty between Egypt and Israel and the Framework for Peace in the Middle East, September 17, 1978 (Egypt-Israel), reprinted in *International Legal Materials* 17 (1978): 1466.

13. Sol Linowitz was appointed personal representative of the president for the Middle East peace negotiations on November 6, 1979, and served in that capacity for fourteen months. His tenure unfortunately coincided completely with the seizure of the U.S. embassy in Tehran. Sol Linowitz, *The Making of a Public Man: A Memoir* (Boston: Little, Brown, 1985), 216.

14. Saadia Touval, *The Peace Brokers: Mediators in the Arab-Israeli Conflict, 1948–1979,* 309.

15. Framework for Peace in the Middle East, September 17, 1978 (Egypt-Israel), reprinted in *International Legal Materials* 17 (1978): 1466, ¶¶ A1b, A1c.

16. Moshe Dayan, *Breakthrough: A Personal Account of the Egypt-Israel Peace Negotiations* (New York: Knopf, 1981).

17. Jimmy Carter, *Keeping Faith: Memoirs of a President* (New York, Bantam: 1982), 397.

18. Linowitz, 232-36.

19. John Boykin, *Cursed is the Peacemaker: The American Diplomat Versus the Israeli General, Beirut 1982* (Belmont, Calif.: Applegate, 2002), 151.

20. Carter, 491.

21. Dayan, 303-15.

22. For details of the interactive problem-solving workshops that Kelman, Cohen, and others were conducting between Palestinians and Israelis, see Stephen Cohen et al., "Evolving Intergroup Techniques for Conflict Resolution: An Israeli-Palestinian Pilot Workshop," *Journal of Social Issues* 33, no. 1 (1977).

23. Mohamed Heikal, *Secret Channels: The Inside Story of Arab-Israeli Peace Negotiations* (New York, HarperCollins: 1996), 343-51.

24. Don Peretz, *The Arab-Israeli Dispute* (New York: Facts on File, 1996), 80–81.

25. Ibid.

26. Carter, 305.

27. Quandt, 346.

28. See Boykin.

29. Boykin, 127–266.

30. Rashid Khalidi, *Under Seige: PLO Decisionmaking During the 1982 War* (New York: Columbia Univ. Press, 1986), 116-34.

31. Hani al-Hasan, "The PLO's Secret Diplomacy after Lebanon" (paper presented at the conference "Back Channel Negotiations in the Arab-Israeli Conflict," Hebrew Univ., Jerusalem, May 4, 2000).

32. Speech of President Ronald Reagan, September 1, 1982, reprinted in Quandt as appendix H.

33. George Shultz, *Turmoil and Triumph: My Years as Secretary of State* (New York: C. Scribner's Sons, 1993), 85–100.

34. Ibid., 94.

35. Ibid., 102.

36. The Kahan Commission's report of February 7, 1983, details defense minister Ariel Sharon's approval of the Phalange incursion into the camps, the operational collaboration between the IDF and the Phalange forces, and that Israeli leaders could have "foreseen that the danger of a massacre existed if the Phalangists were to enter the camps without measures being taken to prevent them from committing acts such as these." Yitzhak Kahan, Aharon Barak, and Yona Efrat (Kahan Commission), *The Commission of Inquiry into the Events at the Refugee Camps in Beirut:, 1983, Final Report* (Jerusalem: Government of Israel, February 7, 1983).

37. The Kahan Commission also recommended the dismissal of Defense Minister Sharon and the censure of other officials for their wartime failures and for collaborating in the ethnic cleansing in Lebanon. See Kahan Commission.

38. Boykin, 266–307; Quandt, 340-48.

39. Yitzhak Shamir, interview with the author, Tel Aviv, May 14, 2000.

40. Charles Enderlin, *Paix ou Guerres: Les Secrets Des Negociations Israelo-Arabes (1917-1997)* (Paris: Stock, 1997), 476-79, 493.

41. Shimon Peres, *Battling for Peace: A Memoir* (New York: Random House, 1995), 264.

42. Joint Palestinian-Jordanian Accords, February 11, 1985, reprinted in Abdul Hadi, ed., vol. 1; Quandt, 351.

43. Quandt, 351-52.

44. See al-Hasan.

45. Enderlin, *Paix ou Guerres,* 480-84.

46. Ibid., 484, 485.

47. Linowitz, 227. Shimon Peres takes credit for the Gaza-first concept and claims it was rejected by el-Sadat. Peres, *Battling for Peace.*

48. Gazit, interview with author, Tufts Univ., Medford, Mass., December 6, 2000; Enderlin, *Paix ou Guerres,* 486.

49. Quandt, 356.

50. Ibid., 355, and 570n56 for the analysis of the Jordanian-PLO rift.

51. See Charles Smith, *Palestine and the Arab-Israeli Conflict,* 3rd ed. (New York: St. Martin's, 1996), 220-24.

52. Gazit, interview.

53. Enderlin, *Paix ou Guerres,* 489–509.

54. Ibid., 501.

55. Peres, *Battling for Peace,* 264.

56. Yitzhak Shamir, interview.

57. Eitan Haber, interview with the author, Tel Aviv, Israel, May 8, 2000.

58. Mordechai Bar-On, *In Pursuit of Peace: A History of the Israeli Peace Movement* (Washington, D.C.: United States Institute of Peace, 1996), 214.

59. Enderlin, *Paix ou Guerres,* 495-97.

60. Mahmoud Abbas, *Through Secret Channels* (Reading, U.K.: Garnet, 1995), 17.

61. Hanan Ashrawi, *This Side of Peace: A Personal Account* (New York: Simon and Schuster, 1995), 10–11; Uri Avnery, *My Friend, the Enemy* (London: Zed, 1986).

62. Peres, *Battling for Peace,* 265.

63. See the London Document (Three-Part Understanding Between Jordan and Israel), reprinted in Abdel Hadi, ed., document F29.

64. Avi Shlaim, "His Royal Shyness: King Hussein and Israel (Interview of King Hussein)," *New York Review of Books,* July 15, 1999.

65. Peres, *Battling for Peace,* 265.

66. Ibid., 265-70.

67. Shultz, 936-41.

68. Ibid., 942-48.

69. Ibid.

70. Peres, *Battling for Peace,* 262-70.

71. Enderlin, *Paix ou Guerres,* 496.

72. Sari Nusseibeh, interview with the author, East Jerusalem, May 10, 2000; Faisal al-Husseini, interview with the author, 'Ayn Sinya, Ramallah, and East Jerusalem, May 14, 2000; Abbas, 37–43; Bar-On, 234-37.

73. Al-Husseini, interview.

74. Yitzhak Shamir, interview.

75. Enderlin, *Paix ou Guerres,* 513-16.

76. Abbas, 12–18; Muhammad Muslih, *Toward Coexistence: An Analysis of the Resolutions of the Palestine National Council* (Washington, D.C.: Institute for Palestine Studies, 1990), 32.

77. Michael Cohen, "Secret Diplomacy and Rebellion in Palestine, 1936–1939," *International Journal of Middle East Studies* 8 (1977); Government of Palestine, *A Survey of Palestine: Prepared in December 1945 and January 1946 for the Information of the Anglo-American Committee of Inquiry,* 3 vols. (Washington, D.C.: Institute for Palestine Studies, 1946; reprint 1991), 35–57.

78. Zeev Schiff and Ehud Yaari, *Intifada: The Palestinian Uprising–Israel's Third Front* (New York: Simon and Schuster, 1990).

79. Quandt, 364-67; also see Quandt, appendix I for text of invitation letter describing the initiative; see Shultz.

80. Heikal, 385.

81. Quandt, 364.

82. Shultz, 1018-19.

83. Ibid., 1016-19.

84. Ibid., 1020-34.

85. See King Hussein, Speech on Jordan's Disengagement from the West Bank, Amman, 31 July 1988, in Institute for Palestine Studies, appendix 14, 262.

86. Schiff and Yaari, 147.

87. Shultz, 1034.

88. Ari Shavit, "Secret Passage to Oslo," *Haaretz,* February 12, 1999, reprinted in *Journal of Palestine Studies* 28, no. 3 (1999): 157–60.

89. Shultz, 1034-45.

90. Abbas, 23–27.

91. Mohamed Rabie, *U.S.-PLO Dialogue: Secret Diplomacy and Conflict Resolution* (Gainesville: Univ. Press of Florida, 1995), 64–84; Abbas, 23–27; Quandt, 367-80.

92. Quandt, 367-80; Shultz, 1032-45.

93. See Rabie; and Quandt.

94. See George Shultz's recollection of his final official conversation with Yitzhak Shamir in which he related to Shamir the need to have negotiators "who truly represent their own constituencies, not people who think the way you do and easy for you to talk to," predicated on Shultz's experience with Nixon's ethnic desegregation actions. Shultz, 1045-50.

95. See Muslih for an examination of the PLO/PNC political developments. Also see UN General Assembly Resolution 181 (II), Recommending a Partition Plan for Palestine, November 29, 1947.

96. Bar-On, 249-53.

97. Shultz, 1043.

98. Ibid., 1032-45.

99. Yasir Arafat, "Speech to the United Nations General Assembly," Geneva, December 13, 1988; and Yasir Arafat, "Press Conference Statement," Geneva, December 14, 1988, reprinted in Institute for Palestine Studies, appendixes 17 and 18.

100. Quandt, 369-94.

101. The delegations used their own respective languages in the meetings, and Rabie believes their mastery of each others language was below par. See Rabie.

102. Rabie, 99–107.

103. Joel Singer, interview with the author, Washington, D.C., April 4, 2000.

104. Charles Smith, 302-7.

105. Quandt, 390-92; Charles Smith, 302-4.

106. Rabie, 99–107.

107. The South African government wanted to trade Mandela his freedom in exchange for a renunciation of armed struggle by the African National Congress. See Sparks.

108. Nusseibeh, interview.

109. Ezer Weizman, *The Battle for Peace* (New York: Bantam, 1981); Peres, *Battling for Peace*, 202.

110. Yitzhak Shamir, *Summing Up: An Autobiography* (London: Weidenfeld and Nicolson, 1994), 172-73.

111. Quandt, 388-94.

112. Charles Smith, 303-7; see Baker.

113. See Ashrawi.

114. See Baker.

115. Quandt, 404-5; Laura Zittrain Eisenberg and Neil Caplan, *Negotiating Arab-Israeli Peace* (Bloomington: Indiana Univ. Press, 1998), 75–89.

3. The Madrid Peace Conference and the Washington Track, 1991 to 1993

1. Hanan Ashrawi, reflecting on her and Faisal al-Husseini's secret meetings with Shimon Peres and Ephraim Sneh, which were efforts to defuse the "deportation crisis." Ashrawi, 238.

2. Camille Mansour, *The Palestinian-Israeli Peace Negotiations: An Overview and Assessment, October 1991-January 1993* (Washington, D.C.: Institute for Palestine Studies, 1993).

3. Unless we include the failed 1938 St. James Palace conferences in London where Palestinian Arab and Zionist delegations met separately with the British Partition Commission.

4. Quandt, 394–403.

5. Nusseibeh, interview; al-Husseini, interview; Camille Mansour, interview with the author, Birzeit, May 10, 2000; Ashrawi.

6. Zvi Dor-Ner, *The Fifty Years War: Israel and the Arabs* (Boston: PBS, 1999), video recording.

7. Mansour, *Palestinian-Israeli Peace Negotiations*, 7–15.

8. The documents exchanged in the first fifteen months of the track (eight rounds, encompassing the Madrid Peace Conference and the subsequent Palestinian-Israeli rounds) are the subject of a legal analysis by one of the Palestinian delegation's advisors, who notes that the parties did not even agree to a common agenda during that time. See Mansour, *Palestinian-Israeli Peace Negotiations* and the documents annexed thereto.

9. Mansour, *Palestinian-Israeli Peace Negotiations*, 44.

10. Geneva Convention Relative to the Protection of Civilian Persons in Time of War, *United Nations Treaty Series*, vol. 75 (1950), 287–416. Done at Geneva, August 12, 1949, entered into force October 21, 1950.

11. Mansour, *Palestinian-Israeli Peace Negotiations*, 13–14.

12. The two famous UN Security Council resolutions admonish the belligerents in those wars for violating one of the main principles of the UN Charter, the inadmissibility of the acquisition of territory by war, and thus the need to return occupied territory to the rule of its inhabitants in compliance with international law and the principles of peacemaking. Texts to these and many other UN resolutions are found in George Tomeh, et al., *United Nations Resolutions on Palestine and the Arab-Israeli Conflict*, vols. 1–5 (Washington, D.C.: Institute for Palestine Studies, 1975–1999).

13. "The Conference and the negotiations that follow will be based on UN Security Council Resolutions 242 and 338." See U.S. Letter of Assurances, reprinted in Institute for Palestine Studies, document A.2.

14. Eliyakim Rubinstein, interview with the author, East Jerusalem, May 8, 2000.

15. Ben-Zvi predicted in 1989 that the circumstances that had helped the 1973 Geneva Conference would not be repeated; boycott of the plenary by Syria and sidelining of the Soviet Union by offering the possibility of side compensation. Abraham Ben-Zvi, *Between Lausanne and Geneva: International Conferences and the Arab-Israeli Conflict* (Boulder, Colo.: Westview, 1990), 107-9. In fact, the Soviet Union was greatly weakened by the time the Madrid Peace Conference was held, and Syria both attended the plenary and engaged in serious subsequent negotiations with Israel.

16. Eisenberg and Caplan, 75–76.

17. See excerpts from the film footage of the conference in Dor-Ner.

18. Rubinstein, interview.

19. Besides the obvious differences in military and political power, the delegations were subject to their own asymmetrical power dynamic. Israel refused to meet with Palestinian delegates it did not approve of. The unacceptable criteria were East Jerusalem residency, Diaspora membership, and of course, official status within the PLO. Despite this phenomenon in which one party to a

conference had to approve the membership of the other side's delegation, behind the scenes, the PLO was involved in the choice, preparation, and coordination of the Palestinian delegation.

20. Ashrawi, 143.

21. Charles Enderlin, "Researching the Parallel-Secret Negotiations: Overview of the '80s" (paper presented at the conference "Back Channel Negotiations in the Arab-Israeli Conflict," Hebrew Univ., Jerusalem, May 4, 2000.

22. Ashrawi, 160.

23. Ibid., 161-63; Mansour, *Palestinian-Israeli Peace Negotiations,* 10–11.

24. Ashrawi, 244.

25. Hassan Asfour, interview with the author, Ramallah, Palestine, April 29, 2000.

26. Yitzhak Shamir, Israeli prime minister at the time of the Madrid Peace Conference, explicitly sought to prevent Labor leaders from implementing their competing concepts of regional peace, to the extent these concepts implied any real accommodation with the PLO. Yitzhak Shamir, interview.

27. I. William Zartman, ed., *Elusive Peace: Negotiating an End to Civil Wars* (Washington, D.C.: Brookings Institution, 1995), 10; Janice Gross Stein, ed., *Getting to the Table: The Processes of International Prenegotiation* (Baltimore: Johns Hopkins Univ. Press, 1989).

28. Rubinstein, interview.

29. Yitzhak Shamir, interview.

30. Ibid.

31. From May 7 to 10, 1992, PLO's Central Council convened to consider the progress of the negotiations at the critical juncture of the Israeli elections. The council issued a final statement in which it expressed its gratitude for the "delegation of the PLO and of the people." Mansour, *Palestinian-Israeli Peace Negotiations,* 23.

32. Ibid., 24.

33. Shimon Peres says that Faisal al-Husseini characterized it in this way. Shimon Peres, *The New Middle East* (New York: Henry Holt, 1993), 7.

34. Abbas, 88.

35. Asfour, interview.

36. Ashrawi, 254.

37. Mansour, interview.

38. Qurei, interview; Asfour, interview.

39. Terje Rød Larsen, interviewed in Dor-Ner.

40. Singer, interview.

41. Yitzhak Shamir, interviewed by Joseph Harif, *Maariv* June 26, 1992, cited in Avi Shlaim, "Prelude to the Accord: Likud, Labor and the Palestinians," *Journal of Palestine Studies* 23, no. 2 (1994).

42. Ashrawi, 183.

43. Ibid., 218.

44. Nusseibeh, interview.

45. Savir, "Roundtable Discussion."

46. Rubinstein, interview.

47. Ibid.; Haber, interview; Mansour, *Palestinian-Israeli Peace Negotiations*; Mansour, interview.

48. Quandt, 404.

49. Jeffrey Rubin, ed., *Dynamics of Third Party Intervention: Kissinger in the Middle East* (New York: Praeger, 1981); Jeffrey Rubin, Dean Pruitt, and Sung Hee Kim, *Social Conflict: Escalation, Stalemate, and Settlement,* 2nd ed. (New York: McGraw-Hill, 1994); Saadia Touval, "The Superpowers as Mediators," in *Mediation in International Relations: Multiple Approaches to Conflict Management,* eds. Jacob Bercovitch and Jeffrey Rubin (New York: St. Martin's, 1992); Saadia Touval and I. William Zartman, eds., *International Mediation in Theory and Practice* (Boulder, Colo.: Westview, 1985); Saadia Touval and I. William Zartman, "Mediation in International Conflicts," in *Mediation Research,* eds. Kenneth Kressel and Dean Pruitt (San Francisco: Jossey-Bass, 1989).

50. Ashrawi, 171.

51. See Palestinian Delegation, Memorandum to Secretary James Baker, Jerusalem, July 20, 1992, reprinted in Institute for Palestine Studies, document A.11.

52. The six-point incident is described by Ashrawi in her memoirs. Ashrawi, 231-36.

53. Ibid.

54. Ibid., 242–44. See United States of America, draft of Israeli-Palestinian Joint Statement, Washington, D.C., May 12, 1993, reprinted in Institute for Palestine Studies, document A.21.

55. Ashrawi, 244.

56. Ibid., 249-51. See Palestinian Delegation, Ten Point Statement on the Peace Process, Washington, D.C., May 28, 1993, reprinted in Institute for Palestine Studies, document A.22. Also see United States of America, draft of Israeli-Palestinian Joint Declaration of Principles, Washington, D.C., June 30, 1993, reprinted in Institute for Palestine Studies, document A.23.

57. See Ashrawi.

58. The former deputy foreign minister of Armenia recounts that he opened a back channel to Azerbaijan, the neighboring republic with which Armenia was in a state of war, in part to marginalize Russian mediators. Gerard Libaridian (presentation at Program on Negotiation, Harvard Law School, Cambridge, Mass., February 25, 2000).

59. Abbas, 94–95.

60. Mansour, *Palestinian-Israeli Peace Negotiations;* and Mansour, interview.

61. Abbas, 94–95.

62. Ashrawi, 238.

63. Abbas, 96–97.

64. Haber, interview.

65. Ashrawi, 220.

66. Asfour, interview; see Ashrawi; Rubinstein, interview.

67. Rubinstein, interview.

68. David Makovsky, *Making Peace with the PLO: The Rabin Government's Road to the Oslo Accord* (Boulder, Colo.: Westview, 1996), 42.

69. Singer, interview.

70. Al-Husseini, interview.

71. Qurei, interview.

4. Negotiations in the Oslo Channel, 1993

1. Uri Savir reflecting on the clandestine initialing of the Israel-PLO declaration of principles in Oslo. Uri Savir, *The Process: 1,100 Days that Changed the Middle East* (New York: Random House, 1998), 58.

2. Singer, interview; Wanis-St. John, "Negotiations Between the Palestinians and Israel" (Program on Negotiation Working Paper Series 95-4, Program on Negotiation, Harvard Law School, 1995).

3. Larsen would later serve as the UN special coordinator for the Middle East peace process.

4. Savir, *The Process*. FAFO was involved in studying the state of the Palestinian economy in Gaza. Beilin became the minister of justice in the Barak government.

5. Yossi Beilin, *Touching Peace: From the Oslo Accord to a Final Agreement* (London: Weidenfeld and Nicolson, 1999), 18.

6. Ibid., 23.

7. Ibid., 25–30.

8. Peres, *Battling for Peace*, 245-46.

9. Nusseibeh is currently president of al-Quds University in East Jerusalem. Faisal al-Husseini, until his death in 2001, had long been in charge of the most prominent Palestinian political and social institution in East Jerusalem, known as New Orient House. Both are affiliated with Fatah, the main centrist party within the PLO, which is Arafat's power base.

10. Nusseibeh, interview; Beilin, 33–36. The document committed both the Israelis and the Palestinians to a future process of negotiation that included the PLO, invoked UN Security Council Resolutions 242 and 338, and explicitly recognized a Palestinian right to self-determination.

11. Beilin, 40–42.

12. Makovsky, 15–16.

13. The working groups were on water issues, refugees, environment, regional economic development, arms control, and regional security. Israel and all the Arab delegations attended all the working groups simultaneously. Eisenberg and Caplan, 75–86. Also see Rex Brynen, "Much Ado About Nothing? The Refugee Working Group and the Perils of Multilateral Quasi-Negotiation," *International Negotiation* 2, no. 1 (1997).

14. Beilin, 51.

15. Johan Jørgen Holst, "Reflections on the Making of a Tenuous Peace; or, the Transformation of Images of the Middle East Conflict" (presentation given at the School of International and Public Affairs, Columbia Univ., New York, September 28, 1993. Reprinted in *Brown Journal of World Affairs* (Spring 1994): 1–16.

16. Beilin, 52.

17. Ibid., 49–53.

18. Abbas, 43–45.

19. Haber, interview; Abbas, 58–67.

20. Beilin, 54–55.

21. Ibid., 56–59.

22. Ibid.

23. Ron Pundik, "The Oslo Negotiations: From Track II to Back Channel" (paper presented at the conference "Back Channel Negotiations in the Arab-Israeli Conflict," Hebrew Univ., Jerusalem, May 4, 2000).

24. Abu Alaa is currently speaker of the Palestinian Legislative Council, the parliamentary branch of the Palestinian National Authority. He continues to be involved in key Palestinian-Israeli negotiations that followed Oslo, especially back channel efforts. Qurei, interview.

25. Jane Corbin, *Gaza First: The Secret Norway Channel to Peace Between Israel and the PLO* (London: Bloomsbury, 1994), 27–28. The document itself has been provided to the author by Abu Alaa. Ahmed Qurei (Abu Alaa), "Thoughts on the Prospective Dividend and Regional Economic Cooperation" (unpublished manuscript on file with the author, Tunis, 1991).

26. See Ashrawi.

27. See Pundik.

28. Amos Elon, "The Peacemakers," *New Yorker,* December 20, 1993.

29. See Bar-On.

30. Corbin, 30.

31. Beilin, 60–63; Elon.

32. Abbas, 112-13.

33. Ibid., 113. At the time, Abu Mazen was the PLO's director general of international relations and a member of the Executive Committee of the PLO. He eventually met and negotiated draft final status accords with Beilin in Stockholm in 1995. He did not seek a position within the Palestinian National Authority, but he succeeded Yasir Arafat upon the latter's death as both elected PNA president and head of the Fatah faction of the PLO.

34. Beilin, 62.

35. See Holst.

36. The accounts of both Abu Mazen and Yossi Beilin, as the overseers of the Oslo channel, are the best written accounts of what transpired in the first five rounds at Oslo. See translated minutes of these rounds in Abbas, 132-41. Also see Beilin, 64–84.

37. And even then, existence of the Oslo channel was a jealously guarded secret. No cabinet ministers or military or intelligence chiefs were informed until the agreement was initialed on September 19, 1993.

38. Peres, *Battling for Peace*, 255.

39. Abbas, 115-17.

40. Beilin, 73.

41. Makovsky, 23. Makovsky relies on his interviews with Peres and Rabin for this assertion.

42. Beilin, 72–76.

43. Ashrawi, 238. Also see Makovsky, 25; and chapter 3 of the present work.

44. Abbas, 132-34; Beilin, 74–76; Heikal, 433.

45. Details of the fourth round can be found in Abbas; Beilin; Makovsky; and Savir, *The Process*.

46. See Beilin; Makovsky, 40–43.

47. See Abu Mazen's reprint of the draft Oslo declaration in Abbas, 143-49.

48. For the Palestinian perspective on the second phase, the authoritative published primary source remains Abu Mazen's. The Israeli perspective is provided by the memoirs of Uri Savir, Yossi Beilin, and to a lesser extent, Shimon Peres. Makovsky relies on his interviews with many key participants and continues to be a useful reference. My primary sources for the second phase include interviews with Asfour, Abu Alaa, and Singer, conference papers read by Pundik, and Savir, "Roundtable Discussion."

49. Savir, *The Process*, 5–6; Savir, "Roundtable Discussion."

50. Ibid., 23–24.

51. Beilin, 86–88.

52. Ibid., 92–93.

53. Ashrawi, 243–45.

54. Mark Perry, *A Fire in Zion: The Israeli-Palestinian Search for Peace* (New York: Morrow, 1994).

55. Beilin, 93–95.

56. Singer is an attorney in the Washington law firm Sidley and Austin. He was head of the international law department of the IDF and had participated in Israeli negotiations at Camp David in the 1970s, with Lebanon in 1983, and again with Egypt (over the Taba issue) in 1985-86. Singer, interview. Beilin, 88–90.

57. Abu Mazen's minutes of the Oslo rounds mention this question. Abbas, 153-55. The concept would be applied to the Israel-PLO understanding on Palestinian institutions in Jerusalem. Peres addressed a confidential letter to Holst setting forth Israeli acceptance of their presence. An exact facsimile of Peres's letter is reproduced by Abu Mazen in his memoirs. Abbas, appendix 3.

58. Beilin, 95.

59. Ibid., 102-3.

60. See minutes of August 20, 1993, negotiations in Oslo, in Abbas, 179.

61. Qurei, interview; Asfour, interview.

62. Minutes of the round and Abu Mazen's comments are found in Abbas, 159-61.

63. Savir, *The Process*, 38–39.

64. Beilin, 106.

65. Ibid., 108–10; Savir, *The Process*, 41–44.

66. Savir, *The Process*, 44–45.

67. Abbas, 168.

68. Beilin, 110–12.

69. Ibid., 111.

70. See the points of disagreement from the July 25–26, 1993, draft declaration of principles in Abbas, 171-72.

71. Savir, *The Process*, 49–50.

72. Ibid., 47–50.

73. Abbas, 169–70, 195–96.

74. Peres, *Battling for Peace*, 294–97.

75. Beilin, 116.

76. Savir, *The Process*, 52. However, Beilin attributes the precipitous loss of momentum in the Israel-Syria track to the American Middle East peace team's preference for August vacations. Beilin, 114-15.

77. Peres, *Battling for Peace*, 299.

78. "We must hurry," I told our Norwegian friends, "or we may end up with a peace treaty but no government to sign it." Peres, *Battling for Peace*, 298.

79. Makovsky, 69, n24.

80. Beilin, 114-16; Peres, *Battling for Peace*, 298.

81. Makovsky, 68.

82. Beilin, 116.

83. Savir, *The Process*, 53.

84. Abbas, 175-79; Beilin, 116-18; Peres, *Battling for Peace*, 299–300; Savir, *The Process*, 54–56.

85. Savir, *The Process*, 55.

86. Ibid., 56.

87. Heikal, 452.

88. Beilin, 121-22.

89. Rubinstein, interview; Haber, interview.

90. Qurei, interview.

91. Savir, *The Process*, 64–77.

92. The four letters are reprinted in Makovsky, appendixes XI, XII, XIII, and XIX. An exact facsimile of Peres's letter is reproduced by Abu Mazen in his memoirs. Abbas, appendix 3.

93. Rubinstein, interview.

94. Beilin, 128.

95. The functionalist approach is attributed to Moshe Dayan, former defense minister and foreign minister of Israel, and Shimon Peres's ideas about Jordanian-Israeli condominium in the West Bank are predicated on this idea. The territorialist approach is attributed to Yigal Allon, former general and foreign minister of Israel, as well as a mentor of Yitzhak Rabin. Makovsky, 92–93, 122–23.

96. Beilin, 133-34. Emphasis added.

97. Annex I, "Protocol on the Mode and Conditions of Elections," Declaration of Principles on Interim Self-Government Arrangements, September 13, 1993. The text and annexes to the DoP are available on the World Wide Web and were accessed December 31, 2000. See State of Israel, Ministry of Foreign Affairs, http://www.israel.org/mfa; and also Palestine Liberation Organization/Palestinian National Authority, Negotiation Affairs department, http://www.nad.gov.ps.

98. Article VI, "Preparatory Transfer of Powers and Responsibilities," Declaration of Principles (see note 95).

99. Annex II, "Protocol on Withdrawal of Israeli Forces from the Gaza Strip and Jericho Area," Declaration of Principles.

100. Article VII, "Interim Agreement," Declaration of Principles.

101. Article VII.5, "Interim Agreement," Declaration of Principles.

102. Annex III, "Protocol on Israeli-Palestinian Cooperation in Economic and Development Programs;" and Annex IV, "Protocol on Israeli-Palestinian Cooperation Concerning Regional Development Programs, Declaration of Principles."

103. Article X, Declaration of Principles.

104. Qurei, interview. Abu Alaa makes it very clear that having the PLO as the recognized signatory and implementing party was of paramount concern during the conduct of the Oslo channel.

105. See Holst.

106. See Ashrawi; Mansour, interview.

107. Abbas, 165-66.

108. There was an alleged Mossad (Israel's foreign intelligence and clandestine agency) spy at PLO headquarters in Tunis: Adnan Yasin, who worked as an aide to Arafat. Mossad reported to Rabin in his capacity as both prime minister and defense minister and may have informed Rabin of the Oslo channel even before Peres brought it to his attention, assuming that Yasin was privy to such information. Yasin was uncovered on October 26, 1993. The uncovering of Yasin is mentioned in "Chronology," *Journal of Palestine Studies* 23, no. 2 (Winter 1994) and received broad news coverage at the time.

109. Peres, *Battling for Peace,* 102-14.

110. Ibid., 103.

111. Ibid., 115-24.

112. Ibid., 301.

113. Savir, "Roundtable Discussion"; Qurei, interview.

114. This is according to Abu Mazen's transcription of Joel Singer's forty questions in the sixth round of the Oslo channel. Abbas, 155.

115. See Abbas.

116. See Peretz.

117. Savir, "Roundtable Discussion."

118. This point was made clear to me by Camille Mansour, a Palestinian lawyer who founded the Birzeit University Law Centre and was a member of the Palestinian delegation to Washington. Mansour, interview. Uri Savir recalls that Muhammad Abu Koush, the most junior Palestinian negotiator at Oslo, met with Uri Savir in Frankfurt, informing him that Abu Koush was replacing Abu Alaa in the post-Oslo phase. This turned out to be his first and last time as chief negotiator. Savir, *The Process,* 81.

119. Binyamin Netanyahu, Statement to the Knesset on Israeli-Palestinian Declaration of Principles, Jerusalem, September 21, 1993, reprinted in *Journal of Palestine Studies* 23, no. 2 (Winter 1994): 141-43.

120. Singer, interview.

121. Heikal, 437.

122. Abbas, 185-90.

123. See Beilin; Peres, *Battling for Peace*; Qurei, interview; Savir, *The Process*; Savir, "Round-table Discussion."

124. Heikal, 439.

125. I. William Zartman and Jeffrey Rubin, eds., *Power and Negotiation* (Ann Arbor: Univ. of Michigan Press, 2000).

126. Savir, *The Process*, 12.

127. Ibid., 21.

128. Abbas, 136-37, 175-76; Makovsky, 22; Savir, *The Process*, 21, 43, 49-50.

129. See Holst, 6-7.

130. Jan Egeland, "The Oslo Accord: Multiparty Facilitation Through the Norwegian Channel," in *Herding Cats: Multiparty Mediation in a Complex World*, eds. Chester Crocker, Fen Osler Hampson, and Pamela Aall, 31.

131. See Holst, 8-9.

132. Makovsky, 13, 26–29.

133. Asfour, interview.

134. See chapter 3 for the details of the April 11, 1987, London Agreement.

135. Savir, "Roundtable Discussion"; Singer, interview.

136. Savir, "Roundtable Discussion."

137. Ibid.

138. Qurei, interview.

139. This pattern of early Zionist/Israeli negotiations is described by several historians. See Shlaim, *Politics of Partition*; and Caplan, *Futile Diplomacy*, vols. 1 and 2.

140. Haber, interview. Also see Makovsky.

141. Heikal, 433-35.

142. See Makovsky.

143. See Ashrawi.

144. Abbas, 134.

145. The PLO also had political and financial responsibilities with other Palestinian Diaspora populations, such as those in Jordanian and Lebanese refugee camps, and perceived itself as the sole party capable of representing Palestinians living in the West Bank/Gaza, as well as Diaspora groups. This helps us understand why Palestinian permanent status negotiators would resisted bargaining away the refugees in exchange for other Israeli concessions. Creative solutions to the refugee issue have been noted to be discussed officially during the last-ditch Taba talks that took place January 21-27, 2001, and are discussed more fully in chapter 6.

146. Singer, interview.

147. Qurei, interview; Savir, "Roundtable Discussion."

148. Ibid.

149. Qurei, interview.

150. Savir, "Roundtable Discussion."

151. Qurei, interview.

152. Savir, "Roundtable Discussion."

5. Negotiations During the Interim Phase, 1993 to 1998

1. Yossi Sarid, "Settlements Worth Dying For?" *Yediot Ahoronot*, November 10, 2000.

2. "Chronology," *Journal of Palestine Studies* 23, no. 3 (Spring 1994).

3. Council of Jewish Communities in Judea, Samaria, and Gaza (YESHA), cited in "Chronology," *Journal of Palestine Studies* 23, no. 3 (Spring 1994).

4. Singer, interview.

5. Declaration of Principles on Interim Self-Government Arrangements (Israel-PLO), September 13, 1993. See Annex II, "Protocol on Withdrawal of Israeli Forces from the Gaza Strip and Jericho Area." Article XVII provides that the declaration will come into force one month after signing, that is, October 13, 1993, making the initial withdrawal due on December 13, 1993.

6. Savir, *The Process*, 79–80.

7. Ibid., 99.

8. See Israeli-Palestinian Gaza-Jericho Committee, joint communiqués, Taba, Egypt, October 13, 14, 21, 1993, reprinted in Institute for Palestine Studies, document C.5.

9. Savir, *The Process*, 101-12.

10. Asfour, interview.

11. Article X of the Declaration of Principles: "In order to provide for the smooth implementation of this Declaration of Principles and any subsequent agreements pertaining to the interim period . . . a Joint Israeli-Palestinian Liaison Committee will be established in order to deal with issues requiring coordination, other issues of common interest and disputes."

12. Savir, *The Process*, 113.

13. Savir, *The Process*, 109-13.

14. "Chronology," *Journal of Palestine Studies* 23, no. 2 (Winter 1994).

15. Cairo Agreement (Israel-PLO), February 9, 1994, reprinted in Institute for Palestine Studies, document C.6.

16. Savir, *The Process*, 114-20.

17. This pattern of terror attacks worked both ways of course. Large-scale attacks against Israelis by HAMAS, especially in 1996, quickly eroded faith in the Labor Party and the peace process among Israelis, leading to the consequences analyzed in this chapter.

18. Savir, *The Process*, 121-34.19. Israeli-Palestinian Security Agreement (Israel-PLO), March 31, 1994, reprinted in *Journal of Palestine Studies* 23, no. 4 (Summer 1994): 102-3.

20. Protocol on Economic Relations (Israel-PLO), April 29, 1994, reprinted in *Journal of Palestine Studies* 23, no. 4 (Summer 1994): 103-4. Also see Savir, *The Process*, 142. The protocol was later integrated into the agreement on the Gaza Strip and the Jericho Area as Annex IV.

21. The Declaration of Principles included a provision for the Palestinians to hold elections within nine months of the DoP entering into force (Article III) and set out the principle that Israeli "military forces should be deployed outside populated areas" (Article XIII). Since these were discussed together, the provisions may be interpreted as the parties' intent to implement Israeli withdrawal and Palestinian elections by July 12, 1994.

22. Savir, *The Process,* 159.

23. Ibid., 165-72.

24. Ibid., 172.

25. Ibid., 153-55.

26. Ibid., 159-92.

27. Interim Agreement on the West Bank and Gaza Strip (PLO-Israel), September 28, 1995 (hereafter Interim Agreement).

28. Interim Agreement, chapter 2, "Redeployment and Security Arrangements," Article X, "Redeployment of Israeli Military Forces."

29. Also see Interim Agreement, Annex I, Appendix 1, "Redeployment of Israeli Military Forces," for the details of the initial and further redeployments.

30. See Articles II, III, and X of the Interim Agreement, which are the initial articles of the agreement that deal with the Palestinian elections, the structure of the Palestinian Council, and the Israeli redeployment, respectively. Also see Annexes I and II of the Interim Agreement, which set out the details of the redeployment and security arrangements, and the full elections protocol, respectively.

31. See "Passage Censored from First Edition," in Yitzhak Rabin, *The Rabin Memoirs,* expanded edition (Berkeley: Univ. of California Press, 1996), appendix A, 383-84.

32. Rabin's final speech at the peace rally (most likely written by his speech writer and bureau chief, Eitan Haber), reprinted in Rabin, appendix J, 427.

33. Beilin, 143-45.

34. Ibid., 146.

35. Hussein Agha, Shai Feldman, Ahmed Khalidi, Zeev Schiff, *Track-II Diplomacy: Lessons from the Middle East* (Cambridge, Mass.: MIT, 2004).

36. Beilin, 153.

37. Ibid., 154-77.

38. While this far-reaching agreement had no discernible impact on the peace process during the years covered in this study, President Clinton is said to have used it as a model for his mediation at the Camp David talks in July 2000. See Michael Hirsh, "The Lost Peace Plan," *Newsweek,* September 18, 2000. More importantly, see Framework for the Conclusion of a Final Status Agreement Between Israel and the Palestine Liberation Organization (Abu Mazen-Beilin Agreement or Stockholm Agreement), October 31, 1995, http://unispal.un.org/UNISPAL.NSF/0/.

39. Joint Communiqué, Permanent Status Negotiations, First Session (Israel-PLO) Taba, May 5-6, 1996, http://www.mfa.gov.il/MFA/Peace+Process/Guide+to+the+peace+process/Israel-PLO+Permanent+Status+Negotiations+-+Joint+C.htm

40. Savir, *The Process.*

41. Isaac Molho, interview with the author, Tel Aviv, Israel, May 11, 2000.

42. Interim Agreement, "Guidelines for Hebron," Annex I, Article VII.

43. Dennis Ross, *The Missing Peace: The Inside Story of the Fight for Middle East Peace* (New York: Farrar, Strauss and Giroux, 2004), 263-68.

44. Dennis Ross, United States Special Coordinator on the Middle East Peace Process, On-the-Record Briefing on the Hebron Agreement, Washington, January 17, 1997, reprinted in *Journal of Palestine Studies* 26, no. 3 (Spring 1997): 144-45.

45. Three documents comprise the 1997 Hebron Accords: Protocol Concerning the Redeployment in Hebron (PLO-Israel), Note for the Record (United States Special Middle East Coordinator), and Agreed Minute, Erez Crossing, January 15, 1997.

46. Israeli prime minister Binyamin Netanyahu, Statement to the Knesset on the Protocol Concerning Redeployment in Hebron, Jerusalem, January 16, 1997, reprinted in *Journal of Palestine Studies* 26, no. 3 (Spring 1997).

47. Leaked to *Haaretz*, May 25, 1998, and entire document leaked to *Journal of Palestine Studies* 28, no. 1 (1998).

48. Wye River Memorandum (Israel-PLO), Washington D.C., October 23, 1998, http://www.usip.org/files/file/resources/collections/peace_agreements/wye_10231998.pdf.

49. See "Time Line" annexed to the Wye River Memorandum, ibid.

50. Joel Greenberg, "Scourge of the West Bank Arabs: Israeli Bulldozers," *New York Times*, November 18, 1998. Accessed at http://www.nytimes.com/1998/11/18/world/scourge-of-the-west-bank-arabs-israeli-bulldozers.html.

51. List of Palestinian Unfulfilled Commitments Under the Wye Memorandum, Office of Prime Minister Netanyahu, December 15, 1998, reprinted in *Journal of Palestine Studies* 28, no. 3 (Spring 1999).

52. President Bill Clinton, Letter of Assurances to the President of the Palestinian Authority, Yasir Arafat, April 26, 1999, reprinted in *Journal of Palestine Studies* 28, no. 4 (Summer 1999): 164-65.

53. European Union, Declaration on the Middle East Process, March 25, 1999, reprinted in *Journal of Palestine Studies* 28, no. 4 (Summer 1999): 148.

54. Molho, interview.

55. Ibid.

56. Asfour, interview.

57. Ibid.

58. Molho, interview.

59. Qurei, interview.

60. Savir, "Roundtable Discussion."

61. Hassan Abu-Libdeh, interview with the author, al-Baloa, Palestine, May 3, 2000.

62. Qurei, interview.

63. Saeb Eraqat, interview with the author, Jericho, Palestine, May 12, 2000; Molho, interview.

64. Molho, interview.

65. Eraqat, interview.

66. Beilin, 164.

67. Savir, *The Process,* 94.

68. See Memorandum to Yasir Arafat, reprinted in *Journal of Palestine Studies* 23, no. 3 (Spring 1994).

69. Yitzhak Shamir, interview.

70. Yitzhak Shamir, interview with the author, Tel Aviv, Israel, May 14, 2000.

71. Savir, *The Process,* 86–87.

72. Ibid., 95.

73. Ibid., 95.

74. Ashrawi, 276-79.

75. Haber, interview.

76. Molho, interview.

77. Ibid.

78. Molho, interview.

79. Asfour, interview; Qurei, interview.

80. Singer, interview.

81. Savir, *The Process,* 85.

82. Ibid., 129; and *Journal of Palestine Studies* 23, no. 3 (Spring 1994).

83. Netanyahu's interpretation of the principle of "reciprocity" is that Israeli compliance is conditioned upon Palestinian compliance. "I do not know any other interpretation of the word 'agreement.'" Prime minister Binyamin Netanyahu, Statement to the Knesset on the Protocol Concerning Redeployment in Hebron, Jerusalem, January 16, 1997, reprinted in *Journal of Palestine Studies* 26, no. 3 (Spring 1997), 141–43.

84. Letter of Assurances to President Arafat from Hans van Mierlo, President of the European Union Council of Ministers, The Hague, Netherlands, January 15, 1997, reprinted in *Journal of Palestine Studies* 26, no. 3 (Spring 1997): 139-40.

85. Molho, interview; Qurei, interview.

86. Dennis Ross, "Lecture and Discussion" (Columbia Univ., School of International and Public Affairs, New York, September 14, 2004).

87. Molho, interview.

88. Savir, *The Process,* 157-58.

89. Beilin, 181.

90. Savir, *The Process,* 120-40.

6. Endgame or Endless Game? Permanent Status
and Crisis Negotiations, 1999 to 2008

1. Gilead Sher, *The Israeli-Palestinian Peace Negotiations, 1999–2001: Within Reach* (New York: Routledge, 2006), 20.

2. President Bill Clinton, Letter of Assurances to Yasir Arafat, April 26, 1999, leaked and reprinted in American Israel Political Action Committee's newsletter *Near East Report* of May 17, 1999; and also reprinted in *Journal of Palestine Studies* 28, no. 4 (1999).

3. Charles Enderlin, *Shattered Dreams: The Failure of the Peace Process in the Middle East, 1995–2002* (New York: Other Press, 2003), 112.

4. Ross, *Missing Peace,* 497.

5. Sher, *The Israeli-Palestinian Negotiations,* 2.

6. Ibid.

7. Ross, *Missing Peace,* 503.

8. Sher, *Israeli-Palestinian Peace Negotiations,* 8.

9. Ross, *Missing Peace,* 503-7.

10. See Interim Agreement, Article XVI on the West Bank and Gaza Strip (Israel-PLO), September 28, 1995; as well as Annex VII. "Israel will release or turn over to the Palestinian side, Palestinian detainees and prisoners, residents of the West Bank and the Gaza Strip. The first stage of release of these prisoners and detainees will take place on the signing of this Agreement and the second stage will take place prior to the date of the elections. There will be a third stage of release of detainees and prisoners. Detainees and prisoners will be released from among categories detailed in Annex VII (Release of Palestinian Prisoners and Detainees). Those released will be free to return to their homes in the West Bank and the Gaza Strip." See also the affirmation in the Note for the Record, prepared by U.S. envoy Dennis Ross at the request of Arafat and Netanyahu, January 15, 1997.

11. Sher, *Israeli-Palestinian Peace Negotiations,* 10–11.

12. Enderlin, *Shattered Dreams,* 115-19.

13. Michele Kjorlien, "Peace Monitor: 16 May-15 August 1999," *Journal of Palestine Studies,* 29, no. 1 (Autumn 1999).

14. Sher, *Israeli-Palestinian Peace Negotiations,* 8–12.

15. Ross, *Missing Peace,* 508.

16. The Sharm el-Sheikh Memorandum on Implementation Timeline of Outstanding Commitments of Agreements Signed and the Resumption of Permanent Status Negotiations, PLO-Israel, September 4, 1999. USIP Peace Agreements Digital Collection.

17. Savir, "Roundtable Discussion."

18. Enderlin, *Shattered Dreams,* 122.

19. Amnon Lipkin-Shahak, "The Roles of Barak, Arafat and Clinton," in *The Camp David Summit—What Went Wrong?* ed. Shimon Shamir and Bruce Maddy-Weitzman (Portland, Oreg.: Sussex Academic, 2005), 43–44.

20. Enderlin, *Shattered Dreams,* 138.

21. Sher, *Israeli-Palestinian Peace Negotiations,* 16.

22. Ross, *Missing Peace,* 592.

23. Ibid.

24. Lipkin-Shahak, 43–44.

25. Ross, *Missing Peace*, 596–602.

26. Ibid., 593-99. According to one source, President Hosni Mubarak also played a role in having Arafat and Barak resume negotiations. The Egyptian president hosted a three-way summit with Arafat and Barak on March 9 after the two had their private summit on March 7. See Enderlin, *Shattered Dreams*, 139-40.

27. Ross, *Missing Peace*, 598.

28. Enderlin, *Shattered Dreams*, 143.

29. Savir, "Roundtable Discussion."

30. Ross, *Missing Peace*, 602; Enderlin, *Shattered Dreams*, 142-43.

31. Omar Dajani, "Surviving Opportunities: Palestinian Negotiating Patterns in Peace Talks With Israel," in *How Israelis and Palestinians Negotiate: A Cross-Cultural Analysis of the Oslo Peace Process*, ed. Tamara Cofman Wittes (Washington, D.C.: United States Institute of Peace, 2005), 60.

32. Yasir Abd Rabbuh, interviewed by Charles Enderlin, in *Shattered Dreams*, 143-44.

33. Sher, *Israeli-Palestinian Peace Negotiations*, 18.

34. Ross, *Missing Peace*, 603-4.

35. Ibid., 608-9.

36. Ibid., 605-20.

37. Ibid., 591.

38. Ibid., 603.

39. Lipkin-Shahak, 43–44; Sher, *Israeli-Palestinian Peace Negotiations*, 21.

40. Enderlin, *Shattered Dreams*, 123. "But, most important, [they] decided to establish a secret channel of negotiation parallel to the official talks."

41. "Palestinian Official Says Peace Talks Also Held Away from Cameras" (interview with Yasir Abd Rabbuh), Deutsche Presse-Agentur, December 29, 1999, accessed from LexisNexis; "Palestinian Official Says Stockholm Talks Not Secret," interview with Mahmoud Abbas on Arab Republic of Egypt Radio, BBC Summary of World Broadcasts, May 17, 2000, transcript accessed from LexisNexis.

42. Abu Alaa reported to the PLO's Executive Committee on the origin and progress of the back channel after it had been exposed. See "PLO Executive Committee Discusses Peace Process, Secret Talks in Sweden," *al-Sharq al-Awsat*, June 29, 2000, BBC Monitoring, Middle East, accessed from LexisNexis.

43. Sher, *Israeli-Palestinian Peace Negotiations*, 21–39.

44. Enderlin, *Shattered Dreams*, 147-58.

45. Ibid., 148.

46. Shlomo Ben-Ami, *Scars of War, Wounds of Peace: The Israeli-Arab Tragedy* (New York: Oxford Univ. Press, 2006), 253.

47. Dajani, "Surviving Opportunities"; Ross, *Missing Peace*, 603, 619.

48. Salah Elayan, chief of staff of Ahmed Qurei (Abu Alaa), interviews with the author, al-Bireh, Palestine, May 7, 8, 13, 2000. Elayan himself informed the author that negotiators had departed for Stockholm for the back channel talks.

49. Ross, *Missing Peace*, 619-20; Enderlin, *Shattered Dreams*, 148-49.

50. "Chief Palestinian Negotiator Quits," BBC News World Service, May 15, 2000, http://news .bbc.co.uk/2/hi/world/monitoring/media_reports/749100.stm.

51. Ross, *Missing Peace*, 600–602, 625.

52. May 15 is al-Nakba Day for Palestinians, which commemorates the "catastrophe"—the loss of the historical pre-1948 Palestine and the uprooting of the Palestinian refugees from the territories that became the state of Israel.

53. Ross, *Missing Peace*, 614.

54. Interview with the author of anonymous Fatah activist regarding armed resistance, East Jerusalem, June 24, 2000.

55. Ross, *Missing Peace*, 621.

56. See excerpts from the European Union nonpaper in Miguel Moratinos, *EU Non-Paper (Moratinos Report on the Palestinian-Israeli Talks at Taba)*, http://www.usip.org/files/file/resources/ collections/peace_agreements/taba.pdf.

57. Ross, *Missing Peace*, 622.

58. Ibid., 623.

59. Ibid., 624-26; Enderlin, *Shattered Dreams*, 149-51.

60. Ross, *Missing Peace*, 626.

61. Yossi Genosar, "Factors that Impeded the Negotiations," in *The Camp David Summit— What Went Wrong?* ed. Shimon Shamir and Bruce Maddy-Weitzman (Portland, Oreg.: Sussex Academic, 2005), 53.

62. Ross, *Missing Peace*, 627-28.

63. Sher, *Israeli-Palestinian Peace Negotiations*, 21–30.

64. Ross, *Missing Peace*, 606.

65. Ibid., 618–20.

66. Sher, *Israeli-Palestinian Peace Negotiations*, 42.

67. Ibid., 32–33; Ross, *Missing Peace*, 621-23.

68. Ross, *Missing Peace*, 620-49.

69. The concept of ripeness in international mediation is occasionally misused by negotiators who fail and then claim that "the time was not ripe" ex post facto. In reality, the concept posits that propitious moments for international conflict resolution are the result of a confluence of both push and pull factors: the mutually hurting stalemate (MHS) is based on parties' perceptions that they cannot escalate the conflict and achieve unilateral victory. The mutually enticing opportunity (MEO) offers them a way out of the MHS. I. William Zartman and Saadia Touval, "International Mediation," in *Leashing the Dogs of War*, ed. Chester Crocker, Fen Osler Hampson, and Pamela Aall (Washington, D.C.: United States Institute of Peace, 2007).

70. Ross, *Missing Peace*, 629-32.

71. Ibid., 633.

72. Sher, *Israeli-Palestinian Peace Negotiations*, 44.

73. Ross, *Missing Peace*, 635-37.

74. Enderlin, *Shattered Dreams,* 166-67.

75. Ross, *Missing Peace,* 636-43.

76. Arafat is quoted by one of his advisors as having said to Albright, "Madame Secretary, if you issue an invitation to the summit, and if it is held and fails, this will weaken the Palestinian people's hopes for achieving peace. Let us not weaken those hopes." Akram Hanieh, *The Camp David Papers* (Ramallah, Palestine: al-Ayyam, 2000), reprinted in *Journal of Palestine Studies,* 30, no. 2 (Winter 2001): 75–97.

77. Ross, *Missing Peace,* 644; Hanieh, 76

78. Ibid., 646.

79. Ibid., 645-49.

80. Ibid., 649.

81. Enderlin, *Shattered Dreams,* 170.

82. Ibid., 172-73.

83. Ross, *Missing Peace,* 651.

84. Principal sources for Camp David data include the accounts by Dennis Ross in his memoir *Missing Peace;* the accounts by Akram Hanieh, *Camp David Papers;* Shlomo Ben-Ami and Gilead Sher in their respective memoirs; and the interesting and less partisan version published by Charles Enderlin in his book *Shattered Dreams.* All of these are extensively reviewed by David Matz in his comprehensive and thoughtful review essay "Reconstructing Camp David," *Negotiation Journal* 22, no. 1 (January 2006): 89–103.

85. Enderlin, *Shattered Dreams,* 225.

86. Ross, *Missing Peace,* 654–55.

87. Ibid., 654–56.

88. Jerusalem-based French television journalist Charles Enderlin, in *Shattered Dreams,* relied explicitly on interviews with all three sides, U.S., Palestinian, and Israeli, to reconstruct some of the key dialogues, tensions, and possibilities of the summit. His account has considerably less grievance than the Palestinian account and is far less self-serving than the Israeli accounts. Dennis Ross's account, despite being partisan, is also analytical and honest in admitting serious errors in the way the summit was mediated, not least of which were the surrender to Barak's working strategies and proposals and the focus of blame on Arafat whenever the latter rejected an Israeli proposal.

89. "The United Nations General Assembly . . . *Resolves* that the refugees wishing to return to their homes and live at peace with their neighbours should be permitted to do so at the earliest practicable date, and that compensation should be paid for the property of those choosing not to return and for loss of or damage to property which, under principles of international law or in equity, should be made good by the Governments or authorities responsible. *Instructs* the Conciliation Commission to facilitate the repatriation, resettlement and economic and social rehabilitation of the refugees and the payment of compensation, and to maintain close relations with the Director of the United Nations Relief for Palestine Refugees and, through him, with the appropriate organs and agencies of the United Nations." UN General Assembly Resolution 194, December 11, 1948, A/

Res/194 (III) ¶11. Reprinted in George Tomeh, ed., *United Nations Resolutions on Palestine and the Arab-Israeli Conflict* (Washington, D.C., Institute for Palestine Studies, 1999).

90. For example, Shlomo Ben-Ami's expressed reluctance to uphold the "land for peace" principle was cast in these terms during a mediation session on July 14, 2000. Enderlin, *Shattered Dreams*, 195.

91. Hanieh, 80.

92. Ibid.

93. Ross, *Missing Peace*, 658.

94. Ibid., 659-61.

95. Enderlin, *Shattered Dreams*, 186-94.

96. Ibid., 242-52; Ross, *Missing Peace*, 699-700.

97. These proposals were attributed to Israeli negotiator Eliyakim Rubenstein, who was Israel's attorney general during the summer of 2000. Rubenstein had led the front channel Israeli delegation to the Washington talks nine years before the summit and regretted not having a broader mandate to negotiate with the Palestinians at that time. Rubenstein, interview.

98. Neil Caplan, "A Tale of Two Cities: The Rhodes and Lausanne Conferences, 1949," *Journal of Palestine Studies* 21, no. 3 (Spring 1992): 5–34, at 17–26; Shlaim, *Politics of Partition*, 352–54; Enderlin, *Paix ou Guerres*, 111–34.

99. Sher, *Israeli-Palestinian Peace Negotiations*, 247. "Israeli Draft of the Framework Agreement."

100. Enderlin, *Shattered Dreams*, 222-25.

101. Ross, *Missing Peace*, 666-67.

102. Ibid., 665-70.

103. Ross described him as "livid," "shouting," having "let it rip," before he finally "stalked out." Ross, *Missing Peace*, 668.

104. Genosar, "Factors that Impeded the Negotiations," 56–57.

105. Ross, *Missing Peace*, 673-75.

106. Ibid., 671-75.

107. Ross reprints passages from Barak's note in *Missing Peace*, 676-77.

108. Ross, *Missing Peace*, 679-84.

109. Ibid., 686.

110. Ross called this his "shock treatment." Ross, *Missing Peace*, 687.

111. Enderlin, *Shattered Dreams*, 231-32.

112. Ross, *Missing Peace*, 688-89.

113. Ibid., 690-91.

114. Enderlin, *Shattered Dreams*, 233-39; Albright "stalked out" on Arafat after having told him "we are done playing your games." Ross, *Missing Peace*, 693–95.

115. Jane Perlez and Elaine Sciolino, "Against Backdrop of History, High Drama and Hard Talks at Camp David," *New York Times,* July 29, 2000. Internet edition, http://www.nytimes.com/2000/07/29/world/high-drama-and-hard-talks-at-camp-david-against-backdrop-of-history.html?pagewanted=all.

116. Ross, *Missing Peace*, 696-99.

117. Enderlin, *Shattered Dreams*, 257-59; Ross, *Missing Peace*, 704.

118. See Perlez and Sciolino.

119. Enderlin, *Shattered Dreams*, 259-60.

120. Deborah Sontag, "Quest for Middle East Peace: How and Why It Failed," *New York Times*, July 26, 2001.

121. Aaron David Miller, "The Effects of the 'Syria-First' Strategy," in *The Camp David Summit—What Went Wrong?* ed. Shimon Shamir and Bruce Maddy-Weitzman (Portland, Oreg.: Sussex Academic, 2005), 98.

122. Robert Malley, "American Mistakes and Israeli Misconceptions," in *The Camp David Summit—What Went Wrong?* (see note 121), 110.

123. Ben-Ami, 251.

124. Enderlin, *Shattered Dreams*, 271-73; Sher, *Israeli-Palestinian Peace Negotiations*, 122.

125. Sher, *Israeli-Palestinian Peace Negotiations*, 133.

126. Ross, *Missing Peace*, 716-19.

127. Enderlin, *Shattered Dreams*, 277; Sher, *Israeli-Palestinian Peace Negotiations*, 137.

128. Ross, *Missing Peace*, 721-23.

129. Ibid., 727-28.

130. Ibid., 731.

131. Enderlin, *Shattered Dreams*, 306-8.

132. Ross, *Missing Peace*, 738.

133. Yossi Beilin and David Silver, *The Path to Geneva: The Quest for a Permanent Agreement, 1996–2004* (New York: RDV, 2004), 199–202; Enderlin, *Shattered Dreams*, 313-16.

134. Text of Clinton's Sharm el-Sheikh speech is reprinted in Enderlin, *Shattered Dreams*, 316-17.

135. Ross, *Missing Peace*, 741.

136. Ibid.

137. Enderlin, *Shattered Dreams*, 326-27.

138. The Mitchell Committee was thus composed. Enderlin, *Shattered Dreams*, 326.

139. See the committee's report as submitted to President Bush, accessible at http://www.usip.org/files/file/resources/collections/peace_agreements/sharm_el_sheikh_committee.pdf.

140. Ross, *Missing Peace*, 743-44.

141. Ibid., 744-45.

142. Ibid., 747.

143. Enderlin, *Shattered Dreams*, 333; Ross, *Missing Peace*, 748.

144. The transcript of the Clinton ideas is widely available, however. One version was republished in *Journal of Palestine Studies* 30, no. 3 (Spring 2001): 171-73.

145. Dennis Ross, after leaving government, subsequently commented on and summarized the Clinton ideas in a public lecture. Dennis Ross, "Remarks on Camp David and the Clinton Proposals,

Georgetown University Law Center, July 19, 2001," published in *Journal of Palestine Studies* 31, no. 1 (Autumn 2001): 150-53. One clarification that Ross gave in his presentation was the possibility that a land swap could result in an area of 118 square kilometers being added to the Gaza Strip (greatly expanding Gaza's 260 square kilometers).

146. Ross, *Missing Peace*, 749-55.

147. Ibid., 756.

148. Enderlin, *Shattered Dreams*, 337-39.

149. The PLO Negotiation Affairs department, in its statement, queried why the Clinton ideas did not reference more progressive Israeli-Palestinian discussions regarding the refugee issue, for example, or how territorial contiguity would be reconciled with the apportioning of sovereignty to Israel or Palestine in the various parts of East Jerusalem, or how to define the geographical boundaries of Israeli claims to holy sites in East Jerusalem. PLO Negotiation Team, Reservations Concerning President Bill Clinton's 23 December Proposals for an Israeli-Palestinian Peace Agreement, January 1, 2001, reprinted in *Journal of Palestine Studies* 30, no. 3 (Spring 2001): 155-59.

150. Enderlin, *Shattered Dreams*, 344-46.

151. Reuters, "Palestinians Reject Clinton's Peace Proposals," *New York Times*, January 8, 2001.

152. Ross, *Missing Peace*, 757.

153. Enderlin, *Shattered Dreams*, 347. There are various versions of the origin of the idea to make a last attempt at Taba; Arafat, Peres, Barak, and Ben-Ami are all credited with the idea in various media accounts. David Matz, "Trying to Understand the Taba Talks (Part I)," *Palestine-Israel Journal of Politics, Economics and Culture* 10, no. 3 (2003).

154. Associated Press, "Israel, Palestinians, Set for Talks," *New York Times*, January 21, 2001.

155. Data regarding agreement and gaps between the parties are derived from David Matz, who interviewed the majority of those present at Taba in researching "Trying to Understand the Taba Talks (Part I)."

156. Matz, "Trying to Understand the Taba Talks (Part I)."

157. Dajani, "Surviving Opportunities," 61.

158. Beilin and Silver, 234-49, 253; see Moratinos.

159. David Matz, "Why Did Taba End?" *Palestine-Israel Journal of Politics, Economics and Culture* 10, no. 4 (2003): 92–98

160. "European Narrative of What Happened at Taba," reprinted in Enderlin, *Shattered Dreams*, 355.

161. Matz, "Why Did Taba End?"

162. Reuters, "Arafat Says Israel, Palestinians Made Peace Progress," *New York Times*, January 29, 2001.

163. Report of the Sharm el-Sheikh Fact-Finding Committee (Mitchell Report), April 30, 2001, Unites States Institute for Peace, http://www.usip.org/files/file/resources/collections/peace_agreements/sharm_el_sheikh_committee.pdf.

164. Brian Knowlton, "Immediate Ceasefire Needed to Restore Trust Needed: US Endorses Call for Mid-East Truce," *International Herald Tribune,* May 22, 2001. Accessible on IHT Archives at http://www.iht.com/articles/2001/05/22/powell_ed3__0.php?page=1.

165. U.S. Secretary of State Colin Powell, "United States Position on Terrorists and Peace in the Middle East" (remarks at the McConnell Center for Political Leadership, Univ. of Louisville, Kentucky, November 19, 2001), http://www.state.gov/secretary/former/powell/remarks/2001/6219.htm.

166. Ibid.

167. February 22, 2002, draft of the French version of this initiative is entitled "Non Paper on the Revival of a Dynamics of Peace in the Middle-East" and is archived at http://www.bitterlemons .org/docs/french.html.

168. Zinni's plan was in letter and spirit an attempt to get the parties to implement the Mitchell Committee and Tenet Plan provisions. The text can be accessed from http://www.al-bab.com/arab/docs/pal/zinni2002a.htm.

169. The transcript of the president's speech is entitled "President Bush Calls for a New Palestinian Leadership" and is available at http://georgewbush-whitehouse.archives.gov/news/releases/2002/06/20020624-3.html.

170. The separation wall/barrier, by the time of this book's publication, continues to be a highly controversial measure and has drawn the ire of the Israeli courts as well as a condemnatory advisory opinion by the International Court of Justice. See *Legal Consequences of the Construction of a Wall in the Occupied Palestinian Territory, Advisory Opinion, ICJ Reports 2004,* 136, http://www .icj-cij.org/docket/files/131/1671.pdf.

171. UN Security Counsel Resolution 1435 (2002), passed 14–0, with the United States abstaining.

172. "A Performance-Based Roadmap to a Permanent Two-State Solution to the Israeli-Palestinian Conflict" (the Roadmap), April 30, 2003. Accessed at: http://www.usip.org/files/file/resources/collections/peace_agreements/roadmap_04302003.pdf.

173. Ibid.

174. Israel's Road Map "reservations" were reprinted widely, for example, in the Israeli daily *Haaretz,* May 25, 2003, accessible at http://www.haaretz.com/hasen/pages/ShArt.jhtml?itemNo =297230.

175. Beilin and Silver, 253-65.

176. Beilin explains that this exchange is the "heart of the agreement." Beilin and Silver, 264. The complete text of the Geneva Accord, translated into numerous languages and accompanied by highly detailed maps and annexes, is available from the Geneva Initiative Web site at http://www .geneva-accord.org.

177. On September 29, 2008, one week after submitting his resignation under pressure for charges of corruption, Olmert made relatively bold statements recognizing that an eventual peace deal with the Palestinians will require the return of substantially all of the West Bank.

178. B'Tselem, "Guidelines for Israel's Investigation into Operation Cast Lead," February 2009, http://www.btselem.org/Download/200902_Operation_Cast_Lead_Position_paper_Eng.pdf.

7. Back Channel Negotiation: Causes and Consequences

1. Dennis Ross, interviewed by Charles Enderlin, February 19, 2000, Jerusalem, cited in Enderlin, *Shattered Dreams*, 361.

2. Several findings in this chapter were previewed in "Back Channel Negotiation: International Bargaining in the Shadows," in *Negotiation Journal* 22, no. 2 (April 2006), and are integrated here by permission of the publisher, Wiley-Blackwell, which the author gratefully acknowledges.

3. Back channels have been observed in domestic negotiation contexts as well. I have observed back channels emerge in intra- and interorganizational conflicts as well. In the author's experience mediating disputes between labor unions and management, teachers unions and school boards, and within corporations, decision makers resort to back channel communications for many of the same general reasons that international negotiators do so.

4. Herbert Kelman, "Contributions of an Unofficial Conflict Resolution Effort to the Israeli-Palestinian Breakthrough," *Negotiation Journal* 11, no. 1 (1995).

5. Omar Dajani, "Understanding Barriers to Peace: A Palestinian Response," *Negotiation Journal* 20, no. 3 (2004).

6. Several scholars have examined this literature, including Matz, "Reconstructing Camp David"; and Daniel Lieberfeld, "Secrecy And 'Two-Level Games' in the Oslo Accord: What the Primary Sources Tell Us," *International Negotiation* 13, no. 1 (2008): 133–46.

7. Anthony Wanis-St. John, "An Assessment of Back Channel Diplomacy: Negotiations between the Palestinians and Israelis" (Program on Negotiation Working Paper Series 00-7, Harvard Law School, 2000).

8. Savir, "Roundtable Discussion."

9. Herbert Kelman, "Social Psychological Dimensions of International Conflict," in *Peacemaking in International Conflict*, ed. I. William Zartman (Washington, D.C.: United States Institute of Peace, 2007); Janice Gross Stein, "Image, Identity and Conflict Resolution," in *Managing Global Chaos*, ed. Chester Crocker and Fen Osler Hampson (Washington, D.C.: United States Institute of Peace, 1996).

10. Molho, interview.

11. Louis Kriesberg, "Mediation and the Transformation of the Israeli-Palestinian Conflict," *Journal of Peace Research* 38, no. 3 (2001): 373–92.

12. For a vast collection of such contributions (although not all are equally relevant to negotiation challenges), see Max Bazerman, ed., *Negotiation, Decision Making, and Conflict Management*, 3 vols. (Northampton, Mass.: Edward Elgar, 2005).

13. Howard Raiffa, *The Art and Science of Negotiation* (Cambridge, Mass.: Belknap Press of Harvard Univ. Press, 1982); Howard Raiffa, David Metcalfe, and John Richardson, *Negotiation Analysis: The Science and Art of Collaborative Decisionmaking* (Cambridge, Mass.: Belknap, 2003).

14. Jeffrey Rubin, ed., *Dynamics of Third Party Intervention: Kissinger in the Middle East* (New York: Praeger, 1981).

15. I. William Zartman and Maureen Berman, *The Practical Negotiator* (New Haven, Conn.: Yale Univ. Press, 1982).

16. Fred C. Iklé, *How Nations Negotiate* (New York: Harper & Row, 1964).

17. Klieman, *Statecraft in the Dark.*

18. Louis Kriesberg, *International Conflict Resolution: The US-USSR and Middle East Cases* (New Haven, Conn.: Yale Univ. Press, 1992).

19. Kriesberg, "Mediation and the Transformation of the Israeli-Palestinian Conflict."

20. Rubin, Pruitt, and Kim, *Social Conflict.*

21. Howard Raiffa, "Analytical Barriers," in *Barriers to Conflict Resolution,* ed. Kenneth Arrow, et al. (New York: W. W. Norton and Company, 1995).

22. Howard Raiffa, *Lectures on Negotiation Analysis* (Cambridge, Mass.: PON, 1996); Raiffa, *Analytical Barriers.*

23. Sissela Bok, *Secrets: On the Ethics of Concealment and Revelation* (New York: Vintage, 1984), 5–6. Emphasis added.

24. Bok, 102.

25. Ibid., 102-11.

26. Ibid., 6. Emphasis added.

27. Ibid., 175.

28. Jeffrey Rubin and Bert Brown, *The Social Psychology of Bargaining and Negotiation* (New York: Academic, 1975).

29. Dean Pruitt and Sung Hee Kim, *Social Conflict: Escalation, Stalemate, and Settlement,* 3rd ed. (Boston: McGraw-Hill, 2004).

30. Rubin and Brown, *The Social Psychology of Bargaining and Negotiation.*

31. See, for example, the work of Robert Cialdini, *Influence: The Psychology of Persuasion,* rev. ed. (New York: Morrow, 1993).

32. Walton and McKersie, *A Behavioral Theory of Labor Negotiations.*

33. Thomas Schelling, *The Strategy of Conflict* (Cambridge, Mass.: Harvard Univ. Press, 1980).

34. Walton and McKersie, *A Behavioral Theory of Labor Negotiations.*

35. Sewell Chan and Steven Greenhouse, "From Back Channel Contacts, Blueprint for a Deal," *New York Times,* December 23, 2005. Internet edition, http://www.nytimes.com/2005/12/23/nyregion/nyregionspecial3/23how.html?_r=1&scp=2&sq=back+channel&st=nyt.

36. Stephen Stedman, "Spoiler Problems in Peace Processes," *International Security* 22, no. 2 (1997); Stephen Stedman, Donald Rothchild, and Elizabeth Cousens, eds., *Ending Civil Wars: The Implementation of Peace Agreements* (Boulder, Colo.: Lynne Rienner, 2002); Louis Kriesberg, *Constructive Conflicts: From Escalation to Resolution* (Lanham, Md.: Rowman and Littlefield, 1998).

37. See Stedman; and Stedman, Rothchild, and Cousens, eds.

38. See Ashrawi; and Baker.

39. Enderlin, *Paix ou Guerres.*

40. Touval, "Superpowers as Mediators."

41. Louis Kriesberg, "The Relevance of Reconciliation Actions in the Breakdown of Israeli-Palestinian Negotiations, 2000," *Peace and Change* 27, no. 4 (October 2002): 546-71.

42. David Lax and James Sebenius, *The Manager As Negotiator: Bargaining for Cooperation and Competitive Gain* (New York: Free Press, 1986); Walton and McKersie, *A Behavioral Theory of Labor Negotiations.*

43. Roger Fisher, *Facilitated Joint Brainstorming: A Powerful Method for Dealing with Conflict* (Cambridge, Mass.: Harvard Negotiation Project, 1996).

44. Rubinstein, interview.

45. See Ashrawi; Mansour, *Palestinian-Israeli Peace Negotiations;* Institute for Palestine Studies.

46. See Abbas; and Beilin; Qurei, interview; Wanis-St. John, "Back-Channel Negotiation."

47. Ross, *Missing Peace.*

48. Anthony Wanis-St. John and Darren Kew, "Civil Society and Peace Negotiations: Confronting Exclusion," *International Negotiation* 13, no. 1 (2008): 11–36.

49. Eraqat, interview.

50. It will be recalled that at the end of the productive years of the peace process, in mid-2000, Yasir Abd Rabbuh (PLO Executive Council) and David Levy (Israeli foreign minister) resigned their (front channel) negotiation duties to protest the existence of back channels. See chapter 6.

51. Eraqat, interview.

52. Dajani, "Surviving Opportunities," 58. Also, Mansour, interview.

53. Anthony Wanis-St. John, "Peace Processes, Secret Negotiations and Civil Society: Dynamics of Inclusion and Exclusion," *International Negotiation* 13, no. 1 (2008); Wanis-St. John and Kew, "Civil Society and Peace Negotiations."

54. Lee Ross and Andrew Ward, "Psychological Barriers to Dispute Resolution," *Advances in Experimental Social Psychology* 27, 1994: 255–304; Daniel Kahneman and Amos Tversky, "Prospect Theory: An Analysis of Decision under Risk," *Econometrica* 47, no. 2 (1979): 263-92.

55. Dean Pruitt, *Whither Ripeness Theory?* (Institute for Conflict Analysis and Resolution Working Paper 25, Fairfax, Va., George Mason Univ., 2005).

56. Savir, *The Process;* Savir, "Roundtable Discussion."

57. Kriesberg, "Relevance of Reconciliation Actions."

58. Khalil Shikaki, *Willing to Compromise: Palestinian Public Opinion and the Peace Process,* Special Report no. 158 (Washington, D.C.: United States Institute of Peace, January 2006); Jacob Shamir, "Public Opinion in the Israeli-Palestinian Conflict," *USIP Peaceworks,* no. 60, June 2007: 46–51

59. Savir, "Roundtable Discussion."

60. Klieman, *Statecraft in the Dark.*

Bibliography

Associated Press. "Israel, Palestinians, Set for Talks." *New York Times.* Jan. 21, 2001. Internet ed.

Abbas, Mahmoud. *Through Secret Channels.* Reading, U.K.: Garnet, 1995.

Abdel Hadi, Mahdi, ed. *Documents on Palestine.* 2 vols. Volume 1, *From the Pre-Ottoman/Ottoman Period to the Prelude of the Madrid Middle East Conference.* Jerusalem: Palestinian Academic Society for the Study of International Affairs, 1997.

Abu Libdeh, Hassan. Interview with the author. Al-Baloa, Palestine. May 3, 2000.

Agha, Hussein, Shai Feldman, Ahmed Khalidi, and Zeev Schiff. *Track-II Diplomacy: Lessons from the Middle East.* Cambridge, Mass.: MIT, 2003.

Albright, Madeleine Korbel, and Bill Woodward. *Madam Secretary: A Memoir.* New York: Miramax Books, 2003.

Allison, Graham. *Essence of Decision: Explaining the Cuban Missile Crisis.* New York: HarperCollins, 1971.

Anonymous [Fatah activist]. Interview with the author. East Jerusalem. June 24, 2000.

Antonius, George. *The Arab Awakening: The Story of the Arab National Movement.* Philadelphia: J. B. Lippincott, 1939.

Arab Republic of Egypt Radio, BBC Summary of World Broadcasts. "Palestinian Official Says Stockholm Talks Not Secret (Interview with Mahmoud Abbas)." LexisNexis. May 17, 2000.

Asfour, Hassan. Interview with the author. Ramallah, Palestine. Apr. 29, 2000.

Ashrawi, Hanan. *This Side of Peace: A Personal Account.* New York: Simon and Schuster, 1995.

Avnery, Uri. *My Friend, the Enemy.* London: Zed, 1986.

B'Tselem. "Guidelines for Israel's Investigation into Operation Cast Lead." Feb. 2009.

Baker, James. "The Road to Madrid." In *Herding Cats: Multiparty Mediation in a Complex World,* edited by Chester Crocker, Fen Osler Hampson, and Pamela Aall, 183–206. Washington, D.C.: United States Institute of Peace, 1999.

Bar-On, Mordechai. *In Pursuit of Peace: A History of the Israeli Peace Movement.* Washington, D.C.: United States Institute of Peace, 1996.

Bazerman, Max, ed. *Negotiation, Decision Making, and Conflict Management.* 3 vols. Northampton, Mass.: Edward Elgar, 2005.

BBC News World Service. "Chief Palestinian Negotiator Quits." May 15, 2000.

Beilin, Yossi. *Touching Peace: From the Oslo Accord to a Final Agreement.* London: Weidenfeld and Nicolson, 1999.

Beilin, Yossi, and David Silver. *The Path to Geneva: The Quest for a Permanent Agreement, 1996–2004.* New York: RDV, 2004.

Ben-Ami, Shlomo. *Scars of War, Wounds of Peace: The Israeli-Arab Tragedy.* New York: Oxford Univ. Press, 2006.

Ben-Gurion, David. *My Talks with Arab Leaders.* New York: Third Press, 1973.

Ben-Zvi, Abraham. *Between Lausanne and Geneva: International Conferences and the Arab-Israeli Conflict.* Boulder, Colo.: Westview, 1990.

Bok, Sissela. *Secrets: On the Ethics of Concealment and Revelation.* New York: Vintage, 1984.

Boykin, John. *Cursed Is the Peacemaker: The American Diplomat Versus the Israeli General, Beirut 1982.* Belmont, Calif.: Applegate, 2002.

Brynen, Rex. "Much Ado about Nothing? The Refugee Working Group and the Perils of Multilateral Quasi-Negotiation." *International Negotiation* 2, no. 1 (1997).

Bush, George W. "President Bush Calls for a New Palestinian Leadership." White House speech, June 24, 2002, http://georgewbush-whitehouse.archives.gov/news/releases/2002/06/20020624-3.html.

Caplan, Neil. *Futile Diplomacy.* Vol. 2, *Arab-Zionist Negotiations and the End of the Mandate.* London: F. Cass, 1986.

———. *Futile Diplomacy.* Vol. 1, *Early Arab-Zionist Negotiation Attempts.* London: F. Cass, 1983.

———. *Futile Diplomacy.* Vol. 4, *Operation Alpha and the Failure of Anglo-American Coercive Diplomacy in the Arab-Israeli Conflict, 1954–1956.* London: F. Cass, 1997.

———. *Futile Diplomacy.* Vol. 3, *The United Nations, the Great Powers, and Middle East Peacemaking 1948–1954.* London: F. Cass, 1997.

———. "A Tale of Two Cities: The Rhodes and Lausanne Conferences, 1949." *Journal of Palestine Studies* 21, no. 3 (Spring 1992): 5–34.

Carter, Jimmy. *Keeping Faith: Memoirs of a President.* New York: Bantam, 1982.

Chan, Sewell, and Steven Greenhouse. "From Back Channel Contacts, Blueprint for a Deal." *New York Times.* Dec. 23, 2005. Internet ed.

"Chronology." *Journal of Palestine Studies* 23, no. 2 (1994): 160–78.

"Chronology." *Journal of Palestine Studies* 23, no. 3 (1994): 167–86.

Cialdini, Robert. *Influence: The Psychology of Persuasion.* Rev. ed. New York: Morrow, 1993.

Cohen, Michael. "Secret Diplomacy and Rebellion in Palestine, 1936–1939." *International Journal of Middle East Studies* 8 (1977): 379–404.

Cohen, Stephen, Herbert Kelman, Frederick Miller, and Bruce Smith. "Evolving Intergroup Techniques for Conflict Resolution: An Israeli-Palestinian Pilot Workshop." *Journal of Social Issues* 33, no. 1 (1977): 165–89.

Corbin, Jane. *Gaza First: The Secret Norway Channel to Peace Between Israel and the PLO.* London: Bloomsbury, 1994.

Dajani, Omar. "Surviving Opportunities: Palestinian Negotiating Patterns in Peace Talks with Israel." In *How Israelis and Palestinians Negotiate: A Cross-Cultural Analysis of the Oslo Peace Process*, edited by Tamara Cofman Wittes, 39–79. Washington, D.C.: United States Institute of Peace, 2005.

———. "Understanding Barriers to Peace: A Palestinian Response." *Negotiation Journal* 20, no. 3 (2004): 401–8.

Dayan, Moshe. *Breakthrough: A Personal Account of the Egypt-Israel Peace Negotiations.* New York: Knopf, 1981.

Deutsche-Presse Agentur. "Palestinian Official Says Peace Talks Also Held away from Cameras (Interview with Yasir 'Abd Rabbuh)." LexisNexis. Dec. 29, 1999.

Dobrynin, Anatoly. *In Confidence: Moscow's Ambassador to America's Six Cold War Presidents (1962–1986).* New York: Random House, 1995.

Dor-Ner, Zvi. *The Fifty Years War: Israel and the Arabs.* Video recording. Boston: PBS, 1999.

Egeland, Jan. "The Oslo Accord: Multiparty Facilitation Through the Norwegian Channel." In *Herding Cats: Multiparty Mediation in a Complex World*, edited by Chester Crocker, Fen Osler Hampson, and Pamela Aall, 529–46. Washington, D.C.: United States Institute of Peace, 1999.

Eisenberg, Laura Zittrain, and Neil Caplan. *Negotiating Arab-Israeli Peace: Patterns, Problems, Possibilities.* Bloomington: Indiana Univ. Press, 1998.

Elayan, Salah. Interview with the author. Al-Bireh, Palestine. May 7, 8, 13, 2000.

Elon, Amos. "The Peacemakers." *New Yorker.* Dec. 20, 1993.

Enderlin, Charles. *Paix Ou Guerres: Les Secrets Des Negociations Israelo-Arabes (1917–1997).* Paris: Stock, 1997.

———. "Researching the Parallel-Secret Negotiations: Overview of the '80s." Paper presented at the conference "Back Channel Negotiations in the Arab-Israeli Conflict," Hebrew Univ., Jerusalem, May 4, 2000.

———. *Shattered Dreams: The Failure of the Peace Process in the Middle East, 1995–2002.* New York: Other Press, 2003.

Eraqat, Saeb. Interview with the author. Jericho, Palestine. May 12, 2000.

Fisher, Roger. "Facilitated Joint Brainstorming: A Powerful Method for Dealing with Conflict." Unpublished manuscript, Harvard Negotiation Project, Harvard Law School, Cambridge, Mass., 1996.

Fisher, Ronald. "Coordination Between Track Two and Track One Diplomacy in Successful Cases of Prenegotiation." *International Negotiation* 11, no. 1 (2006): 65–89.

———. "Interactive Conflict Resolution." In *Peacemaking in International Conflict: Methods and Techniques,* edited by I. William Zartman, 227–72. Washington, D.C.: United States Institute of Peace, 2007.

———, ed. *Paving the Way: Contributions of Interactive Conflict Resolution to Peacemaking.* Lanham, Md.: Lexington, 2005.

———. "The Potential Contribution of Training to Resolving International Conflict." *International Negotiation* 2, no. 3 (1997): 471–86.

Framework for the Conclusion of a Final Status Agreement Between Israel and the Palestine Liberation Organization (Abu Mazen-Beilin Agreement, or Stockholm Agreement), October 31, 1995. Accessed at http://unispal.un.org/UNISPAL.NSF/0/7BA18 696D92A8B6A85256CD3005A6E48.

Framework for the Conclusion of a Peace Treaty Between Egypt and Israel. Signed and entered into force, Washington, D.C., September 17, 1978. *United Nations Treaty Series,* vol. 1138 (1979): 53–55.

Framework for the Conclusion of a Peace Treaty between Egypt and Israel and Framework for Peace in the Middle East. *International Legal Materials* 17 (1978), 1466.

Fromkin, David. *A Peace to End All Peace: The Fall of the Ottoman Empire and the Creation of the Modern Middle East.* New York: Avon, 1989.

Gazit, Shlomo. Interview with the author. Tufts Univ., Medford, Mass. Dec. 6, 2000.

Geneva Accord, Model Israeli-Palestinian Peace Agreement, Draft Permanent Status, 2003, http://www.geneva-accord.org/mainmenu/English.

Geneva Convention Relative to the Protection of Civilian Persons in Time of War, Done at Geneva, August 12, 1949, entered into force October 21, 1950. *United Nations Treaty Series,* vol. 75 (1950): 287–416.

Genosar, Yossi. "Factors that Impeded the Negotiations." In *The Camp David Summit— What Went Wrong?* edited by Shimon Shamir and Bruce Maddy-Weitzman, 51–59. Portland, Oreg.: Sussex Academic, 2005.

Greenberg, Joel. "Scourge of the West Bank Arabs: Israeli Bulldozers." *New York Times,* November 18, 1998. Accessed at http://www.nytimes.com/1998/11/18/world/scourge-of-the-west-bank-arabs-israeli-bulldozers.html.

Haber, Eitan. Interview with the author. Tel Aviv, Israel. May 8, 2000.

Hanieh, Akram. *The Camp David Papers.* Ramallah, Palestine: Al-Ayyam, 2000.

al-Hasan, Hani. "The PLO's Secret Diplomacy after Lebanon." Paper presented at the conference "Back Channel Negotiations in the Arab-Israeli Conflict," Hebrew Univ., Jerusalem, May 4, 2000.

Heikal, Mohamed. *Secret Channels: The Inside Story of Arab-Israeli Peace Negotiations.* New York: HarperCollins, 1996.

Hirsh, Michael. "The Lost Peace Plan." *Newsweek.* Sept. 18, 2000.

Holbrooke, Richard. *To End a War.* New York: Random House, 1998.

Holst, Johan Jørgen. "Reflections on the Making of a Tenuous Peace, or the Transformation of Images of the Middle East Conflict." Presentation at the School of International and Public Affairs, Columbia Univ., New York, Sept. 28, 1993. Reprinted in *Brown Journal of World Affairs* (Spring 1994): 1–16.

al-Husseini, Faisal. Interview with the author. 'Ayn Sinya, Ramallah, and East Jerusalem. May 14, 2000.

Iklé, Fred C. *How Nations Negotiate.* New York: Harper & Row, 1964.

Institute for Palestine Studies. *The Palestinian-Israeli Peace Agreement: A Documentary Record.* Rev. 2nd ed. Washington, D.C.: IPS, 1993.

Interim Agreement on the West Bank and Gaza Strip (PLO-Israel), September 28, 1995. Accessed at http://www.usip.org/files/file/resources/collections/peace_agreements/interim_agreement_09282005.pdf.

International Court of Justice. *Legal Consequences of the Construction of a Wall in the Occupied Palestinian Territory-Advisory Opinion.* ICJ Reports, 2004.

Joint Communiqué, Permanent Status Negotiations, First Session (Israel-PLO) Taba, May 5–6, 1996. Accessed at http://www.mfa.gov.il/MFA/Peace+Process/Guide+to+the+Peace+Process/Israel-PLO+Permanent+Status+Negotiations+-+Joint+C.htm.

Kagan, Donald. *On the Origins of War and the Preservation of Peace.* New York: Doubleday, 1995.

Kahan, Yitzhak, Aharon Barak, and Yona Efrat (Kahan Commission). *Commission of Inquiry into the Events at the Refugee Camps in Beirut: 1983, Final Report.* Jerusalem: Government of Israel, 1983.

Kahneman, Daniel, and Amos Tversky. "Prospect Theory: An Analysis of Decision under Risk." *Econometrica* 47, no. 2 (1979): 263–92.

Kelman, Herbert. "Contributions of an Unofficial Conflict Resolution Effort to the Israeli-Palestinian Breakthrough." *Negotiation Journal* 11, no. 1 (1995): 19–27.

———. "Informal Mediation by the Scholar/Practitioner." In *Mediation in International Relations: Multiple Approaches to Conflict Management,* edited by Jacob Bercovitch and Jeffrey Rubin, 64–96. New York: St. Martin's, 1992.

————. "Social-Psychological Dimensions of International Conflict." In *Peacemaking in International Conflict,* edited by I. William Zartman, 61–107. Washington, D.C.: United States Institute of Peace, 2007.

Khalidi, Rashid. *Under Siege: PLO Decisionmaking During the 1982 War.* New York: Columbia Univ. Press, 1986.

Khalidi, Walid, ed. *From Haven to Conquest: Readings in Zionism and the Palestine Problem until 1948.* Washington, D.C.: Institute for Palestine Studies, 1987.

Kissinger, Henry. *White House Years.* Boston: Little, Brown, 1979.

————. *Years of Renewal.* New York: Simon and Schuster, 1999.

————. *Years of Upheaval.* Boston: Little, Brown, 1982.

Kjorlien, Michele. "Peace Monitor: 16 May–15 August 1999." *Journal of Palestine Studies,* 29, no. 1 (Autumn 1999)

Klein, Menachem. "Track II Plans." In *The Camp David Summit—What Went Wrong?* edited by Shimon Shamir and Bruce Maddy-Weitzman,178–85. Portland, Oreg.: Sussex Academic, 2005.

Klieman, Aharon. *Statecraft in the Dark: Israel's Practice of Quiet Diplomacy.* Jerusalem: Jaffee Center for Strategic Studies, 1988.

————. "The Use of Back Channels in Israeli Diplomacy." Paper presented at the conference "Back Channel Negotiations in the Arab-Israeli Conflict," Hebrew Univ., Jerusalem, May 4, 2000.

Knowlton, Brian. "Immediate Ceasefire Needed to Restore Trust Needed: US Endorses Call for Mid-East Truce." *International Herald Tribune.* May 22, 2001. Internet ed.

Kriesberg, Louis. *Constructive Conflicts: From Escalation to Resolution.* Lanham, Md.: Rowman and Littlefield, 1998.

————. *International Conflict Resolution: The US-USSR and Middle East Cases.* New Haven, Conn.: Yale Univ. Press, 1992.

————. "Mediation and the Transformation of the Israeli-Palestinian Conflict." *Journal of Peace Research* 38, no. 3 (2001): 373–92.

————. "Nature, Dynamics, and Phases of Intractability." In *Grasping the Nettle: Analyzing Cases of Intractable Conflict,* edited by Chester Crocker, Fen Osler Hampson, and Pamela Aall, 65–97. Washington, D.C.: United States Institute of Peace, 2005.

————. "The Relevance of Reconciliation Actions in the Breakdown of Israeli-Palestinian Negotiations, 2000." *Peace and Change* 27, no. 4 (2002): 546–71.

Lax, David, and James Sebenius. *The Manager as Negotiator: Bargaining for Cooperation and Competitive Gain.* New York: Free Press, 1986.

Libaridian, Gerard. Presentation at Program on Negotiation, Harvard Law School, Cambridge, Mass., Feb. 25, 2000.

Lieberfeld, Daniel. "Secrecy And 'Two-Level Games' in the Oslo Accord: What the Primary Sources Tell Us." *International Negotiation* 13, no. 1 (2008): 133–46.

Linowitz, Sol. *The Making of a Public Man: A Memoir.* Boston: Little, Brown, 1985.

Lipkin-Shahak, Amnon. "The Roles of Barak, Arafat and Clinton." In *The Camp David Summit—What Went Wrong?* edited by Shimon Shamir and Bruce Maddy-Weitzman, 42–50. Portland, Oreg.: Sussex Academic, 2005.

Makovsky, David. *Making Peace with the PLO: The Rabin Government's Road to the Oslo Accord.* Boulder, Colo.: Westview, 1996.

Malley, Robert. "American Mistakes and Israeli Misconceptions." In *The Camp David Summit—What Went Wrong?* edited by Shimon Shamir and Bruce Maddy-Weitzman, 108–14. Portland, Oreg.: Sussex Academic, 2005.

Mansour, Camille. Interview with the author. Birzeit, Palestine. May 9, 2000.

———. *The Palestinian-Israeli Peace Negotiations: An Overview and Assessment, October 1991–January 1993.* Washington, D.C.: Institute for Palestine Studies, 1993.

Matz, David. "Reconstructing Camp David." *Negotiation Journal* 22, no. 1 (2006): 89–103.

———. "Trying to Understand the Taba Talks (Part I)." *Palestine-Israel Journal of Politics, Economics and Culture* 10, no. 3 (2003), http://www.pij.org.details.php?id=32.

———. "Why Did Taba End?" *Palestine-Israel Journal of Politics, Economics and Culture* 10, no. 4 (2003): 92–98.

Miller, Aaron David. "The Effects of the 'Syria-First' Strategy." In *The Camp David Summit—What Went Wrong?* edited by Shimon Shamir and Bruce Maddy-Weitzman, 93–99. Portland, Oreg.: Sussex Academic, 2005.

Molho, Isaac. Interview with the author. Tel Aviv, Israel. May 11, 2000.

Moratinos, Miguel. *EU Non-Paper (Moratinos Report on the Palestinian-Israeli Talks at Taba).* Jan. 27, 2001. http://www.usip.org/files/file/resources/collections/peace_agreements/taba.pdf.

Morris, Benny. *Righteous Victims: A History of the Zionist-Arab Conflict, 1881–1999.* New York: Knopf, 1999.

Muslih, Muhammad. *Toward Coexistence: An Analysis of the Resolutions of the Palestine National Council.* Washington, D.C.: Institute for Palestine Studies, 1990.

Netanyahu, Binyamin. Statement to the Knesset on Israeli-Palestinian Declaration of Principles, September 21, 1993. Reprinted in *Journal of Palestine Studies* 23, no. 2 (Winter 1994): 141–43.

———. Statement to the Knesset on the Protocol Concerning Redeployment in Hebron, January 16, 1997. Reprinted in *Journal of Palestine Studies* 26, no. 3 (1997): 141–43.

Non Paper on the Revival of a Dynamics of Peace in the Middle East (France), February 22, 2002. Accessed at http://www.bitterlemons.org/docs/french.html.

Nusseibeh, Sari. Interview with the author. East Jerusalem. May 10, 2000.

Palestine, Government of. *A Survey of Palestine: Prepared in December 1945 and January 1946 for the Information of the Anglo-American Committee of Inquiry.* 3 vols. 1946. Reprint. Washington, D.C.: Institute for Palestine Studies, 1991.

Peres, Shimon. *Battling for Peace: A Memoir.* New York: Random House, 1995.

———. *The New Middle East.* New York: Henry Holt, 1993.

Peretz, Don. *The Arab-Israeli Dispute.* New York: Facts on File, 1996

Perlez, Jane, and Elaine Sciolino. "Against a Backdrop of History, High Drama and Hard Talks at Camp David." *New York Times.* July 29, 2000. Internet ed.

Perry, Mark. *A Fire in Zion: The Israeli-Palestinian Search for Peace.* New York: Morrow, 1994.

Powell, Colin. "United States Position on Terrorists and Peace in the Middle East." Remarks at the McConnell Center for Political Leadership, Univ. of Louisville, Kentucky, Nov. 19, 2001.

Pruitt, Dean. "Whither Ripeness Theory?" Institute for Conflict Analysis and Resolution, Working Paper 25, George Mason Univ., 2005.

Pruitt, Dean, and Sung Hee Kim. *Social Conflict: Escalation, Stalemate, and Settlement.* 3rd ed. Boston: McGraw-Hill, 2004.

Pundik, Ron. "The Oslo Negotiations: From Track II to Back Channel." Paper presented at the conference "Back Channel Negotiations in the Arab-Israeli Conflict," Hebrew Univ., Jerusalem, May 4, 2000.

Putnam, Robert. "Diplomacy and Domestic Politics: The Logic of Two-Level Games." *International Organization* 42, no. 3 (1988): 428–60.

Quandt, William. *Peace Process: American Diplomacy and the Arab-Israeli Conflict since 1967.* Washington: Brookings Institution, 1993.

Qurei (Abu Alaa), Ahmed. Interview with the author. Al-Bireh, Palestine. Apr. 29, 2000.

———. "Thoughts on the Prospective Dividend and Regional Economic Cooperation." Unpublished manuscript, Tunis, 1991.

Rabie, Mohamed. *U.S.-PLO Dialogue: Secret Diplomacy and Conflict Resolution.* Gainesville: Univ. Press of Florida, 1995.

Rabin, Yitzhak. *The Rabin Memoirs.* Expanded ed. Berkeley: Univ. of California Press, 1996.

Raiffa, Howard. "Analytical Barriers." In *Barriers to Conflict Resolution,* edited by Kenneth Arrow, Robert Mnookin, Lee Ross, Amos Tversky, and Robert Wilson, 132–49. New York: W. W. Norton, 1995.

———. *The Art and Science of Negotiation.* Cambridge, Mass.: Belknap Press of Harvard Univ. Press, 1982.

————. *Lectures on Negotiation Analysis.* Cambridge, Mass.: PON, 1996.

Raiffa, Howard, David Metcalfe, and John Richardson. *Negotiation Analysis: The Science and Art of Collaborative Decisionmaking.* Cambridge, Mass.: Belknap Press, 2003.

Report of the Sharm el-Sheikh Fact-Finding Committee (Mitchell Report), April 30, 2001. Accessed at http://www.usip.org/files/file/resources/collections/peace_agreements/sharm_el_sheikh_committee.pdf.

Reuters. "Arafat Says Israel, Palestinians, Made Peace Progress." *New York Times.* Jan. 29, 2001. Internet ed.

————. "Palestinians Reject Clinton's Peace Proposals." *New York Times.* Jan. 8, 2001. Internet ed.

Ross, Dennis. "Lecture and Discussion." Columbia Univ., School of International and Public Affairs, New York, Sept. 14, 2004.

————. *The Missing Peace: The Inside Story of the Fight for Middle East Peace.* New York: Farrar, Straus and Giroux, 2004.

————. On-the-Record Briefing on the Hebron Agreement, United States Special Coordinator on the Middle East Peace Process, January 17, 1997. Reprinted in *Journal of Palestine Studies* 26, no. 3 (1997): 144–45.

————. "Remarks on Camp David and the Clinton Proposals, Georgetown University Law Center, July 19, 2001." *Journal of Palestine Studies* 31, no. 1 (Autumn 2001): 150–53.

Ross, Lee, and Andrew Ward. "Psychological Barriers to Dispute Resolution." *Advances in Experimental Social Psychology* 27 (1994): 255–304.

Rubin, Jeffrey, ed. *Dynamics of Third Party Intervention: Kissinger in the Middle East.* New York: Praeger, 1981.

Rubin, Jeffrey, and Bert Brown. *The Social Psychology of Bargaining and Negotiation.* New York: Academic, 1975.

Rubin, Jeffrey, Dean Pruitt, and Sung Hee Kim. *Social Conflict: Escalation, Stalemate, and Settlement.* 2nd ed. New York: McGraw-Hill, 1994.

Rubinstein, Eliyakim. Interview with the author. East Jerusalem. May 8, 2000.

el-Sadat, Anwar. *In Search of Identity: An Autobiography.* New York: Harper and Row, 1978.

Sarid, Yossi. "Settlements Worth Dying For?" *Yediot Ahoronot.* Nov. 10, 2000.

Saunders, Harold. "Possibilities and Change: Another Way to Consider Unofficial Third Party Intervention." *Negotiation Journal* 11, no. 3 (1995): 271–75.

Savir, Uri. *The Process: 1,100 Days that Changed the Middle East.* New York: Random House, 1998.

————. "Roundtable Discussion: Strengths and Weaknesses of the Method." Paper presented at the conference "Back Channel Negotiations in the Arab-Israeli Conflict," Hebrew Univ. of Jerusalem, May 4, 2000.

Schelling, Thomas. *The Strategy of Conflict*. Cambridge, Mass.: Harvard Univ. Press, 1980.

Schiff, Zeev, and Ehud Yaari. *Intifada: The Palestinian Uprising—Israel's Third Front*. New York: Simon and Schuster, 1990.

Sebenius, James. *Negotiating the Law of the Sea*. Cambridge, Mass.: Harvard Univ. Press, 1984.

Shamir, Jacob. "Public Opinion in the Israeli-Palestinian Conflict." *USIP Peaceworks* 60 (June 2007): 46–51.

Shamir, Shimon, and Bruce Maddy-Weitzman, eds. *The Camp David Summit—What Went Wrong?* Portland, Oreg.: Sussex Academic, 2005.

Shamir, Yitzhak. Interview with the author. Tel Aviv, Israel. May 14, 2000.

———. *Summing Up: An Autobiography*. London: Weidenfeld and Nicolson, 1994.

Sharm el-Sheikh Fact-Finding Committee. *Report to President George W. Bush (Mitchell Report)*. Apr. 30, 2001. http://www.usip.org/files/file/resources/collections/peace_agreements/sharm_el_sheikh_committee.pdf.

Sharm el-Sheikh Memorandum on Implementation Timeline of Outstanding Commitments of Agreements Signed and the Resumption of Permanent Status Negotiations (Israel-PLO), September 4, 1999. Accessed at http://www.usip.org/files/file/resources/collections/peace_agreements/sharm_el-sheikh_09041999.pdf.

al-Sharq al-Awsat, BBC Monitoring. "PLO Executive Committee Discusses Peace Process, Secret Talks in Sweden." LexisNexis. June 29, 2000.

Shavit, Ari. "Secret Passage to Oslo." *Haaretz*. Feb. 12, 1999. Reprinted in *Journal of Palestine Studies* 28, no. 3 (1999): 157–60.

Sher, Gilead. *The Israeli-Palestinian Peace Negotiations, 1999–2001: Within Reach*. New York: Routledge, 2006.

———. "Lessons from the Camp David Experience." In *The Camp David Summit—What Went Wrong?* edited by Shimon Shamir and Bruce Maddy-Weitzman, 61–67. Portland, Oreg.: Sussex Academic, 2005.

Shikaki, Khalil. "Willing to Compromise: Palestinian Public Opinion and the Peace Process." *USIP Special Report* 158. Jan. 2006.

Shlaim, Avi. "His Royal Shyness: King Hussein and Israel (Interview of King Hussein)." *New York Review of Books*. July 15, 1999.

———. *The Politics of Partition: King Abdullah, the Zionists and Palestine 1921–1951*. Oxford: Oxford Univ. Press, 1998.

———. "Prelude to the Accord: Likud, Labor and the Palestinians." *Journal of Palestine Studies* 23, no. 2 (1994): 5–19.

Shultz, George. *Turmoil and Triumph: My Years as Secretary of State*. New York: C. Scribner's Sons, 1993.

Singer, Joel. Interview with the author. Washington, D.C., Apr. 4, 2000.

Smith, Charles. *Palestine and the Arab-Israeli Conflict.* 3rd ed. New York: St. Martin's, 1996.

Smith, Gerard. *Doubletalk: The Story of SALT I.* New York: Univ. Press of America, 1985.

Sontag, Deborah. "Quest for Middle East Peace: How and Why It Failed." *New York Times.* July 26, 2001.

Sparks, Allister. "The Secret Revolution." *New Yorker.* Apr. 11, 1994.

Stedman, Stephen. "Spoiler Problems in Peace Processes." *International Security* 22, no. 2 (1997): 5–53.

Stedman, Stephen, Donald Rothchild, and Elizabeth Cousens, eds. *Ending Civil Wars: The Implementation of Peace Agreements.* Boulder, Colo.: Lynne Rienner, 2002.

Stein, Janice Gross, ed. *Getting to the Table: The Processes of International Prenegotiation.* Baltimore: Johns Hopkins Univ. Press, 1989.

———. "Image, Identity and Conflict Resolution." In *Managing Global Chaos,* edited by Chester Crocker and Fen Osler Hampson, 93–111. Washington, D.C.: United States Institute of Peace, 1996.

Tomeh, George, Regina Sherif, Michael Simpson, Jody Boudreault, Ida Audeh, and Katherine LaRiviere, eds. *United Nations Resolutions on Palestine and the Arab-Israeli Conflict.* 5 vols. Washington, D.C.: Institute for Palestine Studies, 1999.

Touval, Saadia. *The Peace Brokers: Mediators in the Arab-Israeli Conflict, 1948–1979.* Princeton, N.J.: Princeton Univ. Press, 1982.

———. "The Superpowers as Mediators." In *Mediation in International Relations: Multiple Approaches to Conflict Management,* edited by Jacob Bercovitch and Jeffrey Rubin, 232–48. New York: St. Martin's, 1992.

Touval, Saadia, and I. William Zartman, eds. *International Mediation in Theory and Practice.* Boulder, Colo.: Westview, 1985.

———. "Mediation in International Conflicts." In *Mediation Research,* ed. Kenneth Kressel and Dean Pruitt, 115–37. San Francisco: Jossey-Bass, 1989.

Walters, Vernon. Interview with the author. July 24, 2000.

———. *Silent Missions.* Garden City, N.Y.: Doubleday, 1978.

Walton, Richard, and Robert McKersie. *A Behavioral Theory of Labor Negotiations: An Analysis of a Social Interaction System.* 2nd ed. Ithaca, N.Y.: ILR, 1991.

Wanis-St. John, Anthony. "An Assessment of Back Channel Diplomacy: Negotiations Between the Palestinians and Israelis." Program on Negotiation Paper Series 00-7, Harvard Law School, Cambridge, Mass., 2000.

———. "Back-Channel Negotiation: International Bargaining in the Shadows." *Negotiation Journal* 22, no. 2 (2006): 119–44.

———. "The Negotiations Between the Palestinians and Israel: Short-Term Breakthrough or Long-Term Failure?" Program on Negotiation Working Paper Series 95-4, Harvard Law School, Cambridge, Mass., 1995.

———. "Peace Processes, Secret Negotiations and Civil Society: Dynamics of Inclusion and Exclusion." *International Negotiation* 13, no. 1 (2008): 1–9.

Wanis-St. John, Anthony, and Darren Kew. "Civil Society and Peace Negotiations: Confronting Exclusion." *International Negotiation* 13, no. 1 (2008): 11–36.

Weizman, Ezer. *The Battle for Peace.* New York: Bantam, 1981.

Wye River Memorandum (Israel-PLO), Washington, D.C., October 23, 1998. Accessed at http://www.usip.org/files/file/resources/collections/peace_agreements/wye_1023 1998.pdf.

Zartman, I. William, ed. *Elusive Peace: Negotiating an End to Civil Wars.* Washington, D.C.: Brookings Institution, 1995.

Zartman, I. William, and Maureen Berman. *The Practical Negotiator.* New Haven, Conn.: Yale Univ. Press, 1982.

Zartman, I. William, and Jeffrey Rubin, eds. *Power and Negotiation.* Ann Arbor: Univ. of Michigan Press, 2000.

Zartman, I. William, and Saadia Touval. "International Mediation." In *Leashing the Dogs of War,* edited by Chester Crocker, Fen Osler Hampson, and Pamela Aall, 437–54. Washington, D.C.: United States Institute of Peace, 2007.

Zinni Paper, Second US "Joint Goals" Proposal, March 26, 2002 (United States). Accessed at http://www.usip.org/files/file/resources/collections/peace_agreements/joint_goals .pdf.

Index

Anthony Wanis-St. John is an assistant professor at American University in Washington, D.C. He earned his Ph.D. and Master of Arts in law and diplomacy from the Fletcher School, Tufts University and was a Doctoral Fellow at Harvard Law School's Program on Negotiation.

Dr. Wanis-St. John is an advisor to the United States Institute of Peace and has consulted with the World Bank. He has facilitated several Track II workshops for Palestinian and Israeli official negotiation staff and advisors.

He has taught in graduate programs at University of Massachusetts' Dispute Resolution Program, the Fletcher School at Tufts University, Johns Hopkins University's Nitze School of Advanced International Studies, and in the executive education programs at Harvard Law School. He has also lectured at the Command and Staff College of U.S. Marine Corps University; Notre Dame University in Beirut, Lebanon; and the Ecole de Management of the Université de Bordeaux in France.

His published work has appeared in *Negotiation Journal* and *The Handbook of Dispute Resolution*.